At the Intersection of Hermeneutics and Homiletics

At the Intersection of Hermeneutics and Homiletics

Transgressive Readings for
Transformational Preaching

EDITED BY
Yung Suk Kim

◆PICKWICK *Publications* · Eugene, Oregon

AT THE INTERSECTION OF HERMENEUTICS AND HOMILETICS
Transgressive Readings for Transformational Preaching

Copyright © 2025 Wipf and Stock Publishers. All rights reserved. Except for brief quotations in critical publications or reviews, no part of this book may be reproduced in any manner without prior written permission from the publisher. Write: Permissions, Wipf and Stock Publishers, 199 W. 8th Ave., Suite 3, Eugene, OR 97401.

Pickwick Publications
An Imprint of Wipf and Stock Publishers
199 W. 8th Ave., Suite 3
Eugene, OR 97401

www.wipfandstock.com

PAPERBACK ISBN: 978-1-6667-7491-7
HARDCOVER ISBN: 978-1-6667-7492-4
EBOOK ISBN: 978-1-6667-7493-1

Cataloguing-in-Publication data:

Names: Kim, Yung Suk, editor.

Title: At the intersection of hermeneutics and homiletics : transgressive readings for transformational preaching / edited by Yung Suk Kim.

Description: Eugene, OR: Pickwick Publications, 2025. | Includes bibliographical references.

Identifiers: ISBN 978-1-6667-7491-7 (paperback). | ISBN 978-1-6667-7492-4 (hardcover). | ISBN 978-1-6667-7493-1 (ebook).

Subjects: LCSH: Preaching. | Bible—Homiletical use. | Bible—Hermeneutics.

Classification: BV4211 A85 2025 (print). | BV4211 (ebook).

VERSION NUMBER 03/18/25

Scripture quotations are from the New Revised Standard Version Bible © 1989 Division of Christian Education of the National Council of the Churches of Christ in the United States of America. Used by permission. All rights reserved worldwide.

Contents

Acknowledgments | vii
List of Contributors | ix

Part I: Introduction

1 At the Intersection of Hermeneutics and Homiletics | 3
—Yung Suk Kim

2 Alleviating Homiletical Myopia | 9
—Teresa L. Fry Brown

3 Transgressive Preaching Philosophy, Hermeneutics, and Context | 26
—Jacob D. Myers

4 Black Liberation Hermeneutics and Homiletics | 42
—James Henry Harris

Part II: Interpreting the Book of Ruth and Homiletic Overtures

5 Biblical Irony and Emancipatory Proclamation: The Book of Ruth as Exemplary Locus for Feminist Homiletics | 57
—Carolyn J. Sharp

6   Invisible Labor and the Erasure of Ruth | 78
    —Song-Mi Suzie Park

7   Ruth as Model Victim, Hidden Scapegoat, or Groomed Surrogate: A Womanist Reading | 96
    —Cheryl A. Kirk-Duggan

8   Love Makes a Family?: Queer Readings of the Book of Ruth | 119
    —Rhiannon Graybill

9   Decolonizing Ruth, Reading and 'Un-reading' Ruth with African Eyes: Masculinity, Disability, and Survival | 139
    —Robert Wafawanaka

Part III: Interpreting Matthew 15:21–28 and Homiletic Overtures

10 A Womanist Reading of the Canaanite Woman (Matt 15:21–28): Dehumanization, and the Politics of Respectability and Inclusion | 165
    —Mitzi J. Smith

11 The Colonial Christ, the Canaanite Woman, and the Crumbs of Insufficiency | 184
    —Demetrius K. Williams

12 The Matthean Jesus and the Canaanite Blues | 202
    —Hugh R. Page Jr.

13 Crumbs are Never Enough: Decentering the White Supremacist Jesus | 218
    —Katherine A. Shaner

14 The Good News of a Struggle to Care (Matt 15:21–28): Challenge and Opportunity for Intercultural Caregivers | 239
    —Daniel S. Schipani

Bibliography | 263

Acknowledgments

I COLLABORATED WITH MY dedicated and caring colleagues from the beginning of this book's creation. Editing a volume with contributions from such esteemed individuals required additional support, and I was fortunate to have their invaluable input. Carolyn Sharp at Yale Divinity School was instrumental in encouraging me to pursue this volume project and suggested including a queer reading contributor. Following her guidance, I found a talented scholar in my research, Rhiannon Graybill, and included her in the project. Additionally, Carolyn Pressler, the professor emerita at United Theological Seminary of the Twin Cities, recommended a couple of Hebrew Bible colleagues. Valerie Bridgeman at Methodist School in Ohio also recommended a few scholars. My esteemed colleagues at Virginia Union University, James Henry Harris and Robert Wafawanaka, supported me wholeheartedly and contributed to this volume. During a visit to Atlanta, I had the pleasure of meeting with my dear colleague, Mitzi J. Smith, at Columbia Theological Seminary, and we had a fruitful discussion about this volume. During our conversation, she suggested that each chapter needs a short sermon after interpretation, an idea that greatly improved the shape of the book. I am enormously grateful to all my previous and current students at the Samuel DeWitt Proctor School of Theology, whom I have had the privilege of teaching biblical interpretation for two decades. Lastly, I express my utmost appreciation and love to my family, whose unwavering support has been a constant source of strength.

Contributors

Yung Suk Kim, editor and contributor, is Professor of New Testament and Early Christianity at Virginia Union University. He holds a PhD in New Testament studies from Vanderbilt University. He has written nearly twenty books, including *How to Read the Gospels* (2024), *Monotheism, Biblical Traditions, and Race Relations* (2022), *How to Read Paul: A Brief Introduction to Paul's Theology, Writings, and World* (2021), *Toward Decentering the New Testament* (Cascade 2018, co-authored with Mitzi J. Smith), and *Christ's Body in Corinth: The Politics of a Metaphor* (2008). He edited four volumes, including *Paul's Gospel, Empire, Race, and Ethnicity: Through the Lens of Minoritized Scholarship* (Pickwick, 2023), *1–2 Corinthians: Texts at Contexts* (2013), and *Reading Minjung Theology in the Twenty-First Century* (Pickwick 2013, co-edited with Jin-ho Kim). His research interests include mental health and the Bible, parables and political philosophy, and comparative wisdom literature.

Teresa L. Fry Brown is the Bandy Professor of Preaching and Associate Dean for Academic Affairs at Candler School of Theology at Emory University in Atlanta, Georgia. She has authored five monographs and written sixty reviews, chapters, and commentaries on homiletics and womanism in various publications. Her books include *Delivering the Sermon: Voice, Body, and Animation in Proclamation* (2008), *Can A Sister Get a Little Help: Advice and Encouragement for Black Women in Ministry* (2008), *God Don't Like Ugly: African American Women Handing on Spiritual Values* (2000), and *Weary Throats and New Song: Black Women Proclaiming God's Word* (2003).

Rhiannon Graybill is Marcus M. and Carole M. Weinstein & Gilbert M. and Fannie S. Rosenthal Chair of Jewish Studies and Professor of Religious Studies at the University of Richmond in Richmond, Virginia. She is the author of *Texts after Terror: Rape, Sexual Violence, and the Hebrew Bible* (2021) and *Are We Not Men?: Unstable Masculinity in the Hebrew Prophets* (2016). Together with John Kaltner and Steven L. McKenzie, she is co-author of *Jonah: A New Translation with Notes and Commentary* (2023) and *What Are They Saying about the Book of Jonah?* (2023). She has published widely on feminist, queer, and literary approaches to biblical texts and co-edited multiple books, including, most recently, *Lee Edelman and the Queer Study of Religion* (2023). She holds a PhD in Near Eastern Studies, with a Designated Emphasis in Critical Theory, from the University of California, Berkeley.

James Henry Harris is the Distinguished Professor of Homiletics and Pastoral Theology and Research Scholar in Religion and Humanities at the Samuel DeWitt Proctor School of Theology, Virginia Union University and the Senior Pastor of Second Baptist Church both in Richmond, Virginia. He is the author of many articles and books including *Beyond the Tyranny of the Text* (2019), *Black Suffering: Silent Pain, Hidden Hope* (2020), *N: My Encounter with Racism and the Forbidden Word in an American Classic* (2021), *No Longer Bound: A Theology of Reading and Preaching* (Cascade, 2013), *The Word Made Plain: The Power And Promise of Preaching* (2004), and *Preaching Liberation* (1995). He has also taught Preaching at Princeton, Luther Seminary, and McCormick Theological Seminary as well as the Ministers Division of the National Baptist Congress of Christian Education.

Cheryl A. Kirk-Duggan, PhD—Consultant, Scholar, Preacher, Author, Poet, Mentor, and Musical Performer; ordained minister in the Christian Methodist Episcopal Church—is the founder and CEO of Dr. Cheryl Enterprises, LLC. Kirk-Duggan works with people of many nationalities and religious affiliations. Her client circle, by design, is intergenerational and interracial, with whom she focuses on two areas, grief support and writing. She is the author and editor of numerous volumes (twenty-five published volumes) and many articles. She is a sought-after speaker. As an internationally recognized Womanist Scholar, her research interests include the Bible and culture, theology, music, spirituality, justice, violence, sexualities, and sexual misconduct. She works extensively with womanist studies, including women's religious history, leadership, and gender theory. Other focal areas are rage, grief, and transformation. Her most recent publications are *Breaking Free to Write: From Fear to Finish*, and *Baptized Rage, Transformed Grief: I Got Through, So Can You.*

Jacob D. Myers serves as the Wade P. Huie, Jr. Associate Professor of Homiletics at Columbia Theological Seminary. He is an ordained minister of Word and Sacrament in the PC(USA). He has written numerous essays and books, the latest of which is entitled *Stand-up Preaching: Homiletical Insights from Contemporary Comedians* (Cascade, 2022). He has two books forthcoming. The first is entitled *Preaching Philosophy: French Thought for Gospel Proclamation*. Co-authored with Sunggu Yang, this book will soon be published by Baylor University Press. Also in press with Lexington Book's Religion and Pop Culture series is a book entitled *Theology, Ethics, and Stand-up Comedy*, which he is co-authoring with Nicole Graham, a religious studies professor at King's College London. He provides online homiletical resources and sermon coaching.

Hugh R. Page, Jr. is Professor of Theology and *Africana* Studies; and Vice President for Institutional Transformation and Advisor to the President at the University of Notre Dame. He holds a PhD in Near Eastern Languages and Civilizations from Harvard University. His research interests include early Hebrew poetry; *Africana* biblical interpretation; the role of mysticism and esotericism in Anglican and *Africana* spiritualities; and the Blues aesthetic as theological and interpretive paradigm. He is the author of *Israel's Poetry of Resistance: Africana Perspectives on Early Hebrew Verse* (2013); general editor of *The Africana Bible: Reading Israel's Scriptures from Africa and the African Diaspora* (2010); and one of the co-editors for the *Fortress Commentary on the Old Testament and Apocrypha* (2014); *Esotericism in African American Religious Experience: "There is a Mystery"* (2015); and *Black Scholars Matter: Visions, Struggles, and Hopes in Africana Biblical Studies* (2022).

Song-Mi Suzie Park is the Associate Professor of Hebrew Bible at Austin Presbyterian Theological Seminary. She received her doctorate in Near Eastern Languages and Civilizations with a focus on the Hebrew Bible from Harvard University. She also has an MDiv from Harvard Divinity School and a BA from Amherst College. Her research focuses on literary readings and interpretations of the Hebrew Bible with a particular interest in issues of identity and gender. She is the author of *Love in the Hebrew Bible* (2023); *2 Kings: A Commentary* (2019); *Hezekiah and the Dialogue of Memory* (2015); and, with colleague Dr. Carolyn Helsel, *The Flawed Family of God: Stories about the Imperfect Families in Genesis* (2021).

Daniel S. Schipani is Professor Emeritus of Spiritual Care and Counseling at Anabaptist Mennonite Biblical Seminary and serves as an affiliate professor of pastoral and spiritual care at McCormick Theological Seminary and San Francisco Theological Seminary. He holds a Doctor of Psychology degree from Universidad Católica Argentina and a PhD in Practical Theology from Princeton Theological Seminary. He has written extensively for scholarly collections on practical and pastoral theology and education. He coedited *Through the Eyes of the Another: Intercultural Reading of the* Bible and *New Perspectives on Intercultural Reading of the Bible.* He is a member of several professional and academic organizations and the current board president of the International Association for Spiritual Care. His research and teaching interests include formation and transformation processes, intercultural reading of the Bible, and intercultural and interfaith pastoral care and counseling.

Katherine A. Shaner is Associate Professor of New Testament at Wake Forest University School of Divinity. She holds a BA from Luther College, an MDiv and a ThD from Harvard Divinity School. She is the author of *Enslaved Leadership in Early Christianity* (2018) and "The Danger of Singular Saviors: Vulnerability, Political Power, and Jesus's Disturbance in the Temple (Mark 11:15–19)" as well as numerous other articles about the legacies of slavery in New Testament texts. She is also an ordained pastor in the Evangelical Lutheran Church and preaches and teaches regularly in congregations around the US. She writes lectionary commentaries and columns for *Workingpreacher.org* as well as the *Christian Century.* She lives in Winston-Salem, NC, with her family and her dog, Karl Bark, who between naps works on his manuscript of *DOG-matics* fur *Everyone.*

Carolyn J. Sharp, professor of homiletics at Yale Divinity School, researches the narrative art and theology of biblical texts as resources for homiletical theory and praxis. She explores ways in which preaching can catalyze the formation of Christian community via insights from biblical studies and feminist perspectives on power. Sharp is the author of eight books, including a commentary on Micah (2025); a commentary on Jeremiah 26–52 (2022); a commentary on Joshua (2019); and *Irony and Meaning in the Hebrew Bible* (2009). Professor Sharp has edited or co-edited eight volumes, including *Irony in the Bible: Between Subversion and Innovation* (with Tobias Häner and Virginia Miller, 2023), *Feminist Frameworks and the Bible: Power, Ambiguity, and Intersectionality* (with Juliana Claassens, 2017), and *The Oxford Handbook of the Prophets* (2016). She is the founding series editor of the T&T Clark Library of Homiletics.

Mitzi J. Smith is the J. Davison Philips Professor of New Testament at Columbia Theological Seminary, Decatur, GA. She earned a PhD in Religion (New Testament) from Harvard University, an MDiv from Howard University School of Divinity, and an MA from The Ohio State University. Smith's recent publications include *Chloe and Her People: A Womanist Critical Dialogue with First Corinthians* and *Bitter the Chastening Rod: Africana Biblical Interpretation After Stony the Road We Trod in the Time of BLM, SayHerName, and MeToo* (co-edited with Angela Parker and Ericka Dunbar). She lectures, preaches, and hosts the *Beyond the Womanist Classroom* podcast and is a contributor to workingpreacher.org.

Robert Wafawanaka, ThD, is Associate Professor of Biblical Studies and Old Testament at the Samuel DeWitt Proctor School of Theology, Virginia Union University. His research interests include poverty and wealth in the Bible and contemporary society, ethics and social justice issues, as well as postcolonial studies. He is the author of *Am I Still My Brother's Keeper? Biblical Perspectives on Poverty* (2012). He has also published numerous articles in refereed journals and essays in peer-edited books including "Toxic Masculinity in Africa and the Bible: The Strong-Man Model and the Co-optation of Feminist Biblical Interpretation," in *Old Testament Essays*; and "Righteous Rage and the Politics of Subsistence Economies: A Socio-economic Reading of the Books of Amos and Micah from an African Perspective," in *Contemporary African Perspectives on the Bible* (2024).

Demetrius K. Williams is an Associate Professor in the Global Studies Department at the University of Wisconsin-Milwaukee, offering instruction in the Comparative Literature and Religious Studies programs. He is also senior pastor at the Community Baptist Church of

Greater Milwaukee with over 42 years of ministry experience. He is the author of *Enemies of the Cross of Christ: The Terminology of the Cross and Conflict in Philippians* (2002), *"An End to This Strife": The Politics of Gender in African American Churches* (2004), and *The Cross of Christ in African American Christian Religious Experience: Piety, Politics, and Protest* (2023). He is coauthor/editor of *Onesimus Our Brother: Reading Religion, Race and Culture in Philemon* with Matthew V. Johnson and James A. Noel (2012). He anticipates the publication of a book on African American preaching titled, *Black Preaching: White Backlash, Black Indifference—Hope for the Future* (2025).

PART ONE
Introduction

1

At the Intersection of Hermeneutics and Homiletics

Yung Suk Kim

This book is a result of my dedication to contextual critical biblical interpretation and homiletic transformation. Biblical texts do not carry inherent meaning, as meaning emerges from the reader's engagement with the text, whether it is historical, literary, or reader driven. In addition, every interpretation is contextual, so what is required is critical reading that challenges any fixed interpretations. The reader interprets texts and takes a particular stance while remaining open to other critical voices. Often, problems arise when readers are confined by their knowledge or tradition, hindering them from delving deeply into the text from contextual critical perspectives. Some people hesitate to break free from perceived norms, while others need the tools to read texts boldly. This book offers an opportunity to engage with the text in a transgressive and transformative manner.

Transgression means going beyond the limits or norms, and it is needed because of the human tendency to prefer the status quo. In certain ways, the Bible records myriads of stories of transgression. Notably, God breaks into human spheres to challenge the exploitation of people by empire. On the other hand, prophets resist all forms of evil and the power of elites. Transgression is a form of resistance, reformation, and renewal. In the Hebrew Bible, some women transgress male culture and patriarchal society. The book of Ruth, rife with stories of transgression, is a never-ending story taught and preached in traditional ways. However, this story needs transgressive interpretations because there is much room to transcend known perspectives and preaching modalities. On the other, Jesus transgresses traditions that do not support the weak and poor. He goes beyond traditional boundaries, healing the sick on the sabbath and traversing gentile territory. In the New Testament, the encounter between Jesus and the Canaanite woman in Matt 15:21–28 poses many interpretive questions and challenges. Jesus's exclusive and degrading language has been traditionally explained away in the context of Christology or soteriology.

While hermeneutics involves a comprehensive study of the text, ranging from historical to literary to reader-focused approaches, homiletics is concerned with a selected theme/message and composition and delivery of sermonic discourse set toward a particular audience. However, the border between hermeneutics and homiletics is blurred because both require readers to engage the text from their respective contexts. This book bridges the space between hermeneutics and homiletics. The relationship between them is symbiotic. Transgressive hermeneutics leads to transformational preaching, which requires a critical interpretation of the text first.

This collected volume explores the intersection of hermeneutics and homiletics by exploring two revelatory texts—one from the Hebrew Bible, the book of Ruth, and one from the New Testament, Matt 15:21–28 (a Canaanite woman's encounter with Jesus), which reflects still-agonizing issues readers must tackle: migration, family/community, identity/agency, race/ethnicity, gender, class, culture, economy, and religion, among others.

A diverse group of seasoned scholars brings their transgressive perspectives to the above texts. Exploring uncharted areas of interest, inquiry, or insight, they will transgress against authoritative readings of texts, fashion hermeneutical horizons in dialogue with the text, and forge homiletic trajectories for contemporary audiences. Without limiting interpretation to a box, this volume seeks to register bold voices to perennial issues in our day. Homiletic transformation occurs through the relentless, resistant reading of the text and reimagining our world.

In Part One, "Introduction," there are three introductory chapters besides this one, written by homiletics professors who set the tone for the volume, emphasizing the importance of critical, contextual biblical interpretation to preaching. In chapter 2, "Alleviating Homiletical Myopia," Teresa Fry Brown tackles the naive reading of the text, lack of self-exegesis, and poor understanding of listeners and their context. Life is a text, and the preacher's job is a critical reinterpretation of a biblical text given the listeners' context and needs. Moreover, she emphasizes the importance of self-exegesis through a series of questions relating to interpretation and preaching. To reduce homiletical myopia, one must balance the text, the preacher, and the context. In chapter 3, "Transgressive Preaching Philosophy, Hermeneutics, and Context," Jacob D. Myers discusses preaching and transgressive preaching philosophy, based on deconstruction or postmodern philosophy. He details why a deconstruction way of reading the text is required for transformational, transgressive preaching. He argues that transgressive preaching needs transgressive philosophies from poststructuralists. Lastly, in chapter 4, James Henry Harris writes "Black Liberation Hermeneutics and Homiletics" and explains what black liberation hermeneutics means and why it is crucial to black homiletics. He also emphasizes the importance of dialectic notions of self, community, hermeneutics, and homiletics. One's experience in a particular context forms one's selfhood and his/her homiletic identity. This means black preaching must address all forms of evil in people, institutions, and society and should not ignore the pain and agony of others.

In Part Two, "Interpreting Ruth and Homiletic Overtures," five Hebrew Bible scholars read the book of Ruth from their contextual, critical perspectives, engaging with hermeneutical horizons and forming homiletic overtures culminating in a short sermon (homily). The contributors are given the same text of the book of Ruth and asked to interpret it transgressively. They consider the text seriously in various contexts, asking themselves why they read and bringing their homiletical messages to real people at the end.

In chapter 5, "Biblical Irony and Emancipatory Proclamation: The Book of Ruth as Exemplary Locus for Feminist Homiletics," Carolyn J. Sharp theorizes feminist homiletical convictions and preaching praxis, based on the preacher's appreciation of communities' urgent need for strong women characters in Scripture. Exposing the insistent ironies that fracture Ruth's overly idealistic and simplistic readings, she encourages feminist preachers to offer decolonizing discourse, stand in solidarity with those who suffer, and honor polyphony in text and interpretation.

In chapter 6, "Invisible Labor and the Erasure of Ruth," Song-Mi Suzie Park reads the story of Ruth through a feminist, deconstructive lens and points out the striking disappearance of Ruth whose story and ethnicity are erased in the end. As a Korean American feminist reader, she relates the discomfort of Ruth's "disappearance" to the modern issue of invisible labor, especially that of immigrant women. Her study compels readers to rethink the service of many unrewarded and unacknowledged labors among women, immigrants, and the poor in contemporary society.

In chapter 7, "Ruth as Model Victim, Hidden Scapegoat, or Groomed Surrogate: A Womanist Reading," Cheryl Kirk-Duggan reads the book of Ruth from a womanist perspective and explores matters of context, identity, characterization, irony, and misogyny. Likewise, she reveals the Levirate code as a contextual, controlling device in a patriarchal, misogynistic world. According to the reversals of identity and characterizations of Ruth and Naomi, Ruth is the scapegoat in the name of alleged redemption. Kirk-Duggan's homiletic overtures emphasize the fullness of women's inclusion, friendship, faith, and family, rising above the traps of misogyny.

In chapter 8, "Decolonizing Ruth, Reading and 'Un-reading' Ruth with African Eyes: Masculinity, Disability, and Survival," Robert Wafawanaka reads the book of Ruth from an African (Zimbabwean) American male, postcolonial perspective and engages with it in the African cultural context replete with issues of masculinity, disability, and the survival of marginalized women. Aptly applying masculinity theory and disability studies to the book of Ruth, he demonstrates that Ruth and Naomi are victims of a male-dominated society and argues that women should be independent and accomplished without being shackled by tradition.

In chapter 9, "Love Makes a Family: Queer Kinship in Ruth," Rhiannon Graybill explores the interpretations of the book of Ruth from a queer perspective, examining how oppression, migration, and power can impact the pursuit of queer happiness. She defies any fixed notions of queer reading in the book of Ruth, and readers must be open to complex possibilities of queer or queer kinship in the story.

In Part Three, "Interpreting Matt 15:21–28 and Homiletic Overtures," five scholars read Matt 15:21–28 from their transgressive, transformative perspectives, engaging their hermeneutical horizons and bringing their implications for homiletic overtures. In chapter 10, "The Canaanite Woman, the Politics of Inclusion, and the Weaponization of Faith," Mitzi

J. Smith brings her womanist reading to the text and places the story in critical dialogue with African women's experiences of inclusion. She argues that the mere inclusion of women, racial and ethnic minorities, and non-binary individuals in spaces and systems originally established to uphold the dominance of a particular group offers nothing more than a façade of equality and fairness. She delves into the manipulation and exploitation of faith as a price for accessing healing capabilities. In a persuasive homiletical move, she challenges the weaponization of faith and its detrimental impact on the marginalized.

In chapter 11, "The Colonial Christ, the Canaanite Woman, and the Crumbs of Insufficiency," Demetrius K. Williams read the story of a Canaanite woman from an African American postcolonial perspective and relates Jesus's encounter with a Canaanite woman to European Christian colonial encounters with indigenous and native "others." He argues that European colonialism produces a white colonial savior figure who welcomes others only if they accept their subordinate status. In his argument, he suggests that the colonial Christ is unable to address the needs of justice for the marginalized and that the Black Christ is necessary to overcome the legacy of the colonial Christ. He also points out the woman's defiant, challenging faith for her daughter, herself, and the community of the marginalized.

In chapter 12, "The Matthean Jesus and the Canaanite Blues," Hugh R. Page, Jr. reads the story of a Canaanite woman through performative Blues hermeneutics, seeing the power of a nameless woman's challenging faith and courage. She is a model to follow in today's world where the marginalized by oppressive structures find their voice, confront power dynamics, and resist forces that seek to harm them. This perspective also allows for critical questioning and preaching that challenges any interpretations glossing over troubling aspects of Jesus's actions and statements in the gospel accounts.

In chapter 13, "Crumbs are Never Enough: Decentering the White Supremacist Jesus," Katherine A. Shaner analyzes the story of a Canaanite woman, using feminist rhetorical-critical methods. She examines how Matthew's story perpetuates the logic of supremacist groups within the American political context. Shaner uses a reparative hermeneutical approach that emphasizes the wholeness and transformative power of the Canaanite woman, her family, and her community. In this story, she challenges mainline protestant communities to decenter an all-powerful, unquestionably correct Jesus.

In chapter 14, "The Good News of a Struggle to Care (Matt 15:21–28): Challenge and Opportunity for Intercultural Caregivers," Daniel S. Schipani reads the story of Jesus's encounter with a Canaanite woman through Latin American liberation hermeneutics and sees critical insights of transformation in the borderlands for intercultural caregivers. He points out the risk of misunderstanding and causing harm when encountering differences and contrasts while emphasizing the chance to gain insight through openness to creative collaboration and healing. In his sermonic movement, he addresses caregivers and emphasizes a path to wisdom and grace. His approach to the text is interdisciplinary, liberative, and practical.

This collaborative volume aims to explore the reading and preaching of biblical texts in a way that is mindful of real people's experiences. It is important not to feel comfortable with known traditions and interpretations. From a contextual hermeneutical perspective, the interpreter's task is not to stay in the ivory tower and disseminate knowledge. Rather, it is to engage difficult or complex texts, exposing oppressive voices and effects, unraveling abusive ideologies behind, within, and in front of the text, and uncovering "transgressive" teaching that redresses the wrong and empowers all who suffer and labor in inhumane conditions. As the essays in this volume demonstrate, transgressive readings of texts move away from the known to unfold ever-new layers of meaning.

2

Alleviating Homiletical Myopia

TERESA L. FRY BROWN

Introduction

HAVING LISTENED TO SERMONS for seven decades, preached forty-plus years, and taught homiletics for forty years, the necessity of transgressive critical hermeneutical engagement and ultimately transformative practice of homiletics remains central to my pedagogical endeavors. The core of pedagogical contention is that the purpose of preaching is to present the acknowledged Word of God, regardless of translation, verbally and nonverbally (vocally or not vocally), with presence, power, passion, and purpose, engaging the listener or observer, through all one's senses to impact perceived truths resulting in an impulse of change or conversion in their life joy of possibilities and promise. It seeks to engage the preacher and the listener through an oral-aural-psychological-spiritual-theological-social-physical-emotional-ethical endeavor.[1]

This sacred rhetoric connects the community to a divine/human encounter that celebrates God's presence, power, promise, and plan for humanity. The marriage of God's word and human creative language can be a symphony of hope and healing or a lament of defeat and depression, depending on the skill and intent of the orator. Such holy speech is a "divine activity" where the Word of God is proclaimed or

---

1. Brown, "The Action Potential of Preaching," 52.

announced concerning contemporary, often contradictory issues with a view toward the ultimate response to God. It is priestly and prophetic, a well-researched, carefully crafted, and intentionally delivered yet deeply experiential, extemporaneous, and passionately shared intent on transforming individual and communal worlds. However, a possible barrier to this utopian-like definition of the intersection of hermeneutics and homiletics is homiletical myopia.

Myopia is scientifically defined as a near-sighted or narrow view. A person with myopia can clearly see things up close but has difficulty seeing things in the distance or may lack foresight or discernment. Societally, this is manifested in ego ethnocentrism or privilege, viewing oneself and one's racial-ethnic group as the moral and cultural center of all things, the hegemonic ideal, the gold standard of life, or belief that one's ideals are universally right.[2] Homiletically, it is manifested when one performatively employs the often privileged and, at times, indelibly narrow meanings or interpretations attributed to biblical texts in commentaries, biblical text sidebars, and language from pulpits to the exclusion of the voices of women, racialized persons, the disabled, LGBTQIA+ individuals, children, youth, seniors, those outside of the academy, the unchurched, the de-churched, spiritual not religious, varied denominational views, philosophical readings, non-traditional readings, among others. Determinants of dynamic, excellent, salvific, and relevant preaching are approved by cisgender males at times nostalgically preaching excellence with the so-called "father of expository preaching" John Albert Broadus's 1853 "On the Preparation and Delivery of Sermons," "A Legacy of Preaching: Two-Volume Set—Apostles to the Present Day: The Life, Theology, and Method of History's Great Preachers," regardless of the abundance of twenty-first century hermeneutical and homiletical voices.

Nigerian novelist Chinua Achebe's 1958 novel, *Things Fall Apart*, reiterates a Nigerian proverb, "Until the lions have their historians, tales of the hunt shall always glorify the hunter."[3] This saying provides a compelling interpretive lens for attending to various voices and the preacher's agency to move, divert, reframe, transform, and alleviate homiletical myopathy through three homiletical preparation steps. This essay will review a close reading of the text, an introspective reading of the preacher, and the necessity of reading the homiletical room.

2. Mills, *The Racial Contract*, 135.
3. Achebe, *Things Fall Apart*.

A Close Read of the Text

A commonly held definition of hermeneutics is the art of understanding the method and techniques to make the text understandable in a world different from the one in which it originated. Exegesis is supposed to stimulate the imagination to pick out exciting points to investigate indirect wrestling with the text. Textual interpretation is how we communicate about the divine, expressing understanding and the world. Stephen Farris indicates interpretation is the primary task of the preacher.[4] Preachers are challenged to expand their hermeneutical horizons to ensure the selected text is accessible and understandable to contemporary readers/listeners. Like any literary work, the biblical text requires attention to detail, characters, plot, movements, resolution, challenges, reality interpretation, covert and overt meanings, comparison to other works, questions of authorship, origin, and possible application for the reader's life.

In *The Concise Encyclopedia of Preaching*, Richard Hays posited that if the sermon is not informed by careful scripture study, the preacher will likely offer the congregation recycled common sense rather than the proclamation of the Word of God.[5] Expansion of the preacher's hermeneutical worldview may lead to broadened homiletic horizons. It is theological meaning-making and meaning location within the selected text and the world in front of it.[6] However, contemporarily, social media channels, live streaming, public broadcasting, preaching classrooms, preaching conferences, denominational gatherings, pulpits, and personal podcasts are pulsating sites of superficial, poorly researched, dispassionate, vague, childhood understandings of biblical texts and cloned preaching. Soaring metrics of persons tuning in to vapid sermons outweigh the validity of interpretation with integrity. Scathing social critiques of sound hermeneutics associated with the absence of the "Holy Spirit" or consideration of the vernacular or culture of the congregation are legion. One tool for preaching with integrity is developing a close read of the text.

The 1966 Reading Is Fundamental Program immersed children in books, language, and words to broaden their educational horizons.[7] Children were encouraged to read broadly with particular attention to

---

4. Farris, "Hermeneutics."
5. Hays, "Exegesis," 126–27.
6. "ClassicsWrites: A Guide to Research and Writing in the Field of Classics."
7. "Reading is Fundamental."

phonics (phonetics) fluency, vocabulary, sight words, and word comprehension. These basics are critical to sound exegetes and sound preachers. An initial step would be for preachers to develop or reconnect with a habit of reading. Research through Google or Artificial Intelligence increasingly limits purposeful investigation or individual engagement with biblical courses.

Cleophus Larue, adapting William Stidger's paradigm, assesses preachers based on their reading habits and suggests several tools for improved preaching[8]: Good preaching emanates from the natural flow of one's experiences, associations, and ideas. The preacher decides what to reduce, expand, or eliminate from the textual study. The use of word study, devotionals, lectionary, theme, dictionaries, commentaries, social topics, or local church plans may provide intentional and immediate reflective discussions on focused texts. It has been said that a well-read preacher is a good preacher. Reading outside of "it's time to write a sermon," casual or incidental reading, or expanding one's usual genre of reading leads to enhanced illustrations and possibly better connection with diverse listeners. Observation of language, imagery, conversational patterns, and tone characteristic of journals, magazines, blogs, news flashes, and some social media posts incrementally aid in preaching vernacular. Preachers may also seek to read religious and nonreligious works and demographically inclusive sermon collections and academic homiletics books. These habits undergird one's intentional preparation for reading the biblical text. Unfortunately, for too many preachers and students, assigning readings or serious exegetical work results in cries of "not enough time." Adaptive intelligence will find the answer quicker. "I heard the text preacher before", "My Pastor always uses . . . ," "So why not just use textbook's interpretation," or "That is too much work "excuses."

Close reading is carefully analyzing a passage's language, content, structure, and patterns to understand what it means, what it suggests, and how it connects to the larger work. A close reading delves into what a passage means beyond a superficial level and then links what that passage suggests outward to its broader context. Close reading aims to help readers see facets of the text that they may not have noticed before. To this end, close reading entails "reading out of" a text (exegesis) rather than "reading into" (eisegesis) it. The reader actively notices, describes, and interprets evidentiary details of the already written text rather than

---

8. LaRue, "Preaching Out of the Overflow," 243–46.

imposing one's personal agenda on the text. As the name suggests, with or without resources, one interrogates the text for what it says, implies, or contextually connects to a listening or particular social context.

Mary Foskett, a reception history biblical scholar, stipulates the area of interpretation as focusing on how biblical texts have changed over time.[9] It attends to how texts are interpreted in different cultures and communities through translation, reading, retelling, and reworking. Interrogates how people have received, appropriated, and used biblical texts throughout history. It explains how cultural appropriations, art, literature, music, drama, social media, or film adaptations like the classics *Ben Hur*, *The Ten Commandments*, or *Green Pastures* impact both hermeneutics and homiletics. Deborah Organ stipulated the transformative nature of cultural hermeneutics: "Engagement with a text from various cultural perspectives yields new meetings within a given cultural context and between cultural contexts as communities read the Bible together. The role of the preacher is to interpret the Word and preach in the cultural idioms familiar to the congregation so that the community can recognize The Word alive in their midst."[10]

Broadening one's view of both the preacher's textual interpretation and the infinite possibilities of listener explication while taxing is an inviolable part of homiletics. Transitioning between exegesis and sermon writing is a continuum rather than two disparate parts. Similarly, Walter Bruggeman indicates that the text is the word of life, viewed with a vested interest in a particular community. Faith is formed through varied contextualized readings of a text. Believing the text is an act of faith and canon formation. The community sets the standard of authority and significance of a text. The listener chooses his or her own exception or rejection of a particular text.[11] Reading against the text through a cultural lens has proved problematic for some biblical interpreters. At the same time, Hans-Georg Gadamer believed all biblical interpretations were valid, while others reported that some interpretations were more "correct" than others. The reality of subjective, imaginative cultural interpretation paired with historical criticism allows preachers to infuse the text with vibrant congregational or contextual authority and relevance.

Critical biblical interpretation is a "means of conscientization" to address embedded oppressive ideologies and communal lived experiences

9. Foskett, *Interpreting the Bible*, 56.
10. Organ, "Cultural Hermeneutics," 143–46; "What Is Reception History?"
11. Brueggemann, "The Social Nature of the Biblical Text for Preaching."

in the worlds behind and before the text, purports womanist biblical scholar Mitzi Smith.[12] Critical reflection is deep homiletical work that broadens the inclusivity of the oral and aural preached word. Questions explored include: What takes place beyond the text? What does God do in the larger story beyond the focus text? What does this passage tell us about who we are? Who is God? What are we asked to believe? What is God instructing and enabling us to do? What does the cross and resurrection say to Christians concerning themes raised in the text? What would you use as the primary point in a sermon developed from the text? These and other questions are critical elements of the homiletical enterprise. Homiletic myopathy is relieved as the reader excavates the text, peeling away social-political barriers and unearthing elements that speak to the existential realities of identity, content, and lived faith. The late ethicist Katie Geneva Cannon advocated "opening the biblical text wide enough to locate oneself within."[13] She employed cultural imperatives to write about Black women's hermeneutical and homiletical engagement: "One ear to the ground hearing the cries of the people and the other ear at the mouth of God" or "Making it plain" as guides for preaching tasks. Attention to the racist-sexist interpretation of the biblical text, understanding one's preaching context, indelible societal characterization of Black people, the Words of God as incarnate, God's divine activity with all of God's creation, community intellectual and social life, androcentric language, awareness of and engagement with contemporary issues, the gift of imagination, the preacher as the arbiter of communal intellectual/moral life, vital nature of cultural oral traditions, and the divine privilege and power of the preacher "Say a word" are non-negotiables. As a standard homiletical preparation and delivery routine, the preacher interrogates entrenched "othering" in the text, prejudicial characterizations, exposing who is missing from the text, stereotypes, and cultural meanings. Sound homiletical preparation is achieved through a diverse, habitual, broad, and close text reading. For example, a critical engagement of the biblical text in womanist homiletics means sermons are well-researched, linguistically filtered, exegetically sound, culturally relevant, transportable, and topically sensitive to the context.

---

12. M. J. Smith, *Womanist Sass, and Talk Back*, 2–4; M. J. Smith, *I Found God in Me*, 8.

13. Cannon, "Womanist Interpretation and Preaching in the Black Church," 113–21.

An Introspective Read of The Proclaimer

Homiletical myopia occurs when the proclaimer fails to account for diverse listeners in the room. The preacher views the text and sermon from their often-privileged perspective. It is the entrenched "expertise" stance that erects hermeneutical and homiletical "keep out" barriers reinforced by statements of "owning" the text and relegating others to interpretive margins. It is evident in sermons exhibiting excellence in exegesis with little or no consideration of the context or listeners. It is conversely apparent in context-based sermons with vapid exegesis. It either necessitates changing the metanarrative so that the first and last word on the meaning of a text or context rests with the preacher only. The proclaimer's identity, experience, knowledge, ideas, principles, education, creativity, and values elucidate the text through a particular lens. These attributes also affect the sermon's reception through the listener's hermeneutical lens.

The preacher is the oral interpreter of the written text in the life of a particular context at a time for a specific purpose. Preaching is dialogical. It is not a monologue. It is a communal event. Black feminist Patricia Hill Collins states that the first stage of "coming to voice" is "breaking silence."[14] One identifies the cultural domains of power and what shackles muteness in others. What is the intersectionality of gender, race, class, age, ethnicity, institutions, economics, denomination, nation, organizations, sexuality, and neural divergence?[15] How does one understand one's context and who one represents in reading, interpreting, or preaching a particular text? How much time and effort will one invest in deconstructing textual inequity and presenting a humanizing, inclusive read of the text? Hill Collins writes that this usually occurs when an individual speaks out against some kind of institutional knowledge or authority to advance the cause of a collective group. It means speaking out not only as a verbalized discovery of inequality but also as a public testimonial about unequal power relations, which marginalized groups have long understood. Homiletician Donna Allen concurs in her published dissertation, Toward a Womanist Homiletic: Katie Cannon, Alice Walker, and Emancipatory Proclamation,[16] detailing a type of preaching that identifies and deconstructs rhetorical devices that present sexist or racial constrictions

---

14. P. H. Collins, *Fighting Words*, 2–32.
15. Hill Collins and Bilge, *Intersectionality*, 2–15, 25–32.
16. Allen, *Toward a Womanist Homiletic*, 16–20.

language and creates expressions that empower and embrace vast lived experiences, particularly as a praxis-oriented analysis.

Language is the framework in which we live. It gives structure and meaning to our existence with different sociolinguistic frameworks. This results in gaps in the interpretation of texts and life applications. Depending on who has been designated the "authoritative" inside power broker, another's interpretation may be dismissed or related to the unlearned margins. Adapting to representative research on scriptural interpretation is complex but essential. Finally, Hill Collins stipulated equity is increased when one prioritizes coalitions, resistance, global politics, relationality, social context, praxis, and the complexities of the work. As Katie Canon is quoted, the preacher's aim in a realistic cultural context is to attempt to "Slough off memories that no longer have relevance while proclaiming the religious inheritance for ancestral mothers and fathers that enhances narrative variation for audience responses in new situations."[17] Effective eradication of homiletical myopia is work, not accusatory or shaming. Regardless of background, each must linguistically do not harm. Trafficking in introspection before researching and writing a sermon is an ethical necessity responsive to the message's emotional, political, psychic, and intellectual implications.

An Introspective Reading of the Preacher

William Shakespeare, in the *Tragedy of Hamlet*, Prince of Denmark, Act 1, Scene 3, presented Polonius's speech to his son Laertes as Laertes prepared to travel abroad. The resounding, "This above all things, to thine own self be true." lends itself to the preacher's responsibility to be authentic. It encourages preachers to speak in their own voice rather than imitate the peculiarities of other preachers, to stand on their own beliefs instead of pandering to listeners, and to do their own textual homework for sermon preparation rather than taking digital shortcuts. The person of the preacher infuses the interpretation and preaching of the biblical text with integrity. Regardless of the number of books read, sermons heard, or preached, the number of supportive complements or dismissive critiques, the preacher's depth of study, faith claims, and personality will eventually emerge. Elements such as the preacher's

---

17. Cannon, "Womanist Interpretation and Preaching in the Black Church," 113–21.

attentiveness, imagination, and self-exegesis further illustrate introspection of the self and the facility with text.

Sights, sounds, movement, and distractions constantly engulf us. Depending on one's schedule, time set aside for responsible hermeneutical investigation and sermon preparation ranges from months to minutes. According to 2024 research sources, the average adult attention span varies from 8–47 seconds to 15–20 minutes or 5–6 hours.[18] The current reality is that some overly engaged or cognitively divergent preachers may not retain research information or be able to concentrate long enough to understand the research and fully translate it into sermonic material. The operating question is when do preachers have undivided attention to study even newer hermeneutical resources?

Homiletical imagination may be stymied by the tremendous bank of resources and the fingertip accessibility of fully and improperly vetted information. By some estimates, "328.77 million terabytes of data" are created daily for "5.35 billion internet users, "resulting in individuals creating approximately "15.87 TB data" per day.[19] Preachers must decide what is "authoritative," scholarly, valid, and correct interpretations. The preacher's conventional, empathetic, and visionary imagination is essential to developing a corrective vision of the text.[20] Other preachers or theologians have used the text in sermons, songs, and liturgies. Is the preacher aware of the experiences of the persons they preach with? How does the preacher imagine the God of the text is active in the world in which one preaches? Finally, what is the preacher's moral imagination?[21] How does a preacher work the text to signify God's ethical imperatives and divine wisdom, whether written in sacred texts or articulated in secular spaces, to describe a world of order, peace, and virtue where all persons, ethnicities, classes, and nations benefit?

The necessity of self-exegesis or a preacher's introspection before research or preaching widens one's vision of the focus text and context. It allows one to consider the influence of one's personal background, personality, faith claims, social-political identity, sermon influencers, previous textual interpretation, personal biases, and homiletical experiences. Self-exegesis heightens awareness of why and how one interprets

---

18. "Attention Span by Age"; "How to Sharpen Your Attention."
19. "Big Data."
20. Troeger, *Imagining a Sermon*, 14.
21. Kirk, "The Moral Imagination."

the text, determines sermon content, chooses to relate to the audience, and delivers the sermon. Queries may include:

- Who taught me about God?
- What do I believe?
- What is my theology?
- What is my image of God?
- What is my Christology?
- What is my belief regarding pneumatology?
- How are God's promises actualized in my life?
- How is God active in my life?
- Why do I preach?
- What are my hopes?
- What angers/disappoints me?
- Do I self-critique?
- Do I believe what I am saying?
- What is my comfort level for self-disclosure/personal testimony?
- Who are my preaching models?
- Who are my preaching mentors?
- Who are my preaching partners?
- Who is in my company of preachers?
- Who do I watch preach most often?
- What are my political beliefs?
- How often do I engage persons of different faith systems, varied racial-ethnic backgrounds, ages, sexual identities, physical or cognitive abilities, economic levels, or educational degrees?
- Who do I trust with what God has given me to preach?
- Whose critique do I accept/reject? Why?
- What is my agenda for the sermon?
- Is my work originative or derivative?
- What is my favorite or heart text?

- Do I mainly preach from the Hebrew Bible or the New Testament?
- What comprises my denominational canon?
- What texts do I avoid? Why?
- What translation(s) do I primarily research? Why?
- What extra-canonical resources do I reference?
- Do my hermeneutical resources/commentaries align with my context?
- (As Toni Morrison suggested), What is my collective/cultural memory, personal re-memory, intentional repurposing, use, or appropriation of the text(s)?

A monthly self-exegesis clarifies one's hermeneutical and homiletical textual engagement and connection with listeners. This process is essential to pastoral and prophetic preaching and the preacher's humility. It absolves us of the belief that the preacher is the sole voice or expert on a particular text but rather a member of a long history of seminary-educated and lived faith-educated biblical interpreters.

Reading the Homiletical Room

One essential yet often overlooked element of effective preaching is awareness of and engagement with the listeners. Relevant sermons engage the context rather than exhibit a preacher's presupposed idea of the sermon's purpose and effect. Preachers who compose and deliver sermonic content relative to an understanding of communal theologies, ethics, social involvement, politician leanings, denominational polity, gender, sex, age, education, economic status, history, and faith development become holistically conversant. The homiletical room is the space and place, the culmination of the hermeneutical enterprise that impregnates the sermon. The merging of text, preacher, congregation, community, and world populate the walls, ceiling, and floor cultural homiletical rooms.

Culture is our way of making sense of the world. Culture is more than skin tone, hobbies, vocation, neighborhood, denomination, gender sexuality, family structure, political bias, residence, speech pattern, food choices, or education. It includes what we've inherited from others, their understanding of the life around them, their belief system, and the way they deliver or discuss what they believe. How we name ourselves or navigate and negotiate the world is cultural. Pastoral theologian Lee Butler stated each person's sense of identity begins with one's relationship to their primary familial group. Community and group dynamics undergird the acceptance or rejection of the self, decerning "Who am I?"[22] Homileticians are interlocutors with God and the people. The preacher has a responsibility to communicate a humanizing word. Responsible preachers should be aware that the status of named and nameless women in the Bible is not the current women. There are gross differences in the lived experiences of white women and Black women, Black women and Latin women, Latin women and Asian women, Asian women and biracial women, transwomen and cisgender women. The social-historical faith-centered healing text requires careful evaluation of whether one is using the first language of a disabled person or a person with disability descriptors. Knowing the difference between healing and cure of a health challenge in the biblical text and medical technology lessens the possibility of narrow faith claims. Microaggressions bubble up frequently in sermons through misuse of references to LGBTQIA+ individuals proffered from four or five texts. Before preaching a topic, ask the person how they want to be named. Careful erasure of ageism is crucial when referencing texts about children, elders, and young adults (such as Jesus and disciples), and their expectations of contemporary demographics. Denominational polities, textual canons, and preaching authority determinants are important contextual considerations. Biblical literacy, despite increased access to varied translations, in 2022 was evidenced by 39% of self-identified Christians reporting they no longer read the Bible.[23] The assumption that the listener has heard or understands the text widens the chasm between the comprehension of the sermon and any interpretive points the preacher attempts.

At its foundation, communication is the mutual creation of meaning, and "culture" is the coordination of meaning and action within a group. It follows that "intercultural communication" is the mutual creation of meaning across cultures. Intercultural communication is how people of different groups perceive and try to make sense of one another. When one effectively reads the room, difference enriches sermonic material. While there are no guarantees that people will respect the differences they encounter in this process, it is undoubtedly a criterion of good

---

22. L. H. Butler, *Liberating Our Dignity, Saving Our Souls*, 3–4.
23. "Biblical Literacy in the Postliterate Age."

communication that people seek to understand each other's intentions in non-evaluative ways. According to homiletician Frank Thomas, equality is a representative physical presence of envisioned freedom.[24] Thomas recommends preachers employ ancient text wisdom, proven faith truths, sincere empathy, awareness of God's mystery, carefully cultivate poetic language, and avoid scapegoating or blaming culture to establish a communicative room of interpretive mutuality.

The following statements are frequently heard in introductory preaching classes: "My Bible says . . ."; "I do not understand what you mean"; "Where does it say that?"; "That's not what the text says"; "You are being too progressive (conservative)"; "But my pastor says." "How can you really believe that?" Countless experienced preachers or avoiding preaching students are confronted, dismissed, or supported with new or different textual meanings for the first time after decades of indoctrination of "this is the whole truth and nothing but the truth" biblical translations, text meanings, and faith claims in seminary. This context of hermeneutics may be generative, or pain-filled accusation of education heresy. Some delve into the hermeneutical process with abandon. Others execute the syllabus requirements yet revert to old patterns in their home church preaching contexts.

Meaning-making is a function of context. It refers to the immediate surroundings or location where messages are encoded. A sermon must be contextually congruent with the context in which it is preached. The preacher must be aware of with whom they are preaching. No one sees the world exactly alike; they use their glasses, optic nerves, and brain. Few take off their glasses to assess how others view life. The result is blurred vision if sources do not venture into another's perspective. The preacher and congregation's literal and figurative worldviews must be appraised. One's cognitive processes and how we process social and educational thought information are not a function of ethnic origin. All "normal" people in any culture can think. People in different cultures tend to arrive at similar conclusions with different processes. One's way of expressing ideas or linguistic form reflects what is important in that culture, i.e., the English tense is past, present, and future. At the same time, other languages may only deal with the "now" or Kenya-life events that begin when the people arrive. One's behavioral patterns—how we act— "formal or informal" cultural definitions of the right and wrong way to act,

---

24. F. Thomas, *How to Preach a Dangerous Sermon*, 45, 76.

establish acting according to codes of conduct or behavior. One's social structures and interactions are important. It involves who communicates with whom, how it affects the outcome and emotions, when to communicate, and what type of message. One's media influence includes the means for channeling the message, the message context, who is sending, who is receiving the information, its organization, content, and style. Finally, one's motivational resources and decision-making style affect how one perceives and receives the message.[25]

Charles Taylor stipulated communicators should intuit social imaginaries.[26] These are "ways people imagine their social existence, how they fit with others, how things go on between them and their fellows, the expectations normally met, and the deeper normative notions and images underlying these expectations."[27] The homiletic room changes from preacher to congregant, service to service, denomination to denomination, week to week, and demographic to demographic. Intercultural communication incorporates strategies that encourage us to attribute equal humanity and complexity to people not part of our group. Intercultural communication is to derive the value of cultural diversity. The potential of diversity is to offer alternative perspectives and approaches to tasks, thus contributing to innovation and creativity. However, the actuality is that diversity is frequently suppressed or eliminated in the name of unified action: "my way or the highway." Visionary preachers are not only aware that there are varied perspectives, truths, communities, and faiths but that there are infinite opportunities to "hear each of them into speaking."

Problematically, there are times when twenty-first-century preachers relegate others to linguistic balconies, erect verbal "Us Only" or "Keep out" barriers or compose unwritten devaluing "Just–Us" and "I Am Better than You" laws and codes to shove others to the margins of the room. One may begin to believe the rhetoric if one constantly hears the language of erasure, disdain, dismissal, or disenfranchisement. The exegete and the proclaimer must work to avoid excluding voices and people in the room. Othering is a way of defining and securing one's positive identity through stigmatizing an "other."[28] Othering convinces

25. Bennett, "Intercultural Communication"; Hesselgrave, *Communicating Christ Cross-Culturally*, 76–305

26. C. Taylor, *Modern Social Imaginaries*, 23–24.

27. C. Taylor, *Modern Social Imaginaries*, 23–24.

28. Morrison, *The Origin of Others*, xii, xv, xiv, 36.

us of some divine or natural delineation between people. Othering leads the proclaimer to intentionally or unintentionally make statements that rhetorically erase, dismiss, marginalize, disenfranchise, separate, or ridicule any person viewed as different. A significant challenge to today's preachers reminds us that we can never preach without being attentive to and remembering the other—our neighbors and strangers.[29] Biblical scholar Gail O'Day reports that the preacher is charged to converse with the listeners so that congregation members can imagine their lives transformed and renewed by the possibilities of the biblical texts.[30] However, the preacher should attend to so-called homiletical traps, such as if the congregation does not know the text. There is a communal shared hearing of the text the preacher may or may not anticipate. Additionally, listeners use technology to simultaneously "fact check" the preacher's sermonic employment of scripture, compare the text to other interpreters, or compare it to the contextual understanding of the passage.

Borrowing from pedagogical genius bell hooks, preachers should work "to decolonize our minds" by cultivating awareness.[31] This implies that interpretations of preaching and understanding may not be correct or relevant in contemporary contexts, regardless of how something was traditionally preached or interpreted. Calcified hermeneutics lead to spiritual cataracts. Intentional awareness of the context, the homiletical room, the variety of inhabitants, the seating chart, the focus text, the acoustics, the liturgical season, the hurting, the previously excluded, the standard of good preaching, authority figures, and message recipients must be considered and if necessary revised and revitalized. Womanist homiletics seek the utilization of a liberating discourse for God's people with metamorphic boldness. Preachers are advised to step out of the status quo and seek sermonic language and content that shakes dungeons and makes chains fall off. Sacred orators are to be responsive to the message's emotional, political, psychic, and intellectual implications while placing sermon material in a realistic cultural context. Homiletical critical engagement means one strives to learn from as many different people as imaginable, thus eliminating boxes of sermonic content often constructed for people.[32] The proclaimer examines and reexamines the biblical texts and life texts to locate themselves and what God says to and

29. McClure, *Otherwise Preaching*, 1; Blount, *Cultural Interpretation*, 4.
30. O'Day, "Shaped by Hearing," 3–9.
31. hooks, "Talking Race and Racism."
32. Floyd-Thomas, *Deeper Shades of Purple*, 78.

about them. It recognizes that no one has all the answers or the correct answers.

Preachers are rhetoricians of the varied translation of a sacred text using formal and informal language, imagery, illustrations, idioms, or phrases to make faith claims to a particular community at a particular time. An appropriation of the theoretical strategies offered by Molefi Kete Asante is a viable tool to address obstructive linguistic power that frequently occupies the homiletical room.[33] His typology begins with the understanding that we are each a part of a rhetorical community. There are communal deliberations, discourses, actions, and purposes resulting in a collaborative good for a specific gathering of people. The people cohesively, in some cases, and fragmentedly, in others, work or struggle linguistically together to resist internal and external forces against their personhood or faith. The use of certain terminology in group sayings, dialects, colloquialisms, vernacular, or coded language provides a rhetoric of affirmation leading to a liberating sense of status, being, meaning, and social and historical responsibilities. Finally, Asante's rhetoric of possibility acknowledges the power of language or Nommo to channel increased persuasion, sharing information, searching, and exploring opportunities in the social and human condition. The homiletician is positioned to sustain or destroy a faith comment based on the weaponization or restorative nature of their speech.

Supplemented by contemporary theories of invitational rhetoric, the exegete and the preacher construct a communicative relationship rooted in equality, intrinsic value, and self-determination.[34] This emphasizes the need to hear rather than judge or denigrate other perspectives. Invitational rhetoric provides a means for transformative communication with an appreciation for all occupants' faith development or belief positionality. The alleviation of homiletical myopia begins and ends with a thorough evaluation of who is in the room. The efficacy of the message is impacted by the listeners' belief that the exegete and the rhetor contemplated the possibility of their existence. The heavy work is learning to read the in-person or digital room while writing, delivering, and receiving feedback following the preaching presentation. Our linguistic performance is generated and sustained in a community. Regardless of the location of the homiletical room, home, church, conference,

---

33. Asante, *The Afrocentric Idea Revised*, 71–91; Banks, *Remix*, 86–87.
34. Foss and Griffin, "Beyond Persuasion," 79–88.

classroom, hospital, chapel, academy podcast, television, or live stream, the preacher's awareness of who is listening is critical. Research the room. Ask questions about the occupants' beliefs, demographics, attention span, expressiveness, current issues, problems, politics, preferred translation, or acceptance of difference. Avoid the assumption that all rooms are alike. Remember the linguistic and rhetorical power of both the speaker and the listeners.

Conclusion

The text, the preacher, and the context are critical elements of the sermonic moment. The exegete rigorously interprets the ancient text with an inclusive view of contemporary listeners' broad differences. During the sermon preparation process, homiletical myopia occurs when the possibilities of difference are obfuscated. This reality may be alleviated through attention to radical subjectivity, raising the preacher's and audience listeners' consciousness about the possibilities of liberation and justice for all persons in the biblical text. It may mean deconstructing and reconstructing communalism and our responsibilities to each other as heirs to God's promise. Having completed a self-exegesis, the preacher may better understand themselves while dismantling the nearsighted concept that there are monolithic preachers, one textual interpretation, one preaching style, and uniformity of preaching contexts.

3

Transgressive Preaching Philosophy, Hermeneutics, and Context

Jacob D. Myers

In this chapter, I offer a framework for interpreting Scripture for sermon development that critically and creatively engages philosophy. It opens a way toward *transgressive preaching*. Transgressive preaching philosophies resist ways of reading and proclaiming Scripture that delimit the thriving of all. Since transgressive philosophies rarely appear in homiletics courses and texts beyond a random name drop here or a bit of fancy-sounding jargon there, I will present these insights as clearly and compellingly as I can. Philosophy—especially that of the transgressive variety—can intimidate and even spook us. I know it did for me when I first encountered it. Because philosophy's fundamental tenant is to question all assumptions, when those assumptions shape how we have learned to understand the functioning of language and interpretation, it can be tempting to go full-ostrich, burying our heads in the theological sand to avoid grappling with the philosophical assumptions baked into our homiletical systems.

The strand of philosophical hermeneutics that has been most life-giving and invigorating for my preaching and teaching falls under the broad (and contentious) designation of "French theory," which conjoined phenomenology, structuralism, and psychoanalytic philosophies in the late 1960s.[1] The more we engage the work of such philosophies, the further we drift from the familiar biblical environs of Jerusalem and Athens, for it was in Paris that the seeds of transgressive thinking first bore fruit. Nietzsche planted these seeds in Bonn and Marx in Berlin; Heidegger propagated them in Marburg, Husserl in Freiburg, Saussure in Leipzig, and Freud in Vienna. But they were harvested by a coterie of Parisian philosophers including Emmanuel Lévinas, Jacques Derrida, Michel Foucault, and Luce Irigaray.[2]

Even a cursory glance at twentieth-century French philosophy can overwhelm a preacher. You're not even a page into such texts before you stumble over their abstruse vernacular. If your experience has been anything like mine, you've likely found yourself reading and re-reading sentences, trying to make sense of what these writers are trying to say. The way these Francophone thinkers broach philosophical topics and engage their philosophical forebears can make you feel like you're the only person on the dance floor who doesn't know the steps to the music. To make things even more complicated, Continental philosophers are notorious for inventing words—many of which require a working knowledge of Greek, Latin, German, and French. I know I struggled when I first tried to make sense of concepts like the *ego cogito*, ipseity, alterity, *Weltanschauung*, *Epochē*, *Unheimlichkeit*, epistemē, *dépouillement*, *différance*, *grand récit*, and Écriture *féminine*. It can feel like these great thinkers are messing with us as if they take some perverse delight in making us feel dumber by reading their works rather than smarter. After slogging through their texts for a while, it can be tempting to hurl the book across the room and be done with it. The learning curve is steep, to be sure; but I hope to bear witness to the fact that such effort yields profound insights for how we make meaning from and with biblical texts for Christian proclamation. Such hermeneutics condition our capacity to challenge unjust sociopolitical structures, enabling us

---

1. French theory arose amid a time of intense sociopolitical foment. The French student and worker revolts of May 1968 gave rise to a critical reception of many inherited philosophical precepts, structuralism first and foremost among them. In a nutshell, the so-called poststructuralists argued that texts are able to make meaning due to linguistic and sociopolitical structures that condition our hermeneutical possibilities a priori. For more on this development and its homiletical significance, see Myers and Yang, *Preaching Philosophy*.

2. For a compelling narration of the movement of philosophy from Germany to France in the twentieth century, see Lawlor, *Thinking Through French Philosophy*.

to bear witness to the God who came to live and dwell among us so we might have life in all its fullness (John 10:10).

The hermeneutical approach I find most adept at facilitating transgressive preaching is called *deconstruction*. Deconstruction is not as destructive as it might sound. It is a hermeneutical approach that acknowledges the fact that our ways of seeing and hearing arise from the languages, social norms, values, and sociopolitical structures in which we find ourselves. Amid such acknowledgment arises a healthy respect for the contingency of our sociopolitical and linguistic structures. John Caputo puts it well: "Deconstructors cultivate a congenital disposition to look at things *otherwise*, to pick up views that have fallen out of favor or dropped through the cracks of the tradition."[3] Just by asking a few questions, we cultivate capacities to discern not only what but *how* texts mean.[4] But what kind of questions enable us to regard Scripture otherwise? That's what we're going to investigate in the following pages.

Learning Transgression Through a Children's Story

—Be wise. Be brave. Be tricky.[5]

As I mentioned above, philosophies, in general, and transgressive philosophies, in particular, can easily confuse and frustrate us. This steep learning curve can thwart our efforts to interpret and preach the Bible otherwise. So, in the remainder of this chapter, I will explore how to identify the constructed and contingent nature of texts and traditions and thereby open other ways that biblical texts might mean for Christian preaching. And the subjunctive mood is key here. Texts do not *have* meanings. They have meaning-potential.[6] Just as a fallen tree requires an aural mechanism—such as the one in our middle ears—to make sound manifest as such, apart from such a mechanism the fallen tree produces only vibrations. Accordingly, we might speak of a tree's sound potential rather than a sound intrinsic to the tree. So it is with texts that their potential energies await a structure of signification sufficient to *make* meaning.

---

3. Caputo, *Hermeneutics*, 10.
4. Hence the subtitle of my first monograph: *Making Love with Scripture*.
5. Gaiman, *Coraline*, 143.
6. M. J. Smith and Kim, *Toward Decentering the New Testament*, 14: "Biblical texts do not mean anything without the reader."

There are a few texts that can help us understand the complex processes of transgressive biblical interpretation than Neil Gaiman's haunting children's tale, *Coraline*. In case you haven't read it, here's a quick overview of the book's plot: The story's protagonist is named Coraline Jones, and the story begins when she moves with her parents into a new flat. As a curious and adventurous nine-year-old, Coraline quickly grows bored with her new surroundings and preoccupied parents. One rainy day, Coraline becomes interested in a locked door that opens to a brick wall in the drawing room of her new residence. Mysteriously, the following day, Coraline discovers that the brick wall has vanished, opening onto a corridor. When Coraline sets out to explore where the corridor leads, she finds that on the other side exists a parallel universe bearing an uncanny resemblance to the one she left behind. She finds an alternate version of her flat inhabited by a couple who resemble Coraline's parents. They call themselves her other mother and other father.

When Coraline returns to her flat from the parallel universe, she discovers that her real parents have gone missing. Mustering her courage, she decides to go back to the other flat to search for her parents and the other souls sequestered over the years by the other mother. Coraline's intrepid exploration leads her to undertake a series of perilous adventures in the other universe as she battles the other mother's pernicious machinations. Coraline ends up discovering incredible strength within herself through these adventures, and through her experiences, she is able to see her own world with new eyes.

There are many touchpoints between *Coraline* and our efforts to read and preach Scripture transgressively. Let's follow Coraline's narrative journey to discern some of the key aspects of reading deconstructively, along with the transgressive preaching it engenders. In my use of *Coraline* I am aligning the novel's eponymous protagonist with the preacher/interpreter, the other flat as the "world of the work," and the other mother as the arbiter of meaning-making bent on constraining the hermeneut's understanding.[7] Linking Gaiman's tale with biblical hermeneutics, I argue that interpretation remains incomplete unless the reader "appropriates" the world of the work. Such an appropriation requires the reader to loosen the reins of interpretation governed by the "narcissistic ego"; rather than "taking hold of things," the reader instead follows the

---

7. The "world of the work" constitutes "a proposed world, a world that I might inhabit and wherein I might project my own most possibilities." Ricoeur, "The Hermeneutical Function of Distanciation," 143.

direction of thought opened by the text.[8] At the risk of spoiling the ending for you, it's important to identify several dominant themes in *Coraline*. These oscillate around matters of identity and naming; decorum and defiance; texts and contexts; and vision and blindness.

Identity and Naming

> *Now, you people have names. That's because you don't know who you are.*[9]

Like we who go to Scripture in search of a Word from God for the people of God we are called to serve, Coraline is something of an explorer. Coraline presents herself to the reader as one with all the makings of a fine preacher: she's inquisitive, thoughtful, relentless, and unwilling to follow the rules when those rules restrict the flourishing of herself or others. Perhaps this is why I find her a kindred spirit for we who are called to and equipped for the task of exegetical exploration for the betterment of human and non-human others.

Here's the first thing we must get straight: we read biblical texts and proclaim those texts out of our lived experiences. Always. This means that no matter how deftly we wield our interpretive scalpel, we cannot excise our cultural contexts from our efforts at meaning-making. Merold Westphal puts this point clearly: "Our interpretations are relative to (conditioned by) the presuppositions we bring with us, and those presuppositions, as human, all too human, are themselves relative (penultimate, revisable, even replaceable) and not absolute."[10] Some of these presuppositions are the product of our education—both formal and informal. We intuit ways to interpret biblical texts out of our ecclesial and cultural contexts. This means that every act of interpretation for sermon development takes place from a particular angle of vision of the world.

As it is for all biblical interpreters, Coraline is indelibly marked by the world around her. I love how Gaiman fosters narrative drive by placing this obstacle between our protagonist and her needs, wants, and desires; when her temperament drives her to the outside, her circumstances constrain her to the inside. The generative tension between the freedom we claim as relatively autonomous subjects and those social conditions

---

8. Ricoeur, *Interpretation Theory*, 94.
9. Gaiman, *Coraline*, 35.
10. Westphal, *Whose Community, Which Interpretation?*, 14–15.

that delimit our freedom shapes all possibilities of interpretation. It is this tension that piques the interest of deconstructors such as myself.

In homiletics, generations of scholars have worked hard to cultivate homiletical utopias to protect preachers from the hermeneutical specters lurking and leering at us from behind the chancel. To name but one example, homiletician HyeRan Kim-Cragg summons the specter of white supremacy from the shadows and into the light by challenging homileticians who fail to name the ways our race, gender, sexual orientation, ability, etc. shape the kinds of meanings the biblical text yields for teaching and preaching.[11] By virtue of my intersectional identity as a mostly straight, cisgender, presently able-bodied, white man in America, I was embarrassingly far along in my theological education before I realized that my ways of interpreting scripture reinforce my sociopolitical privilege. It didn't help that when I went to the "experts" in the commentaries to bolster the viability of my interpretations, those white, male biblical scholars had already rendered an interpretation that confirmed mine in advance because they were reading Scripture from the same intersectional place as I.

The first step toward transgressive preaching is to name ourselves before the text. Knowing and naming who we are enables us to grapple with the myriad ways of being and belonging conditioning our hermeneutics a priori.

Decorum & Defiance

> *Coraline wasn't allowed in there. Nobody went in there.*
> *It was only for the best.*[12]

The story of *Coraline* proceeds from an act of defiance. Coraline finds herself in her family's drawing room where they keep all the expensive (and uncomfortable) furniture they'd inherited from Coraline's grandmother. Gaiman tells us explicitly that Coraline wasn't allowed in there. Guess where she goes the instant she has a chance? That's right, the drawing room.

The following day, Coraline bumps into a few of her neighbors. She visits a pair of elderly women who invite her for tea before bumping into

---

11. Kim-Cragg, "Unfinished and Unfolding Tasks of Preaching," 6–7. See also Valle-Ruiz and Wymer, *Unmasking White Preaching*.

12. Gaiman, *Coraline*, 6.

the "crazy old man upstairs." This unnamed neighbor informs Coraline that his pet mice have a special message for her. He says their message for her is this: "Don't go through the door." Amid the absurdity of a man passing along a secret message from his mice not to go through a door that is bricked up emerges a scenario that is fundamentally human and deeply philosophical. Any act of transgression requires a concerted effort to question and defy received norms and traditions when they impinge upon the flourishing of all. As my Columbia Seminary colleague Mitzi Smith puts it, "To expect communities most impacted by social injustice to ignore their oppressions in the process of interpretation places a greater and often unbearable burden on them as readers of sacred texts."[13]

Thinking about biblical interpretation, some of the most profound and politically potent readings of Scripture arise from similar acts of defiance. Only when certain rules or norms are imposed upon us can an act of transgression take place. Coraline is commanded twice—by her mother and the mice—that the drawing room and its mysterious door are out of bounds. Similarly, due to the accretion of hermeneutical wisdom and the purported sin of eisegesis, certain readings of texts are deemed off-limits or out of bounds. More on this later.

Moving toward a transgressive hermeneutic calls us to disregard decorum in the name of justice and freedom. With Coraline, we are wise to question both the necessity and veracity of our received norms. When reading texts that cut against the grain of "malestream" interpretations,[14] we would do well to question why such readings are out of bounds and who holds the power to enforce such boundaries. We might further press this point, asking who stands to benefit from maintaining such norms. We ought to interrogate the grounds upon which such lines of true or false readings are drawn. Are such grounds necessary or are they contingent upon beliefs that benefit those who already hold power? As my Columbia Seminary colleague Raj Nadella argues, no situated viewpoint is sufficient for rendering a final judgment on what a biblical text ought to mean.[15] Boundary keepers and boundary breakers face off between restriction and resistance. Hence, our hermeneutical hackles should be raised whenever we are told that a

---

13. M. J. Smith, *Womanist Sass and Talk Back*, 1.

14. This neologism is Elisabeth Schüssler Fiorenza's. See her *Jesus and the Politics of Interpretation*.

15. Nadella, *Dialogue not Dogma*, 130–31. See also Blount, *Cultural Interpretation*.

text *must* be interpreted in such and such a way. Coraline's defiance is a model worthy of homiletical emulation.

Some days later, Coraline returns to the drawing-room door. Gaiman writes, "Coraline stopped and listened. She knew she was doing something wrong; she was trying to listen for her mother coming back, but she heard nothing. Then Coraline put her hand on the doorknob and turned it; and, finally, she opened the door."[16] To transgress boundaries and borders in the spirit of Coraline, the preacher must go rogue, or even become a kind of rogue for the sake of the gospel.[17] By transgressing boundaries, the preacher can enter this other world of language *in a certain way*. This attitude or approach of defiance—of wanting to discern what is hidden, what is present in its absence, what is necessarily excluded, what is other in the world of language—features centrally in readings attuned to the constructed and thereby contingent nature of texts—even biblical texts.[18]

Texts and Contexts

> *There was something very familiar about it . . . She knew where she was: she was in her own home. She hadn't left.*[19]

It will not surprise you to hear that texts are constructed. But what if I told you contexts are constructed as well? When we speak of contexts, we refer to the social, political, and linguistic strata that constitute our ways of being, behaving, and belonging. The constructed—and thereby contingent and deconstructable—nature of our contexts appears less obvious to us than do texts. We can hold texts in our hands. We can feel the texture of the paperboard, cloth, or leather binding the pages together. Our contexts are far more ethereal and conceptual. Our contexts condition our interpretive capacities. When we apply said capacities to texts, those texts, in turn, impact how we understand ourselves in relation to our contexts. Paul Ricoeur describes this process as an

---

16. Gaiman, *Coraline*, 24.
17. Derrida, "The Rogue That I Am."
18. "If we are to approach a text, it must have an edge . . . [But] a 'text' . . . is henceforth no longer a finished corpus of writing, some content enclosed in a book or its margins, but a differential network, a fabric of traces referring endlessly to something other than itself, to other differential traces." Derrida, "Living On," 256–57.
19. Gaiman, *Coraline*, 25.

ever-expanding vertical spiral.[20] Meaning emerges from interactions between our world and the world of the text, which continues through subsequent reading and reflection.

When we talk about accessing biblical wisdom, we frequently employ spatial metaphors. Even the interpretive modalities delimited by exegesis and eisegesis presuppose a directionality and a movement out of or into the text (the Greek prefix *ex-* equates to the English prepositions "out of" or "away from" while the Greek prefix *eis-* equates to the English prepositions "in" or "into").[21] Here is where the hermeneutical method intervenes, purporting to provide "proper" access to biblical wisdom. But the method will not save us. Interpreting biblical texts is far less straightforward than following instructions to assemble a piece of furniture. The hermeneutical method is frequently commended to deliver the would-be interpreter to the promised land of biblical understanding. But such a utopian vision presents as many problems as it solves.

A utopia is, by definition, a non-place—u-topia (from the Greek *ou* = "no/non" + *topos* = "place").[22] This is how I learned to interpret scripture. I was taught that if I followed the precise steps for a "proper" interpretation, I would wield the keys to unlocking the mysteries of God. The first step in this approach was to bracket all bias from my reading. I was inaugurated into that mythical land where my gendered, ethnic, and culturally ingrained ways of being, behaving, and belonging held little bearing upon textual meaning. It was because of a utopian vision that I strove to master historical-critical methods of biblical interpretation. This utopia was a haven constructed to protect me from the sin of all sins: eisegesis. We were taught the "science" of exegesis, by which we read out of the text what God wanted to say rather than reading into the text what we wanted it to mean. It took me a long time before I discerned the futility—nay, impossibility—of a reading that sufficiently bracketed my culturally conditioned perspectives to discern a capital-M Meaning free from my ideological prejudices. It was a profound wakeup call when I discovered that biblical meaning-making was indelibly marked, or contaminated, by my ways of being and belonging.[23]

20. Ricoeur, *Time and Narrative*, vol. 1, 54–64. The technical term for this is threefold mimesis.

21. "All exegesis [is] ultimately eisegesis." Segovia, *Decolonizing Biblical Studies*, 152.

22. On this point, see Foucault's 1967 essay, "Of Other Spaces: Utopias and Heterotopias."

23. The fear of eisegetical contamination was profound in my Southern Baptist

When Coraline passes through the corridor to arrive in the other flat, where she encounters her other parents and other neighbors, she discovers a world very much like the one she left behind. Gaiman narrates, "The house looked exactly the same from the outside. Or almost exactly the same" (33). Here's the primary takeaway from this for our present concerns: understanding the "world of the work" can only arise from a pre-understanding based on sameness. However, as Heidegger first recognized, our pre-understandings often remain hidden from us. Another way to say this is that we always begin to interpret from where we already are. Heidegger spoke of this in terms of our "thrownness" into the world of culture that indelibly shapes our interpretive possibilities. Like the proverbial fish that remains oblivious to the water in which it swims, our "facticity" or "factual life" determines, in part, what we see and how we see.[24] This means that every interpretation of the world presupposes a prior interpretation by the world. Our hermeneutical efforts cannot arise from a naive perspective that denies or brackets our facticity. When we start from no-place, we end nowhere.

Tentatively venturing into this new space that was simultaneously the same and different from her own, Coraline encounters a man and a woman who bear an unsettling resemblance to her own parents and yet they were very much not her parents. They are disturbingly intent that Coraline remains with them. Upon a subsequent trip to the other drawing room, she discovers that the door is locked and that she cannot return to her own flat. She leaves the other flat through the front door that opens not into the world she had known, but to another world. This was a world suffused with mist. Gaiman explains that it felt like she was walking into nothingness: "The world she was walking through was a pale nothingness, like a blank sheet of paper or an enormous, empty white room.... For a moment she wondered if she might not have gone blind. But no, she could see herself, plain as day. There was no ground beneath her feet, just a misty, milky whiteness."[25]

Because deconstruction is also hyper-vigilant about how language structures reality, it calls us to interrogate how our linguistic structures enable and constrain our understanding. This drives to the heart of

---

ecclesial context. See Derrida, "Violence and Metaphysics," 129, where he asserts that all phenomena and every interpretation "supposes original contamination by the sign [i.e., language]."

24. See Heidegger, *Ontology*, 5.
25. Gaiman, *Coraline*, 70–71.

deconstruction's provocative, and often misunderstood, tagline: "There is no outside-text."[26] This doesn't mean that there is no such thing as reality, or that all is language. Rather, it means that language, as a constant movement of differences in which we find no stable resting point, makes it impossible to appeal to reality as a refuge independent of language. Everything acquires the instability and ambiguity that is inherent in language. Deconstruction works to unveil the constructed reality of the contingent, dreamlike world established by language. Reality depends on the language we use to label it. Deconstruction blurs the lines between language and reality, between text and context. After all, "every text is a text on a text under a text, without any established hierarchy."[27] Deconstructors understand that there is no way outside of the linguistic world, that the so-called "real" world can in no way supervene upon the "other" world fabricated in and through language. The real world has always already escaped and is beyond our reach amid the endless play of differences necessary to simulate sameness. The fancy philosophical word for this is *mimesis*.

By attending to a certain troubling of language, deconstruction can open our facility with language in and through Christian preaching. Deconstruction arises out of a transgression of language; that is, a use of language that infringes upon linguistic codes.[28] Preachers who adopt this way of seeing will begin to detect philosophical and theological commitments underwriting certain patterns of discourse, and they will seek to insert themselves upon those codes in fidelity to the gospel

26. Derrida, *Of Grammatology*, 158. Derrida's much abused observation, *il n'y a pas de hors-texte*, does not mean there is no reference, but that there is no reference without difference, without *différance*. "When I say there is nothing outside the text," explains Derrida, "I mean there is nothing outside the context." Derrida, "Hospitality," 79.

27. Bennington, *Jacques Derrida*, 92. Bennington continues, "But if we thus place in doubt the distinctions between text and context on the one hand, object-language and metalanguage on the other, we are not flattening everything into a single homogeneous text: on the contrary, we are multiplying differences within the text, whose unity and closure were given only by the context supposed to surround it . . . the context is already remarked in the text, the object-language already infiltrated with metalanguage: to this extent we ought to be able, up to a point, to find resources for reading 'in' the text being read" (93).

28. See Derrida, *Of Grammatology*, 158: "[T]he writer writes in a language and in a logic whose proper system, laws, and life his discourse by definition cannot dominate absolutely. He uses them only by letting himself . . . be governed by the system. And the reading must always aim at a certain relationship, unperceived by the writer, between what he commands and what he does not command of the patterns of the language that he uses."

of liberation. This is why so many so-called "postmodern" theologians and philosophers employ hyphens, parentheses, and slashes in our scholarly dis-course.

Vision and Blindness

> *It was funny, Coraline thought. The other mother did not look anything like her own mother. She wondered how she had ever been deceived into imagining a resemblance.*[29]

Transgressive preaching calls us to hold text and context together. Doing so opens our eyes to the ways texts delimit freedom for some while bolstering that of others. As Mitzi Smith avers, "When we turn a blind eye to biases and violence in our sacred (con)texts, the likelihood is great that we will learn to internalize the oppression in (con)texts and read as oppressed people, rather than as a people who value and seek freedom for ourselves and others."[30] Here Smith leads us to a final point of connection between biblical interpretation and *Coraline*. Why, we might wonder, would any preacher "turn a blind eye" to violence and oppression? That's not a very Jesusy way to be. Here is where the dialectical motifs of vision and blindness become imperative for transgressive preaching.

Deconstruction is first and foremost a way of seeing. As John Caputo puts it, "Instead of a phenomenology of the bedazzling brilliance of givenness, deconstruction is 'writing in the dark,' groping like a blind man feeling his way with his stick (or stylus), producing at most a self-interrupting, quasi-phenomenology of 'blindness' and of expectant faith—*il faut croire* [one must believe]—in something coming, I know not what, something I cannot see, something *tout autre* [wholly other]."[31] A major feature of the other mother's insidiousness in *Coraline* pertains to Coraline's capacity to see the other world. Gaiman writes,

> "So," said her other father. "Do you like it here?"
> I suppose," said Coraline. "It's much more interesting than home."
> They went inside. "I'm glad you like it," said Coraline's mother. "Because we'd like to think that this is your home. You can stay here forever and always. If you want to." . . .

---

29. Gaiman, *Coraline*, 126.
30. M. J. Smith, *Womanist Sass and Talk Back*, 3.
31. Caputo, *Collected Philosophical and Theological Papers*, vol. 3, 128.

"If you want to stay," said her other father, "there's only one little thing we'll have to do, so you can stay here forever and always."

They went into the kitchen. On a china plate on the kitchen table was a spool of black cotton, and a long silver needle, and, beside them, two large black buttons.

"I don't think so," said Coraline.[32]

The "one little thing" required for Coraline to remain in her other parents' utopia is to surrender the one thing enabling her to see the other flat for what it is: her vision. As her other parents have buttons for eyes, they want her to forsake her own ability to see, forcing Coraline to "see" just as they see—which is to not *really* see, i.e., they wish to rob her of her hermeneutical capacities.

Interpretation is a function of our ways of seeing and hearing. It is conditioned by the ideologies and prejudices transmitted to us without our being aware of it. So, how might we see and hear biblical texts so that our readings and proclamatory efforts do not substantiate the status quo but are liberating to those relegated to the margins of society by virtue of their intersectional identities? A way beyond this impasse is to forefront hermeneutics by acknowledging the culturally conditioned nature of our ways of seeing and hearing, of our understanding.

Here we have a final signpost on our road of hermeneutical deconstruction: our boldness in venturing to read scripture otherwise than we've always heard it read makes the text strange again. The text itself has not changed, but our perception of the text has shifted. It's the same text, but it now appears different, other. This leads us to another motif in *Coraline* that plays between vision and blindness. We've already witnessed the obscuring quality of the mist suffusing the other world. Thematically, the mist holds a pivotal role. It not only limits Coraline's desire to explore but also restricts her ability to see the other world truly.

But *Coraline* illuminates our capacities to resist an imposed blindness in another way. Before transgressing decorum and traversing the distance between her flat and the other flat, Coraline receives from one of her neighbors a boon: a small stone with a hole carved through it. As the other mother's fabricated world grows increasingly perilous, Coraline discovers that when she peers through the hole, she can see souls that the other mother has trapped and hidden in the other flat. Just

---

32. Gaiman, *Coraline*, 43.

having the stone in her pocket clears her head—"as if she had come out of some sort of fog."[33]

Coraline models a hermeneutic that resists conformity in favor of liberation. This liberation is just as much for herself as it is for the others, who, like her real parents, are constrained by constructs delimiting their freedom and agency (i.e., they are the other mother's prisoners). When she peers through the stone, Coraline recognizes the real from the imaginary. Through it, she comes to see one of her other neighbors as "just a bad copy."[34]

Upon her return to her world from the other world created by the other mother, Gaiman writes, "The light that came through the picture window was daylight, real golden late-afternoon daylight, not a white mist light. The sky was a robin's-egg blue, and Coraline could see trees and, beyond the trees, green hills, which faded on the horizon into purples and grays. The sky had never seemed so sky, the world had never seemed so world."[35]

Gaiman renders narratively what Ricoeur describes philosophically. Our engagement with texts from our respective contexts can broaden our horizon for self-understanding.[36] Moreover, far from saying that a subject already mastering her own way of being in the world projects her self-understanding on the text and reads it into the text, Ricoeur contends that textual interpretation discloses new modes of being, behaving, and belonging; it gives to the subject a new capacity for understanding.[37] In terms of Gaiman's tale, it is only *after* Coraline has perceived the ways that entering the other flat curbed her ways of making sense of the other world that she can perceive her context afresh; the blindness she experienced in the text conditions her vision beyond it.

Conclusion: Transgressing the Same

> *"She wants something to love, I think," said the cat.*

---

33. Gaiman, *Coraline*, 67.
34. Gaiman, *Coraline*, 118.
35. Gaiman, *Coraline*, 135.
36. Ricoeur, "Metaphor and the Main Problem of Hermeneutics," 107.
37. Ricoeur, *Interpretation Theory*, 94.

> "Something that isn't her. She might want something to eat as well. It's hard to tell with creatures like that."[38]

Gaiman's loquacious cat offers Coraline and us an insight so subtle it's easy to overlook its profundity. It is this distinction between a love that consumes the other's otherness and one that preserves it that makes all the difference for a transgressive preaching philosophy. Between erasing and underscoring otherness rests the difference between destruction and deconstruction. Deconstruction, Derrida says, amounts to an act of "loving even the invisibility that keeps the other inaccessible."[39] Such an approach to the other recognizes a very Western tendency to reduce otherness to sameness. Derrida, for whom Lévinas's ethics of otherness is also a profound lesson, proffers a way of reading and writing that elevates every other to the wholly other (*tout autre*). Because the other is "infinitely other," the other remains, at its core, inaccessible, so that not even an infinite amount of time spent in contact with the other ego will bridge that gap. For Lévinas, this gap is not merely an epistemic gap that must somehow be crossed—though this is what many proponents of historical-critical hermeneutics presume—but an ethical "abyss" to be affirmed and honored. Such is the condition of love.[40]

The other mother's declared intention that she created the other flat out of love for Coraline is not without its conditions. The other mother says, "Now, if you will be a good child who loves her mother, be compliant and fair-spoken, you and I shall understand each other perfectly and we shall love each other perfectly as well."[41] We find a parallel sentiment expressed by Coraline's other father a bit later in the story: "Stay here with us," said the voice from the figure at the end of the room. "We will listen to you and play with you and laugh with you. Your other mother will build whole worlds for you to explore, and tear them down every night when you are done. Every day will be better and brighter than the one that went before."[42] Such a utopic vision might seem enticing, but notice the steep entry fee for inhabiting this world. To fully immerse herself in the other mother's reality requires that Coraline surrender the very aspects of her

---

38. Gaiman, *Coraline*, 63.
39. Derrida, *Sauf le nom*, 74.
40. Lévinas, *Ethics and Infinity*, 67. True love for Lévinas "is a relation with that which always slips away."
41. Gaiman, *Coraline*, 88.
42. Gaiman, *Coraline*, 43.

identity that make her Coraline. Transposing this encounter onto our homiletical concerns means prohibiting any transgression of the imposed hermeneutical norm. What her other parents highlight as care and concern ends up looking more like consumption. One cannot presume to love the other while devouring the very things that make them *other*.

Deconstruction provides the transgressive preacher a way to approach the otherness of the text as *other*. It marks every assertion as to the meaning of the biblical text as finite and conditional. It fosters in us as readers of sacred texts and contexts a disposition that seeks above all the other's flourishing—whether that other be other reading communities beyond our own, the others populating the text, or the divine otherness rendered in and through Scripture. The degree to which we resist the temptation to totalize textual meaning will enable us to preserve its hermeneutical possibilities. As Raj Nadella observes, "It may be that, regardless of the essence and nature of a text, its reception is mostly determined by the interpretive choices made by the reading communities. Specifically, their openness to indeterminacy and the degree to which assumptions about scripture shape their reading."[43] When we receive hermeneutical indeterminacy as a mark of love rather than as a deficiency in our reading strategies, we will foster alternative modes of understanding and proclaiming biblical texts that are more, rather than less, faithful to Scripture as such. Or, as Yung Suk Kim poetically puts it,

> Because of this kind of complexity involved in our interpretation, there is a holy, even mystical chasm between the text and the reader; so let it go like a forever running river, which runs all the way to the sea, with detours and meanderings. Yet the goal of the river is to provide a source of life for the people around it. So our interpretation of the Bible, like an ever-flowing river, provides a rich source of life for all only when we engage it through a critical, creative lens locked in human transformation.[44]

---

43. Nadella, *Dialogue not Dogma*, 137.
44. Kim, *Biblical Interpretation*, 16.

4

Black Liberation Hermeneutics and Homiletics

JAMES HENRY HARRIS

Introduction

THE BLACK CHURCH INFORMS my theology and philosophy at every level, whether expounding on my cortical understanding of the mind-body dialectic or a notion of univocity inherent in efforts to maintain a strong sense of selfhood in light of the psychological, spiritual, and social realities of the preacher in the Black church. My work is not just homiletical and hermeneutical, but it is phenomenological. I mean that the absolute and necessary move toward consciousness and selfhood is an unending process explored in different ways and leading to a transformative action. On a very basic level, phenomenology is to be conscious of the meaning and value of one's experience as a particular human being in a particular context. For W. E. B. Du Bois, consciousness is highly correlated with educational enlightenment and understanding of Black oppression and injustice. Black preachers are compelled to augment their understanding of the meaning of consciousness by reading, rereading, and unreading texts (scripture, congregational contexts, social and political policies, practices, etc.) and reinterpreting them to foster freedom and selfhood. This reinterpretation is the cornerstone of my social imaginary, pragmatic linguistic term of *unreading* since America as a "text" is enveloped by metastatic racism that is omnipresent, albeit often disguised as something else or at least scaffolded by something else, i.e., the white church, religion, politics, economics, etc. Du Bois' concept of double consciousness and the veil prompts me to ask: What *is* their practical impact on society's current political interest in rewriting, sanitizing, and even erasing American history? This is another place where interpretation or hermeneutics and Black preaching or homiletics intersect.

It is important to understand that Black life, in general, is a testament to a selfhood that is continuously overcoming the "thing-hood" ascribed to it by the oppressor and explicated by G. F. W. Hegel in *Phenomenology of Spirit*. Blacks have historically possessed not only a strangely unstable sense of self but a self-surpassing understanding of the self which has manifested its mode of being as a type of emphatic otherness. This is contrary to the Eurocentric oppressor who appears to have a systemic lack of consciousness which seeks fulfillment and satisfaction in its possession of the objectified other as slave or something less than the self that needs the other only to satiate its erotic self. This is related to what philosopher William Desmond terms "erotic selving," which is akin to what Hegel called "self-determining negativity," which is an ancestor of Sartre's "self as nothingness: desire is an insatiable lack that wants to devour omnivorously that which is other to itself; it even wants to devour the divine and, in the process, become God."[1] This is the essential problem with proponents and architects of slavery and the dichotomous language of master/slave. It is all about the ungodly white self —seeking to be[come] God. Moreover, the Black self is not only the "I am somebody" of Martin Luther King, Jr. and Jesse Jackson but the "I can do all things through Christ who strengthens me" (Phil 4:13) and the "I will" grounded in the hope and aspiration of scripture and Black religion as practiced in the Black church.

Intersections of Homiletics and Hermeneutics

Preaching is an interpretation event such that it is an interpretation of an interpretation. Every phase of the written and spoken word or

---

1. Desmond, *Ethics and the Between*, 403. See also Sartre, *Being and Nothingness*. Also see especially chapter 3 of Catalano, *A Commentary on Jean-Paul Sartre's Being and Nothingness*. In addition, I endeavor to place the Black self in a larger social and spiritual context correlating Hegel, Sartre, and Desmond's philosophy of religion with the meaning of Black life.

sermon is involved in elements of guessing, divining, understanding, and explaining a text, whether it's the self as text, the congregation as text, the biblical text, and/or the sociocultural context as text. Therefore, the correlation between preaching and hermeneutics is a positive nexeological[2] reality that is evident every time sermonic discourse is developed through writing or speaking.

Black preaching, in its particular authenticity, is compelled to consider, engage, and critique the social situation or the existential reality of Black life. This means that the joys, pain, and suffering of poor, Black, struggling, and disenfranchised people loom large over the preachers as they prepare and deliver sermons. Black preachers do not have the luxury of ignoring the pain and agony of others, too often evident in whiteness, where alterity is practically a dirty word that cannot be uttered in white religion—especially white churches on Sunday mornings. Paul Ricoeur is certainly idealistic and hopeful in thinking and writing of self as other or "oneself as another."[3] This means that the white church and academy tend to think of the Other as a negativity, a less-than-self rather than an extension of the self. Let's face it white Christianity in America has placed its *imprimatur* on chattel slavery, lynchings of Blacks, the bombing of Black churches, etc., while simultaneously building more churches, Christian schools, and worshipping their own white supremacy ideology which in my view has become a deity.

Allow me to tell you the story of a recent experience. One of my church members, let's call him Jacob, graduated from college with a bachelor's degree in exercise science. He got a job teaching physical education at Richmond Christian School, a K–12 establishment in Chesterfield County, Virginia. The young Black man, in his late 20s, taught physical education in their lower, middle, and high school. He was also the basketball coach and the assistant coach in several other sports. Well, on Maundy Thursday, he was fired for speaking "inappropriately" to several boys whom he taught and coached. How do we interpret this situation?

The fact is we have a young Black male teacher with "locs," braids, or plaits. This hairstyle is negativized and associated with a certain [mis]understanding and [mis]interpretation of Blacks. It is a bias against Black and African culture. This deliberate [mis]interpretation is used to develop narratives of negativity that morph into the ontological negation of

---

2. I use this term as a derivative of the Latin and Greek word *nexeo* to mean association or connection.

3. Ricoeur, *Oneself as Another*.

young Black males—professional or otherwise. This type of "otherwise-than-being" tends to dehumanize the individual and create a fear-based narrative based on skin color and hairstyle.[4] Be mindful of the fact that none of this is ever "said." It is all unsaid as a pretext for something else. This is why Jacob, the teacher, was placed on an "improvement plan" because the white parents of their misbehaving children who were disciplined in Jacob's classes complained to the school administration about the teacher. The Black teacher was placed on a punitive plan to improve *his* behavior, while the white students were allowed to continue to disrupt and interrupt his class. This is Kafkaesque and reeks of blatant racism and injustice. But, like most private Christian and church-based schools this school, like thousands of others across the nation, was formed and organized in response to the Supreme Court decision of Brown versus Board of Education of Topeka, Kansas, in 1954.

Imagining Getting in Front of the Text to Create a New World

Being a serious theological student, prophetic pastor, or preacher is about negotiating human affairs such that it demands understanding and explaining the meaning and depths of the economic, racial, and social issues that Black folk face in church and society. In other words, the center of Black cultural and religious understanding is exegetical and hermeneutical, thereby servicing the contextual relevance of sermonic discourse. The Black preacher is compelled to function in the dialecticism of an American imperialist and hostile sociopolitical environment (antithesis) and the loving world of the Black church and community (thesis). Therefore, it is incumbent upon the preacher to read, interpret, and reread her or his socioeconomic location/context by creating another more hopeful world for oppressed and poor people. This is what I call "reading the situation" in the spirit of Jesus Christ and human beings like Frederick Douglass, Sojourner Truth, Fannie Lou Hamer, Martin Luther King, Jr., and Ella Baker among many others.

Rescripting life is what the Black preacher is called to do every Sunday and every day of the week. The script that's been given needs a thorough rewrite which demands reading, rereading, and unreading before it can be uttered to the people. Rescripting the biblical text and unreading the text are the same. It's a liberating process—an event that

---

4. See Lévinas, *Otherwise Than Being*.

must become a habitual practice. This is the Black hermeneutical circle or, more precisely, what I am naming: the "hermeneutical triangle" of reading, rereading, and unreading to create an understanding of Black folk being constantly and systematically thrown into a world of trouble, i.e., pain and suffering undergirded and sustained by racism, injustice, and oppression. In Black preaching, this is where the intersectionality of hermeneutics and homiletics has its birth and future life. This requires boldness and fearlessness, which only the black preacher currently possesses. It is my observation and assessment that white preachers seem to be following along in a linearity that began in slavery and continues in the white church today. For example, the slaves were forbidden to read and write by the metonymical and metaphorical nature of the "master," who was the personified *defacto* law more sovereign than God. The slave master was the god of the American plantation and, in concert with the federal, state, and local government, the nucleus of the slavocracy. He was both supreme judge and jury—a deity whose judgment could not be questioned or appealed.

While I am not suggesting equivalence, I am, however, indicating strongly that the white church's lukewarm and tepid preachers seem to stand in fear of their congregations, refusing to address the issues of white racism and white supremacy, inequality, sexism, injustice, and basic human decency towards Blacks and other oppressed peoples. Frantz Fanon, the French Martinican philosopher and psychiatrist, says that "white people struggle to be human."[5] And, please explain to me how and why current and modern-day Black folk would want to participate in a white church, especially when the slaves who were forbidden by American culture and law to read or write would nevertheless say that "They would rather hear a Black preacher any day than to hear the white slave master's preacher."[6]

The Hermeneutic and Homiletic Triangle: Reading, Rereading, and Unreading

In my preaching classes, it is an interactive, heuristic, and pedagogical practice to read texts (scripture, novels, memoirs, philosophical and

---

5. See Fanon, *Black Skin, White Masks*; Bernasconi, *Critical Philosophy of Race*.

6. See, for example, Stampp, *Peculiar Institution*; Raboteau, *Slave Religion*; Stuckey, *Slave Culture*. See also "Born in Slavery."

theological books, essays, etc.) out loud—an oral and aural exercise. I do this so that students can hear themselves read and for me and others to hear them read, to encourage better listening skills, and to connect what is being heard and spoken to what is seen on the written page. Often, there is a disconnect between the two things where students see one thing with their eyes but read another with their mouths. This is a type of "rewriting" of someone else's written text or a redacting of the written text. Most of the time, this is inadvertently done; however, sometimes, the reader will intentionally interpret, misinterpret, or reinterpret what's on the given page by inserting words or excising words from the text, thereby reinterpreting the given text. This can be construed as a form of creativity; however, that's a positive assessment that is often more generous than it should be. But, it is the reading and rereading that count here as the beginning of exegesis and hermeneutics. When some students read orally, I immediately recognize the degree to which God has gifted them. Their voices are often so beautiful and captivating that they command attention. The hearer is forced to look up and pay attention because of the aural aesthetic quality embedded in their sweet-sounding voices. There is a natural smoothness and tonality coupled with syncopated rhythm and cadence that compel me to take notice and to communicate to them something on the order of "*God has blessed you with a powerful preaching voice. Now, it is incumbent upon you to seek to bless God by learning to preach something meaningful, transformative, and creative when you speak the sermon into existence.*" Moreover, I seek to make it plain and clear that they have never studied music or had a voice or dramaturgy coach, yet they have such a commanding presence made evident through the power of their voice. Accordingly, they need to thank God every day for the grace and kindness bestowed on them. They, like others, did not earn this and don't deserve it in any way. It's all DNA driven and grace given, so let's not abuse the gift by displaying arrogance and hubris. I also try to point out that their evaluations in my classes are based on hard work, not the natural God-given gifts they had when they walked into the classroom.

Martin Luther King, Jr., in his "Letter from Birmingham City Jail," said that when he walked past the white church with its steeple spiraling toward heaven, he wondered, "Who is their God?" The steeple is a symbol and sign of the institutional church and Christians' religious beliefs and practices. It is a sign of those individuals who inhabit the sanctuary believing that their eschatological rituals, doctrines, and spiritual community practices are in synchrony with their perception of the will of God as manifested in their community's interpretation of scripture. The statement by King, however, is a sign of the need for a corrective reading of their beliefs and practices. Like other social theorists and liberation theologians, King's observation is intended to cause those who are part of the white church to begin to correlate scripture with their contextual actions and beliefs, i.e., practices within the church community. This basic theological question grew from his social ontology and frustration with the intractable presence of pandemic injustices and oppression. If the philosopher and religious scholar Peter Ochs is correct in defining Charles Peirce's pragmatism as a corrective reading of itself and others, then Black religion and Black preaching, in particular, is the ultimate pragmatic corrective to traditional religious theory and practices. Peter Ochs writes:

> My thesis is that pragmatic definition is not a discrete act of judgment or classification, but a performance of correcting other, inadequate definitions of imprecise things . . . It is a corrective activity . . . My thesis is therefore not a thesis in the usual sense. Since my claim is that to define pragmatically is to correct and that to correct is to read, my thesis is better named my "corrective reading" . . .[7]

Ochs goes on to say that the aforementioned definition is lacking because pragmatism as correction is a complicated phenomenon that makes continuous correction normative in the Peircian model. I am more interested in the concept and practice of correction that characterizes and constitutes the hermeneutic and homiletic enterprise. Black preaching has necessarily been practiced in an oppressed community of the faithful in a double context of a microcosmic community of care and simultaneously in a macrocosmic community of evil hatred, and disinterest in the Other. The intertextuality of these two worlds constitutes the social context of the Black preacher. And, being caught in the "metaxological"[8] reality of these two contexts, the Black preacher has had to use scripture as a corrective to both—with a particular focus on the Black community. The converse is also true. The Black lived experience is often a corrective to particular experiences as seen in scripture.

---

7. Ochs, *Peirce, Pragmatism and the Logic of Scripture*, 4–5.

8. The term "metaxological" is found in Desmond, *Being and the Between*, 178. Metaxology emphasizes a plurality of the between.

This Du Boisian dilemma has characterized the pragmatics of Black sermonic discourse from slavery to the present.

Getting in front of the text means reading, rereading, and unreading the text as a sociocultural hermeneutical move that allows the preacher to develop and maintain contiguity with the people in the congregation and the local community. Getting in front of the text also means understanding the text in a way that creates proximity between the text and the people. In reading, rereading, and unreading, one has to encounter the biblical world, the modern and postmodern world, and the world of the preacher and the hearer. Getting in front of the text is a spiritual, rational, and emotive enterprise because there are several sides of the same triangle to speak spatially and metaphorically. I am postulating that each generation has to read the text to get in front of it and make it contextually relevant for today and tomorrow. Any preaching that does not get in front of the text to unread white supremacy, injustice, and evil in the world is conformist and afraid to speak truth to power. In this sense, getting in front of the text is hermeneutical and exegetical as well as a social and contextual move designed to create new horizons and a new world absent of oppression and injustice or at least creates an affront to the church and world in their current state.

Prerequisites to Black Preaching: Reading as an Act of Holiness and Meditation

My preaching teacher, Miles J. Jones, had a working definition of preaching that speaks to my thesis. While he implored his students to learn and memorize a definition of preaching advanced by G. Ray Jordan in his book *The Art of Preaching*, by the time of his death in 2002, he had advanced beyond his earlier dependence on other more well-known scholars and literary theorists such as Paul Tillich and I. A. Richards. He developed the correlation method of preaching based on his understanding of Tillich's theology and method of correlation as advanced in Tillich's work in systematic theology.[9] Clearly, the sermon is a work of art; however, it is more than that. It is a work of hermeneutic creativity. And this is what Miles Jones did with the very dense language used by Paul Tillich in his systematic theology. Miles Jones read, reread,

---

9. See Tillich, *Systematic Theology*, vol. 1, 30–31, 59–60, 64–66; Tillich, *Systematic Theology*, vol. 2, 13–16.

and unread what Tillich said about the correlation method. And in his unreading, he was able to appropriate this in such a way that he made it palatable for preachers to understand and practice. This means that Miles Jones was able to make this method his own, which is one of the purposes of exegesis and hermeneutics. Jones demonstrated his own authenticity by unreading and rewriting much of what he gleaned from theologians and philosophers.

Therefore, the best way for the preacher to communicate with the congregation is to figure out how to correlate her experiences with their experiences. This means that the preacher is called to live among the people symbolically and actually. The preacher's experience and the people's experience become more meaningful at the point of intersection.

The witness of the Black preacher is critical to communication. This means, in my constructive approach, that the inner history of the preacher helps to form the sermonic narrative and the theological perspective of the preacher and the people. When this witness and testimony is motivated by love, the understanding of the hearer and the meaning of the preacher are evidenced by an "Aha!" This brings me back to the more advanced definition of Black preaching that Miles Jones had written before he died. In a handout to his students, he wrote the following definition of preaching: "Preaching is the action that creates the avenue for love's entrance into human affairs."[10] In this definition, Miles Jones began to distance himself from the decades-old definition he had used to define the homiletic task. He was no longer satisfied with the mechanical, detached, and sterile definitions of preaching he had advanced for so long. The sermon as a "statement of faith" was now inadequate and invalid—unable to express the deep meaning that preaching held for him. He expounded upon his new definition by saying,

> As "action," the sermon becomes more than statement; it is statement with a dimension of depth that includes the recognition of deed in order to participate in the next level of proclamation. The sermon as statement only, begs for an expression of performance that validates the exhortation and affirms the imperative that is implied in the proclamation itself.[11]

---

10. Harris, *The Word Made Plain*, 39.

11. Miles Jones' working definition of preaching in an unpublished handout to his class on the preparation and delivery of sermons, 1995–2001.

The sermon is an action or deed that is expressed through the act of preaching. Preaching is a performative act that creates something new—something that did not exist heretofore. The sermon has pro-creative power resident in the act of preaching. This language of sexuality signifies creation and newness. Jones states, "The stimulus for the arousal is attributed to the pro-creative relationship inherent in the matter of sermonizing. Preaching implies an engagement between two entities of what is (the situation) and that which works on the situation, namely, the creative potential of the word."[12] This is classic Miles Jones because the structure of his argument remains correlative and thus didactic. Action is correlated with consequence. Preaching is engagement between situation and scripture—like writing is the interplay between situation and story.[13]

Black Preaching, Hermeneutics, and Black Phenomenology

Black preaching is, in fact, a phenomenological hermeneutic in its expressions and embodiment which bears witness to the human pain and anguish of Jesus in the temples, the streets, and on the cross. Moreover, for Blacks in America, the issue is indeed one of Black struggle, oppression, and ubiquitous suffering; however, this is not a question of theodicy for me, but a question of meaning and remembrance. Hermeneutics, homiletics, and phenomenology are interrelated or what I term "nexeological" such that Black people are always interrogating their condition of existence. Jean-Paul Sartre, the existentialist philosopher, says, "We're thrust into freedom" yet we don't know how, why, who, or when we were born. This existential phenomenology exceeds the aporias embedded in Christian theology just as being Black does. Therefore, phenomenology seeks to get back to a consciousness of the things themselves. For Blacks, the relevant question is: How do we get back to understanding and explaining an exile that was not warranted and not wanted? The question is really serious and hard to swallow. This is indeed what Samuel DeWitt Proctor refers to as the certain sound of the trumpet and how they shall hear, which are also titles of two of his books.

---

12. Miles Jones' working definition.
13. See, Harris, *The Word Made Plain*. Also, see Gornick, *The Situation and the Story*.

Agapeic Interlocution and Perlocution-Hermeneutics in Action

Speaking and writing are two sides of the same coin. I often say that my soul speaks to me before I can write a single sentence on the page. And, organically, I am a speaking self, which means that I literally speak sermonic words onto the page verbally and simultaneously as my hand seeks to keep pace with these illocutionary habits. This is something I learned in the Black church long before I ever heard of Paul Ricoeur or his philosophical hermeneutics and phenomenology. The Black church was/is the incubator and promoter of eloquent speech and rhetorical flair. For example, Miles Jerome Jone and Paul Nichols, like many others, preached in "demonstration of the spirit and of power."[14] This practice is instrumental in developing preaching as an art grounded in speech, scripture, experience, theory and practice, reading and rereading. And, central to my theology as action, "unreading" is the most critical component of the hermeneutic and homiletic process, which is intended to foster understanding, explanation, and social transformation. The sermon is a revolutionary act of love and creation, which means that the world as it is must be prompted and pushed, i.e., intentionally challenged to become something other than what it is. This serious and continuous prompting and encouragement is the power of the Black preacher's sermon, which is designed to create a new world. This revolutionary act of creation is an act of agapeic love. Indeed, Fannie Lou Hamer, Martin Luther King, Jr., bell hooks, and the Danish philosopher Soren Kierkegaard are right, "love is a revolution."[15]

The Homiletics of Unreading in the Interpretation of History

The modern Black preacher, as an activist and public intellectual, is compelled to augment her understanding of the meaning of consciousness by reading, rereading, and unreading texts and contexts, including scripture, congregations, poems, books, social/cultural contexts, policies, and practices, etc. and reinterpreting them to foster freedom and selfhood. This reinterpretation is the cornerstone of my pragmatic linguistic term "unreading" inasmuch as America as a "text" is enveloped by metastatic racism

---

14. See 1 Cor 2:4–5; Rom 1:16.

15. See King, *Strength to Love*; Kierkegaard, *Works of Love*; Perkins, ed., *The International Kierkegaard Commentary*.

that is omnipresent, albeit often disguised as a pretense towards something else, i.e., diversity, equity, and inclusion or even white fragility.

In three hundred years or more of American history, the slave system is the evil that has no rivalry. It alone is the ultimate "game of thrones" where power and money are often the expressed desire of the white few without apology or pretense—characterized by extreme Christian/white supremacy and racial prejudice with no interest in alterity. The driving force at work here is the advancement of self. Power, at all costs, is the unabashedly evil goal! There is no "Other," except the self as other in a very ego-driven, maniacal, and mendacious quest to become the embodiment of siloistic power. This is the white American interpretation of the Ricouerian concept of "Oneself as Another," where the self always violates, cancels, and destroys the non-white other.[16] There is no such thing as the Black "Other" human being.

Forward Thinking: Getting in Front of the Text as Unreading

> "Beloved, I do not consider that I have made it on my own, but this one thing I do: forgetting what lies behind and straining forward to what lies ahead, I press toward the goal for the prize of the heavenly call of God in Christ Jesus." (Phil 3:13–14)

Memory is the enigmatic presence of absence. It can be characterized as the dredging and delving into some event, some past experience—either trauma, something terrible and terrifying, or something jubilant and joyous. We love to remember something happy, something filled with anamnestic emotions and enjoyment. Memory is a past that never really dies, and it is not even past if we can recall regardless of how deep it is. It is buried in our consciousness, our unconsciousness, through force, delusion, or delay. Not only that, but we keep our memories alive through photographs—pictures framed and tamed—photoshopped and airbrushed to capture and maintain our wrinkle-free youth and to remember days and years long gone, erased by the passage of time.

For the slaves, transported from their homeland to Maryland, Virginia, and points south, the evil of slavery was to erase all memories of family, religion, and culture from their consciousness by first taking away their language, names, starving them, beating, maiming, raping and murdering them with a brutal, cruel, and violent caravan of inhumane actions.

---

16. Ricoeur, *Oneself as Another*.

Forgetting is a threat to both history and memory, and it's always lurking in the shadow of our minds and on the horizon of our remembering. And yet, some people and some things must be forgotten and forgiven. The scripture text above (Phil 3:13–14) is certainly about moving forward, but it is also a prescription for how to reach one's goal. How to overcome the obstacles to success and how to keep your eyes on the prize of the upward call of God. In other words, we, as a people, must learn how to keep stepping—one foot at a time, not being deterred by the roadblocks and negative energy from folk around us, no matter who they are or what their motives are. Even if it's your memory, your mental monsters harassing and hampering your hopes and dreams, confusing your mind to make you think you are incapable of doing what God has equipped you to do. Forget that! "Beloved, I do not consider that I have made it my own, but this one thing I do: forgetting what lies behind . . ."

This is deliberate. It is freedom from restraint and restriction. It is an escape from the debilitating power of memory. It is a dangerous disremembering of the past in search of moving forward and creating a future. This is my point: we forget not to erase traces of our past. No. We must not forget that forgetting has a specific and singular purpose. Forgetting is not a reflection or even a distancing of ourselves from our history and memory, but forgetting is a forward action —propelling us to new heights, new horizons, new hopes, new dreams, and new experiences unburdened by the past. Forgetting what's behind and pressing, straining, struggling, moving forward to what's ahead. That's my goal, and I can't reach it without forgetting some ugly and debilitating stuff. It's behind me now. It's back there. It's still looking and lurking in my history, my memory, but I'm not back there anymore. We as a people are now free from what's behind us. "One thing I do: forgetting what lies behind and straining forward to what lies ahead . . ." It's just one thing I do. It's an action. It's a *doing!* Forget and move forward in synchronized steps. I forget in order to move forward, and we move forward in order to never forget knowing and believing that Christ Jesus has made us his own.

PART TWO

Interpreting the Book of Ruth and Homiletic Overtures

5

Biblical Irony and Emancipatory Proclamation

The Book of Ruth as Exemplary Locus for Feminist Homiletics

CAROLYN J. SHARP

Introduction

HOW MIGHT FEMINISTS PREACH on the book of Ruth? This exquisitely crafted novella from antiquity presents superb opportunities to consider issues of belonging, gender, and power from the pulpit. Expert homiletical engagement of biblical narratives requires that preachers steep themselves in Scripture, searching out themes and intertexts to which the focal text alludes, listening for subtleties in characterization and dialogue, and the like. One vital purpose of preaching is to draw believers into Scripture, guiding them into an emancipatory Word that deepens their capacity to discern the ways of God. Effective preaching should catalyze holy curiosity in hearers about the treasure to be found in sacred texts. The book of Ruth offers treasure indeed.

As a public-facing discipline within practical theology, homiletics explores theological and ethical issues via sermons and homilies, testimony, and other modes of witness in community. Since antiquity, preaching has constituted a major site of theological and ethical reflection, catechetical instruction, and pastoral engagement for communities of conviction. Preachers testify to divine grace in the creation of the world and the healing of its brokenness; grace in the calling and redeeming of people obedient to God's purposes; grace in the witness of healers, artists, writers, activists, and others to the catalytic truth of divine love; and grace anticipated in a radiant eschatological future. Divine grace is explored in the Hebrew Scriptures through narratives and poetry about Israel and Judah journeying with God through defining moments of belonging, halakhic observance, and conflict, prophetic vision and wisdom, and the tragedies and triumphs of geopolitical history. Divine grace is explored in the New Testament in plurivocal ways that draw on the witness of the Hebrew Scriptures to ground and proclaim the new thing God has done in Jesus of Nazareth, acclaimed by Christians as the Messiah.

Among diverse purposes of Christian preaching, classic homiletical foci have included preaching as logocentric theology, preaching as a witness for social justice, preaching as spiritual formation, and preaching as a sacramental sign of the inbreaking reign of God. Three fresh approaches will help frame my exploration of Ruth as a resource for feminist homiletics: preaching as decolonizing discourse, preaching as coalitional relationality, and preaching as radical solidarity with those who suffer.

First, Sarah Travis urges that preachers resist colonizing discourses that render as natural the exploitation of those perceived through derogatory ideologies of ethnicity, race, economic class, or migration status. "We preach in the interstices of empire," she observes, thus a crucial homiletical goal is "to aid listeners in constructing a worldview attentive to the effects of empire, a profound and loving ethical engagement with a multiplicity of others, and an identity not limited to what the empire seeks to construct and endorse."[1] Because in many cultural formations, including biblical texts, "the colonized other is inserted into the discursive space fully formed in the colonizer's own image,"[2] preachers on the book of Ruth will need to be alert to ways in which Moabite identity is construed there. Travis argues, "Preaching addresses all who have been implicated in the systems of empires—perpetrators, victims, and bystanders."[3] Her point is relevant not only to listeners in the sanctuary but to all throughout the history of reception who have heard interpretations

---

1. Travis, *Decolonizing Preaching*, 38.
2. Travis, *Decolonizing Preaching*, 79.
3. Travis, *Decolonizing Preaching*, 93.

ignorant of, complicit with, or disruptive of imperial power. Travis affirms that postcolonial biblical interpretation for the pulpit "does not collapse or homogenize various interpretations, but reads contrapuntally; that is, approaches the text with a simultaneous awareness of multiple perspectives, including colonized and colonizer, metropolis and periphery, and others," with the aim of "exposing threads of colonial/imperial domination embodied in biblical texts and subsequent interpretations of those texts."[4] Key to my reading of Ruth is making visible the text's ironic disruption of imperial domination.

Second, Donyelle McCray has drawn insights for womanist preaching from a 1999 event in which the voices of Alice Walker, Angela Davis, and June Jordan were hosted. McCray analyzes the event as an exemplary instance of Black feminist collectivity in public proclamation, something that may be taken implicitly to contest the monologic authority of the preacher's voice in the traditional pulpit. Noting, "Blackness has historically accompanied a struggle to be heard and seen in one's complexity amid the forces of white reduction,"[5] McCray offers a reframing of homiletical practice via Black feminist relationality: "Black feminist care encompasses a broad array of public and private practices of succor and mutual encouragement that cultivate delight, creativity, and self-definition in Black women," including "candid . . . engagement with the coalescing effects of race, class, gender, sexuality, and experiences of migration on human experience."[6] McCray suggests that "layered proclamation" of the "multi-angled story" of the Gospels is vital for the decolonization of preachers' imaginations and for fostering relationships of mutuality in a polyphony of perspectives.[7] She is interested in dialogical preaching practices, proposing a "triptych" model in which three homilists might preach in a single worship service to yield a "kaleidoscopic and coalitional vision of preaching."[8] My own work has focused on the literary interpretation of Scripture deepened by feminist ideology critique

---

4. Travis, *Decolonizing Preaching*, 112–13. Postcolonial interpretations analyze multiple discursive levels of ideological subjugation and social exclusion. Some biblical traditions that articulate the speaking subject's trauma also reperform discursive violence against enemies (as in prophetic oracles against the nations and psalms of imprecation). In such cases, it is ethically imperative that preachers honor the text's truth-telling about trauma while declining calls for vengeance.

5. McCray, "Black Feminist Triptych," 12.

6. McCray, "Black Feminist Triptych," 6.

7. McCray, "Black Feminist Triptych," 8, 13.

8. McCray, "Black Feminist Triptych," 10.

and shaped by hermeneutics informed by postmodern approaches to poetics. McCray and I share an interest in polyphony as destabilizing hegemonic views of agency and authoritarian constraints on meaning. Honoring polyphony is essential to my reading of Ruth.

Third, Megan McKenna affirms that "preaching is the process of integrating the Word into our own person" and striving "to translate it for our community, with their help . . . . witnessing and revealing to others what obedience to" God's emerging kingdom might mean by "uncovering God's hidden presence loose in the world."[9] McKenna avers, "The Word and our preaching must teach compassion and solidarity with others' suffering, their forsakenness, being outcast, abandoned, left behind, excluded . . . . This is God-seeing life . . . to help the lost find themselves again, and in doing so, being 'found' ourselves, becoming human."[10] McKenna's incarnational theology underscores the importance of the preacher's leadership in fostering empathy. Preachers should explicate vividly the ways in which biblical texts represent cruelty and compassion, deprivation and deliverance, forsakenness and fortitude. Preaching should honor the depth and richness of the human story with its yearnings and conflicts, its moments of desperation and bitterness as well as joy and trust, as an invitation to radical solidarity. Further, the exegete should take seriously the wildness and hiddenness of the God of Scripture. When we lose ourselves in the toxicity of political and social violence against others, whether such violence be encountered in biblical rhetoric, theology, or politics, we return to our humanness not by conforming ourselves to distorted social norms but by opening our hearts and minds to the "summoning Mystery"[11] whose ways are not like our ways (Isa 55:8–9). Embracing solidarity with those who suffer is at the heart of the mystery of divine love (Luke 4:16–21).

In what follows, I explore dimensions of ironic storytelling in Ruth that can help preachers engage the homiletical goals identified above: 1) to disrupt colonizing ideology, 2) to honor polyphony in the preaching event, and 3) to ground our humanness in solidarity with the suffering Other.

---

9. McKenna, "Navigating Mystery," 19.
10. McKenna, "Navigating Mystery," 25.
11. Brueggemann, *Deep Memory, Exuberant Hope*, 122.

Hermeneutical Horizon

My interpretation of Ruth constitutes a transgressive reading over against several kinds of consensus views: rabbinic celebration of Ruth as a paradigmatic convert to Judaism;[12] the age-old Christian claim that Ruth is an exemplary model of faith; many feminist interpreters' conviction that the relationship between Naomi and Ruth is mutually supportive; and the focus in traditional homiletics on "the" message of a biblical text, as versus listening for polyphonic possibilities in biblical signifying.

Literarily Astute Reading and Feminist Homiletics

The present essay is positioned at the nexus of two trajectories of scholarly inquiry that have been explored for decades in the humanities but are still emerging as loci of engagement within homiletics: analysis of the effects of literary irony on meaning-making in and with biblical texts, and feminist hermeneutics informed by contemporary gender studies.

Literary Analysis of Irony

Analysis of the operations of literary irony has a long history in criticism. The reader eager to delve into literary irony may consult works by Katharina Barbe, Wayne Booth, Paul Duke, Joana Garmendia, Edwin Good, Linda Hutcheon, Uwe Japp, Søren Kierkegaard, Hannele Kohvakka, Edgar Lapp, Douglas Muecke, Mark Nanos, Richard Rorty, and others.[13] My own definition of literary irony highlights the interplay between surface meanings presented as contextually unreliable and potential meanings that may be deemed truer or more contextually appropriate:

> Irony is a performance of misdirection that generates aporetic interactions between an unreliable "said" and a truer "unsaid" so as to persuade us of something that is subtler, more complex, or more profound than the apparent meaning. Irony disrupts cultural assumptions about the narrative coherence that seems to ground tropological and epistemological transactions, inviting

---

12. See Brady, "Conversion of Ruth."

13. For works by these and other scholars of irony, see the bibliographies in twenty essays in Häner, Miller, and Sharp, eds., *Irony in the Bible*.

us into an experience of alterity that moves us toward new insight by problematizing false understandings.[14]

The ironized "said" and the truer "unsaid" are inextricably intertwined in readers' and hearers' processes of meaning-making. The insufficient or misleading ostensible meaning triggers a response of hesitation, then outright balking, in the astute reader who understands that the purposes of the text are likely more complex or different than what the ostensible "said" would seem to suggest.[15]

Interpreting an ironic Scripture text for the pulpit faces several challenges. First, the exegete must be literarily adept in order to recognize irony and explore it in sermon preparation. The preacher should know deeply the biblical book from which the focal passage is drawn. The preacher should be familiar with the book's characteristic ways of signaling character development, plot development, ethics, and theology, such that hyperbole or understatement, gaps, inconcinnities, and distorted perspectives in the focal passage become evident and their potential role in the meaning-making of the biblical book comes into view. This could pose a challenge to any preacher who has not studied, at least at an advanced high-school level, how literature works.

Second, the homiletical exegete should have a keen sense of literary, theological, and cultural features of the biblical corpus within which a biblical book is situated, so as to hear distinct emphases in the focal text. How Hosea and Ezekiel work with the Exodus traditions is strikingly different from how those traditions are featured in Deutero-Isaiah; the Gospel of Matthew is saturated with allusions to the Hebrew Scriptures in a way that is powerfully significant for meaning-making in the First Gospel; and so on. To train oneself in the larger biblical corpus presents a challenge for preachers whose busy schedules make it difficult to set aside time for Scripture study apart from quick tactical research on a specific pericope.

A third challenge in preaching on an ironic text has to do with sermon delivery. Without waxing overly didactic about irony, the preacher needs to communicate how the "said"—the surface meaning of a biblical story or poem—is not, in fact, the direct message of the text. While maintaining a joyous, energetic affect that draws listeners toward the Word of God, the preacher must offer an explication of ironizing elements that are

---

14. Sharp, *Irony and Meaning*, 24.
15. Sharp, *Irony and Meaning*, 15; Booth, *Rhetoric of Irony*, 24.

meant to catalyze balking and reassessment on the part of listeners who may not know the passage well or may never have studied literature. This challenge will be compounded for preachers in Christian traditions that promote the mistaken view that a woodenly "literal" reading is the only faithful way to interpret Scripture.

Feminist Interpretation for the Pulpit

Feminist theology, in all its variegated beauty and power, holds much potential for homiletics. Some feminist writers address ongoing overt discrimination against women in ecclesial traditions in which women are barred from holy orders and forbidden to preach or are allowed by male authorities to preach only in services that are not the principal Eucharistic celebration. In these contexts, as Laurie Lyter Bright observes, female preachers may constitute a "prophetic . . . disruptive, resistant presence" entirely apart from the content of any sermonic message they may offer[16]; the same is true of trans and nonbinary preachers in contexts that do not welcome their presence and their voices. Other feminist interpreters inhabit Christian traditions in which women are no longer blocked from ordination and preaching, yet there remains important work to do to deconstruct misogyny, sexism, racism, homophobia, classism, discrimination against those living with disability, and devaluing of non-human creaturely life.

Feminist, womanist, and queer biblical interpretation has generated important readings for several decades, explicitly theorizing gender and power relations, yet it is still unusual to find sustained scholarly engagement of this work in homiletics books and articles. There are historical studies of women preachers that go nowhere near feminist theory or mention only in a brief, descriptive way the oppressive gender norms with which women preachers throughout history have had to contend. Such studies are to be commended for their contributions to historical knowledge, to be sure, but they ought not necessarily to be considered feminist in perspective or methodology simply because women are the constituency being studied. Some studies persist in making essentialist claims about women preachers—characterizing certain epistemological approaches and pastoral leadership styles as "women's ways"—with

---

16. Bright, "Woman in a Man's Pulpit," 109; see also Yarber, *Gendered Pulpit*, 22–49; Shercliff, "Towards a New Homiletic," 51–52.

scant reference to contextual particularities of economic class, racial or ethnic identification, sexual orientation, access to education, and other features of lived experience rightly foregrounded in womanist homiletics and intersectional research on gender more broadly. Gender essentialism, absent a theoretical framework situating that standpoint as a provisional strategy, may be considered a reflection of second-wave feminism that, however well-intentioned, fails to break free of distorted patriarchal enculturation.

Relevant to this essay is my subject position not only as a biblical scholar and professor, but as a white, educationally privileged Episcopal priest, pacifist, and ally of LGBTQ+ and gender-nonconforming persons; as one who worked with Southeast Asian refugees in communities where they faced racism, social marginalization, and assault; as one living with difficult memories of financial precarity from childhood through age 25 but now economically secure; and as one blessed with a trusted life partner for decades. What I see and cannot see in Ruth is unquestionably related to those aspects of my lived experience.

Elsewhere I have articulated three goals for my feminist work with sacred texts in community.[17] Here, I translate these into goals for feminist Christian preaching. First, the feminist preacher should *honor all subjects*, making sure to listen to those whose experiences and perspectives have been discounted, distorted, or erased in biblical texts and trajectories of interpretation. Second, the feminist preacher should *interrogate relations of power*, resisting the harms of ecclesial and other traditions and inviting listeners into Gospel possibilities for renewed life, as disciples and as believing communities seeking to follow Jesus Christ. Third, the feminist preacher should invite hearers to *reform community* as a capacious space in which all are welcome, helping listeners envision and work toward lifegiving modes of relationality that allow every living being to flourish as God intended.

---

17. Sharp, *Jeremiah 26–52*, 49. My feminist work there seeks to "critique and destabilize ideologies of subjugation" by "exposing oppressive uses of power, including suppression of the reality of harms experienced from antiquity to the present day by women, girls, and gender-expansive persons, and harms experienced by men and boys." I have sought to "facilitate the movement away from gender essentialism, which impoverishes persons of every gender, and . . . to contest race and class hierarchies, which replicate the commodification of bodies and imaginations to serve the material gain of particular elites" (49–50).

Interpretation

The book of Ruth, likely composed in the postexilic period in Judah, is a dramatic story of challenges and reversals. Characters are limned with depth and nuance through dialogue that unfolds in intense and suspenseful scenes. The plot moves through defining moments of displacement, loss, and manipulation as the main characters, a bereaved and bitter Judean mother and her widowed Moabite daughter-in-law, struggle to flourish in a landscape that proves both familiar and unfamiliar. Naomi and Ruth negotiate their way from a situation of loss and despair to a fresh claim on landed belonging and kinship in the Bethlehem community. The ending of the book presents a stunning surprise: a Moabite migrant worker turns out to be the ancestor of the Judean king David. This well-crafted narrative alludes to and reconfigures a number of Hebrew Bible traditions in creative ways. In centuries of rabbinic and Christian reception history, many fascinating valences of potential meaning have been explored, amplified, and contested.[18]

Irony and Feminist Preaching on Ruth

The literature on Ruth is vast. Many interpreters see the book as a celebration of women's tenacity and the fruitfulness of harvest, though some acknowledge ambiguities at multiple moments in the text. I find particularly generative the 1999 literary-critical reading of Tod Linafelt, the 2007 carnivalesque reading of Nehama Aschkenasy, the 2018 intertextual queer reading of Stephanie Day Powell, the 2021 affect-studies reading of Rhiannon Graybill, the 2022 psychological reading of Ilana Pardes, and the 2022 ecological reading of Alice Sinnott.[19] A minority of readers have seen—correctly, in my view—that far from being an idyll, the story of Ruth reveals troubling dynamics of exploitation and threat. Early roots of a negative reading can be unearthed in the Targum to Ruth, which claims that the deaths of Mahlon and Chilion happened

---

18. See Kowalski, "Rewriting of the Old Testament in the Book of Ruth"; Fischer, "Book of Ruth"; Fischer, *Rut*, 95–112, 263–66; Eskenazi and Frymer-Kensky, *Ruth*, lvi–lxx. On Ruth as problematizing wisdom tropes in Proverbs and subverting gender norms, see Quick, "Book of Ruth," esp. 55–56, 61–65.

19. Linafelt, *Ruth*; Aschkenasy, "Reading Ruth through a Bakhtinian Lens"; Powell, *Narrative Desire and the Book of Ruth*; Graybill, "Even unto This Bitter Loving"; Pardes, *Ruth: A Migrant's Tale*; Sinnott, *Ruth*.

because they transgressed the divine prohibition against marrying women from other nations.[20]

In interpretations presenting Ruth as a beautiful tale of collaboration and resilience, hyperbole—a classic signal of irony across cultures—often goes unremarked; Naomi putting Ruth at risk of assault from field laborers is passed over in silence, despite clear signals of that danger in the text; Naomi's scheme for Ruth to entrap Boaz sexually in a venue notorious as a site of sex work (Hos 9:1) is downplayed. Powell argues that it is vital to honor dimensions of grief, shame, and conflict in Ruth, for the book "carries forward a history of unassimilated losses born of social strife, ethnic tension, and repudiated loss. If listening to the wounds of others is to serve as the basis of history"—or homiletical theology—"then we must listen for what the story of Ruth does not tell, between the lines on the page."[21] Precisely. Positive readings of Ruth have spotted elements present in the text, but in such readings, I believe the razor-sharp irony of the narratology has been missed.

Irony in the Book of Ruth

Interpreters debate whether the portrayal of this Moabite migrant has been designed to contest postexilic ideologies that reject outsiders, as in Ezra-Nehemiah, or, conversely, has been crafted to demonstrate the appropriateness of suspicion of outsiders. Does "in the days when the judges ruled" in Ruth 1:1 signal that what follows is a counter-example of fidelity and flourishing over against the spiraling moral decay and violence of Judges, or does the story exemplify the negative appraisal that in those days, everyone did "what was right in their own eyes" (Judg 17:6; 21:25) rather than following the Torah? In Ruth 1:4, does the verb *nāśā'*, used of Mahlon and Chilion marrying Moabite women, evoke resonances with Judg 21:23, where Benjaminite men abduct and forcibly "marry" (*sic*—hold captive and subject to repeated sexual violation) female dancers at

---

20. Michael Moore, who reads Ruth as an idyll, characterizes targumic expansions to Ruth 1 as yielding "a xenophobic diatribe against Israel's enemies," objecting, "*Targum Ruth* consistently and deliberately converts one of the Hebrew Bible's most beautiful narratives about diversity and tolerance into a manifesto for ethnoreligious extremism" ("Ruth the Moabite," 213, 215). Readers who understand the book of Ruth to be marking Moabite foreignness as undesirable might interpret those targumic amplifications as fully consonant with the ironic subtext of the book.

21. Powell, *Narrative Desire and the Book of Ruth*, 161.

Shiloh, or does the verb suggest repair of that harm?[22] Similar questions about many other textual details have been posed.

I have analyzed Ruth in three earlier publications and will summarize those arguments here. In 2009,[23] I observed that interpretations that valorize Ruth overlook many ironies of gendered and sexualized agency in the renegotiation of kinship bonds and land. Ruth clings to her mother-in-law despite Naomi's fierce protestations, saddling the older woman with truly unwanted economic liability. Ruth sexually manipulates Boaz on the threshing floor, returning with a payment of barley that should be construed as the trading of sex for economic security.[24] Israel's cultural anxiety about foreign women (expressed in many texts in the Deuteronomistic History) would seem to be well founded—this is the narratorial perspective as I understand it—if a "Moabite can easily seduce her way into a sizable inheritance in a community she has never seen before."[25] The words of ostensible blessing spoken by Judeans in the town gate identify as precedent Tamar's seduction of her father-in-law Judah, which involved veiling herself as a sex worker (Genesis 38). "Survival gained through prostitute-like dissembling . . . runs all through the heritage of the illustrious David" whose genealogy comes as the shocking twist at the end of the story.[26] David has been shown to be "ethnically hybrid and morally compromised" by the narratives of Tamar and Ruth as ancestors in his bloodline.[27]

In 2014, I urged interpreters to move beyond simple exposition toward skilled literary work with the complex nature of biblical narratology, "in light of the virtually infinite possibilities for signifying and contestation" that discerning readers have spied in textual representations of biblical characters, dialogue, and narrative plots.[28] I identified three goals of feminist criticism: "to interrogate and destabilize ideologies of subjugation," to press "cultural systems to move beyond essentialism

22. For commentators who link the violence at the end of Judg 21 to concerns about Ruth's exogamous status, see Matheny, "Ruth in Recent Research," 15.

23. Sharp, *Irony and Meaning*, 116–22.

24. Sharp, *Irony and Meaning*, 117.

25. Sharp, *Irony and Meaning*, 118.

26. Sharp, *Irony and Meaning*, 118.

27. For scholars' negative appraisals of David, as well as proponents of the consensus positive reading of Ruth as an idyllic tale of fidelity and fruitfulness, see Sharp, *Irony and Meaning*, 287–89, nn85–98.

28. Sharp, "Feminist Queries for Ruth and Joshua," 230.

with regard to gender, race, sexual identity, and other dimensions of human identity and relationship in community," and "to facilitate rigorous and creative work for justice and shalom."[29] Regarding Ruth, I probed "fractures within official narrations of identity and the hybridity that is required of women (and non-normative men) in patriarchal cultures," pointing to four key moments: the clash of perspectives between Ruth and Naomi in Ruth 1[30]; Naomi rendering Ruth as invisible when they first meet the women of Bethlehem (1:19–21), something mirrored in Ruth's erasure at the conclusion of the story; ways in which Ruth's discourse may be manipulating Boaz even as her Moabite "otherness" is emphasized in Ruth 2; and Ruth's offer of sex on the threshing floor, received by a grateful Boaz with acknowledgment of the economic implications when he says Ruth has "not made herself sexually available to a younger man, 'whether poor or rich'" (3:10), a point that would be unnecessary if economics were not at the center of this transaction. I argued that the reading of Ruth as a valorous ancestor of David is misguided in taking as earnest what is, in fact, the unreliable ironic feint of the surface level of the narrative.[31] The dread of foreignness, a motif audible in Pentateuch traditions, pervasive in Deuteronomistic literature, and virulent in Ezra-Nehemiah, indicates that scribal "production of the Judean communal 'self'—the cultural construction of God's people over against Others in the Hebrew Bible—has had to wrestle, in fruitful and disturbing ways, with persistent anxiety about potentially foreign or ungovernable elements within the faithful community itself."[32]

In 2017, I probed ambiguities in the characterization of Naomi to expose subterranean tensions in the narratology of Ruth. My methodology lifted up feminist dissensus and celebrated the elusiveness of textual signifying as a "potentially subversive resource with which to dismantle oppressive structures and ideological distortions,"[33] whether those be found within ancient texts, in reception history, or in contemporary

---

29. Sharp, "Feminist Queries for Ruth and Joshua," 231.

30. Jione Havea comments that given the "complex realities that migrants face," Naomi's attempt "to turn her daughters-in-law back while they were on the way" and inhabiting the liminal status of widowhood, would be tantamount, from an islander perspective, to Naomi paddling a canoe past the fringing or barrier reef and then telling "her daughters-in-law to jump off and swim back home" (Havea, *Losing Ground*, 82–83).

31. Sharp, "Feminist Queries for Ruth and Joshua," 245–47.

32. Sharp, "Embodying Moab," 106.

33. Sharp, "Is This Naomi?," 151.

appropriations. I drew on the work of Madipoane Masenya, who highlights the exploitation of daughters-in-law by their mothers-in-law in tribal communities in South Africa[34]; analyzed the threats to Jewish identity presented in two other Second Temple novellas by the assimilation of Jews in diaspora (Joseph being assimilated into Egyptian culture and Esther into Persian culture) as a way of demonstrating that "diaspora changes the indigene, and not for the better";[35] and argued that Naomi—the protagonist of the book of Ruth—is being depicted in the ranks of those who return from exile "unrecognizable," having learned to "commodify the labor of others for their own survival."[36] On the genealogy concluding Ruth 4, I argued that "the machinations of Ruth and Naomi foreshadow David's own corruption," as evidenced in David's extortionate "protection" of Nabal (1 Sam 25:2–42); the mercenary affiliation of David and his disreputable militia with the Philistines (1 Sam 27:1–28:2; 29:1–11); several instances of targeted assassination and mutilation of adversaries, per David's direction or due to David's weakness in failing to restrain his murderous army commander Joab (2 Sam 2–4, 8, 18, 20); and David's sexual use of Bathsheba and cold-blooded betrayal of her husband, the loyal soldier Uriah, earning a direct statement of divine disapprobation and fatal consequences for Bathsheba's child (2 Sam 11–12).[37] In Ruth 4:18–22, the recitation of the lineage of David reveals a stunning ironic twist: a Moabite woman acting as a sex worker has made her way into Judean land holdings as the king's ancestor, the narratology "(un)masking the violence and commodification that have riven the Judean body politic" during David's rule.[38]

The points above are discernible to those who read biblical texts carefully, without allowing dominant views in the history of interpretation to constrain their vision. Preachers should not assume that readings in the reception history of a text are reliable guides to a text's meaning. As homileticians know well, contextual factors shape every reading of Scripture. Consider the negative light in which Jephthah is portrayed in Judges 11. This mercenary warrior is portrayed as the son of a sex worker (11:1), which undermines his lineage beyond repair when

34. See Masenya, "*Ngwetši* (Bride)."
35. Sharp, "Is This Naomi?," 153.
36. Sharp, "Is This Naomi?," 156.
37. For incisive analysis of negative biblical traditions about David, see Halpern, *David's Secret Demons*.
38. Sharp, "Is This Naomi?," 157.

framed in the social mores of Israelite antiquity (let me be clear that the shaming of sex workers is not a value I share). The impetuous vow he makes before battling the Ammonites leads to the ritual sacrifice of his beloved daughter (11:30–40), something deplorable to the biblical narrator. The internecine conflicts in Judges dramatize the depths of moral corruption to which the Israelite tribes have sunk in the absence of the monarchy; one example is the incident in which Jephthah and Gileadite troops kill forty-two thousand Ephraimites (12:1–6). Jephthah is no hero in these stories—yet he is lionized in the list of exemplars of fidelity in Heb 11:1–40. The preacher whose focal text is Judges 11 should not be unduly influenced by Hebrews 11.

In Ruth, the ironic subtext may be portraying Ruth as a scheming, sexually immoral Moabite woman whose presence in the lineage of David adumbrates the king's manipulative and morally dubious ways of seizing Judean land. I reject any implication that women's bodies and sexuality should be controlled by male authorities, and I find abhorrent any ideology that trades on xenophobia and racialized "othering." The book constitutes an exemplary locus for feminist homiletics not because preachers should reperform the book's excessive marking of Ruth's foreignness or implicit shaming of her sexual agency—far from it!—but because preachers must equip listeners to grapple with such issues. Preaching responsibly on Ruth requires that the preacher speak publicly about the circumstances of women under patriarchy, including the economic disprivilege facing widows not attached to a patrilocal kinship group in many cultures and the commodification of women's labor and sexuality to secure patrilineal claims on land and other resources.

Homiletic Overtures

Preachers wishing to lift up Ruth as an icon of fidelity and resilience are free to do so, but they should realize this interpretation may be transgressing the intended ironic meaning of the text. Such a reading may be misreading the book's biblical allusions, mistaking Boaz's lauding of Ruth for the narrator's own view, and trading on the unlikely assumption that the actions of a sexually aggressive[39] Moabite migrant to secure

---

39. Justin David Strong argues that Ruth sexually assaults Boaz in Ruth 3, as Lot is raped by his daughters (Gen 19:30–38), Jacob is tricked into nonconsensual sex with Leah (Gen 29:20–25), Judah is deceived into nonconsensual sex by Tamar (Gen 38:12–26), and Joseph is sexually assaulted by Potiphar's wife (Gen 39:7–20). See Strong,

Judean economic resources should be understood as a positive credential in the genealogy of David.

Preachers who see subversive ironizing in this story might preach on how the narrative exposes the predations of empire beneath the surface of official history; or they could model resistance to ways in which ethnic stereotypes and sexualized representations of marginalized groups have long animated racist ideologies; or they could lift up the plight of migrants as exploited labor. Preachers eager to invite hearers into the ambiguities of this ancient story might craft a series of sermons, inhabiting in each proclamation a distinct approach to the text. One sermon might read Ruth as the progenitor of the "golden era" of Israel's united monarchy, highlighting the tenacity and ingenuity of Naomi and Ruth as inspirational for those struggling with loss, displacement, or economic precarity. A second sermon might teach about anti-Moabite sentiment in the Hebrew Bible, tying the Davidic genealogy to Num 25:1–5 (Israelite idolatry linked to sexual relations with Moabite women), Deut 23:3–6 (the mandate to exclude Moabites from the worshipping assembly in perpetuity) and the searing biblical critique of David for his violent abuses of power; in this frame, Ruth becomes a resource for prophetic resistance to the brutality of empire. A third sermon might acknowledge the flawed nature of social hierarchies, affirm that God can work good even through harm perpetrated by human actors (cf. Gen 50:20), and read the Matthean genealogy (Matt 1:1–17) as foreshadowing God's redemption not only of individuals but of the entire sweep of political history. The preacher could convene a fascinating sermon discussion group after the series.

Homily

"The Polyphony of Grace": A Feminist Homily on Ruth 1:1–18

How might one design an emancipatory proclamation on Ruth for listeners who may not know the biblical story? For congregations ordering their worship according to the Revised Common Lectionary, only two lessons from Ruth come up in three years: Ruth 1:1–18 for Proper 26B and Ruth 3:1–5; 4:13–17 for Proper 27B. In 2024, Proper 26B falls on November 3; the major feast of All Saints will be transferred to that Sunday in the Episcopal Church and other traditions, the feast's lessons

---

"Rape of Men in the Hebrew Bible."

displacing those of Proper 26B. Realizing that worshippers in RCL traditions therefore would not hear Ruth 1:1–18 for five years, I chose this as my focal text for a homily in Marquand Chapel at Yale Divinity School on 29 January 2024.

Most of my hearers would not have engaged Ruth in depth. A Hebrew Bible introductory course covers Ruth and other topics in one 50-minute lecture in April; for years, the sole assigned reading on Ruth has been a basic overview, twelve paragraphs long, given mostly to plot summary. What Walter Brueggemann observes about the challenges of biblical preaching in congregations is relevant here:

> The preacher has on her hands a Subject who is not obvious and a mode of speech that is endlessly open and demanding . . . [which] makes preaching deeply demanding in a congregation schooled in one-dimensional, technological certitude . . . Faithful speech about God is sure to be faithful speech about the complicatedness of being human . . . The *irascible* character of God and the *elusive* rhetoric of the text mean that . . . textual testimony is deeply *polyvalent*, that is, it speaks with many voices and is profoundly open to rich variation in rendering . . . Almost none of this, moreover, is available to or recognized among most of our listeners.[40]

Another context note: political tensions were volatile on campus concerning the Israel/Hamas conflict in Gaza. I preached this homily sixteen weeks after the atrocities committed by Hamas on 7 October 2023, when hundreds of Israelis were murdered and almost 300 were taken hostage. Israel's militarized response was relentless: cities in Gaza were being obliterated by Israeli Defense Force bombardment as I created the homily, and the Gazan death toll had climbed over 25,000, most of those noncombatants.[41] Gazan families were facing dire food shortages and severely limited access to medical care. Resonances with the book of Ruth pressed insistently upon my homiletical imagination as I considered the famine that drove Elimelech, Naomi, and their sons to Moab and the precarity faced by Naomi and Ruth upon their return to Judah.

---

40. Brueggemann, *Deep Memory, Exuberant Hope*, 4; emphasis original.

41. In July 2024, Agence France Presse estimated 796 Israeli civilians murdered during the Hamas attack and 252 Israelis taken hostage, dozens of whom have since died or been executed. As of this writing, the Gazan death toll has soared over 39,000.

Homily

When I married my partner, a friend made me a lovely piece of embroidery that said, "Where you go, I will go. Where you lodge, I will lodge," and so on, from the book of Ruth. In those days, the third wave of feminism was cresting; it would break upon the shores of academia less than a year after our wedding.[42] As a feminist, I was moved by her gift, but not thrilled at the sentiment. What did Ruth's declaration of abject submission—for so I heard it—have to do with feminist life?

These days, I see more in Ruth.

Precarity and resilience. Earnest hope and callous exploitation. Intimacy and erasure.

All that, too, is the book of Ruth. And it assuredly has a word for us today!

Many biblical texts reflect on diaspora, remembering Judeans in exile who turned toward home, toward the place where they knew most deeply who they were as God's beloved people. The prophet Isaiah envisions a highway for the return of Jews from diaspora, a road on which "the redeemed of the Lord shall return, and come to Zion with singing" (Isa 35:8–10). Imagine younger returnees—those born in diaspora—joyous on the road, their eyes alight with expectation as they strain to glimpse the magnificent Jerusalem Temple.[43] But for seasoned members of the community, returning is more complicated. They sing the songs of Zion with tears in their eyes. They carry memories of wrenching loss, haunted by what they'd had to abandon decades earlier. You don't just get over something like that.

Loss and displacement put entire communities at risk, with dire consequences far into the future. We're watching this unfold right now in Gaza. Traumatized families are living in the rubble of their homes;

---

42. All footnotes to the homily are original; I have added a few minor amplifications for this essay. On third-wave feminism: for convenience, many scholars identify the beginning of the third wave of feminist advocacy for gender justice with the 1990 publication of Judith Butler's book, *Gender Trouble*.

43. The narrative setting of Ruth is the time of the judges, when Solomon's Temple had not yet been built, but of course, the setting within a story should not be confused with the time when the piece of literature was actually composed. Here, I imagine returnees coming back to the rebuilt Temple of the Persian era, in line with the position of many scholars that the book of Ruth was likely crafted in the Second Temple period. I am persuaded that Ruth addresses the complexities of lineage and return from a postexilic perspective.

starvation is looming for many.[44] The Palestinian death toll has climbed past 25,000—two thirds of the dead are women and children—while global political discourse remains mired in dogmatism.

Dogmatism is "the tendency to lay down principles as undeniably true"[45] while ignoring evidence and the counter-positions of others. Dogmatism thrives on social media, but you can hear it anywhere, including at kitchen tables and in classrooms. Dogmatism is toxic. It shuts down dialogue and distorts authentic, honest community, turning "belonging" into something coercive.

The good news is, there's a remedy for dogmatism: polyphony. A fancy multisyllabic word, right? Well, "polyphony" just means "many sounds,"[46] many voices. Many voices.

In music, polyphony describes the use of two or more melodic lines in a single harmonious composition. Each line has its own integrity, being melodically independent *and* responsive to the larger composition. In literature, polyphony describes unmerged narrative voices, some antithetical to others, that together create a rich interplay of perspectives. If you're in a book club (I mean, other than the giant book club that is Yale), you know polyphony is huge in novels right now.[47]

The book of Ruth invites us into polyphony—into harmony and dissonance, point and counterpoint, movements of resistance and growth that make up real life in God. In polyphony, we encounter grace: God's redeeming love at work, not in some monolithic fairy tale but in a dynamic network of entangled truths!

Ruth gives us polyphony. The bereaved Naomi is leaving Moab to go back to Judah, and her Moabite daughter-in-law Ruth wants to accompany her. In the polyphony of this exquisite book, the first melody we hear is fidelity: Ruth's famous declaration to Naomi: "Where you go,

---

44. In January 2024, I cited these sources: World Food Programme, "Gaza—Food Security Assessment," 14 December 2023; *The New Yorker,* "Gaza Is Starving," 3 January 2024; *Time,* "How Experts Believe Starvation Is Being Utilized in Gaza," 6 January 2024; Islamic Relief, "Gaza Now the World's Worst Hunger Crisis and On the Verge of Famine," 9 January 2024; Reuters, "Fears of Famine in Gaza as Hunger Hits Crisis Levels," 17 January 2024; *The New York Times,* "Gaza's Food Crisis," 29 January 2024.

45. "Dogmatism," in the *Oxford English Dictionary* (OED) online.

46. "Polyphony" is "a multiplicity of sounds or voices," per the *OED* online. https://www.oed.com/dictionary/polyphony_n?tab=factsheet#29580040.

47. My ethical resistance to capitalist exploitation of migrant laborers has been strengthened by two novels that use polyphony: Jess Walter's 2021 novel, *The Cold Millions,* and Sofía Segovia's 2019 novel, *The Murmur of Bees.*

I will go; where you lodge, I will lodge; your people shall be my people, and your God my God." Yearning for home. But Naomi is not having it, this burden to continue supporting her daughter-in-law economically. She snarls, "NO—it has been far more bitter for me than for you!" Ruth will not be deterred, and Naomi lapses into silence. Not a warm, companionable silence. A bitter silence.

Bitterness is the second melodic line in this artful composition. Arriving back in Judah, Naomi is unrecognizable, her face ravaged by what she's suffered. The women of Bethlehem literally don't know who she is. She says: "My name is no longer Naomi. Call me Mara"—bitter— "because the Almighty has dealt bitterness to me."[48] She does not mention Ruth. Naomi ignores this unwanted Moabite standing right next to her. That's how Naomi returns: not singing, as Isaiah had envisioned, but broken by loss, disfigured by bitterness, and publicly cruel to the Moabite immigrant standing next to her.

All kinds of unpleasantness ensue. I've got to lay it out.

- First: Ruth is marked excessively, over and over again, as "the Moabite," underscoring her affiliation with Israel's despised enemy and making her hope of belonging, "your people shall be my people," seem heartbreakingly naïve in retrospect.

- Second: Ruth proposes that she work alone in a random field. Though she'll be at serious risk of harassment, Naomi says, "Go ahead," without a word of warning.[49] Ruth gleans for hours without stopping, with no guarantee of compensation. Migrant labor with no protection.

- Third: Naomi dispatches Ruth late at night to the threshing floor, where only male laborers and sex workers will be, having instructed Ruth how to lure a wealthy landowner into sleeping with her. This sexual entrapment plan puts Ruth at extreme risk, something that's explicitly clear in the storytelling.

---

48. The NRSV translation, "the Almighty has dealt bitterly with me" is poor English; the adverb implies that it is the deity who is bitter. I prefer to render קְרֶאןָ לִי מָרָא כִּי־הֵמַר שַׁדַּי לִי מְאֹד as, "Call me Mara, for Shaddai has made exceeding bitterness my lot." In this homily, I cannot change many words from the NRSV text listeners have heard without explaining, so I have chosen "has dealt *bitterness* to me," the noun in English being the most economical way to move forward.

49. The threat of sexual violence is openly acknowledged by this ancient text; see Ruth 2:8–9 and Matheny, "Ruth in Recent Research," 16–17.

- Naomi's strategy works, and Ruth is "acquired" by the landowner—that's his insulting language when he announces it in the public square. Ruth gives birth, and Naomi immediately appropriates the baby as her own. Ruth's labor, in the fields and in childbirth, has been commodified by the community, and she's erased from the rest of the story.

Feminist and decolonizing readers have seen many parallels between Ruth's story and what happens to migrant laborers, persons trafficked for sex work,[50] and refugees treated as "perpetual foreigners."[51] Others still manage to read Ruth as an idyllic tale of fidelity and abundance. Polyphony: those elements are there, though I believe they're being heavily ironized. Still others cherish the book as a queer love story. Polyphony: I honor that reading, even as I call out how heartless Naomi is toward Ruth at every turn. The melodic line that's most audible to me is the grim fate of migrants oppressed by the economic predations of empire—the Davidic monarchy, named at the end of the book as the result of all this,[52] and relevant also for later extractive economies, including our own late capitalism.

Friends, we have to tell the whole truth! That's how we remember who we are, how we remember where home is. We worship an incarnate

---

50. The last time Ruth speaks is when she goes home after sleeping with Boaz and tells Naomi, the woman who sent her there for sex work, "Look, he gave me six measures of barley, for he said, 'Do not go back to your mother-in-law empty-handed.'" It is a wrenching moment, the vulnerable Ruth showing Naomi that her sex work, which had put at risk Ruth's physical safety and social reputation (transparently evident from Boaz's reflection, "'It must not be known that the woman came to the threshing floor,'" 3:14), did yield the hoped-for economic benefit.

51. On the complexities of characterization in Ruth, see the essays in Athalya Brenner, ed. *Ruth and Esther*, esp. those by Bonnie Honig, Laura Donaldson, Judith McKinlay, and Athalya Brenner; Linafelt, *Ruth*; Sharp, *Irony and Meaning*, 116–21; Yee, "She Stood in Tears Amid the Alien Corn"; Halton, "An Indecent Proposal"; Fulata Lusungu Moyo, "Traffic Violations"; Koosed, *Gleaning Ruth*; Graybill, "Even unto This Bitter Loving."

52. The Davidic genealogy appended to the story (Ruth 4:18–22) reveals predatory imperialism as a factor in local stories that may seem innocent on the face of it. Some scholars read the purpose of the genealogy as being apologetic in favor of David, but this case is difficult to sustain. I believe the ancient author intends to mock David's linkage to non-Judean and non-Israelite peoples by associating him with a Moabite woman who gains Judean resources through scheming and sexualized entrapment. That Ruth is lauded by the cuckolded Boaz and the same women of Bethlehem who did not recognize Naomi earlier in the story should not be read as the position of the *narrator* and the author of the story.

Holy One whose polyphony of grace calls us to tell all of these truths. To celebrate feminist and queer solidarity while candidly naming the wounds of intersectional injustice. To praise God for the abundance of harvest while advocating fiercely for the rights of migrants and other disenfranchised workers.

There is incarnational good news in the polyphony of our sacred texts! These entangled witnesses tell the incarnational truth of love and woundedness. When dogmatism threatens to make your ethics brittle, your theology narrow, or your notion of community into something coercive: RESIST!

Resist—and lift up the polyphony of grace, as you turn, with so many others, toward home. Amen.

Conclusion

Sophisticated biblical narratives invite the preacher to consider depths and ambiguities of characterization, subtle trajectories of irony, and the play of multiple perspectives as resources for homiletical reflection. Meaning-making with sacred texts should engage all that we can discern in the Word of God: not only the events unfolding in the plot, dialogue among characters, and narratorial comments, but also the layered allusions, freighted silences, and shimmering subtexts that animate this ancient literature. Considering Ruth in the pulpit, feminist preachers should be emboldened, taking Scripture as their warrant to offer decolonizing discourse that disrupts systemic exploitation, to model coalitional relationality by honoring polyphony in text and interpretation, and to ground the congregation's mission in radical solidarity with those who suffer.

6

Invisible Labor and the Erasure of Ruth

Song-Mi Suzie Park

Introduction

The disappearance of Ruth is sudden and subtle. Despite being the center of action throughout most of the book, Ruth mysteriously disappears at the end of her namesake work. Though abrupt, her disappearance is also discreet. Readers, flying through this short narrative, might remain unaware of the sudden and inexplicable evaporation of one of the book's main characters. Wrapping up at warp speed after the neat and succinct resolution of the protagonists' central dilemma—the lack of an appropriate male heir—the book seems uninterested in the whereabouts of the person who has done much of the work to conceive and birth the long-awaited child. Like a temporary employee, once she has completed her job, she is summarily dismissed.[1]

Ruth's disappearance raises some unnerving questions, especially when this ancient story is read through the lens of modern concerns. What purpose does her disappearance serve within the story and also "outside" of it when the tale is brought into conversation with current events? Why is Ruth abruptly dismissed at the end, and how does her disappearance affect our reading of this tale? What messages and possible homiletical trajectories does her absence evince?

1. Fewell and Gunn, *Compromising Redemption*, 105.

Focusing on these questions, this chapter offers a transgressive reading of Ruth. Using a feminist, contextual, and deconstructive lens, I argue that the vanishing of Ruth at the end of the book reveals a discomfort with her ethnicity and gender, a discomfort that is subtly present throughout most of the work. This unease, I argue, manifests in an attempt to undermine and erase her contribution and her labor. Moving from ancient text to modern context by reading the tale as a Korean American feminist reader, I assert that this discomfort, which is manifest in Ruth's absence at the end of the book, speaks to the current issues facing women and immigrants today.

Hermeneutical Horizon

We begin our reading and interrogation of the text by reiterating the central question at the heart of this examination: Where is Ruth at the end of the book (4:13–17)? The last we hear of her, she has seemingly conceived and given birth to a son, much to the delight of her mother-in-law, Naomi. Her disappearance at the end is disconcerting, to say the least.

In terms of academic interpretations of her story, Ruth's absence has not generated much attention. The usual explanation, so apparent that it is rarely acknowledged, is that the main problem of the story has been resolved: Ruth has birthed the requisite male heir, and, in so doing, she has saved Naomi and herself from a lack of "food, husbands and heirs."[2] With her job done, her story is complete. What happens next is no longer the concern of the narrative and, therefore, no longer the concern of the reader who, despite wanting to continue this literary journey, faces a closed door—the same closed door that meets all readers at the end of a compelling tale.

Even the strange final scene where the women of the town celebrate Naomi instead of Ruth (4:14–17) can be explained as due to the contours of the tale.[3] Naomi, after all, is one of the co-protagonists of the book. Indeed, as an Israelite, she is perhaps the book's main protagonist as it is her problem caused by her childlessness, her age, and the deaths of all the male members of her family that serve as inciting events that begin her and Ruth's journey. As it is Naomi's problem that is central to the narrative, it is fitting that she reemerges at the end to celebrate and mark its

2. Brenner, "Naomi and Ruth," 390.
3. For an overview of the problems with this verse, see Fentress-Williams, *Ruth*, 81.

resolution. Hence, according to this interpretation, the focus on Naomi and, therefore, the lack of interest in Ruth—and her sudden disappearance at the end of the tale—fits the narrative's trajectory: As it is Naomi whose sad tale begins the narrative, so the book concludes with Naomi with Ruth mainly serving "as a vehicle for Naomi's restoration."[4]

Athalya Brenner offers a different reason for the disappearance of Ruth. She argues that this feature results from the work's compositional history.[5] According to Brenner, two "separate, although parallel, folk-tale or novella"[6] with similar structures, topics, and themes—a Naomi story and a Ruth story"[7]—were combined to form a single story that is found in Ruth.[8] This combined version resulted in an uneven narrative, textured with inconsistencies and seams. As a result, it is unclear in the narrative who—Naomi, Ruth, or both—is the main character and who is ultimately redeemed at the end. This is the reason why "there is no clear-cut distinction as to whose child the new-born is: It is as if he belongs, directly or simultaneously, to both of them."[9]

Brenner's interesting idea of the composition of Ruth initially appears to resolve the problem of the disappearance of Ruth—at least, indirectly. Ruth disappears at the conclusion of the book, not only because her story is complete, but because of the text's compositional history. Ruth originally served as the main and sole protagonist of only *one* of the two stories, which were imperfectly combined to form a single tale. When the two stories were blended, she received less airtime, and her role became obfuscated.

On closer inspection, however, Brenner's argument does not resolve the issue so much as refocuses and adjusts it. In particular, the narrative of Ruth features a series of "displacement on top of a displacement,"[10] one of which is Ruth's disappearance and replacement by Naomi. The argument that Ruth's disappearance results from the compositional history of the work fails to explain why displacements occur so frequently in this work. That is, replacements—such as the replacement of Ruth by Naomi

---

4. Eskenazi and Frymer-Kensky, *Ruth*, 88.
5. Brenner, "Naomi and Ruth," 391ff.
6. Brenner, "Naomi and Ruth," 385.
7. Brenner, "Naomi and Ruth," 385.
8. Brenner, "Naomi and Ruth," 391.
9. Brenner, "Naomi and Ruth," 391.
10. Koosed, *Gleaning Ruth*, 104.

at the end—appear to be a key feature of the book, not just an unintended by-product of its compositional past.

Jennifer Koosed, for example, notes that it is not just Ruth who is displaced by Naomi when Ruth 4:16 cryptically states that it was Naomi, an adopted grandmother, and *not Ruth* who "nurses" the child.[11] Rather, Boaz, as the Levirate redeemer, also serves as both the replacement and the replaced. He replaces Mahlon, the dead heir, in impregnating Ruth. However, he is also displaced in that he, as a redeemer, is not designated as the "real" father of the child.

According to Koosed, the displacements act in concert with the themes of boundary crossing and gleaning to create a patchwork sense of family and kinship that is liminal and transgressive: "Naomi and Ruth transgress the borders of Israel and Moab, transgress borders of conventional kinship, glean in the fields, and, since their kinship 'is seen to be self-consciously assembled from a multiplicity of possible bits and pieces,' glean their family ties as well."[12] As such, according to Koosed, the replacement and displacement—including that of Ruth—seem to be a deliberate and meaningful feature of the book, and not a byproduct of a faulty and imperfect textual integration process.

This edgy vision of family and therefore identity, and the tensions reflected by it, is exacerbated by the most significant displacement found at the end of the work. As we now have it, the book of Ruth ends with neither of the female protagonists nor Boaz. Rather, the narrative concludes with a supplemented genealogy that elucidates how Obed, the child born to Ruth and perhaps adopted by Naomi, will be the forefather of King David (4:18–22). It is David who is the last biblical character mentioned in Ruth. Indeed, David is the last word—and therefore, one can assume, the culmination—of Ruth.[13]

The supplementary as well as supplanting nature of the inserted genealogy has been acknowledged by scholars.[14] In terms of its literary effect, the concluding genealogy recasts the narrative, rendering Ruth, Naomi, and Boaz secondary and transforming them from main characters into "supporting roles to Obed and David."[15]

---

11. Chapman, "'Oh that you were like a brother,'" 38; La Cocque, *Ruth*, 143; Palmer, "Naomi the Nurse," 277–88; Yee, "'Take This Child,'" 1–10.

12. Koosed, *Gleaning Ruth*, 107.

13. Park, *Love in the Hebrew Bible*, 106–7.

14. Nielsen, *Ruth*, 7; Sasson, *Ruth*, 178–86; Schipper, *Ruth*, 186.

15. Fentress-Williams, *Ruth*, 83.

For our purposes, this supplementation of the genealogy at Ruth 4:18–22 revives and further stresses the disappearance, displacement, and absence of Ruth at the end of the tale. With the genealogy, the work done by Ruth and, to a lesser extent, Naomi, is made deeply ambivalent—simultaneously enhanced and undermined. On the one hand, the genealogy in so far as it leads to Israel's most important king, David, enhances the value of the work done by these women. Without them, there would be no David, no City of David, no Solomon, no Temple, no Davidic dynasty, and, according to the contours of the New Testament, no Jesus. The accomplishment of an impoverished elderly Israelite widow and her impoverished, foreign, immigrant daughter-in-law is singular and world-altering—at least according to the biblical writers![16]

On the other hand, the genealogy also undermines, deconstructs, and devalues the work of Ruth and Naomi. With the genealogy, the women's importance is reduced to their maternal function.[17] As Ruth's work leads to King David, the genealogy asserts that her most important function, the central purpose of her travels and travails, is to give birth to David's forebearer. That is, to be the broodmare for the male greatness to come. As such, the genealogy further underlines and, therefore, upholds and justifies the idea that Ruth's and therefore women's central role is to be "baby-makers."[18]

If the genealogy is understood as evincing this gendered message, it clarifies Ruth's disappearance: Ruth has done her duty *as a woman*, that is, to provide a male Israelite heir who can inherit patrimonial land. Once this task is accomplished, she is now superfluous and unneeded. As such, the genealogy redefines Ruth's story as simply a prelude to and background for the more important story of the male character that is to come. In so doing, it therefore disturbingly resolves the question of Ruth's disappearance by answering that she is not that important anyway. Rather, her significance centers on her incubation and birth of the forefather of David.

This disheartening answer to the central question of this essay—Where is Ruth, and what is the purpose of her disappearance?—has a motivational effect, however. Namely, it compels the reader to push back; to re-read and reinterpret Ruth so as to find a different resolution, perhaps

---

16. On foreigners as a source of blessing, see M. Moore, "Ruth the Moabite," 203–17.

17. Fewell and Gunn, *Compromising Redemption*, 105.

18. Eskanzi and Frymer-Kensky also argue that the genealogy can be read as having both a positive or negative function (*Ruth*, 93).

even a different answer to the above question revealed by the book's ending. Most importantly, it pushes the reader to redress and rectify Ruth's disappearance by uncovering her unfair treatment in the narrative; and in so doing, to reveal similar unfair treatment of people like Ruth today.

Interpretation

Ruth's disappearance, which I have argued centers on the fulfillment of her maternal function, overlaps with and is mirrored in the sense of unease that runs throughout the work. This ambivalence is evident in the tension between Ruth's characterization and her identity. In terms of her identity, Ruth is repeatedly identified and therefore defined as a Moabite (1:4, 22; 2:2, 6, 21; 4:5, 10). Hence, the writers and editors of the text appear to be particularly focused on and interested in who she is—that is, her identity as a foreigner. Indeed, the writers emphasize her outsider status by depicting Ruth identifying herself as such when she meets Boaz: "Why have I found favor in your sight, that you should take notice of me, when I am a foreigner?" (2:10).

It is difficult to think that this interest in her ethnicity is neutral, especially in light of the description and mention of Moab in other parts of the Hebrew Bible. Indeed, the very first mention of Moab entails a salacious and unsavory narrative about the nation's birth and origin. Genesis 19 tells of how the unnamed daughters of Lot, Abraham's nephew (Gen 11:27), in the wake of the destruction of Sodom and Gomorrah, get their father drunk and rape him. This leads to their pregnancies and the births of Lot's sons/grandsons, Moab and Ammon. The risqué nature of the story suggests that its purpose was to ridicule and denigrate Israel's neighbors. At the very least, this story portrays these countries unfavorably, especially in light of the prohibition in Leviticus 18 against sexual relations between close family members.[19]

More importantly, in terms of identity, Genesis 19, among other things, demarcates and stresses the rejected status of Lot, Moab's father, as heir to the Abrahamic Promise. Indeed, it is telling that, after the birth narrative of Moab and Ammon, Lot disappears from the Hebrew text. Though earlier in the narrative, Lot is hinted as a possible heir to Abraham (Gen 12:5; 14:16), this deed with his daughters confirms

---

19. Tellingly, the Hebrew text does not forbid relationships between father and daughters, however (Schipper, *Ruth*, 41).

the separation of nephew and uncle. Lot and his descendants, the text stresses, are indeed distinct from those of Abraham. Therefore, the text affirms that Lot's children are not part of the promises God made to the Israelite patriarch.

Moab's origin narrative, therefore, serves to contrast the divinely elected Israelites from their unelect neighbors, the Moabites.[20] And the repeated mention of Ruth's Moabite identity seems to evince a similar sentiment. Ruth, as the narrative keeps pointing out, is *not* an Israelite—and therefore *not* part of the chosen people of God, and therefore *not* part of the divine promises made by the Israelite God. She, in other words, is technically excluded from the considerations of God and God's people. This idea has a theological purpose. To show the magnanimity of Israel's God who is depicted as gracious enough to extend his help and care—his *hesed*, as it were—to those outside the covenant as well. However, even this theological sentiment relies on and emphasizes Ruth's foreignness and, therefore, the fact that she, as a Moabite, is undeserving of such divine favors.

What makes the narrative so interesting, however, is that it is not univocal in its disparagement of Moabites. That is, the story of Ruth cannot be said to evince a strong anti-Moabite, xenophobic, or endogamous sentiment. Rather, Ruth the Moabite, as I will discuss shortly, is depicted rather positively. Moreover, the Hebrew Bible as a whole is ambivalent about Lot and his descendants. For example, though the origin tale of the Moabites in Genesis 19 can be said to be unsavory, the surrounding narratives depict Lot in a generally favorable manner. Though Lot is ultimately rejected as heir to the Abrahamic Promise, he is, however, shown to be almost cherished by the Israelite patriarch. Not only does Abraham twice rescue Lot (Gen 14; 18), but the patriarch even bargains with God for the welfare of Sodom and Gomorrah because his nephew resides there (Gen 18:22–33). Considering that Abraham fails to intercede for his heir, Isaac, when he is endangered (Gen 22), but does so with Lot speaks to his high regard for his nephew.

Even Moab's incestuous origin story in Genesis 19 cannot be interpreted as wholly negative. The depiction of Lot, the father of Moab, is again somewhat favorable. When the angels show up to Sodom and Gomorrah, Lot is the only one to offer them hospitality. In so doing, he mimics his uncle, Abraham, who, in the immediately preceding chapter,

---

20. Donaldson, "Sign of Orpah," 161–62; Siquans, "Foreignness," 447.

also hospitably greets the same divine entourage that stops by his place for a meal and a chat (Gen 18).

Not just Lot, but his daughters' actions in Genesis 19 can also be somewhat explained. As commentators have noted, the daughters seem to believe they are the lone survivors and therefore necessary repopulators of a worldwide cataclysm.[21] The daughters, moreover, in getting Lot drunk and raping him deliver a narrative comeuppance for his earlier overzealous hospitality. When the men of Sodom and Gomorrah show up to demand that Lot offer up his angelic guests, Lot offers to send out his daughters instead (Gen 19:8). For this disturbing lack of paternal care, the daughters later do unto their father what their father offered to do (or to have been done) unto them. Though horrifying and disturbing, narrative-wise the daughters' actions balance the narrative "scales." Moab's origin tale, hence, is not wholly condemnatory so much as ambivalent and uneasy.

Other biblical passages offer equally varying accounts of Israel's Moabite cousins. At points, Moab is described as Israel's enemy (Judg 3:12–30; 2 Sam 8:2; 2 Kgs 3:4–27; 13:20; 24:2; 1 Chr 18:2; the Mesha Stela [ANET, 320–21]) and condemned by the prophets (Isa 15:1–16; Jer 48:1–47; Amos 2:1–2; Zeph 2:9; cf. Ps 83:609). Alongside the Ammonites, Moabites are even prevented from entrance into the assembly of the Lord because of their inhospitable mistreatment of Israelites during their wilderness journey (Deut 23:3–6; Judg 11:17–18; Neh 13:1–2). Most important for the story in Ruth, marriages between Moabite women and Israelite men are forbidden lest they lead to religious infidelity and apostasy (Num 25:1–5; 1 Kgs 11:1–2; Ezra 9:1–2; Neh 13:1–2). Indeed, some rabbinic interpretations interpret the deaths of Mahlon and Kilion as punishment for their marriages to Moabite women (Targum Ruth 1:4–5; Ruth Rab. 2:9).

Moabites in the Hebrew text are not universally maligned or scorned, however. Exogamous marriages, including with Moabites, are at times regarded neutrally or even favorably (Gen 38:2; 1 Chr 2:3–4; Ruth 4:12; 4:22). For example, Judah and Saraph, who are said to be descendants of Judah, are stated, without much fanfare, to have married Moabites (1 Chr 4:22). Individual Moabites are also well-regarded. Aside from Ruth, Ithmah the Moabite, for example, is named as one of David's mighty warriors (1 Chr 11:46). Finally, in contrast to the

---

21. Rashkow interprets the story of Lot and his daughters as about child abuse (*Taboo or Not Taboo*, 104–13).

wilderness traditions that describe negative interactions between Moabites and Israelites, other traditions in the Hebrew text commend Moab's behavior during the wilderness period. For example, the Israelites, during their wilderness journey, are warned not to "harass Moab or engage them in battle" (Deut 2:9) because Moab allowed Israel to pass peaceably through their land and sold them food and water during their travels (Deut 1:28–29; Num 21:11–20]. In short, Israelites seem to feel about Moabites like how many of us feel about our less luminous family members: At points, you hope they decline the invitation to the next family gathering; and at other points, when in the mood for some drama, you hope they show up to liven up the place.

This ambivalence is reflected in the narrative in the complicated portrayal of Ruth. As I noted earlier, Ruth's Moabite identity is repeatedly mentioned, therefore signaling that she is different and alien. That she is marked as a native of Moab is significant considering how this country is portrayed, especially in the book of Ruth. Despite the mixed portrayal of Moab in the Hebrew text, in the book of Ruth, the depiction of Moab is more straightforwardly bleak. Described as a land of sickness and decimation, it is a death trap, especially for male Israelites. The Israelite family at the heart of the tale experiences little but suffering and pain there. As Naomi so heartbreakingly bemoans to the townspeople when she returns: "I went away full, but the Lord has brought me back empty" (1:21).

Considering that Naomi's husband and sons all expire on this foreign land and considering that both sons marry foreign women, the book connects foreigners, especially foreign women and foreign land—that is, Moabitesses and Moab—with sickness, suffering, and death. In short, the very things opposite of the life-giving and life-enhancing land (and people) of Yahweh.

This connection undoubtedly has gendered implications. Moab, the land of death, is associated with foreign women whose marriages precede the demise of the Israelite grooms. The subtext is undeniable: Had this family remained in Israel and had the sons married nice Israelite women, they might have been saved from all this trouble. The suffering and tragedies of this Israelite family can be blamed on the Other—foreign places and foreign people, especially foreign women. It does not help that the warnings about foreign women are rampant throughout the Hebrew text, especially in the book of Proverbs (1 Kgs 11; Ezra 10:11; Neh 13:26–27; Prov 2:16, 5:20, 6:24, 7:5, 23:27). Especially dangerous were those temptresses who enticed and entrapped impressionable young Israelite men to a life of apostasy and religious/sapiential "demise."[22]

Yet to say that Ruth as a Moabitess is therefore portrayed unfavorably in the book is also incorrect. Rather, what is peculiar about the book is that, despite the emphasis on her foreignness, Ruth is depicted favorably throughout most of the work. Portrayed as loyal, hardworking, and deferential to her mother-in-law, Ruth, some have argued, embodies *hesed*. *Hesed*, as commentators have noted, is a key idea and term,[23] which is mentioned in nearly every chapter of the work (1:8, 2:20, 3:10).[24] As Koosed puts it, Ruth embodies "all of the virtues explicated in Proverbs 31 and attributed to the perfect wife."[25]

Indeed, so flattering is Ruth's portrayal that rabbinic sources envision her as a convert[26] and compare her to Abraham.[27] According to this reading, Ruth turns her back on her native country, family, and customs so as to align herself with a poor Israelite widow. In so doing, she becomes a significant part of Israel's history and trajectory.[28] Her blessings from the Israelite deity confirm the rightness and righteousness of her choice to side with Israel and the Israelites. As foreshadowed by Boaz's statement at their first meeting, for leaving her "father and mother and homeland" the "Lord, the God of Israel, under whose wings [she has] come to take refuge" will indeed repay and richly reward Ruth for her deeds (2:11–12). So integrated does Ruth become to Israel and its people that the elders who bless Boaz's relationship liken her to Israel's great matriarchs, Rachel and Leah (4:11).

In short, some argue that Ruth becomes a quasi-Israelite or adopted Israelite heroine in the tale. At the very least, she increasingly moves away from being considered just a Moabitess. Rather, her identity becomes complicated and hybrid.[29] And as such, by the end of the book, Ruth's

22. Tan, *The "Foreignness" of the Foreign Woman*, esp. 101–5, 106–11.

23. Glueck, *Hesed in the Bible*, 1–118; Sakenfeld, *The Meaning of* Hesed, 1–288.

24. Saxegaard, *Character Complexity*, 3–6. Goh, 'Ruth as a Superior Woman of חיל?"

25. Koosed, *Gleaning Ruth*, 92.

26. Eskenazi and Frymer-Kensky, *Ruth*, 19.

27. Hubbard, *Book of Ruth*, 165. Indeed, Ruth's risk is greater as "unlike Abraham, Ruth leaves home without any promised security and with every prospect of a future life of poverty and alienation" (Eskenazi and Frymer-Kensky, *Ruth*, 38).

28. M. Moore, "Ruth the Moabite"; Niggemann, "Matriarch of Israel."

29. Lau, "Another Postcolonial Reading," 22–26. Niggemann concurs, writing that Ruth's portrayal "underscores the difficulty in deciphering the boundary between Israelite and non-Israelite, Jew and non-Jew" and that "Ruth dwelled on this boundary"

opposite is shown to be, not an Israelite, but another Moabitess: Orpah, the other Moabitess daughter-in-law who chose to remain in Moab and, as a result, remains the foreign Other—the "counter-narrative" or "anti-Pocahontas" to Ruth's Pocahontas.[30] For her decision to remain in Moab, Orpah suffers total erasure in the biblical narrative. In contrast, Ruth, despite her Moabite ancestry, is made the mother of the ancestor of Israel's greatest king. That is, at the end, Ruth moves from being a foreigner and an outsider to something approaching an ideal immigrant.

This does not mean all is forgiven and forgotten, however. Indeed, as with so many immigrants, full acceptance is impossible to obtain, and "her otherness cannot be expunged."[31] Rather, the tension between Ruth's identity, which is negative, and her characterization, which is positive, remains; and with it, a lingering sense of unease. The abrupt ending of the book reflects this tension. As I noted earlier, Ruth, after the birth of her child, disappears, first replaced by Naomi[32] and then by David. The absence of Ruth and her replacement by Naomi as a nurse, Jennifer Koosed argues, stems from a lingering apprehensiveness about Ruth's foreignness: Though the child "grew in a foreign woman's womb . . . he can ingest only the milk produced by an Israelite body."[33]

That is, despite Ruth's hard work and travails, she still remains a foreigner at the end. Indeed, as Gafney starkly states: "She will never be one of them, no matter what she does; whether she is remembered as the grandmother of David, Israel's messiah-king, or the ancestress of Yeshua, the Christian Messiah, Ruth is remembered as a non-Israelite."[34] Ruth, in other words, continues to be considered a Moabite in Israel, not a Moab-Israelite, which, according to text, is an oxymoron.[35] And

("Matriarch of Israel," 377).

30. Donaldson, "Sign of Orpah," 166–67.

31. Lee, "Ruth," 149. On the complexity of the depiction of Ruth, see: Saxegaard, *Character Complexity*, esp. 105–42.

32. Laffey and Leonard-Fleckman, 147–48. Gafney even argues that Naomi's directions to Ruth about her encounter at the threshing floor entails Naomi's "sexploitation" of Ruth ("Mother Knows Best," 31).

33. Koosed, *Gleaning Ruth*, 117.

34. Gafney, "Mother Knows Best," 31.

35. The designations of Ruth throughout the work as a Moabite, a foreign woman, the wife of the dead man/Mahlon/Machlon shows that despite her actions, she remains foreign according to Niggemann ("Matriarch of Israel," 358). However, according to Matheny, Ruth is also called "daughter" (3:11), "woman of valor" (3:11), "wife of Boaz" (4:10), "better than seven sons" (4:15), which seems to indicate that Ruth's identity is ambivalent and shifting ("Ruth in Recent Research," 19).

as such, though Ruth "may embody all of the virtues explicated in Proverbs 31 and attributed to the perfect wife," she persists as "the foreign woman who seduces the righteous Israelite man."[36]

No wonder the narrative abruptly abandons and erases Ruth at the end, replacing her with Naomi.[37] As Cynthia Chapman notes: "Whether literal or symbolic, Naomi's breastfeeding is the ritual action required to confer upon Obed unquestionable Judean ethnicity."[38] In so doing, the story "removes the child from any Moabite stigma."[39] Indeed, it is telling that ten generations—that is, an epoch[40]—separate Ruth and David. According to Eskenazi and Frymer-Kensky, epochs "express a community's ideology about its identity, or to establish the legitimacy of certain structures or individuals."[41] As such, the genealogy at the end of Ruth suggests that enough generations have passed to diminish and wash the foreignness out of David. And despite the work done by Ruth, she endures as an outsider in and of her namesake book, which fittingly begins and ends with bonafide Israelites.[42]

Homiletic Overtures

The rich tale of Ruth evinces a sense of ambivalence and unease about foreigners, especially foreign women. In so doing, it reflects and speaks to current issues, pushing us to think about them anew. Especially pertinent are concerns about women and immigrants—issues that I am especially attuned to as an Asian American Biblicist.[43] My identity undoubtedly affects my reading of Ruth as a narrative about a hardworking immigrant

---

36. Koosed, *Gleaning Ruth*, 92. In contrast, Siquans argues that the purpose of Ruth is to show how foreign women are dangerous seductresses ("Forgiveness," 449–52).

37. Alice Ogden Bellis and Surekha Nelavala, in contrast, argue that Ruth shows two women cooperating with each other (Bellis, "Ruth: Sweet or Salty," 66–67; Nelavala, "Patriarchy," 91–97).

38. Chapman, "'Oh that you were like a brother,'" 39. According to Chapman, the description of Naomi's nursing of Obed "convey a transference of her Judean ethnicity to this child of a Moabite mother" (38).

39. Koosed, *Gleaning Ruth*, 117.

40. Eskenazi and Frymer-Kensky, *Ruth*, 93.

41. Eskenazi and Frymer-Kensky, *Ruth*, 93.

42. Fewell and Gunn, *Compromising Redemption*, 103.

43. Indeed, according to Sun, Ruth is a favorite character for readings through an Asian American lens ("Recent Research on Asian and Asian American Hermeneutics," 243).

woman who is unfairly dismissed. In this section, I highlight and elucidate the unfair treatment of Ruth, namely the lack of acknowledgment of her struggles and work, by reading Ruth alongside current concerns.[44]

The first issue reflected in the book of Ruth is the negative or ambivalent feelings about immigrants, especially poor immigrants. Like Ruth and Naomi, economic hardships continue to motivate people to immigrate. Despite the understandable reasons for relocation, immigrants, however, are viewed with suspicion and sometimes even met with hostility and violence by those in their host countries.[45] Stereotyped as lazy and freeloading, they are also feared oxymoronically as overly industrious and hardworking—so much so that they are blamed for taking jobs and increasing competition for the more deserving "true" citizens. Despite evidence of the significant contribution of immigrants,[46] their work is questioned, undermined, and ignored.

The ambivalence that society has towards them, especially in the United States where I reside, mirrors the ambivalence and unease towards foreigners reflected in the book of Ruth. Though Ruth's contributions are acknowledged by Naomi and the chorus of Israelite women, her disappearance at the end of the book and her concomitant displacement by the genealogy suggests an attempt to bypass or undermine or, at the very least, take the focus off Ruth, an immigrant woman, and her work. Indeed, though Ruth is accepted to some degree into Israelite society, especially as a mother of an Israelite heir, her absence at the end of the narrative raises questions about the level of acceptance she really achieves. Ruth, despite her work, remains foreign, so foreign that the tale feels the need to shift away from her towards more bonafide Israelites at the end of the story.

The attempt to blur and undermine Ruth's contributions highlights another issue. As I noted earlier, Ruth disappears at the end of the narrative and is replaced by, first, Naomi and then by the list of male patriarchs that lead to David. This shift of attention from the foreign female character who has done most of the work to her male descendants recalls similar instances where the work done by women and other

---

44. V. Ndikhokele N. Mtshiselwa offers a similar reading by looking at Ruth through the lens of modern socioeconomic concerns in South Africa ("Reading Ruth 4 and Leviticus 25:8–55," 1–5).

45. So also Dagley, "Women's Experience of Migration," 211.

46. Hamad, "Immigrants," 1–3; Hirschman, "Contributions of Immigrants," 26–47; Nadadur, "Illegal Immigrations," 1037–52.

marginalized groups are ignored, overlooked, or dismissed. That is, the issue of invisible labor. Sociologist Arlene Kaplan Daniel coined the term "invisible labor" to refer to work that is unpaid, unacknowledged, and unregulated.[47] As usually applied, this term refers to work done by women and other marginalized groups, such as child-rearing and the maintenance of the household, which require time and effort but remain largely unrecognized and unremunerated.[48]

This extra work, as researchers have noted, goes beyond the home. In the workplace, women and others from marginalized communities, such as those who are minorities, LGBTQ+, or have disabilities, do much more invisible labor to support, mentor, and help employees, and to promote diversity, equity, and inclusion (DEI).[49] On top of their jobs, Arlie Hochchild argues that women and other marginalized groups frequently take on "the second shift" by continuing to do the bulk of the labor to take care of the household.[50]

It might seem strange to discuss invisible labor in reference to the story of Ruth as the tale is centered on her work. That is, Ruth's actions—namely relocating to Israel with her mother-in-law, gleaning food, following Naomi's instructions to compel Boaz to serve as a kinsman-redeemer, and finally providing an heir for Naomi and her family—in so far as they serve as the main plot points appear to be well-acknowledged by the text. Indeed, as I noted earlier, Ruth is explicitly praised for her aid of Naomi by Boaz during their initial meeting (2:11–12) and by other Israelite women at the end of the book (4:14). Though Ruth's labors are unpaid and unregulated, they are, one can argue, robustly noted in the text.

While it is true that Ruth's labors constitute the main points of the plot and are acknowledged to some degree, the reason and purpose behind the recognition problematizes this conclusion. Though the women praise Ruth, she is tellingly absent. Rather, it is Naomi (and the readers) who hear the women's praise of Ruth, one which is centered on Ruth's aid of Naomi, an Israelite. Boaz's praise of Ruth is similar: Centered on Ruth's generous hard work to help Naomi. This lauding of Ruth, in sum, concerns what she has done for others, namely, other Israelites. That is, the praise is focalized around her contribution to Israelite society by taking care of and providing for its elderly.

47. Daniels, "Invisible Work," 403–15.
48. Budd, "Eyes See," 3–27.
49. Gordon, Willink, and Hunter, "Invisible Labor," 285–96.
50. Hochschild, *The Second Shift*, 3–33.

These plaudits serve a dubious purpose. Like praise given to girls for being nice or to women for keeping such a clean home, these compliments are not only an acknowledgment of Ruth's labors but also a kind of manipulation and attempt at control. It is a way to set up expectations to continue to obtain free aid and labor. That is, the praise of Ruth conveys the message that such self-sacrifice is what is expected and required of all respectable women, especially foreign women who hope for some measure of acceptance into Israelite society.

For all of Ruth's work, however, her reward remains ambiguous. In the end, it is unclear what she receives besides putting herself in danger to carry and give birth to a child—a child that is ultimately adopted by Naomi (4:16). Rather, it is Naomi and, more largely, the nation of Israel who are the true recipients of the fruits of Ruth's work. Naomi, as the women note in Ruth 4:14, gets an heir—her "social security"—while Israel is rewarded with a famous future king. In contrast, for all Ruth's toil, all she gets is indirect praise, which she does not hear, and which seems to push her and others like her to continue to give their efforts.[51]

Aside from economic loss, invisible work also exacts an emotional and physical price.[52] As such, the toll of labor, especially unremunerated and unacknowledged labor, leads easily to a discussion of women's health, especially the effects of pregnancy. If we imagine Ruth as a modern figure, the lack of mention of Ruth's whereabouts after giving birth is deeply troubling. Her absence intersects with concerns about maternal health and mortality. Recent reports, for example, note that women, especially women of color face mistreatment and discrimination during their pregnancy.[53] After birth, mothers are also susceptible to serious health ramifications, such as postpartum depression and post-traumatic stress disorder.[54] Indeed, pregnancy and childbirth can be deadly, especially for women of color.[55]

---

51. Gafney writes, "Naomi has received her social security; she has become the surrogate mother of the messiah. Ruth is a non-Israelite cultural outsider who abandons her family, land, ancestors, and gods, siding with her abductors and those who exploited her. For her troubles, she is not permitted to name her own child, as was the custom among Israelite women, nor is she named in the genealogy of her most famous descendant in 4:17" ("Mother Knows Best," 31–32).

52. Hochschild, *Invisible Labor*, 217.

53. Rabin, "One in Five Women," n.p.

54. Pearson, "Life," n.p.

55. Miller, Kliff, and Buchanan, "Childbirth," n.p.

These modern problems, when applied to Ruth, compels us to ask some disturbing questions about her disappearance. Is Ruth missing because she is struggling with postpartum complications and related health effects, such as depression? Indeed, did Ruth survive childbirth? And if she did, was she incapacitated or unable to care for her child for some reason? Ruth 4:16 cryptically states it was Naomi, an adopted grandmother, and *not Ruth* who "nursed" or adopted the child. Was Naomi taking care of the baby because Ruth was unable to? Most disturbing of all is the obvious lack of care or concern displayed by the narrative. Once Ruth fulfilled her maternal, familial, and national duty, the writers apparently felt no need to explain her sudden absence. Like so many women—but especially foreign, impoverished, immigrant women—after giving of her time and her labor, Ruth is rudely dismissed, her fate and her whereabouts deemed moot and irrelevant.

Homily

One way to argue against and counteract the disturbing, dismissive conclusion to and outcome of Ruth is to remember her anew—to evoke her in our current discussions and our sermons. As such, let us now turn to a succinct homily on Ruth. This sermon, which argues that one be cautious and conscious of the detrimental messages slyly evinced from the stories, is directed to any who find the biblical text enduringly relevant. It is also aimed at those who seek in the biblical text the voices of the unfairly lost, marginalized, or ignored.

Lauded in the Bible and by readers of the text, Ruth is remembered as a model woman and a model immigrant. She does all the things that good immigrants and good women are supposed to do: She leaves behind her birth country to follow her elderly mother-in-law back to her homeland. Once there, though the work is hard and dangerous,[56] and her situation, fragile, she dedicates herself to her new home and works feverishly to provide for her family.

Despite the challenges, Ruth, with some sage "dating" advice from her mother-in-law, makes it—well, makes it, at least in terms of what success means in the biblical text: She becomes pregnant by Boaz, the owner of the field on which she gleans, and gives birth to a son who,

---

56. Dagley, "Women's Experience of Migration," 211; Eskenazi and Frymer-Kensky, *Ruth*, 35; Schipper, *Ruth*, 116; Shepherd, "Ruth in the Days of Judges," 528–43.

due to complicated inheritance laws in ancient Israel, stands to inherit a piece of property in Israel. Her mother-in-law, Naomi, is overjoyed and, as the inheritance is connected to Naomi and her family, Naomi becomes a kind of adoptive parent to Ruth's son. This son, as we find out from the last chapter of the book, is not just any child but the ancestor of the great King David!

According to the biblical tale, Ruth is a resounding success—a triumphant story of a hardworking immigrant woman who through her continual labor succeeds in a new country, so much so that she becomes a foremother of a great Israelite hero and leader. Indeed, according to many interpreters, the story of Ruth embodies and defines this untranslatable word and concept, *hesed*—a term usually translated as loving-kindness, but which denotes an untranslatable sense of God's blessing and help.

Yet in lauding Ruth and in rejoicing with her, we must also be mindful—indeed, we must be critical and suspicious. We must ask what purpose this story serves and for whom. What message is it trying to subtly evince and why? And when we look at the narrative through glasses a little less rose-colored, we realize that this hopeful rags-to-riches plot line hides a dangerous message—one that can easily be manipulated to justify injustice or even abuse, especially of marginalized people. This message is that your main duty as someone like Ruth—as a poor woman, an immigrant, or an outsider—is to self-sacrifice. Your main duty is to work your fingers to the bone, to sacrifice your body and health, to give your all to your family, your community, and your country—especially the country that has stooped to let you in. That the value of your life depends on what you can give to others without complaint.

Hence, though presented and usually read as a happy story about a successful immigrant woman, Ruth also conveys a disturbing message, one which helps to justify the lack of acknowledgment or appropriate remuneration for the marginalized. It can send the message that women immigrants or poor people should constantly work, going above and beyond, despite inadequate pay or treatment. Even more disturbingly, Ruth can be said to convey the message that the labor of the powerless should be given away for free or for a far lesser sum than their true worth. That doing so—that constantly giving of yourself—is the price you pay for acceptance.

Conclusion

The book of Ruth, which is centered on the rags-to-riches tale of a poor, female immigrant oddly ends with Ruth's disappearance. Her disappearance, when coupled with the supplementation of David's genealogy at the end of the book, undermines and subverts Ruth's work. This rude conclusion stems from ambivalent feelings about immigrants, especially about immigrant women, which runs throughout the book as a whole. In particular, I have argued that the narrative is generally positive in its portrayal of Ruth. However, the focus on her Moabite identity and the portrayal of Moab in the Hebrew biblical text speak to a lingering sense of ambivalence about Moab and, therefore, of Ruth the Moabitess.

These problematic feelings mimic those that current society still has of its marginalized members. The narrative of Ruth compels us to think about how the labors of some are unfairly devalued, disregarded, unremunerated, and rendered invisible. In particular, the descriptions of the unrewarded and unacknowledged labors of Ruth coupled with her disappearance send the disturbing message that work done by women, immigrants, or the poor should be given away, without compensation or even acknowledgment. Only by giving such work for free will someone be considered a good woman, a good immigrant, and a good citizen.

7

Ruth as Model Victim, Hidden Scapegoat, or Groomed Surrogate

A Womanist Reading

Cheryl A. Kirk-Duggan

Introduction

Only two books bear women's names in Bibles that do not include the pseudepigraphic or apocryphal texts: Esther and Ruth. Both women's stories involve metaphorical and actual famines, feasts, and families. Ruth and Naomi shift between the roles of mother and daughter amid metaphors of famine and feast. Both women's lives intersect with issues of anger, identity, sexuality, boundaries, creativity, and pain. Both stories reflect a shift in power, a politics of displacements, a juxtaposition of emptiness and fullness, and tensions around the roles of these women amid the presence of a hidden God. Female relationships, such as those within Ruth, between Ruth and Naomi, and the community women provide a context for intriguing understandings of theological anthropology.[1] The initial absence of food in Ruth prompts the storyline. Tensions, women's roles, relationships, and impact of faith develop amid a patriarchal, misogynistic world.

1. Kirk-Duggan, "Black Mother Women and Daughters," 192–93.

The cultural world of the biblical ancient Near East so oppressed women, with no rights as they were the property of their fathers or husbands. Thus, the most important thing was for the right woman to marry the right man to bear a son to inherit the land. Women had few options and few choices about their identity and actions. Dreams were nonexistent.

This essay explores the challenges and opportunities for critical thinking when exegeting and interpreting the book of Ruth to explore Ruth and Naomi from a womanist biblical perspective. After providing the Hermeneutical Horizon, which includes a brief overview of my womanist biblical hermeneutics, and Naomi and Ruth's story, the essay explores an interpretation of cultural matters and focuses on the story as a soap opera where the Levirate code reflects contextual devices in a patriarchal, misogynistic world viewing the reversals of identity and characterizations. Then, this essay discusses Homiletic Overtures, which honor questions of inclusion, and Ruth as the redemptive scapegoat or trickster.

Hermeneutical Horizon

Bringing expansive, creative, pedagogical, pastoral, and scholarly lived experiences and skills to the book of Ruth is an interesting adventure of reading, exegeting, and interpretation. The cultural norms then and now are glaringly different and jarring to contemporary ears. The inherent oppressive, biased systems in the biblical world in conversation with contemporary global white supremacist patriarchal colonial capitalist misogyny require careful analysis to find relevant meaning. Not all audiences care about the questions I ask. Some traditional faith readings of Ruth allow for systemic oppression and pain to remain hidden in plain sight. A womanist lens provides the space and energy to explore my concerns.

My Kaleidoscope: The Womanist Lens Through Which I Peer

The term Womanist emerges from the term "womanish" in African Diasporan communities, and refers to a Black feminist who takes seriously oppression meted out against women. Alice Walker's definition of womanist is complex and fertile as a significant rubric for critical, textual analysis and vibrant living.² Along with components of survival, loving, of taking charge, the term Womanist also imparts a living vitality, a search for knowledge, an intergenerational wisdom, and a desire for freedom for all. Womanist sensibilities foster the freedom of being able to love all people, sexually and nonsexually, and give credence to the manifestation of a woman's culture and life. Many black women scholars of religion have embraced the term womanist as a category of analysis and a way of life, to name and critique systemic oppressions around gender, race, class, sexual orientation, age, and ability.

Reading from my womanist biblical perspective generates provocative questions about life and texts, uncovering the imagination and violence of humanity and God. My critical lens uses suspicion with sensitivity to grasp what I read, question biblical texts and their power for believers, appreciate the careful work of biblical scholars, honor tradition, and acknowledge its misuse to justify bad causes. This is complex work where some questions will be left unanswered via tempered cynicism. A creative ear listens to how my life experience may contribute to, benefit from, and take exception to other interpretations and traditions. With courage, a comparative analysis provides a way to juxtapose various biblical stories with other texts³ to find common themes of life-giving or death-dealing power, even if they seem antithetical. A commitment to hearing these texts in their ancient contexts affords opportunities to discover both the irreconcilable and a just, appropriate ethical contemporary living of these texts. A candor emerges that assures the naming of oppression and questions how we have used these texts amid faith. My curiosity supports searching scripture to see how relationships between God and humanity unfold to honor inclusivity, mercy, justice, and love. Such serious work calls for the comedic, reminding us not to take ourselves so seriously that we fail to grow and respect other ways of seeing; and to be upfront about texts I find jarring and unjust, while others may disagree. My personal story, research, lived experiences, creative curiosity, and commitment to liberation and love undergird my methodology. My life's metaphor: "Laughing, Dancing, and Singing with God," provides the context from which I read, as our conversation shifts to the contextual realities of the book of Ruth.

---

2. Walker, *In Search of Our Mother's Gardens*, ix.

3. Analysis can include other types of literature, music, film, art, dance, and personal/communal stories.

Their Story: The Biblical Contexts

The book of Ruth, named after a foreign (Moabite), non-Jewish woman in the Messianic lineage, engages issues of immigration, sexuality, gender, race/ethnicity, class, nationality, and assimilation, and provides a scenario where we can read our own stories into the complex narrative of Ruth and Naomi. Gale Yee notes that the book of Ruth provides a significant lens for reading otherness and foreign aliens as stereotypical configurations where race/color for blacks and citizenship for many Asians, where cultural and institutional racism always defines persons other than white male Protestants as perpetual resident aliens. She notes that often Chinese Americans get trapped into the double bind of being a perpetual foreigner and not being American enough while being cast as a model minority stereotype, both a critique and a denigration. The latter signifies the US as a just society while overlooking the systemic oppression that targets nonwhite persons, the poor, and women. Yee cautions us in our readings to be open and embrace ambiguity and be intentional about exploring matters of economic exploitation, ethnicity, racism, and the sexuality of foreigners in the text, being aware of the stereotypes that emerge in the idea of model minority. Model minority weaponized becomes a way to ostracize and critique black and brown persons as if they are underperforming, not taking into consideration systemic oppression. As perpetual foreigners, some view Asian Americans as a threat to white students who think Asian students distort the grading curve. Personal and cultural perceptions often position foreigners as a threat. In a broader sense, *gēr* a*nd nokriya* categorize foreigners in Ruth.[4]

Gēr defines foreigners who have immigrated and now live in an area minus familial or tribal relations. Whereas Elimelech and his family going to Moab make him a *ger*, Ruth technically is not, although her gleaning like the poor implies she is a *gēr*. When Ruth calls herself a *nokrî* (Chapter 2), which connotes negation and otherness, this illuminates her status as part of a tribe hated by Israel. For some, Ruth is a model foreigner or a perpetual foreigner. In the Hebrew Bible, foreign women are often connected to sexual insatiability and erotic allure. This perspective underscores Ruth's case, where earlier incest between Lot and his daughter (Gen 19) produces progeny, the Moabite lineage. In addition to gender and immigrant issues, viewing the status of Naomi and Boaz as elite reflects the commodification of Ruth. Boaz owns the land; Ruth

---

4. Yee, "She Stood in Tears Amid the Alien Corn."

works the land as she gleans, and Naomi does not work the land but depends upon Ruth and ultimately becomes Ruth's pimp, as Naomi sets Ruth up with Boaz.[5] Conversely, the story opens where Naomi, her husband Elimelech, and their sons Mahlon and Chilion have immigrated or moved from Judah to Moab, due to a famine. The text does not see them as dishonorable foreigners, as they left for food. Nor does the text explain why the family decides to go to Moab, given the famine in Bethlehem "house of bread/food," occupied the land. Moab is problematic, biblically, because of the apostasy resulting when Israelite men were sexually engaged with Moabite women (Num 25:1–2), Moab oppressed Israel (Judg 3:12ff), and Moabites were forbidden in Israel's religious assembly (Neh 13:1). These accounts signal Israel's negative view of Moab.[6] Some biblical scholars look to Genesis 19 and the saga of Lot and his unnamed daughters, who get their dad drunk and rape him on subsequent nights, to have offspring as though they were the last people on earth. While some see this text as a negation of the Moabites, other scholars note that Lot's daughters help to preserve the male lineage, to ensure God's promise of Jacob's inheritance (Gen 22). One can see Lot's daughters in a similar light to Tamar and Rebecca (Gen 38), making their conception a righteous act. Jennifer Koosed reminds us that several encounters across the Torah signal ambivalence around relationships between Israel and Moab—sometimes positive, sometimes negative. With the book of Ruth, many commentators see the marriage of Mahlon and Chilion to the Moabites, Ruth and Orpah, as an abomination, a violation of biblical law. Thus, many make a hermeneutical move of censure. Whereas the text does not condemn multi-faith marriages, reading from the perspective of Genesis, Numbers, and Deuteronomy, they are problematic. How we read also concerns the dating of Ruth, before or after the monarchical period—not a priority here. Ultimately, we get ambiguous readings of intermarriages and must be aware of our biases as we read.[7] The need for the family's departure, the famine, assumes punishment by God: a simple story of survival, a complex story of human drama. As this drama unfolds, we wonder how they navigated their travels and what challenges arose around markers of identity and their safety.

Named for the Moabite woman, questions of ethnicity, gender, loyalty, and outsider/immigration emerge. Challenges and crises begin and

---

5. Yee, 130–32.
6. Sakenfeld, *Ruth: Interpretation*, 10.
7. Koosed, *Gleaning Ruth*, 29–34.

end the four-chapter book. Famine, migration/displacement, multiple deaths, and bareness are prologue. Ruth, Naomi, Elimelech, and their sons leave Judah because of a famine. Famine, a storytelling device, plays a significant role in Genesis and Esther as a literary device, a trope, to create tension and serve as a mechanism of divine wrath and destruction. The famine moves Abraham's kin from Haran to Egypt. Multiple factors, including conflict and climate, cause famines. A famine is not a natural disaster but a result of human actions or lack of action to prevent it. Famines do not happen overnight but develop over time until they cause massive harm and suffering. The Integrated Food Security Phase Classification (IPC) describes the severity of food emergencies in a five-phase scale that warns governments and humanitarian organizations to take action: from food security to food insecurity and acute food and livelihood crisis, to humanitarian emergency and then famine. Famines destroy futures, fuel violence and insecurity, and destroy societies. Famine signals change, a curse, and a new beginning.[8] Drought and famine, which caused twenty-first-century tragedies, concerned those in the biblical ancient Near East.

Chance or happenstance and nature as we understand it today were nonexistent in the ancient Near East. When God was pleased, things were good; if God was angry or displeased, usually people were disobedient. Famines could reflect a national catastrophe where either the entire people or their representative monarchs were disobedient. Famine as a narrative device— rather than as a theological tool—is found regularly throughout the Bible. In the Hebrew Bible, writers used famine as the motivation for major changes in character's lives, signifying the impact of famine in the ancient world. In sum, famine triggers Naomi, Elimelech, and their family to move from Judah to Moab and back. Preserving family and transgressive human faithfulness crosses boundaries and offers readers an opportunity to think about communal and personal identity, destiny, and inclusion.[9] Since moving is one of the most stressful human activities, one wonders about their feelings in those moments.

Focusing on feelings, Graybill sees the book of Ruth as one of hardship, from death and famine to tears. With lesbian and queer readings of Ruth and Naomi, while paying critical attention to structures of exploitation, Graybill invites readers to take seriously backward and unhappy

8. "What Is Famine?" International Rescue Committee (IRC).
9. Lee, "Ruth," 142–45. Streete, *The Strange Woman*, 68. Kim, "Ruth vis-a-vis Esther," 20–24, 29–34.

feelings. Is the text one of inspiration and affirmation, of the model refugee or devoted loyalist, or one of exploitation by Naomi of Ruth while forcing a happy ending? Graybill notes that various cultural artifacts or other genres may provide space where we can imagine lesbian lives, however the endings must be unhappy. She sees a delicate space of love between women that morphs into marriage and baby plots. In a queer reading, Naomi as an alleged moderate lesbian lover becomes Naomi the trickster/pimp. Bitter, Naomi uses Ruth to support her survival. Ruth may be Naomi's pawn or bargaining chip. Exploitative relationships mixed in with intimate relationships involve friendship, failure, and backward feelings—sensations from love and desire to abuse, mixing past and present, even promise.[10] These families had so many challenges. Considering their inner spiritual lives and culture, their names mirror their reality.

Naomi, "fair, pleasant, delightful, sweet," and her husband Elimelech, "God is my King," with their two sons, Mahlon, "to be sick or to entreat," and Chilion, "finished, complete, or perfect," go to Moab. Their immigration is logical during a famine, though the text does not paint the Ephramites as foreigners in Moab. Lack of food meant they had to leave. Perhaps, additional food was not available nearby in Judah. Initially, we learned nothing about any property Elimelech may have left behind in Judah. We don't know how long Elimelech lived in Moab or about his relationship with Naomi or their sons. Shortly after their move, Elimelech dies. How tragic: Naomi now has no husband. So many issues are left to the reader's imagination. For example, after Elimelech's death, the two sons marry two Moabite women: Ruth, "friend or companion," and Orpah, "neck, stiff-neck or gazelle." How do Naomi's boys meet Ruth and Orpah? Was it an arranged marriage? Were they hoping to marry so that they could have a son, to inherit land at some point (Gen 12:1–3)? After a decade in Moab, the women are widows, commodities—the property of dead men. What happened during those ten years? Were no Israelite women available? Were the men sterile, the women unable to conceive, or unable to carry a fetus to term? Is barrenness a theological device to signal Divine displeasure? Were they farmers? The text provides no information regarding the relationship of Naomi, her sons, and their wives. After ten years, both sons die. Is this a literary device? Did an illness kill many people? Questions about Naomi's immediate family, trigger those of her married relations.

---

10. Graybill, "Even unto This Bitter Loving," 308–22.

In addition to being kin by marriage, a *go'el*, a redeemer—who is Boaz? In chapter 3, he uses the endearment of "his daughter" when referring to Ruth and suggests that she works with "his women." Who are these women? Are they servants or kin? Boaz learns of Ruth's kindness to Naomi, and he invokes the power of God to bless Ruth and promises to make sure she is protected. Naomi reassures Ruth that being with Boaz is best and for her to continue to glean with the other young women. Sometimes, Boaz comes across as a patron or big brother; other times, he seems to be a lover or suitor who gets what he wants and needs to direct the relationship. Ruth gets encouragement from Naomi and Boaz. Both support Ruth staying close to the other women gleaning in the field as if a hidden danger lurks.

Naomi desires security, a protector/husband for Ruth. She prepares Ruth to approach Boaz. Is Naomi functioning as a mother or madam? Naomi blesses Boaz for his kindness to Ruth and for honoring the legacy of her dead husband, Elimelech. That Boaz indicates Ruth will be blessed and is a worthy woman, and insists that no one knows they slept together begs the question of power and consent. Is it consent or coercion, where Ruth benefits from following cultural norms yet has limited options? Is this a "love triangle," where Naomi and Boaz orchestrate the dance, and Ruth is a pawn in a chess game? Is this a threesome, or a twosome of Ruth/Boaz orchestrated by Naomi? Were the three deaths a curse? A literary twist? Something more nefarious? Did Naomi's sorrow include guilt? Anger? Terror? The men's one-sentence obituaries and epithets make us ask: what difference did their lives make? How does one's culture shape life and death? Our stories and thoughts inform how we interpret.

Interpretation

Cultural Contextual Devices and the Challenges

The stories we hear and read concern our perceptions of self, culture, and our curiosity. Some focus on this text as Ruth's story. Some argue that the end game of who gets the child makes it Naomi's story. Athalya Brenner convincingly argues that the received MT (Masoretic Text) Book of Ruth is a compilation of a Ruth story and a Naomi story. The two stories explain many textual challenges, where the women's roles seem interchangeable. Like the ancient Greek Demeter-Persephone myth, one could read Ruth-Naomi as two sides of the same Eve. The structure and topics of both stories are similar, with differing subthemes. The parallel stories in the flood story (Gen 7–8) and the Tower of Babel (Gen 11), and the strands in Esther of Mordecai and Haman, Esther and Vashti, all use double structures. Harmony emerges as Ruth and Naomi are a team. With Naomi as the senior and Ruth, as the junior partner, the community women note that Ruth is worth more than ten sons. In a patriarchal culture, such a value reflects Ruth's profound expressions of love and loyalty.[11]

With family, immigration, levirate, love, and intrigue, the book of Ruth juxtaposes cultural traditions, family inheritances, and two women's stories. The concerns around the Moab/Judah proximity remind us of the twenty-first-century immigration questions, particularly considering the Statue of Liberty's base inscription: "Give me your tired, your poor, your huddled masses yearning to breathe free," along with desirable versus undesirable immigrants. Much of the unexplained connects with the textual dance between Ruth and Naomi. Ruth is faithful to Naomi. However, the community women take the child sired by Boaz with Ruth from them and give him to Naomi. Brazenly, they reduce Ruth to a broodmare, a commodity. Naomi replaces Ruth as Obed's mother, making her indispensable. Much of the action occurs through the women's direct speech acts. Their speech acts create a power base and express women's wisdom and a female audience. That Naomi suggests her daughters-in-law return to their "mother's house" after their husbands have died, reflects women's shaping of their destiny, and the gifts of female authority, maternity, amidst sexuality and motherhood. Binary oppositions color the text: foreigner vs. native, Naomi vs. Ruth, Naomi's married relative vs. Boaz as *goʾel*, and Moab vs. Judah, along with the need for Obed to be the grandfather of David, as the Messiah must be from the root of Jesse, David's dad—the story is rife with intrigue and has numerous options for interpretation and preaching.[12]

Ancient stories assume readers have a cultural knowledge of traditions, like levirate marriage, rather than explain them. Levirate marriage was a provision where a male relative (often the next oldest brother) assumed the responsibility of impregnating a widow whose husband died without progeny, a male heir (Gen 38; Deut 25:5–10). Inference of levirate occurs several times: Naomi's sorrow that she cannot bear other

---

11. Brenner, "Naomi and Ruth," 70–74, 81–83.
12. Brenner, "Introduction," 8–19.

sons to marry Orpah and Ruth (1:12–13); the threshing floor dialog between Ruth and Boaz (chapter 3); the conversation between the nearest kin and Boaz (chapter 4); and preserving Elimelech's name, though the text names Boaz as the child's father, not Elimelech or Mahlon. Morally, levirate provides for Ruth and legally handles the right of land redemption.[13] Levirate traditions seem abhorrent today. They assume heterosexual marriages and patriarchal power where women are the property of their dad or husband. Perhaps a metaphorical application to care for family following grief might include a levirate variation. Late in the narrative (4:3), Naomi has come to sell the land owned by Elimelech, and Boaz inquires if the other kinsman has an interest. Boaz appropriately negotiated the levirate. He approaches the ten other male kinfolk, a minion. With the land acquisition, Boaz owns Ruth. Similarly, many complications arise for children of formerly enslaved and contemporary domestic workers, who experience abuse under white supremacist patriarchal colonial capitalistic misogyny.

Such anxiety is alive and well. The development of a deep-seated white fear and its impact on culture and democracy in the United States—fear of losing a particular way of life, power, and economic standing, as a future looms where white people will become a racial minority continues to fester, intensify, and heighten in visibility.[14] Systematic white male oppression arrived from Europe with the intent to conquer and take the land as part of manifest destiny and American essentialism, rooted in Tacitus' notion of Anglo-Saxon superiority, 98 CE.[15] Land becomes a commodity of exchange, identity, and relationships.

Land connects Elimelech, Mahlon, and Ruth. After the kinsman rejects the invitation, Boaz claims his acquisition to everyone, and they link this process to Rachel and Leah, producers of progeny, with the House of Perez, reflecting Tamar and Judah. The negotiation connects back to the Abrahamic covenant (Gen 12:1–3)[16] and the Messianic line. As the genealogy provides benediction, the communal women may subvert familial and patriarchal protocol. Other assumptions of a willing redeemer, of women as totally dependent, and that land is available for inheritance are not realistic today, ethically and theologically.

13. Sakenfeld, *Ruth: Interpretation*, 6–7.
14. See Martin, *White Fear*, 1–6.
15. Brown Douglas, *Stand Your Ground*, 3–89.
16. YHWH promises Abram to make his name great—have relationships with his people in perpetuity, have a son, and have land.

To make theology and religion relevant requires new interpretations related to various contexts, notably in Old Testament or Hebrew Bible studies. The Old Testament is a collection of various genres and literary communicative forms arising out of multiple processes, from oral traditions to canonization amid numerous manuscripts creating multiple contradictions and incongruities. Thus, hermeneutics and homiletics are complex. We question circumstances, people, history, or theological ideas behind and in the text: its form, texture, composition, and synchronic nature; and issues before the text, including the "reader," the lens the reader uses, biases, assumptions, and socio-historic context of the interpreter, who then determines meaning and outcomes of the exegetical method. W. P. Human sees Ruth as a transforming theology of Deuteronomic Law, encouraging solidarity, creating hope for the Second-Temple community, portraying a distinctive Israelite identity with a future identity, and a counter-narrative to the exclusionary practices of Ezra 10 and Nehemiah 13 against mixed marriages.[17] He suggests that Ruth expands the levirate code in Deuteronomy 25. A redeemer is available via Elimelech's relative (4:1), but he refuses to act to avoid jeopardizing his situation (4:6) when Boaz inquires. Boaz, a wealthy, close clan member, not a brother-in-law, honors the social obligation. By re-interpreting the earlier Levirate code, Human contends that the book of Ruth changes the law into a life-giving theology.[18] While persuasive, he fails to address Ruth's commodification, her erasure at the text's end, and the gift of the child to Naomi.

In her comparative analysis between the foreign woman, Ruth, and the Gibeonites (Levite's, Judg 19) concubine, Orit Avnery engages liminality, common to both stories. In Ruth, liminality or quality of disorientation or ambiguity that happens in the middle of a rite of passage occurs as spatial, temporal, and identic. Spatial involves entrance to the city, of being inside or outside. Temporal relates to the threshing floor, along with the period the text comes into being, whether monarchial or post-exilic. The identic liminality unfolds as the text names all of the players. Ruth, though an immigrant, becomes a major player in Bethlehem as an unprotected person. Yet, in the end, Ruth achieves status by having Obed, and a great value occurs when the communal women bless Ruth saying she is worth seven times that of a son (4:15).[19] Avnery concludes that rectification and

17. Human, "Re-interpretation as Transformation."
18. Human, "Re-interpretation as Transformation."
19. Avnery, "On the Threshold," 232–33, 236–40, 243–45.

continuation of social order closes the book. Beyond causing a disruption, the women's actions erase Ruth: they named the child and gave him to Naomi as her son. Relationships then and now can be dicey.

Koosed questions Ruth and Naomi's relationship. Is their relationship about Phyllis Trible's notion of *hesed* where two women connect to survive patriarchy, and female relationships run the narrative as the two bond amid generational, ethnic, and religious differences? Readings by Danna Nolan Fewell, David Miller, and Athalya Brenner address questions about Ruth's devotion given Naomi's antagonism, amid tensions, mercurial feelings, and contrasts in speech style. Rebecca Alpert, Mona West, and Jeannette H. Foster view the two women in love with each other amid gender and sexual ambiguity and the blurring of characters that can express heterosexual, lesbian, and/or bisexual realities. Intriguingly, some of the Masoretic text's examples indicate that Naomi says she will go to the threshing floor in Ruth's place (Ruth 3:3–4). The Masoretes alter the text so that Ruth acts on the threshing floor. Koosed sees Ruth and Naomi as sparring partners, where Ruth's first hyperbolic words situate her as an oral trickster of words. Initially, Ruth expresses loyalty and commitment to Naomi. With the mixing of positions, identities, and subverting binaries, many scholars assume reciprocity between Ruth and Naomi. However, there are tensions, times of silence, connections, disconnects, and miscommunication. The uses of powerful speech acts, hyperbole, and complicated women's conversation, signal we should not oversimplify a complicated text.[20] For example, who instigates the activity on the threshing floor: Ruth, Naomi, or Boaz?

The threshing floor incident where the language of "to lie down," to enter, and to know, reflects Ruth's sexual vulnerabilities and the realities and struggles of a woman who has limited options for survival, amid danger, secrecy, and ambiguity. Ruth daringly suggests Boaz make good on his promise to "spread his cloak over her," to marry her as kinsman (3:9), echoing Tamar's story (Gen 38). Amid the intrigue and role reversals, Boaz confesses Ruth's worthiness (3:11).[21]

Several times, the gender roles get reversed from standard patriarchy and highlight some perverse sexuality. Ruth gets valued at more than seven sons (4:15). Gail Corrington Streete reminds us that the family matters of land and lineage conjure up sexual perversity, incest, danger, and hostility

20. Koosed, *Gleaning Ruth*, 50–63.
21. Lee, "Ruth," 147.

that frames Lot and his daughter's legacy (Gen 19:37), the whoring after foreign gods (Num 25:1–5), and issues of dangerous immigration when Naomi's two sons marry Moabite women. The death of Naomi's husband, Elimelech, and her two sons, without them having sired male children, leaves Elimelech without an heir, exiled to a foreign land. This reflects the challenge that rankles with God's promise to Abram, cited earlier. Thus, the right man must marry the right woman so that she can bear him a son to inherit the land. Several other reversals occur. Christy Cobb notes that Ruth is a superb text for exploring political issues like gender roles, immigration, sex, and consent. Cobb incorporates bell hooks' concept of "engaged pedagogy," to heighten student's self-awareness, humanity, and passion for subjects as a parallel for working with homiletics and congregants. With numerous impressions and issues important to our global world, we can use pedagogical strategies within our homiletic practice, by using the arts and technology for illustrations. Rhetorically, questions can encourage listeners to become audience participants. By focusing on geography, we can explore the question of immigration and juxtapose the reception of Naomi, Elimelech, Mahlon, and Chilion going into Moab, with the return of Naomi and Ruth to Judah; with Haitian and Latinx immigrants. The text is silent on the family's reception in Moab and assumes well-being for ten years after the famine. After the deaths of her husband and two sons, Naomi returns to Judah, assuming an ease of reception. Intriguingly, the texts repeatedly call our attention to Ruth's foreign status.[22] Returning to Bethlehem, Naomi suggests that the two daughters-in-law return to their mother's homes, not their father's. That Ruth avoids Naomi's advice and "clings to" her mother-in-law as a wife would relate to a husband (Gen 2:24) is misguided and often misused at weddings. Enigmatically, Naomi becomes Ruth's pimp, suggesting she seduce and have sex with Boaz, her ultimate *go'el*, or redeemer[23] Then, and now, family matters involve dense stories, shaped by traditions and power brokers who share narratives: some weld religious doctrine, others inspire mythic scenarios and warped beliefs.

---

22. Cobb, "Learning Design," 117–22.
23. Streete, *The Strange Woman*, 67–72.

No Hallmark Soap Opera: A Hermeneutical Focus

Hallmark, long a multimedia conglomerate that began with greeting cards, now hosts television programming of original dramas, made-for-TV movies, and comedies. The company dubs itself as a leader for feel-good and family-friendly entertainment with a 100-year legacy. The formulaic storyline includes personal ties to some previous relationship, and years later, person one meets person two. Initially antagonistic, a romance soon happens. The relationship goes well, a conundrum occurs, and the couple falls apart. Serendipitously, the couple finds they really love each other and everything ends, "happily ever after," every time, for every story. Ruth's saga is no hallmark soap opera. Focusing only on Ruth's transgressive faithfulness for Naomi, all is well. But, upon the return of Ruth and Naomi to Judah, there is irony, upheaval, sexual entendre, power, and politics.

Naomi hears that God decided to give people food, so she returns to Judah; the famine is over. The text does not say who informed Naomi and why they could not stay in Moab, nor is it clear why Naomi suggests her daughters-in-law "return to their mother's house" in a patriarchal society. While blessing the two women with a prayer for security and a husband, she kisses them, and they cry aloud. The text intimates Levirate code reversal when Naomi reminds them that she is too old to bear sons. After tears, Orpah leaves and Ruth clings to Naomi, expressing *hesed*—faithfulness and loyalty. When Naomi and Ruth return to Bethlehem, though the townspeople greet her excitedly, Naomi ties her plight to divine punishment and changes her name to Mara since YHWH made her life bitter and brought her back empty. While Naomi states she went away full with family, she blames God that she was empty with no food (1:20–21).

While much of Ruth's storyline unfolds through dialog, there are five major silences: (1) Naomi's silence when Ruth decides to accompany her to Bethlehem; (2) Naomi's silence on their arrival to Bethlehem; (3) Naomi's initial silence about her relationship to Boaz by marriage; (4) Ruth's silence about the threshing floor encounter; (5) Naomi's silence regarding Ruth at Obed's birth. Ultimately, Naomi's bitterness and emptiness shifted to security. In the mix, rhetorical ambiguity, praise, and irony emerge. Dana Fewell and David Gunn remind us of the irony of Naomi's position—that a foreign woman who challenges patriarchal values—provides restoration. Naomi and readers know the community women stating the child belongs to Naomi is rhetorical. These assumptions problematize seeing Ruth as the generator of change.[24] However, the text erases Ruth. Both women maneuver within a patriarchal system, so Ruth as privileged is not certain. The communal women privilege Naomi. Thus, despite biology, we are left with irony, rhetoric, and ambiguity, significantly around motherhood.

Wil Gafney explores motherhood in Ruth, as the rape marriages, or "forced conjugal cohabitation," of Orpah and Ruth—the sexual exploitation used to legitimate and establish Israel's offspring. There was no consent or negotiations between families, parents, or the woman. Deuteronomy 21 sanctions rape marriages of women dubbed enemies. Legally, Israel's men can kidnap, rape, and humiliate by shaving a woman's head. Viewing Naomi's treatment of Ruth as sexploitation, the story proceeds around provision and progeny. In exploiting Ruth, and coaching her in seducing Boaz, Naomi exploits Ruth's body, Ruth's commitment to Naomi, and Boaz's inebriated sexuality. Boaz also implores Ruth to "keep things undercover" in multiple ways. He does not want anyone to know Ruth has slept with him. Ruth, a foreign immigrant outsider, gives up everything—her family, beliefs, and cultures, to help Naomi, and she adopts Naomi's god, her faith, land, and customs. Ruth received kudos for embodying *hesed*. At what cost?[25] The women in the relationship appear to support survival, but the men disappear in Chapter 1.

Given that male characters, Dad Elimelech and sons Mahlon and Chilion, all die after being in Moab for ten years, the women are major players. Analysis from a womanist perspective, one must take seriously inherent cultural and personal lenses and biases when reading and interpreting the text. The statements by Naomi and Ruth allow them to exert power. Contextually, Ruth's words move her from the margins to stability. Naomi's words make her the central character who goes from Moab and bitterness to Judah, return, and redemption. Naomi's insistence on her daughters-in-law returning to their mothers emphasizes the importance of women's relationships, a rarity in the Hebrew bible. Just as Ruth has the last word with Naomi (1:16–18) given the former's refusal to leave her mother-in-law in Judah, Ruth has the last word with Boaz (2:10–13). After Ruth brings Boaz into Naomi's life, the power shifts and Naomi sees Boaz as a redeemer, the solution to their problem. Leaving Naomi's script of letting Boaz initially instruct her, Boaz ultimately becomes

---

24. Fewell and Gunn, "A Son is Born to Naomi, 233–39.
25. Gafney, "Mother Knows Best," 23–36.

the redeemer, and the reversal of power occurs again at the end—both women gain power through discourse and doubling.

Doublings occur in character relationships and the rhythm or movement of the plot, sometimes in opposition. The dance between famine and fullness weaves through the narrative. Poetry mingled with dialog, wordplay, and the way certain phrases bracket and help develop the plot constitute doubles. The doublings and pairings frame the relationships—the confluence of twos: ethnicities, cultures, religions, and women—all inform the book's structure, themes, characters, and plot. The bifurcated, oppositional readings of Ruth herself, given that her interior thoughts remain silent, and her dialogue, exaggerated actions, and what she does and says, make Ruth the consummate double, a trickster.[26] Being a trickster heightens our awareness of power dynamics, critical in all relationships. People have power over, power under, or shared power.

As readers and interpreters, we work to make sense of the power dynamics, based on our experiences, which prompts diverse interpretations. How we read determines what we privilege or ignore, what we place at the center, and what we marginalize.[27] Readers learn of Ruth's personality as she interacts with the other characters in the story. Not only is one's character formed and expressed through relationships, but one's character is also embedded in a social context and geographical location. Questions of society and land are also important, especially in Ruth, where the agricultural setting is key to the plot. In the three "Agricultural Interludes," Koosed explores Ruth's world—the land she inhabits, the food she eats, and the fields she works. In pre-industrial worlds, women had power, though circumscribed by patriarchy. To be a self-sufficient household, all family members had to participate in a function of gender balance, not hierarchy. Food and famine shape major components of Ruth, including ethnicity, sexuality, gender, and reproduction. Naomi's lack of response to Ruth's passionate vow of loyalty introduces ambiguities around gender and sexuality that occur throughout the book, alongside the impact of access to grain and bread production. The lack of access and how Ruth gains provision reflect her vulnerability and the impact of poverty. With this awareness, the story becomes a fascinating lens through which to consider the plight of immigrants/foreigners, and poor people in a world that commodifies them, that is connected globally by technology, and

---

26. Koosed, *Gleaning Ruth*, 2–6.
27. Greenstein, "Reading Strategies and the Story of Ruth," 211, 218, 223.

where the impact of climate change is formidable.[28] Often, immigrants/foreigners get demonized and blamed for any ills of the primary country, yet they often fail to realize that immigrants/foreigners do the manual labor, construction, and harvesting that natural-born citizens will not do. Regarding economics, alleged first-world countries could not thrive if all so-called illegal immigrants/foreigners left immediately, notably in the United States—topics for sermons. Critical to one's homiletic process is identifying the socio-cultural, spiritual, and economic issues that shape our daily lives, including human vocal mechanisms, and verbal and nonverbal communication.[29]

Homiletic Overtures

Engaging Ruth presents several themes regarding homiletical options. Making the text come alive today is an opportunity to ask provocative, profound, passionate questions about rules and relationships, understanding and undercurrents, commitments and commodification, personalities and perceptions, immigration and inspiration, heart and health, Creator and creation, being, beliefs, and belonging. After prayer and reviewing the lectionary, I select a pericope, read the original and several English translations with the Holy Spirit's inspiration, and develop the thesis and three points, mindful of current events and the preaching context. My audience has in-person and virtual intergenerational audiences, primarily African American, with mixed class, heterosexual and homosexual members, with a mission statement of a church that "Loves God, and Loves God's people." The Ruth and Naomi stories are important to me for personal reasons.

The names Ruth and Naomi anchor my identity as these are the first and middle names of my mother, Naomi Ruth (1927—1989). Mother was an incredible woman, daughter, wife, mother, grandmother, sister, cousin, singer, executive secretary, seamstress, cosmetologist, cook, cheerleader, champion, confidante, community leader, a keen observer of life, romance novel aficionado, a woman of faith. Ruth Naomi (1930–) is the name of the mother of my twin from another mother, Allison Brewster Franzetti. Ruth Naomi is also an amazing woman of faith. She is a phenomenal woman, daughter, wife/widow, mother,

---

28. Koosed, *Gleaning Ruth*, ix–xi.
29. Fry Brown, *Delivering the Sermon*, 2–4.

grandmother, aunt, cousin, friend, one-of-a-kind trailblazer, loving matriarch, absolutely brilliant, opinionated with reason, business entrepreneur, inspirational cheerleader, community leader, and a savvy strategist. Naomi Ruth was Christian. Ruth Naomi is Jewish. These two powerhouses have expressed passionate power far beyond their namesakes. Born of these two awesome women, Allison and I share many experiences of biology, talent, and commitment.

Our birthdates are the same, five years apart. We began performing as children and have undergraduate, masters, and doctoral degrees. We value God, family, social justice, and love of neighbor. My twin predicted that I would marry someone like the man I did, she was a bridesmaid for our wedding, and our relationship continues. Her daughter is my niece, and I was family at a Passover Seder a few years ago hosted by Ruth Naomi. We are kindred spirits: musicians, moms, sisters, wives (me now widow), professors (me now retired and an entrepreneur). We perform, research, teach, and coach. We have collaborated on musical projects. She has composed and arranged numerous works; I have composed and published books and articles. We both travel globally and belong to professional guilds, with an over four-decade friendship. To this text, I bring love, curiosity, and appreciation.

From the Book of Ruth, I selected Ruth 1:3–5, and 3:6–16, with the sermon title: "Naming Things Hidden in Plain Sight: Journeys to Inclusion." The thesis is: Our character transcends our labels, allowing us to love universally. Connecting the congregation with its mission and the text, the significance of reading, living, and thinking critically about the text frames the message. Principles to engage and to avoid, the importance of healthy communication, and the impact of love as we process loss and grief weave through the message.

Homily

One day a grandmother sat on her porch on her recliner rocker, with pieces of fabric on her lap, as she pieced a quilt for the new grandbaby on the way. An older grandchild came over and asked her Grannie what she was doing. Her Grannie replied, "I'm making a family quilt. Each block will refer to some of our ancestors, long dead. There will also be a block of each of my children and their children, including you, your siblings, and cousins." "What makes you want to make that kind of quilt,

Grannie?" Grannie smiled and said, "In each square, I sew a bit of love, and I honor a memory. We are blessed to have four generations alive and well. We've had good times and bad ones. When we learned to share our stories and name the secrets, those traumatizing events no longer had power over us. While our earlier generations were not wealthy in finances, we have loved you and been able to help you and your cousins get educations, and some now have businesses. We had to move from the South. Some moved to the West Coast. Some moved to the Northeast. Many have returned. We immigrated when there were no jobs, and the racist terror that existed meant it was not safe for us to remain in the South back in the 1950s. Long before George Floyd, Trayvon Martin, Breonna Taylor, Atiana Jefferson, and Sonya Massey—the latter three murdered in their own homes by police—other black people were murdered and lynched; some disappeared for looking at a white person in the eye or speaking to them. There are so many stories. The murder of Emmett Till helped galvanize the 1960s civil rights movement. Some were made scapegoats and blamed for doing things that never happened. Other times women who were pregnant and not married were condemned before the church, but their male partners received no such shaming. Our family story of being in exile and then returning home reminds me of the story of Ruth in the Bible."

The book of Ruth has many family stories about inheritance, power, privilege, and identity. Many situations are challenging for twenty-first-century people to understand. How can we begin to imagine the idiosyncrasies and lives of Ruth and Naomi? They had no electricity, running water, indoor plumbing, or status of any sort. While many today live in similar situations of exile, needing to immigrate to survive, most people in the West have no clue. These women had no social media, designer clothing, microwaves, online ordering, or access to education, spas, airline travel, or global foods. As women, they could not own property. They were considered property themselves. So, what can we learn from their experiences? What is the good news about Ruth and Naomi that can serve as rays of hope today?

First, texts of confusion and terror show us how to live, and what to avoid. So much pain occurs in the book of Ruth. Because of famine, Elimelech's family fled to Moab. In short measure, Naomi loses her husband. In those days a woman was the property of her father or husband; they worked at home and were not taught to read or write. After ten years, Naomi loses both her sons. One can either become a victim of life's circumstances or figure out how to survive and thrive. People who become victims are in prison outside—they're not behind metal bars, but their mindset and their fears keep them in mental and emotional strait jackets. What is Naomi's motivation? Is Ruth conscious of who she is and the options before her? With so many losses and being immigrants in a foreign land where religious differences could have caused major trouble, Naomi and Ruth learn to live together in conjunction with Boaz as married relatives. Ruth is a chameleon—a willing participant, and a trickster on the threshing floor, who gets erased in the end. Today, these texts remind us that where terror occurs, we have options. Though the voice of God is implied, Naomi views her life in dialogue with God. Ruth pledges to follow the God Naomi follows. We can trust that the God who made us in divine image, who is within us, never leaves or forsakes us, in times of trouble or triumph. We learn to avoid being trapped by our circumstances and to not react from a place of emotional fear. Moments of terror are opportunities to be prayerful, communicate, and explore options for well-being.

Second, clear communication supports healthy intergenerational families. The text does not disclose the inner thoughts of Ruth or Naomi. Orpah leaves the story early and returns home. We have no idea what happened to her. We do learn about the threesome of Naomi, Ruth, and Boaz. There are many twists and turns in the plot, to the point that we wonder about their values and ethics, especially sexual ethics and intergenerational family dynamics. With ongoing global domestic violence and sexual assault, we need to take seriously the power dynamics between the three. Too often in our families and faith communities, we avoid having conversations about sex, sexuality, and the biases of a patriarchal, misogynistic culture where there is a need to control women's bodies, where reproductive justice continues to shrink, but men can have vasectomies and take pills for erectile dysfunction without any required therapy or laws that regulate their behavior. Men almost get props for being promiscuous. Promiscuous women get labeled sluts and whores. Too often, we fail to talk about sexual violence and how rape victims end up being on trial when they are the ones who have been violated. Ruth's story is one where we can explore our identities and healthy boundaries, and develop a healthy spirituality of sexuality. We can use scripture to work through the facts of life and be clear about expectations, then and now. Further, many times we want a simple solution to life's complexities, where lines get blurred. Ruth's story reminds us of the importance of family therapy and the importance of having candid conversations before serious dating and marriage, especially discussions around communication—when there are marked differences in the number of siblings, communication styles, children, finances, and sexuality. With multiple generations, prior family history must be explored to help heal the traumas. If these traumas, whether over gender issues, ethnicity, class, or other categories of difference are not understood, the residual effects will continue to the detriment of all. So many problems result when we fail to deal with our total well-being.

Third, faithful love supports us through our experiences of loss and grief toward restoration. The deaths of the three men early on slam the family with horrific losses and subsequent grief. Losses concern the absence of someone or something, as an event. Losses are inescapable, part of the circle of life. Losses include the death of a loved one, job loss, loss of dreams, an empty nest, loss of pets, anticipatory loss around aging and mental illness, divorce or a bad breakup, and retirement. Grief, a healthy response to loss, involves mental, emotional, physical, and spiritual engagement, toward personal and communal healing and restoration. Ruth is full of words that express the pain and angst of dislocation and loss. Naomi kisses both the daughters-in-law and weeps aloud with them (1:9). The entire town is stirred when Naomi and Ruth return. Was this an experience of surprise and appreciation? Was their hope, given the return? What was the expectation of the community? Were they stirred because Naomi returned without her husband and sons since she left with them? Are we concerned that Naomi was suffering from a type of Munchausen syndrome by proxy (MBP), now called "fabricated or induced illness by caregivers" (FIIC) where a person either fakes or produces symptoms in someone else, usually their child? Ruth's tireless faithfulness reminds us of what it means to love neighbor, to be present during loss; to offer support when profound loss has occurred. In situations of such distress, we need professional help. We have little compunction about going to doctors or therapists for physical ailments; yet stigma still exists around mental illness, though the devastation of covid has brought conversations around mental illness to the forefront. With social media bullying, teen suicide has increased. We need to protect and support our families and communities during a crisis. Whatever her feelings, Naomi's bitterness intensifies as she links her horrific loss with divine sanction (1:20–22). This makes for an interesting experience of theodicy: why bad things happen to good people. Is it easier to blame

God for the pain that occurs in our lives? Is this bad luck or an intergenerational curse? Given the impact of global warming from famines and floods to tsunamis and tornadoes, Ruth's story reminds us that we are part of creation: we need to be better stewards of our world. Such loss is an opportunity for us to think through our relationship with God. Are we afraid of God? Is God a bully? Our faithful love provides a framework for us to embrace a relationship with God and each other that honors the beauty of creation and the gift of life while realizing, that we can experience restoration and new identities amidst horror and confusion. That God exists and we can share faithful love is good news!

Conclusion

Every story has context, content, and characters. The stories of the characters matter in fiction and nonfiction. In my life, the stories of Ruth and Naomi are autobiographical and biblical. In both instances, issues of relationships, love, faith, power dynamics, and a patriarchal culture frame reality. Suspicion with sensitivity framed my womanist lens, mind, and heart as I lived with the book of Ruth as a scholarly endeavor, rooted in in-depth research and a prominent faith. Many questions that arose remain unanswered because of textual silence on those matters. Reading, mindful of the power of these texts for believers and the creative, careful work of biblical scholars, the exegetical and homiletical work was a wonderful adventure.

The adventure brought me to explore levels of intimacy and love, various interpretations of the roles of Naomi, Ruth, and Boaz, and the space of inclusion, immigration, and how our lives intersect with creation. Despite myriad unanswered questions, amid great suspicion, my work resulted in heightened awareness of human nature and curiosity about how we perceive women and relationships between named, biblical women. We have to admire the courage of the women, how they navigate cultural traditions, even levirate, and their fierceness amid challenges. A comparative analysis between Naomi and Ruth and contemporary women provides an excellent case study to discuss how people come to know their authentic selves and the consequences of human actions. Some elements of the book of Ruth are life-giving; others are death-dealing. Amid hermeneutics and homiletics, Ruth provides numerous scenarios for exploring appropriate ethical contemporary, familial living. The story indicates the importance of intergenerational lives, the impact ecology/nature can have on family well-being and mobility, and the ever-present impact of economics and land. That Naomi indicates God's implicit presence, but no one interacts directly with the divine, offers opportunities to explore how modern people live their faith. While some listeners believe women are inferior and subservient to men, this story debunks that lie and encourages a move toward their liberation. The book of Ruth offers a wealth of material for sharing about family, faith, and friendship, particularly to help women rise above the traps of systematic misogyny to the fullness of inclusion.

8

Love Makes a Family?

Queer Readings of the Book of Ruth

RHIANNON GRAYBILL

Introduction

THE HEBREW BIBLE DOES not always seem like a friendly space for queer readers or queer readings. Much of this is due, of course, to the history of using the Bible to discipline, punish, or endorse violence against gay, lesbian, bisexual, transgender, intersex, nonbinary, and gender nonconforming people. One possible response to this history is to reject the texts themselves as homophobic, transphobic, or otherwise "texts of terror." Another response is to reread the Bible with an eye to its queer possibilities. Perhaps the text is not such a hostile space after all, or at least not uniformly so. Perhaps there is a possibility of excavating buried queer stories or alternative traditions. Perhaps, instead of a justification of violence, we might even find in the Hebrew Bible stories of queer love and queer kinship.

Queer love? Queer kinship? Though queer exegesis has explored a remarkable number of biblical stories—there is even a queer commentary on the entire Bible, now in its second edition[1] —a few narratives remain especially significant, especially for readers seeking a positive

1. West and Shore-Goss, eds., *The Queer Bible Commentary*.

representation of queerness, queer identities, or alternative models for love, sex, and relationships. David's bond with Jonathan, which he himself describes as "surpassing the love of women" (2 Sam. 1:26), has long been celebrated for its homoerotic overtones (and perhaps more explicit homoeroticism as well). But David, however much he may love Jonathan, and in what capacity (as a friend, as a companion-in-arms, as a lover) does not establish lasting kinship bonds with him.[2] For this, interpreters look instead at the other key story for queer readings of the Hebrew Bible: the book of Ruth.

Just four chapters long, the book tells the story of two women, the Israelite Naomi and her Moabite daughter-in-law, Ruth. Together, they struggle to survive tragedy, famine, and migration—and eventually find their own happy ending, in the form of a marriage, a baby, and a new chosen family. As even the briefest summary suggests, much may be queer here, on both the level of love and kinship. Ruth is often celebrated as a queer or bisexual figure; her bond with Naomi, in particular, has a lengthy history in queer reception of the biblical text. Interpreters have also speculated that both Naomi and Boaz can be understood as queer. And the family unit that forms at the book's end—two women, a man, and a baby who seems to possess three parents—also invites readings as a queer chosen family. Is this, at last, the queer text we have been looking for?

At the same time, the book of Ruth is not all queer sweetness and light. It also contains troubling suggestions of exploitation. Does Naomi exploit or abuse Ruth? In bringing her to Israel, does she engage in labor trafficking, or even sex trafficking?[3] Does Naomi steal Ruth's baby (Ruth 4:16–17)? However we answer these questions, the book is also undeniably filled with famine, untimely death, and trauma. All this suggests that even if the book of Ruth is the biblical text that is most available for a queer love and kinship reading, we as readers and interpreters must proceed with caution.

A queer reading that erases or ignores violence and oppression is not, ultimately, a reading in the service of queer liberation. This chapter, therefore, will explore how we can undertake a queer reading of Ruth and help create queer "spaces to breathe" in the text while also taking

---

2. One notable exception is that David subsequently brings into his household Jonathan's son Mephibosheth (2 Sam. 9:1–8). Mephibosheth is also notable as one of the few openly physically disabled characters in the Hebrew Bible.

3. See Graybill, "Even unto This Bitter Loving," 308–31.

seriously the feminist, critical race, and labor critiques that interpreters have raised against the book.[4] Our goal, in the final analysis, is a richer, more critically queer reading of a beloved, imperfect, beautiful, and infinitely compelling text. Ruth deserves no less.

Hermeneutical Horizon

In this section, I have two main goals: first, to trace the hermeneutical horizons of existing queer readings of the book of Ruth, and second, to explore some of the limitations such readings face. I aim to provide the necessary backgrounds for the queer interpretations I outlined in the following section.

In this essay, I will use the term "queer biblical interpretation" intentionally and loosely, as a catch-all term for the related fields of LGBTQIA+ interpretation. There are of course nuances here, which have been addressed lucidly elsewhere and in greater detail: "lesbian and gay" interpretation is often linked to specific identity categories, while queer interpretation is intentionally more open and flexible. The term queer, borrowed from the field of queer theory more broadly, is a former slur that has been repurposed as a flexible, dynamic alternative. Its specific meaning is the subject of some debate. David Halperin, for example, argues that queer simply marks an opposition to dynamic power structures; Lee Edelman claims that "queerness can never define an identity; it can only ever disturb one."[5] Other interpreters tie "queer" more closely to specific sexual identities, including but not exclusively lesbian, gay, and bisexual. These debates and discussions are important; they are, however, somewhat beyond our focus here.[6] My key interest is in readings of the book of Ruth that adopt any or all of these perspectives, without necessarily privileging one branch of criticism over another (though my own preferences for certain forms of queer reading will become clearer in the next section).

Queer interpretation is a relatively new field of biblical interpretation, coming into its own in the past twenty-five years.[7] But the queer

---

4. I adopt the metaphor of space to breathe, and the broader idea of a "queer aspiration" from Sara Ahmed. See Ahmed, *The Promise of Happiness*.

5. Halperin, *Saint Foucault*, 62; Edelman, *No Future*, 17.

6. For a good overview of the issue and several possible genealogies for a queer approach, see Brintnall, "Queer Studies and Religion."

7. See, to begin, Goss and West, *Take Back the Word*; Stone, *Queer Commentary and*

reading of the book of Ruth did not begin with queer biblical scholarship. Instead, it is in the reception (and literary reimagining) of biblical texts that we find this interpretation first flourish. Queer readings of Ruth are central, for example, to such lesbian classics as Jeanette Winterson's *Oranges are Not the Only Fruit* (1985) and Fannie Flagg's *Fried Green Tomatoes at the Whistlestop Cafe* (1987, followed by a film adaptation in 1992).[8] The queer readings of Ruth and Naomi that flourish in lesbian and queer literature have been joined, as well, by scholarly readings. Rebecca Alpert's short essay "Finding Our Past: A Lesbian Reading of the Book of Ruth" is an early classic of lesbian reading and reclamation. Alpert argues that when we view the book of Ruth with lesbian eyes, we are able to perceive the love between women within it.[9] Though she stops short of arguing for Ruth and Naomi as actual lesbians—identities, after all, are historically positioned and conditioned things—she nevertheless lifts up the lesbian possibilities of the book.

While the lesbian trajectory remains the dominant one in queer readings of Ruth, other interpreters have suggested that bisexuality is a more fitting category, at least for the book's heroine. Celena Duncan, for example, has argued that Ruth's loving relationships with both a woman (Naomi) and a man (Boaz) are best understood through the framework of bisexuality.[10] Brett Krutzsch has shifted focus from Ruth and Naomi to Boaz, putting pressure on the assumption that Naomi's kinsman and Ruth's future husband is heterosexual (consider the classic queer slogan "HOW DARE YOU ASSUME I'M STRAIGHT").[11] Krutzsch argues, instead, for a queer Boaz. And Mona West has suggested that in their unconventional family unit—Naomi, Ruth, Boaz, and baby Obed—the characters in the book offer a model for queer kinship and queer procreation strategies.[12]

These queer readings, varied as they are, help show the breadth of current queer interpretations of Ruth. We can also note some general tendencies. All of the readings challenge the assumption of what

---

the Hebrew Bible.

8. Winterson, *Oranges Are not the Only Fruit*; Flagg, *Fried Green Tomatoes at the Whistle Stop Cafe*. On these works and their relation to Ruth, see Powell, *Narrative Desire and the Book of Ruth*.

9. Alpert, "Finding Our Past," 95.

10. Duncan, "The Book of Ruth."

11. Krutzsch, "Un-Straightening Boaz in Ruth Scholarship."

12. West, "The Book of Ruth."

Adrienne Rich termed "compulsory heterosexuality."[13] They offer alternative portraits of sex and identity—often focused on Ruth, but also extending to the figures around her. Attending to tone, the readings also share an attitude of hopefulness or positivity toward the biblical text. The Bible may seem a hostile place for queer people and queer interpretation; Ruth, however, offers a respite. Furthermore, the book may even serve as a model for progressive and liberation-oriented readers seeking to reclaim other biblical texts, or even the Bible as a whole. If we seek to "take back the word," to borrow the title of a classic work of queer biblical interpretation, then this taking back may well begin with Ruth.[14]

The sanguine view of Ruth that is prominent in queer interpretation (as well as many feminist interpretations) is not, however, shared by all readers and interpreters of the book. Readers attuned to ethnicity, social class, and power have directed attention to another set of readings, which highlights Ruth's vulnerability as a single foreign woman. From this perspective, Ruth's interactions with Naomi are neither love nor "women working out their own salvation . . . women in culture, women against culture, and women transforming culture" (Phyllis Trible's famous feminist celebration of the text).[15] Instead, Naomi exploits Ruth's labor and perhaps even sex traffics her as well.[16] Ruth, meanwhile, is a mistreated foreign laborer, a discriminated-against ethnic Other, a migrant child, a refugee, and/or a forced surrogate who disappears from the text as soon as her reproductive labor is complete.[17]

These readings are troubling; they are also compelling. It is difficult to hold on to happy readings of Ruth, including or especially readings of the book as a celebration of queer love and kinship, when we look closely at its representations of power. And if we take seriously queer interpretation as part of a larger project of liberation and human flourishing, these critiques become more troubling still. We are in a difficult interpretive space. I am not interested in a queer reading that erases or neglects oppression, or that lifts up sexuality over all other categories of intersectional identity—queer liberation at the expense of racial, ethnic, or class liberation. The good

13. Rich, "Compulsory Heterosexuality and Lesbian Existence."
14. Goss and West, eds., *Take Back the Word*.
15. Trible, *God and the Rhetoric of Sexuality*, 196.
16. Gafney, "Mother Knows Best."
17. Brenner, "From Ruth to the 'Global Woman'"; Melgar, "Ruth and the Unaccompanied Minors from Central America"; Rees, "The Boaz Solution"; Yee, "She Stood in Tears," 134.

news is that most queer theory, and most queer interpreters, are not interested in this sort of liberation either.

Elsewhere, I have written at length about the icky, tricky position these competing interpretations create for the reader who is *both* drawn to the (happy) queer reading and persuaded by the (unhappy) exploitation reading of Ruth. There, I have lingered with the interpretive dilemma, as well as its affective dimensions.[18] I have also explored queer disappointment as an alternative point of entry into Ruth.[19] Briefly, a significant and exciting branch of the academic field of queer theory is interested in disappointment, failure, and other unhappy emotions and experiences. I have argued that this work pairs productively with Ruth, which is a book that in many ways disappoints queer readers (whether with its conclusion in heterosexual matrimony or with its inability to refute the exploitation argument). Building on this work, I am interested here in exploring a broader selection of queer readings of Ruth. I am convinced of the importance of such queer readings precisely because, in addition to critique, we also need queer hope—a point sometimes made by queer theory, and often made by queer peoples.[20] Without forgetting oppression, I aim to sketch some contours of queer possibility and queer hope in what follows.

Interpretation

Ruth is a biblical book with a rich history of queer interpretation, as well as additional under-realized queer potential. In this section, my goal is to proliferate queer readings and a broader set of queer interpretations of Ruth.

Queering Ruth

Ruth's words of devotion to Naomi hold a central place in most queer readings of the book. It is worth revisiting these words here. After Naomi urges her to return home to her mother's house, Ruth replies,

---

18. Graybill, "Even unto This Bitter Loving."
19. Graybill, "After the Idyll Ends."
20. On queer hope and futurity, see Muñoz, *Cruising Utopia*; Floyd and Muñoz, "Queer Principles of Hope."

> Do not press me to leave you, to turn back from going after you, for where you go, I will go, and where you lodge I will lodge, your people will be my people, and your God will be my God. Where you die, I will die, and there I will be buried—may Yahweh do this to me, and more, if death separates me from you! (Ruth 1:16–17)

Ruth's words are both powerful and shot through with feeling. The internal repetition of each verset or colon (the subunit of a verse), as well as the repetition and amplification across the poem as a whole, all add to its overall impact. Tod Linafelt has argued that poetry is used in the otherwise prose book "precisely in order to give the reader access to the inner lives of Ruth and of Naomi."[21] Thus, Ruth's poetic speech reveals an interiority that is otherwise concealed in the text. Furthermore, when we glimpse into this interiority, all we find is Naomi—there is nothing about Ruth's dead husband, nothing about her family of origins or the suggestion that she return to them, nothing about Moab and its gods except a renunciation of fidelity. Instead, we have devotion to a single person, and a devotion that extends even beyond death (consider here the famous exhortation in Song 8:6 that "stronger than death is love"). This devotion is confirmed in Ruth's actions: she remains loyal to Naomi and accompanies her to Bethlehem, where she does everything she instructs. Even the "giving" of Ruth's baby to Naomi in the book's final scene ("a child is born to Naomi!") can be read as an act of love, rather than Ruth's erasure.[22]

It seems clear that Ruth loves Naomi and values her relationship deeply. Less clear is what sort of love this is—romantic, friendship, even familial. The good news is that we don't need to assign Ruth's love to a category in order to conclude that this love, and the text more broadly, is somehow queer. Ruth loves Naomi; this love is unexpected and goes against the norms of text and time (this is what makes Ruth's words such a crucial turning point in the text). Furthermore, and importantly, Ruth's love does not have to be reciprocated or even understood by Naomi in order for it to exist, and to matter. Love is often unreciprocated, missed, ignored—and to hold lesbian or queer love to a different, higher, standard is, inadvertently, to devalue it. Similarly, and importantly, the existence of love in the story, and in 1:16–17 in particular, does not preclude the possibility of exploitation.

---

21. Linafelt, "Narrative and Poetic Art in the Book of Ruth," 127.
22. Contrast Yee, "She Stood in Tears Amid the Alien Corn."

To say Ruth loves Naomi and is simultaneously exploited by her may feel like a disappointing twist. But I would suggest that holding space for this possibility means holding space for the wide range of possibilities for queerness — not all of which are happy. Still, we do important political and ethical work when we hold open a full spectrum of (queer) ways of being, and ways of being in relation.

Queering Naomi

So much for Ruth—what of Naomi? Often, queer readings of the book of Ruth hinge upon readings of Ruth and Naomi's mutual relationship (and not simply on Ruth's love for Naomi). But unlike Ruth, Naomi never expresses feelings of devotion to Ruth—even as she freely expresses other emotions, at other points in the text. Still, there are multiple moments of queerness in Naomi's story. Here, I will highlight three possibilities.

First, we should look closely at Naomi's speech and examine in particular the original Hebrew text. This is because when Naomi speaks to Ruth and Orpah in chapter 1, urging them to return home, something peculiar happens: Naomi refers to her daughters-in-law using masculine grammatical forms (that is, she addresses them as "you [males]" rather than "you [females]." Scholars refer to this phenomenon as "gender discord."[23] But while describing it is simple enough, explaining its meaning is not. One line of argument holds that Naomi's speech is broken and confused because of her grief.[24] Having lost her sons, she addresses their surviving wives as if they were the dead men themselves. Or, perhaps, grief has simply rendered Naomi unable to use language correctly. Gil Rosenberg has suggested another, queerer interpretive possibility. Perhaps Naomi's grammatical gender discord—which also, notably, occurs in chapter 4, a far happier text—is not simply a negative. It may, instead, suggest an effort to create a horizon of queer possibility in the text. By using masculine forms for female characters, the text signals a broader realm of "freedom from male control" and the possibility of new, queer forms of relationality.[25]

Naomi's speech may be queer—the same can be said for her silence. In particular, I want to suggest that her silence in response to Ruth's

---

23. Davis, "The Literary Effect of Gender Discord in the Book of Ruth," 495.
24. Davis, "The Literary Effect of Gender Discord in the Book of Ruth," 501.
25. Rosenberg, "New Authorities, New Readings," 596.

words of love and devotion can be read as a hint that Naomi is a stone butch figure. Emphasizing the significance of "silence and stoicism," K. Allison Hammer notes the impermeability of the stone butch, "a lesbian who refuses to be penetrated by a lover, though the term also describes a type of emotional impenetrability across masculinities and sexual categories."[26] This sounds rather like Naomi. She does not speak in response to Ruth's emotional vulnerability; she refuses to show herself penetrated or touched. Instead, by bringing Ruth with her to Israel, Naomi provides for her security and well-being.

Third, beyond Naomi's relationship with Ruth, we might consider as well other relationships between women. Naomi's conversations, after all, are mostly with the women of Bethlehem. On a structural level, these scenes of verbal exchange resemble the Shulammite's conversations with the daughters of Jerusalem in the Song of Songs (Song 1:5; 2:7; 3:5, 10; 5:8, 16; 8:4). While the Song is principally a series of dialogues between the female Shulammite and her male lover, there are also handful of significant moments where the woman neglects her lover and speaks, instead, to her female companions. Elsewhere, I have argued that these moments are an important queer intervention in the text—not because of the homosociality they introduce (though that is also important), but because of the way they make sex into something public and publicly mediated.[27] Queer theorists Lauren Berlant and Michael Warner have argued for the queer importance of "sex in public"—that is, for taking sex seriously as both public and political, rather than clinging to the fantasy of a pre-political private sexuality.[28] In this context, the conversations with the daughters of Jerusalem do the work of making sex public. So too, I suggest, in Ruth. Naomi's conversations with the women of Bethlehem, especially in chapter 4, do the work of making sex public—itself queer work. From this perspective, it is also notable that the women compare Ruth to Rachel and Leah (Ruth 4:11), whose highly public struggle over sex and childbearing is itself another example of sex in public. Naomi and the women, too, do the work of making sex public and thus queer.

---

26. Hammer, "Epic Stone Butch," 79.

27. Graybill, "Sex in Public in the Song of Songs." My notion of "sex in public" is drawn from Berlant and Warner, "Sex in Public."

28. Berlant and Warner, "Sex in Public."

Queer Kinship

Having considered Ruth and Naomi separately, I want now to explore some queer possibilities for their togetherness, as well as their individual and mutual relationships with Boaz. In chapter 1, Ruth chooses Naomi and the two form a nontraditional dyad. When the two return to Naomi's home in Bethlehem, they are accepted and welcomed by her community. In chapter 2, when Ruth goes to glean in the fields, Boaz meets her, praises her and her devotion to Naomi, and strategizes with her to provide for her safety in the fields (Ruth 2:8–13). This kinship develops further as Boaz enters into and expands the Ruth-Naomi family unit. Following the events of the threshing floor in chapter 3, Boaz marries Ruth in chapter 4, outwitting another, closer kinsman of Naomi's.[29] It is understood that in marrying Ruth, Boaz gains Naomi as well. The closeness of this family unit is confirmed when Ruth gives birth to a child and the women of Bethlehem celebrate "a son is born to Naomi!" (4:17). While this scene of childbearing and child-sharing is sometimes interpreted as a queer moment between Ruth and Naomi (with Boaz sidelined), we can equally read it as confirming a three-way queer kinship. As Mona West notes, the book of Ruth is saturated with the language of kinship and family;[30] the final chapter shows such queer kinship in action—both in the family unit of Ruth, Boaz, and Naomi, and in the support they receive from their community. Thus, West comments, "The actions of the townswomen in naming the son and Naomi in breast-feeding the child provide examples of the ways in which a whole community is involved in the nourishment and growth of its children."[31] This is mutual care beyond the traditional boundaries of the family.

Furthermore, we can productively read the family that forms at the end of the book of Ruth together with more contemporary notions of queer kinship and chosen families. The notion of "chosen families" is common in work on queer kinship but especially associated with Kath Weston.[32] Or consider Josephine Baird's account of her own queer family:

> At the age of two our child met the woman who would become my present wife, Karin. In fact, not long thereafter our child

---

29. On this dynamic, see further Guillaume, "One Plus One Equals Three."
30. West, "The Book of Ruth," 55.
31. West, "The Book of Ruth," 59.
32. Weston, *Families We Choose*. With respect to Ruth, see as well Koosed, *Gleaning Ruth*, 106.

> declared of her own volition one day that my future wife was her parent. We discussed at length amongst the three of us and decided that since our child had decided this and we were all amenable, we would simply form our dynamic that way. For about a year we lived in a polyamorous dynamic, until my former wife and I decided to end our marriage and I married my present wife. During that time and ever since, our child has had three parents. We share responsibilities amongst the three of us, we attend important meetings at school or with doctors, in every respect we are all three our child's parents and she has never consciously known anything else.[33]

As Baird chronicles, it is a struggle to create and sustain a family that crosses "hetero- and cis-normative national, legal, and social lines." This is a struggle many queer (and other) chosen families know well. It is also, perhaps, the struggle of Ruth, Naomi, and Boaz.

Baird's reflections on her own family inspire a final comment on the biblical family unit in Ruth. While I have been describing the book's vision of queer family as Ruth, Boaz, and Naomi together, we should also hold space for reading the relationships in the text, especially romantic or erotic relationships, as sequential, instead of simply as simultaneous. Put another way: Ruth does not have to (still) be in romantic love with Naomi, or even to ever have been in love with Naomi, for the text to offer a model of queer kinship. There are many kinds of love, and many sorts of kinship alignments, that can make a family.[34]

Queer Migration

From kinship, I want to turn to some queer possibilities for reading migration and diaspora in Ruth. The book, after all, is a book filled with movement. Naomi, Elimelech, and their sons move from Israel to Moab. Naomi and Ruth return to Israel. Ruth, even in her migration and her enthusiastic embrace of Naomi, remains marked as "Ruth the Moabite"—she is a "perpetual foreigner" even as she is integrated into the community of Bethlehem, the household of Boaz, and, eventually, the genealogy of David (though her name is absent from the genealogy proper).[35] As

---

33. Baird, "Trans/National Queer Parenting," 201.

34. See further Preser, "Things I Learned from the Book of Ruth," 61–62.

35. On Ruth as a "perpetual foreigner," see Yee, "She Stood in Tears Amid the Alien Corn." Notably, the genealogy in Matthew restores Ruth (Matt. 1:5).

I have already mentioned, postcolonial and other related scholarly approaches have explored in detail the ways in which Ruth's migration is a scene of exploitation or racial or ethnic alienation.[36] I want now to link those arguments to the field of queer diaspora studies, which offers another possibility to take seriously the grimmer side of the book of Ruth while also emphasizing queer approaches.

One useful introduction to queer migration and diaspora studies comes from Martin F. Manalansan IV. As Manalasan describes, this scholarly approach does not simply attend to the movement of queer people across space and national borders (though it certainly can focus on such movements). Instead, more broadly, queer migration studies asks us to consider the ways in which "sexuality is disciplined by social institutions and practices" that regulate migration and movement, including state policies that privilege and naturalize heterosexuality, marriage, biological reproduction, and the family.[37] Sex, sexuality, nation, and borders are thus categories that are bound up with each other. Certain types of sexual subjects are allowed or even encouraged to migrate; others are discouraged or forbidden. Furthermore, who a nation permits to enter, and under what circumstances, also plays a role in the nation's conception of self: thus granting asylum to persecuted queer people can demonstrate to a nation its own laudable progressive values. Or the simple desire of migrants to enter a country may be used to demonstrate the country's desirability. As Eithne Luibhéid observes, migrants "are painted as passionately desiring the nation, as shown by their migration; thus citizens depend on migrants to show that the nation remains lovable."[38] Immigration across borders helps secure the nation's idea of itself.

As this (extremely brief) overview shows, queer migration studies are principally concerned with the present moment, and with the modern nation-state. Still, I suggest, we can glean some insights into Ruth from this literature. First, queer diaspora studies help us put pressure on the appeal and very notion of "home" in the book of Ruth. As Farhang Rouhani writes in another introduction to queer diasporas, "the home is neither a resolution nor a refuge from dominant society but a space that is itself fraught with tension and complexity. Queer diasporic approaches complicate the idea of a sense of home in a way that shows how it is

---

36. See Park and Kirk-Duggan in this volume.
37. Manalansan, "Queer Intersections," 225.
38. Luibhéid, "Queer/Migration," 174–5.

simultaneously desirable and undesirable, possible and impossible."[39] This is certainly true of the book of Ruth. For both Naomi and Ruth, "home . . . is simultaneously desirable and undesirable, possible and impossible." Naomi is forced to leave her home; she desires to return, but when she does, she pronounces herself bitter. Furthermore, in returning to Bethlehem she must ultimately lose her late husband and sons' parcels of land to Boaz. Ruth, meanwhile, expresses a desire to leave her home and follow Naomi. And yet integration into Bethlehem is both "possible" (via marriage and childbearing) and "impossible" (never does she become "Ruth the Israelite.") Perhaps this is why Ruth frames her own desire not as to leave or be in a specific place, but simply to *be with* Naomi.

I also want to suggest that queer migration can help us think more deeply, and compassionately, about Obed, the child born to Ruth and Boaz and given to Naomi. In the previous section, I suggested reading the three parents as a queer family unit. Here, I offer a less hopeful reading. The situation of Obed, a child born to one mother but given to another, also evokes queer reflections on transnational and transracial adoption, especially the work of David L. Eng. In "Transnational Adoption and Queer Diasporas," Eng explores the case of Deann Borshay Liem, a Korean child adopted by White Americans in 1966, as well as Liem's documentary about her own experience of adoption, *First Person Plural*.[40] While Liem believes that bringing together her two mothers, birth and adoptive, will heal her depression, she finds herself psychically torn when the two actually meet. As she tells the camera, "There wasn't room in my mind for two mothers."[41] Eng builds on this confession, exploring the ways in which transnational adoption creates lesbian and gay consumer subjects while transforming infants into global commodities. He also attends to the psychic turmoil and consequences of transnational adoption, which is often framed through "generalized narratives of salvation."[42] We see these dynamics, I suggest, in Obed's transfer from the Moabite Ruth to Naomi, and in Ruth's disappearance from the narrative.[43] A queer-migration-informed reading might

39. Rouhani, "Queer Diasporas," 460.
40. Eng, "Transnational Adoption and Queer Diasporas."
41. Eng, "Transnational Adoption and Queer Diasporas," 1.
42. Eng, "Transnational Adoption and Queer Diasporas," 9.
43. Queer and feminist analyses of surrogacy, especially those that attend to nationality, race, and/or class, are also highly salient here.

help us think more deeply about Obed, and about the border-crossing, mother-leaving movement of children more broadly.

Queer Unhappiness

Reading Obed as a psychically shattered and commodified queer infant is a long way from where we began, with a celebration of Ruth as a figure of queer love. This is perhaps sobering, or disappointing. Where is queer happiness, after all this? In response, I want to make a simple point that I have also offered elsewhere: *the book of Ruth does not have to be a perfect, happy queer story for it to constitute a queer story.* Just as queerness encompasses many forms of sexual subjectivity and ways of being in the world, so too does a queer reading of the book of Ruth hold room for many queer possibilities. And these possibilities extend to disappointment. Our disappointment may arise because the book of Ruth, on closer examination, is not the perfect picture of queer love we imagined it to be, when reading Ruth's words of love to Naomi (after all, it may begin with these words, but it ends with a heterosexual marriage and a baby). We may be disappointed because the book seems more an account of exploitation than of love. We may be disappointed with the treatment of Ruth, the easy cruelty of Naomi, the flatness of Boaz (queer reading or otherwise), the quick transfer of Obed to Naomi (and erasure of Ruth as mother). We may be disappointed that for all these flaws, the story *still* seems to present the best example of lesbian subjectivity or love between women in the Hebrew Bible (there isn't much else to choose from). Or we may be disappointed that the queer readings of the book, such as I have offered above, seem to contradict each other.

In response, I urge us to embrace queer disappointment and even queer unhappiness as part of the larger range of queer affects and emotional experiences. This is related to what Jack Halberstam describes as "the queer art of failure," and traces as part of a queer politics and ethics of relation.[44] It is also part of a vital project of finding space for queer readers and interpreters—and people—to experience a full range of feelings, not simply the happy or the triumphant. Heather Love has argued for the importance of including "backward feelings" in the queer archive, even as we may be reluctant, hurt, or embarrassed to admit them.[45] Ap-

---

44. Halberstam, *The Queer Art of Failure*.
45. Love, *Feeling Backward*.

plying Love's work to Ruth, I have suggested that backward feeling, far from a mistake, may lie at the heart of our own queer engagements with the text.[46] To feel Ruth backward is, also, to feel Ruth queerly.

Homiletic Overtures

Unlike most of the other contributors to this volume, I am not a theologian; neither do I work (or even moonlight) as a preacher or leader in a religious community that treats the Bible as a sacred text. I am simply a biblical scholar; my focus is on literary readings of the texts, including Ruth. And so I am a bit daunted by the prospect of offering a homily, however brief. Still, I will try my best, and I will ask for generosity from my readers as well—especially if you read this homily under the light of the other homilies in the book.

In thinking about my possibilities for writing a homily, I found myself returning to my students. I have spent nearly all of my career teaching 18- to 22-year-old students at two residential liberal arts colleges. These students end up in a biblical studies classroom for a variety of reasons—sometimes, it's genuine interest, often, it's a convenient time for their schedule or a general education requirement. But more often than they expect, they find themselves drawn in by the Bible, and by the ways that biblical versions of the family and "Family Values" are often so different from what they have been told. In addition, I often also encounter students who are struggling to negotiate their own relationships with family and home after coming out. Too often, the Bible is used as a weapon or a threat against these students. I hope to show them other ways of reading. And so in writing this homily, I have kept in mind, first and foremost, my students and their struggle for community.

Homily

The opening line of Tolstoy's novel *Anna Karenina* is famous: "Happy families are all alike; every unhappy family is unhappy in its own way."[47] It's pithy, catchy, easy to quote in a pinch—all the things the rest of the novel is *not*, in my experience of reading, at least. But is Tolstoy right? I'm not so sure. In my experience, at least, happiness and unhappiness

46. Graybill, "Even unto This Bitter Loving."
47. Tolstoy, *Anna Karenina*, 3.

are often mixed together. A happy family can also be an unhappy family, and the opposite too is true.

Imagine a family. Who are the members of the family? What are their relationships with each other? Are they biological or chosen kin, or some mix of both? Are there children in the family? Elders? Friends? Is the family peaceful, or contentious? Do you recognize this family as similar to your own?

And now, I want to describe to you some families from other, more recent books. The first family comes from Jeanette Winterson's coming-of-age novel, *Oranges are Not the Only Fruit*.[48] The family in the novel consists of the teenage Jeanette, her mother, and her father—and a rich church community that Jeanette and her family participate in, and eventually, Jeanette grows apart from. A few other salient details: Jeanette is adopted; the church is a highly conservative Pentecostal church; Jeanette discovers she is a lesbian and has several female lovers over the course of the book. Jeanette's rejection by her mother, and their eventual careful partial reunion, are at the book's emotional core. A happy family, or an unhappy one?

The second family comes from Fannie Flagg's *Fried Green Tomatoes at the Whistlestop Cafe*, a novel adapted into a popular film.[49] The family here consists of two women, Idgie and Ruth, along with Ruth's son Buddy. Ruth first meets Idgie when she is engaged to Idgie's older brother; he dies before the marriage can occur. Ruth and Idgie become close friends and perhaps more than friends. When Ruth finds herself in an abusive marriage, she sends to Idgie for help; Idgie rescues her. Together, the two women form a family, raising Ruth's son together and opening the titular "Whistlestop Cafe," until Ruth dies of cancer. A happy family, or an unhappy one?

The third family comes from Torrey Peters' *Detransition, Baby*.[50] Here, the family—more of a future family, really—consists of Reese, a trans woman who wants to have a baby; Reese's former girlfriend Amy (now Ames), who has detransitioned and is living as a man; and Katrina, Ames' boss. When Katrina unexpectedly becomes pregnant, Ames proposes that Reese join the two of them as a third co-parent. The characters explore this possibility; the novel ends on a (frustratingly) open note,

48. Winterson, *Oranges Are not the Only Fruit*.
49. Flagg, *Fried Green Tomatoes at the Whistlestop Cafe*.
50. Peters, *Detransition, Baby*. I am grateful to Rochelle Malter for the inspired suggestion to read this novel together with the book of Ruth.

unclear as to whether the family will form or Katrina will choose to have an abortion, leaving Reese without the baby she wanted. A happy family, or an unhappy one?

All three of these families push beyond heteronormative assumptions of what a family is or should be. All three of them speak, in complicated ways, to the queer slogan I have borrowed for my title, "Love makes a family." There is love here, but it is complicated, fraught, challenged and challenging. And also, all three of these families call to mind the book of Ruth.

It is true that Ruth plays a role, literally, in the first two novels. *Oranges are Not the Only Fruit* is organized into chapters that are named after the first eight books of the Christian Bible; the final chapter is "Ruth." Jeanette's explorations of her love for women also call to mind the biblical book of Ruth. But it is Jeanette's complicated relationship with her mother that is truly the book's emotional core—and this, too, is a relationship we can understand through the book of Ruth, when we take seriously the semi-maternal connection between Ruth and her mother-in-law, Naomi. After all, if Ruth is "better than seven sons" (4:15), this means that she is a very special sort of daughter. In *Fried Green Tomatoes*, Ruth is the name of one of the two main characters. But the book of Ruth plays other roles as well. When Ruth sends to Idgie for help, she mails her a passage from the King James Bible: Ruth 1:16–17, "Wherever you go, I will go, wherever you lodge, I will lodge, your people will be my people and your God my God. Where you die, I will die, and there I will be buried." Ruth borrows the words of another Ruth to voice her devotion. Furthermore, much like the biblical Ruth and Naomi, Ruth and Idgie's relationship is the subject of much speculation. Are they friends? Lovers? Chosen family? Like the biblical text, readers seem to find what they are seeking in this relationship, even as the various readings contradict each other.

The third family, from *Detransition, Baby*, does not explicitly invoke the biblical text. But no less than the others, it calls to mind the book of Ruth. Reese, Ames, and Katrina, no less than Ruth, Boaz, and Naomi, are exploring the possibility of forming a queer family. This is difficult, messy, emotionally and socially fraught work. There are real risks of exploitation, of multiple kinds. And success is not guaranteed: indeed, the novel leaves the ending open. But there is also a kind of glorious possibility of queer and trans hope.

I have lingered with these three families—Jeanette and her mother, Ruth, Idgie, and Buddy; Ruth, Ames, Katrina, and an unborn baby who may not exist at all—because they help us think more expansively about the idea of family, in the biblical text and in our own lives. They also help us think about queer families in the book of Ruth, and queerness and queer possibility in Ruth more broadly. The book of Ruth is a book rich with queer possibilities. Ruth and Naomi's relationship is perhaps the most famous of these possibilities. The love between these two women is richly sketched through Ruth's words of devotion, as well as through Naomi's actions to care for Ruth and provide for her future. There are many queer ways to read this relationship. Ruth may be, like Jeanette, a lesbian. She may be, like Reese, bisexual. She may love Naomi in a way that resists labeling. And these fictional families, like so much of queer interpretation, also nudge us to question our assumptions. Biblical scholarship challenges the presumption of heterosexuality: why should we assume Boaz is straight, for example?[51] Similarly, *Detransition, Baby* pushes back against cisgender assumptions. Couldn't we also read Naomi as (like) Reese, a woman who desperately wants a baby but is unable to bear one through ordinary pregnancy? Could Ruth be another Katrina, an ambivalent mother looking to pass her child on?

Both the queer novels and the academic field of queer biblical interpretation help us think more generously and flexibly about what queerness means, and where we might find it in the Bible. Naomi and Ruth may be queer, for example, not in the sense of sexuality (which many scholars suggest is a modern concept), but because they insist on the importance of relationships between women. We see this both in their relationship and in the role the women of Bethlehem play in Naomi's life and the narrative. Relationships between women are vital. Or the text may be most queer in how it shows kinship: in Ruth's unexpected, age-defying, countercultural devotion to Naomi; in Naomi's efforts to build a new family for Ruth; in the chosen family that forms at the book's end. Or we can also think about queerness together with migration, and the movement of people in the book: often, queer people are forced to move, even as institutions like nations and borders reinforce the idea that heterosexuality is normal and desirable, and queerness is bad and deviant. Thinking about Ruth as a queer migrant can help hear the voices of contemporary queer migrants—and also think critically about the ways our nation regulates and exploits sexuality (as in the phenomenon of pinkwashing[52]).

---

51. Krutzsch, "Unstraightening Boaz"; West, "The Book of Ruth," 55.
52. See Puar and Mikdashi, "Pinkwatching and Pinkwashing."

I want Jeanette to have a happy ending. I want Ruth and Idgie to have a happy ending together. I want a happy ending for Reese, and for Ames and Katrina. Most of all, I want the book of Ruth to have a happy ending. I want happiness for Ruth, for Naomi, and for all the queer readers who see themselves in the book. But I also know that family is complicated, identity is complicated, and we do not always get the happy endings we want. Perhaps what is queerest of all in the book of Ruth is the way the text holds space for queer possibility, without, however, naively assuming all queer stories are happy stories. Ruth is a book that refracts the endless possibilities of queer people, queer families, and queer lives.

Conclusion

It would be a lovely thing if the book of Ruth were simply, uncomplicatedly a work of queer joy, or a celebration of queer love. But in the biblical text as in the real world, love is complicated, kinship is fraught, relationships are difficult, and *things change*. Ruth may speak the most famous words of devotion in all the Hebrew Bible, and yet there is nothing simple about what follows. Still, this is also the beauty of the text: it refracts the complexities of our own lives, and our own manifold experiences of family, kinship, and queerness.

In this chapter, I have not offered a single reading of the book of Ruth. Instead, I have sought to draw out a wide range of queer possibilities for interpretation, some familiar, some straightforward, others less so. There are, of course, the simple identity-based readings: Ruth is a lesbian, Ruth is bisexual, Naomi is a lesbian, Boaz is queer or at least strikingly unsuccessful at "normal" heterosexuality. And, of course, the Ruth-Boaz-Naomi family unit is a queer family, celebrated and blessed in the text with a child, Obed. These readings are certainly viable; moreover, they have done—and no doubt will continue to do—important work in queer religious spaces.

To these readings, I want to emphasize, once more, a handful of important caveats. First, *love does not preclude complications*. Ruth may love Naomi; Naomi may love Ruth; this does not mean that their relationship is straightforward, or unfolds in a straightforward way. Second, *loving someone does not preclude harming that person*. This is both difficult to accept—why can't we just claim Ruth and Naomi as a glorious love story, without caveats?—And deeply familiar, when we think about our own relationships, and what we know of the world. Sometimes, harm can even become exploitation, as some readings of the book suggested. Third, *relationships are not always symmetrical.* Love is not always returned in the same way. And fourth and finally, *love can change over time*—in type, in object, in intensity, in goal. Ruth can love Naomi and also Boaz. Naomi can feel nothing for Ruth, only to grow to love her, and so on.

Assigning an identity category to biblical characters is not the only way to read the text queerly. We can also take the lead from queer theory and find queerness elsewhere. One possibility is in thinking about queer kinship, tracing the spaces where this may emerge in the story (especially chapters 1 and 4). We can take seriously the queerness of migration, without making a strong claim (or any claim at all) about the sexuality of the characters. We can consider the ways in which the book explores a queer practice of "making sex public" and challenging norms of public and private. And we can allow ourselves to feel queer disappointment with how it all turns out, while also taking seriously disappointment and sadness as queer feelings. The book of Ruth can hold space for all this, and more.

9

Decolonizing Ruth, Reading and "Un-reading" Ruth with African Eyes

Masculinity, Disability, and Survival

Robert Wafawanaka

Introduction

This essay analyzes the book of Ruth from multiple transgressive perspectives.[1] These various interpretive frameworks expand the reader's understanding of this small but important book of the Hebrew Bible. Reading from an African cultural context, I employ socio economic analysis, decoloniality, masculinity theory, and disability studies. The essay wrestles with issues of gender, economics, poverty, patriarchy, decoloniality, and survival. I seek to address women and men as biblical interpreters, students of the Hebrew Bible, and parishioners. My goal is to expose the richness of this book, thereby contributing to new knowledge production.

---

1. I thank Matthew J. M. Coomber for his response to an initial version of this essay at the 2023 SBL/AAR Annual Meeting in San Antonio, TX, and his suggestion of some resources used here. The transgressive act of "reading, re-reading, un-reading, writing, and re-writing" of the same text is James Henry Harris's methodology that he explored in his book. See Harris, *Beyond the Tyranny of the Text*.

The book of Ruth has attracted wide attention among biblical scholars and ordinary readers, particularly because it is named after a woman and features women's struggles to survive in a male-dominated society. The book is also about a Moabite woman's unlikely contribution to the Davidic ancestry. Ruth has been interpreted as a model minority, a role model for women, an oppressed woman, or a committed daughter-in-law. The essay explores themes of crisis, migration, seduction, honor and shame. Ruth provides an intimate portrait of agrarian life in ancient Israel. Ruth and Naomi's story of struggle and survival in a male-dominated society has many resonances with the lives of rural African women. Therefore, I will highlight them as I read to decolonize Ruth from an African perspective.

Hermeneutical Horizon

The historical-critical method has dominated the discipline of biblical studies for centuries, but newer and transgressive methods have decentered its hegemonic place and shed significant light on biblical texts. These methodologies are created by most Bible readers residing in the Two-Thirds World. Majority World readers engage the Bible from diverse social locations which influence their methods and interpretive insights. They read the Bible from the realities of poverty, injustice, colonialism, gender discrimination, migration, oppression, or political domination.[2] Christianity is pervasive in Africa and the Bible is the norm of faith and practice; therefore it is emulated, whether it is problematic or not.

Social-science theory and methods like anthropology and sociology have also enhanced biblical interpretation. Since biblical texts are shaped by their social and cultural environments, social-scientific criticism of the Bible is fruitful.[3] Critics contend that the Bible presents people as they are and "also in the concrete, historically and socially differentiated relationships that make up their lives."[4] Hence, sociological methods seek

2. Dube, *Postcolonial Feminist Interpretation of the Bible*; Dube, Mbuvi, and Mbuwayesango, eds. *Postcolonial Perspectives*; Page, et al. eds, *The Africana Bible*; Felder, ed, *Stony the Road*; Segovia and Tolbert, eds., *Reading from this Place*. Vol 1 and Vol 2; Segovia, *Decolonizing Biblical Studies*; Sugirtharajah, *The Bible and the Third World*; Sugirtharajah, *Postcolonial Reconfigurations*.

3. Wilson, *Prophecy and Society in Ancient Israel*; Wilson, *Sociological Approaches to the Old Testament*; Schottroff and Stegemann, eds, *God of the Lowly*; Elliott, *What Is Social-Scientific Criticism?*.

4. Schottroff and Stegemann, eds., *God of the Lowly*, 4; Gottwald, *The Tribes of*

to "re-create the real life of a given era in a very concrete way."[5] Scholars have recently attended to economic approaches addressing problems of poverty, wealth, loans, debt, and interest. They demonstrate that the ancient Israelites depended on subsistence economies and were at the mercy of empires that extracted their meager resources.[6]

While biblical texts were shaped by their historical environments, interpreters also brought their own presuppositions to reading and interpreting texts, creating new, transgressive, and alternative meanings. These various social locations enable interpreters to ask more critical questions and make discerning judgments that traditional scholars might not ask or make. For example, African biblical scholars interpret biblical texts through the lens of African history, religion, culture, oppression, colonialism, and land struggles.[7] Thus, African biblical hermeneutics engages the Bible from the lived experiences of Africans where many biblical texts resonate with African life and tradition.[8]

This chapter focuses on multiple analytical approaches to Ruth from an African perspective. The social worlds and agrarian contexts of ancient Israel and traditional Africa provide the African biblical interpreter with heightened sensitivity to biblical texts. In both contexts, the struggle for survival was commonplace, and extracting resources from the land was the primary mode of economic productivity. The key questions are, "What did these texts mean then, and what do they mean today?"

Yahweh.

5. Schottroff and Stegemann, eds., *God of the Lowly,* 4.

6. Hudson, *The Lost Tradition*; Husdon and Van De Mieroop, eds., *Debt and Economic Renewal*; Hudson, "Reconstructing the Origins of Interest-Bearing Debt and the Logic of Clean Slates," 7–58; Van De Mieroop, "A History of Ancient Near Eastern Debt?" 59–94; Graeber, *Debt*; West, "Tracking an Ancient Near Eastern Economic System"; Boer, *The Sacred Economy*; Brueggemann, *Money and Possessions*; Coomber, ed., *Economics and Empire in the Ancient Near East*; Wafawanaka, "Righteous Rage and the Politics of Subsistence Economies."

7. Ngũgĩ, *Decolonising the Mind*; West and Dube, eds., "'Reading With African Overtures,'" 1–284; West, "1 and 2 Samuel," 92–104; Brown, ed., *The Blackening of the Bible*; Wafawanaka, "'The Land is Mine!'" 221–34; Wafawanaka, "In Quest of Survival," 349–358; Wafawanaka, "The Global Crisis of Debt in Context," 163–90; and Dube, Mbuvi, and Mbuwayesango, eds., *Postcolonial Perspectives*.

8. Adamo, *Africa and Africans in the Old Testament*; Adamo, ed., *Biblical Interpretation in African Perspective*; West and Dube, eds., *The Bible in Africa*; Dube, ed., *Other Ways of Reading*; Dube, Mbuvi, and Mbuwayesango, eds., *Postcolonial Perspectives*; West, "1 and 2 Samuel;" West, *The Stolen Bible*; Masenya and Ngwa, eds., *Navigating African Biblical Hermeneutics*; and Mbuvi, *African Biblical Studies*.

Additionally, "How should we read them and how prescriptive are they for modern twenty-first-century readers?"

The interpretive framework of Ruth recognizes that it is set in an agrarian context where rural folk depended on land for subsistence living.[9] The book describes a patriarchal context where women depended on the men in their lives, that is, the husband, the father, or the adult son. However, recent studies have reexamined the role and function of women in the social world of ancient Israel and proposed "heterarchy" as a heuristic model that compliments and supplements patriarchy.[10]

Carol Meyers adopts this model from the social sciences as an apt description of vertical and lateral social structures. Through archaeological evidence and the organization of ancient societies, she argues that "patriarchy" is an inadequate term because ancient Israelite society was "complex" and not only hierarchical.[11] Moreover, "the concept *heterarchy* may be more flexible than hierarchy alone for acknowledging the variability, context, and fluctuation of power structures in premodern societies."[12] Meyers claims the concept of heterarchy challenges the view of patriarchy as the dominant model in ancient societies. She argues, "With respect to gender, the heterarchy model challenges the notion of patriarchy by recognizing that certain systems associated with women, each with its own set of rankings, privileges, and statuses, would hold authoritative roles vis-à-vis other systems."[13] She concludes that Iron Age Israel was defined by both hierarchy and heterarchy because "there were multiple systems and multiple loci of power, with women as well as men shaping society."[14]

Meyers arrives at the heterarchy model as her ideas have evolved and matured. In her earlier works, she critiques the patriarchal model and demonstrates the multiple roles women played. She also chronicles the extensive networks of women in the ancient biblical world.[15] Unlike

---

9. Charney, "The Political Economy of Peasant Poverty"; Gottwald, "Abusing the Bible," 196–98; Coomber, ed., *Economics and Empire in the Ancient Near East*.

10. Meyers, "Hierarchy or Heterarchy?"; Shafer-Elliott, "Women and Economics in Ancient Israel and Judah." I thank Matthew Coomber for pointing me to these resources.

11. Meyers, "Hierarchy or Heterarchy?" 246.

12. Meyers, "Hierarchy or Heterarchy?" 249, emphasis original.

13. Meyers, "Hierarchy or Heterarchy?" 251.

14. Meyers, "Hierarchy or Heterarchy?" 251. Heterarchy is a more heuristic model because it "does not eliminate hierarchies within sub-systems," 251.

15. Meyers, *Discovering Eve*; Meyers, "'Women of the Neighborhood' (Ruth 4:17)."

formerly thought, women were active in both private and public sectors. They formed networks of relationships in the new homes of their husbands. These women surround Naomi when she returns from Moab with Ruth. Meyers concludes, "the informal associations of village women in ancient Israel, as well as their links with women in other settlements, represent a more diffuse and thus a more elusive form of female power than that of women in formal or professional groups."[16] While the Bible is silent about women unless they are notable or notorious, this is where most of Israel's women are found.

Shafer-Elliott agrees that while ancient Israel and Judah were "patrilocal and patrilineal," the umbrella term "patriarchy" is an oversimplification of ancient domestic societies.[17] She argues that "*heterarchy* seems to best describe the social structure of Israel/Judah, particularly on a domestic level, which allows the average, ancient Israelite/Judahite woman to be more visible to us."[18] She demonstrates that women contributed greatly to the grinding household economy and were most productive as their reproductive roles waned. Women functioned as household managers, religious leaders, and healthcare professionals.[19]

Thus, the concept of heterarchy supplements that of patriarchy and adds new light to our (mis)understanding of the lives and roles of women in the biblical world. These perspectives will enhance the analysis of women in the book of Ruth. Due to close similarities between ancient biblical women and African women who exist in a male-dominated society, the idea of heterarchy augments their lives. African women occupy and dominate the domestic sector, and they can relate to the story of Ruth and Naomi in several ways.

Interpretation

Historical Context of Ruth

Situated between the books of Judges and Samuel, Ruth interrupts the flow of the Deuteronomistic History. While Judges emphasizes that "there was no king in Israel" (Judg 17:6; 18:1; 19:1; 21:25), 1 Sam 8–12

16. Meyers, "'Women of the Neighborhood' (Ruth 4:17)," 125.

17. Shafer-Elliott, "Women and Economics in Ancient Israel and Judah," 111–12.

18. Shafer-Elliott, "Women and Economics in Ancient Israel and Judah," 112, emphasis original.

19. Shafer-Elliott, "Women and Economics in Ancient Israel and Judah," 112–24.

describes the emergence of kingship in ancient Israel. The rest of the books of Samuel and Kings describe the rise and fall of the monarchy, and David is presented as the ideal king (2 Sam 7). The location of Ruth in this context highlights the model king conceived by the historians. However, in the Hebrew Bible, Ruth is placed among the Writings, as one of the Five Scrolls or *Megilloth*.[20]

Biblical scholars debate the authorship of Ruth and date it anywhere from the period of the judges to the post-exilic era, although the Davidic focus suggests a monarchic date for many scholars.[21] Moreover, its genre is classified as a novella, folk-tale, short story, "a work of history," or "a historical narrative" that describes the ancestry of King David.[22]

The deaths of all the men in Naomi's family plunge her and her daughters-in-law into a precarious economic situation. Hence, the women took on additional roles that the males had played. Their struggle to survive and the mutual acts of kindness among the characters are the hallmarks of this little book of eighty-five verses. The multiple analytical lenses noted above seek to shed better light on Ruth. African women find Ruth to be more than an ancient text; it is their own living text.

African Cultural Context

Like ancient Israelite culture, traditional African culture is also patriarchal, communal, and agrarian. Men are the heads of their families and determine family affairs. They are expected to care for their wives and elderly parents. Men ensure the continuation of the family line through heterosexual marriage and child-bearing, especially sons. The typical African family is not just the nuclear family; it is the extended family including a large circle of relatives on both sides of the couple's families. This sense of communal living extends to the larger society such that in Africa, "everybody is related to everybody else."[23] Communal living involves abiding by moral values like honor and respect for elders, hospitality for strangers, and sharing resources. Mbiti adds, "In traditional life, the individual does not and cannot exist alone except corporately . . . He is simply part of the

---

20. J. J. Collins, *Introduction to the Hebrew Bible*, 4–5, 514.

21. Lau, *The Book of Ruth*, 12–20; Matthews, *Judges and Ruth*, 208–12; Laffey and Leonard-Fleckman, *Ruth,* liv–lxv.

22. Lau, *The Book of Ruth*, 11.

23. Mbiti, *African Religions and Philosophy*, 102.

whole."²⁴ In this communal context, it is shameful to violate social norms and risk disrespecting the family name.

Traditionally, Africans depended on land in subsistence economies. The work on the land to grow crops and produce food is a complex and long process. Families clear the land, cultivate the soil with oxen and plows, grow, weed, and harvest crops, thrash and winnow grain, grind or ferment grain to prepare food or drink. The land is fertilized or lies fallow, and the process is repeated every year during the next growing season. Africans also raise animals like sheep, goats, and cattle for domestic use and consumption. Historically, women worked in the home while men worked in the fields or hunted. This complements the Israelite practice where women dominated the household economy while men governed public spaces. However, as noted above, Israelite women also appear in public spheres, though less frequently than men. The combined presence of Israelite women in both private and public places heightens their contributions to the ancient world. When the men are absent, African women work in the home and also outside, taking on some of the responsibilities of their husbands. With the advent of cities and urban employment, men typically leave their homes for work in the cities. Hence, the traditional work of farming is left to women, in addition to raising children. However, in modern Africa, this image is changing. Some women, particularly the educated and ambitious, are exempt from such traditional life and work in cities or create their own businesses. But most African women are still struggling on the land and dependent on their husbands for survival. They also struggle against sexism, discrimination, and poverty.²⁵

Masenya and Kondemo argue that today heterosexual marriage expected of African women can be troublesome and exacerbate their situation.²⁶ They find problematic the expectation of marriage for Mongo women (of the Democratic Republic of the Congo) who are deprived of education or job qualifications. These women are also burdened by notions of masculinity where "a man is not considered a man unless he has a wife attached to him."²⁷

Various problematic factors affect these African women. They struggle against "economic problems, sexual violence, female prostitution,

24. Mbiti, *African Religions and Philosophy*, 106.
25. Masenya and Kondemo, "What of the Problematic Norm?"
26. Masenya and Kondemo, "What of the Problematic Norm?"
27. Masenya and Kondemo, "What of the Problematic Norm?" 125.

unemployment, poverty, war, unstable political systems, religious conflicts, cultural tension and gender inequality."[28] Hence, they seek the safety of heterosexual marriage as their primary mode of economic security. However, this dependence on husbands is complicated when the men cannot adequately provide for their families and are unfit, scarce, or dead as in the book of Ruth. The life and experiences of rural African women mirror that of biblical women. Both are shackled by tradition and male domination and need to be decolonized.

The decolonial project is more than just getting rid of colonial powers. It is a fight to dismantle deeply embedded systems, ways of thinking and being, and dominant paradigms, and introduce new knowledge creation systems. Ngũgĩ waThiongo argues that colonialism is a system of domination, whether in life, politics, culture, language, or one's very own mind. In the encounter between Africa and European powers, African history, culture, religion, and people were denigrated and destroyed, and the language and culture of the colonizer were elevated. The decolonial project reverses this way of thinking and corrects the narrative. Thus, Ngũgĩ argues for the decolonizing of the mind because "the domination of a people's language by the languages of the colonising nations was crucial to the domination of the mental universe of the colonized."[29] This implies that biblical scholars must think differently about reading and interpreting imperial biblical texts. They have fruitfully employed the transgressive method of postcolonial biblical criticism to engage the Bible from the various life contexts of readers.[30] Therefore, decolonizing any biblical text means "re-reading" and "un-reading" it from non-traditional perspectives to create new meaning, indeed a new world.[31]

African Reading

The story of Ruth and Naomi is one of struggle and triumph for the women characters. The narrative begins with the ironic migrating of Elimelech's family from Bethlehem to Moab, a land not metonymically associated with food. Elimelech's death transitions Naomi into an economically

28. Masenya and Kondemo, "What of the Problematic Norm?" 130.

29. Ngũgĩ, *Decolonising the Mind*, 16.

30. Segovia, *Decolonizing Biblical Studies*; Mbuvi, *African Biblical Studies*; Dube, *Postcolonial Feminist Biblical Interpretation*; Dube, Mbuvi, and Mbuwayesango, eds., *Postcolonial Perspectives*; Moore and Segovia, eds., *Postcolonial Biblical Criticism*.

31. Harris, *Beyond the Tyranny of the Text*, Appendix A and B, 139–49.

precarious widow because widows, strangers, and orphans were among the poor and oppressed in ancient Israel.³² Widows were dependent on the men in their lives, and "when these male persons were nonexistent, then the widow's connection to the kinship structure was severed. She became an *'almānâ*."³³ We can assume that Naomi's sons provided for her after the death of Elimelech for ten years, but the deaths of the three men worsen the social status and economic condition of the three women.

This story has resonances with African women who depend on their husbands as providers but are disenfranchised after they die. In ancient Israel, widows could return to the father's house, remarry, or remain single.³⁴ Traditionally in Zimbabwe, a widow married the surviving brother of her husband, but most widows remained in the homes of their husbands for familial reasons. Since a woman marries into the extended family, leaving may be viewed as abandoning the family. The widow also inherits the property of her husband and maintains it. If the widow has young children to support or adult children to be supported by, these are compelling reasons for her to remain in her husband's home. This choice keeps the children in the family. Even if a biological father is absent, a paternal uncle can act as a father and is addressed as "father" in Shona culture. This is due to close kinship ties in African culture, which are transgressive to Westerners. Hence Mbiti's claim that Africans have literally hundreds of fathers, mothers, wives, or children.³⁵

African kinship ties continue beyond the grave when the deceased become the "living dead."³⁶ Africans have a vibrant spiritual world and

---

32. Bennett, *Injustice Made Legal;* Havice, "The Concern for the Widow and Fatherless," 130–34; Wafawanaka, *Am I Still My Brother's Keeper?*

33. Hiebert, "'Whence Shall Help Come to Me?'" 125–41, esp. 137.

34. Wafawanaka, *Am I Still My Brother's Keeper?* 42–49.

35. Mbiti, *African Religions and Philosophy*, 102. In the Shona culture of Zimbabwe, family relationships are close and may sound strange or too complicated for Westerners. For example, all my brothers' children call me "father" ("*baba*," *not* uncle) and I call them my "children" (*vana*), not nephews or nieces. My nephews and nieces are only the children of my sisters. My father's father did not permit my siblings and I to call him grandfather (*sekuru*). Instead, he *demanded* that we call him "*baba/bambo*" ("father/big father"). Our grandfather (*sekuru*) was only our mother's father. I call all my father's brothers *baba* (father) and my uncles (*sekuru*) are only my mother's brothers. Similarly, I call all my mother's sisters *amai* (mother) and my aunts (*tete*) are only my father's sisters. These relationships extend to strangers such that I would call any man or woman my parents' age father or mother, any man my age brother, any woman my sisters' ages sister, any man or woman my grandparents' age grandfather or grandmother, and any young person, *mwana* (child).

36. Mbiti, *African Religions and Philosophy*, 25–26, 69–70, 81–86. For Mbiti, "the

relationships continue with deceased ancestors who oversee the welfare of their families. Thus, Africans never abandon their traditional homes where their loved ones are buried. In fact, the dead are buried in family plots around each home to oversee the welfare of their families. Thus, Ruth's choice to return to Bethlehem with Naomi is ambiguous. Masenya concurs that in the traditional Northern Sotho context of South Africa, "one's husband's death is not supposed to 'release' the widow from the deceased family, because . . . the grave may not be divorced."[37] Therefore, by leaving Moab, Naomi is abandoning her dead husband and sons and will neither be buried with them nor be able to care for their graves.[38] While Ruth abandons Maḥlon's grave on the one hand, on the other, her marriage to Boaz perpetuates Maḥlon's ancestry in his original family home in Bethlehem (4:10).

Naomi and Ruth return to the homeland of their husbands where there might be an extended family. While Dube detects "the tones of a master-to-slave relationship"[39] between the two women, in African culture, it is typical of how daughters-in-law care for their mothers-in-law. Naomi's return attracts public attention typical in communal African settings rife with chatter, gossip, excitement, and curiosity.

Back in Judah, the women apparently have no access to Elimelech's or Maḥlon's fields. This indicates that Israelite women did not own or inherit property, except for the daughters of Zelophehad who married within their father's clan to inherit his property (Num 27:1–11; 36:1–13).[40] Ruth's work in Boaz's fields is a subsistence task African women perform, especially if men are working in cities. They do not glean in other people's fields because even widows have the property of their husbands to maintain. African interpreters can relate to reaping ripe crops during harvest season when reapers go row by row to the end of the field until the whole field is finished.

Ruth's assimilation into Israelite society is an identity crisis because she is always Moabite first (2:6). As a foreigner in Israel, she could be victimized, bullied, or sexually abused (2:8–9, 15–16, 22). Though Ruth

---

living-dead is a person who is physically dead but alive in the memory of those who knew him in his life as well as being alive in the world of the spirits," 25.

37. Masenya, "Ruth," 88.
38. Laffey and Leonard-Fleckman, *Ruth*, 40.
39. Dube, "Divining Ruth for International Relations," esp. 192.
40. Endogamy is "marrying within a specific group," Matthews, *Judges and Ruth*, 210–11.

"maintains some dignity"[41] through gleaning, her shame is not having a husband or sons to provide for her. Her honor and dignity would be maintained if she did not have to glean at all.

Processing grain is a demanding task familiar to African readers who depend on agrarian economies. After harvesting, one goes to the threshing floor to beat out the grain and sift it in the wind to separate the grain from the chaff. This is why Boaz is on the threshing floor. Meyers and Shafer-Elliott's concept of "heterarchy" demonstrates that women contributed much to the domestic economy and the work was time-consuming and demanding, especially for women past child-bearing age.[42] We can appreciate Ruth's work inside Naomi's home and also in the fields.

Naomi's plan for Ruth to seek the security of marriage is problematic for some modern African women even though marriage is the traditional norm. There is a shifting landscape because, "Nowadays, some women have proved that their security does not depend on a man. Again, women's idea of marriage is changing given that many women have become more independent and active in the economic sphere. They no longer agree to be validated by men through the institution of marriage."[43]

The surreptitious nocturnal rendezvous of Ruth and Boaz at the threshing floor is highly problematic for its sexually suggestive language, setting, and transgression (3:1–18). Ruth's trip is "risky," "dangerous," and "unconventional" because "it transgresses physical and social boundaries."[44] Naomi hatches a daring plan and Ruth faithfully implements it. She sends Ruth on a mission to "seduce" Boaz and perhaps "entrap" him into marriage.[45] More critical scholars view Naomi as prostituting Ruth for economic survival, claiming, "Perhaps the greatest question is whether Naomi wishes Ruth to prostitute herself in some way and how we as readers handle this possibility."[46] Today, prostitution is widespread globally and is either legal or illegal. However, feminist scholars condemn "any situation in which a person is forced into prostitution against her or his will, which includes anything from difficult economic situations

---

41. Lau, *The Book of Ruth*, 130.

42. Meyers, "Hierarchy or Heterarchy?"; Shafer-Elliott, "Women and Economics in Ancient Israel and Judah."

43. Masenya and Kondemo, "What of the Problematic Norm?," 127.

44. Lau, *The Book of Ruth*, 194.

45. Lau, *The Book of Ruth*, 192–93; Halton, "An Indecent Proposal"; Kugler and Magori, "*Hesed* in Ruth," 1–13.

46. Laffey and Leonard-Fleckman, *Ruth*, 103–4; Gafney, "Ruth."

to human trafficking."⁴⁷ Unfortunately, some Mongo mothers emulate Naomi because "the Anamongo women would encourage their daughters to act seductively in order to win the hand of a financially wealthy man in marriage."⁴⁸ It is evident that Ruth and the Anamongo daughters are predisposed to being prostituted. The parallels are alarming as Ruth has a mother-in-law and the Anamongo women have mothers who expose both to being sexually exploited by men.

When Ruth lies down next to Boaz "at the place of his feet" (*margəlōtāyw*; a euphemism for sexual organs), the plot thickens. Lau dismisses the sexual connotations and views Ruth as a social inferior (šipḥâ) submitting to a superior for dependence. However, scholars suggest that Ruth is asking Boaz to marry her, and she is transgressing social boundaries and "doing the unconventional by proposing marriage to a man!"⁴⁹ This is true because, in African culture, a woman never asks a man for marriage. Moreover, a woman visiting a man at night subjects herself to sexual objectification and abuse. The narrator is transgressively silent about what transpired that night. If no sexual intercourse happened, then Ruth's nocturnal visit may not be viewed as a sexual invitation.

The text has several transgressive moves; secrecy pervades the scene. Ruth lies next to Boaz until morning but leaves early before anyone can recognize her. Her identity is a secret until she reveals it to Boaz in the dark. Moreover, Boaz ensures their rendezvous remains a secret. While Boaz gives her food as an altruistic gesture, it has connotations of payment for sex in cases of prostitution (Gen 38:1–30).

Some African women can relate to the experience of marrying rich men for economic reasons. African culture is built on patriarchal and heterosexual family arrangements where the husband is the breadwinner. This marginalizes the unmarried or widows and worsens their economic status. In cities, other women engage in prostitution to support themselves. Women are also endangered by broken economies. Unemployment worsens the status of women who cannot find work, depend on men, or work in the informal sector at marketplaces. Generally, men create social structures that diminish women, and conditions that make poor women vulnerable.

---

47. Laffey and Leonard-Fleckman, *Ruth*, 105.
48. Masenya and Kondemo, "What of the Problematic Norm?" 129.
49. Masenya and Kondemo, "What of the Problematic Norm?" 133.

As the book ends, Ruth's agency suffers when the narrative shifts to Naomi for whom Ruth has born a child. Ruth's significance and status diminish as Naomi's increases. The women bless the Lord who has given Naomi a redeemer, and she takes Ruth's child and becomes his nurse. They exclaim that "a son has been born to Naomi" (4:15–17). This ending aligns with the beginning where the focus is on Naomi and her family. Naomi starts out full but becomes empty when her family members die. In the end, she transitions from emptiness to fullness, from bitterness to pleasantness. Ruth marries an empty husband who dies childless after ten years. In the end, she marries another husband who provides her with a son and restores what she has lost. While this book is about women and their struggles to survive, men have the final word.

Masculinity Reading

Biblical masculinity studies highlight the "manly" acts of characters and their obsession with power, strength, violence, war, killing, domination of others, and fear of weakness.[50] In Africa, masculinity has traditionally been associated with men and male physical attributes, performances, and accomplishments, but some women also exhibit the basic traits of masculinity.[51] I have analyzed the notion of masculinity and deemed it "toxic" because women too, can be co-opted to emulate the negative behaviors of men.[52] Masculinity is a social construct and not a biological attribute, therefore, women too can act and behave like men. However, masculinity tendencies are mainly identified with men and their obsessions, and the few women who exhibit manly tendencies. As such, masculinity is toxic, whether practiced by men or women. In Africa and the biblical world, masculinity studies demonstrate that men have controlled most aspects of society.

Masculinity studies are more revealing in patriarchal contexts. Men are construed as strong, providers, and protectors of their families. Their interests and activities take center stage, yet women too, can act and behave, or even dress like men. The analysis of the book of Ruth pays attention to the roles played by men and women as defined by masculinity.

---

50. Creangă, and Smit, *Biblical Masculinities*.
51. Lindsay and Miescher, eds. *Men and Masculinities in Modern Africa*.
52. Wafawanaka, "Toxic Masculinity in Africa and the Bible."

In Ruth, men are in charge at the beginning but disappear from the text quickly. Elimelech moves to Moab with his family and the men clearly dominate in this family. After the men die, the surviving widows must now play the roles that the men once played. Naomi initiates the return to Bethlehem as Elimelech has led the migration to Moab. Ruth clings to Naomi as Naomi had clung to her husband earlier. In the rest of the story, Ruth acts and behaves like a female husband until the real man appears. She secures food for herself and Naomi from a mighty man of power and wealth whom the text describes in militaristic language as 'îsh *gibbôr ḥayil* (a man of great worth). Naomi also arranges a marriage scenario and Ruth asks Boaz for marriage just as a man would normally do. When Ruth has a son, the child is born to Naomi as it was born to a powerful man like Abraham (Gen 21:2). The masculinity displayed by Ruth and Naomi is not toxic, but for the purposes of survival.

The book of Ruth concludes on a high masculinity pitch. At the end of the narrative, Ruth's male child Obed occupies the Davidic ancestry. Notably, Old Testament genealogies typically include male descendants, and the mention of women is an exception. So, Ruth's omission from the genealogy fits within a typical male-centered listing of ancestors. Just as men rule at the beginning, they overwhelmingly dominate at the end. The narrator stresses peculiar interest in the men who conclude and punctuate the book. The list is extensive: Perez, Hezron, Ram, Amminadab, Naḥshon, Salmon, Boaz, Obed, Jesse, and David. Ten men accentuate the text's interest in men. By ending with David who in the history of Israel and the Bible is presented as the "perfect" or ideal man and king, a man after God's own heart (1 Sam 13:14), the book of Ruth exudes the highest masculinity. David exhibits all aspects of strong masculinity: seasoned warrior, hero, strong, commandeering, and a perfect killing machine. With feminist insight, Laffey and Leonard-Fleckman note that the concluding genealogy excluding women serves patriarchal interests. These men "serve, by their detail, to reinforce the patriarchal contents of genealogies in general and of a society that documents men and men's roles and accomplishments . . . and thereby erases women and their accomplishments."[53] Such erasure of women highlights the "manly" interests of the text and "the heterosexual-male gaze through which Ruth was written and is so often interpreted."[54]

---

53. Laffey and Leonard-Fleckman, *Ruth*, 161. They note genealogies typically begin than end biblical books.

54. I owe this phrase to Matthew Coomber.

Disability Reading

Another perspective that sheds light on the book of Ruth is disability studies. As a hermeneutical framework, disability criticism focuses on the construction and construal of the human body. How is the body made, viewed, described, and what kind of abilities or disabilities are associated with it? William Brown argues, "Like race, gender, and sexuality, 'disability' is more a social identity marker than a diagnostic category . . . disability has to do with interpreting and evaluating human differences based on presumed or real physical features."[55] Furthermore, some bodies are socially construed as able and others disabled. There are also social structures that contribute to the experience of disability, and society tends to marginalize disabled bodies. Disability includes cognitive limitations and the inevitability of the aging process, a normal part of living.[56] In a male-oriented society, Brown believes being female would be considered a disability. Moreover, in a society that views the perfect or ideal body as male and white, "persons of color would also be deemed 'naturally' deficient or disabled."[57] Obviously, this is a racist remark based on white supremacy.

A consideration of Ruth and Naomi from a disability perspective leads us to the conclusion that both would be viewed as disabled by virtue of their gender; they are not men and they do not have the ideal bodies. Ruth is doubly disabled by virtue of her gender and ethnicity, for Moabites are mostly described negatively in the Hebrew Bible. They are imperfect bodies, products of the incestuous bastardly union of Lot and his daughters (Gen 19:37–38). Perhaps to compensate for this, Ruth is presented as an exceptional woman, but the text constantly mentions her "Moabite" identity (1:4, 22; 2:2, 6, 21; 4:5, 10). Ruth and Naomi live in a male-centered society that values the male body and devalues the female body. After the deaths of her two sons, Naomi's old body becomes a crippling factor, for she can no longer bear sons for her daughters-in-law. She is now empty, barren, and disabled because "for women in the ancient world, the most common 'disability' was barrenness, a condition that could threaten the very livelihood of women, given their primary biological and social role in procreation."[58]

---

55. Brown, *A Handbook to Old Testament Exegesis*, 306.
56. Brown, *A Handbook to Old Testament Exegesis*, 306.
57. Brown, *A Handbook to Old Testament Exegesis*, 307.
58. Brown, *A Handbook to Old Testament Exegesis*, 309.

Biblical narratives enshrine stories of women struggling against the inability to have children, a veritable disability. Key figures include Sarah, Rebekah, Rachel, Samuel's mother, and Samson's mother (Gen 11:30; 16:1–16; 17:17; 25:21; 29:31; 30:22; 1 Sam 1:2; Judg 13:2–3). While each of them eventually had her disability reversed, each had the preferred child, a male child whose body is conceived as the ideal body. At the end of the narrative, Ruth gives birth to a male child who sires the grandfather of David, the "perfect" and ideal king of Israel. Now, the Bible celebrates physical beauty because David was "ruddy, and had beautiful eyes, and was handsome" (1 Sam 16:12). The womenfolk view Ruth's child as Naomi's and name him Obed (Ruth 4:17) for the child now removes Naomi's disability to have children at a late stage of life. Naomi signals this by taking and nursing the child, reversing her body's inability to have children anymore.

How the human body is viewed is also clear in the description of Naomi's two sons. While both Ruth and Orpah were married to Mahlon and Chilion for ten years, the text is silent about the couples' ability to have children (1:4–5). Since Ruth later had a child with another man, we can place the inability to have children on the body of Mahlon. The etymology of the names of Naomi's sons connotes significant disabilities. Queen-Sutherland states that "the names Mahlon and Chilion, however, foreshadow sickness, death, and childlessness" and "they pass quickly from the story."[59] Moreover, while the names of the parents connote divine connection and pleasantness, "the names of the two sons, by contrast, sound foreboding or even sinister."[60] Additionally, the parents' names reinforce patriarchy as they describe appropriate roles and behaviors for women and men.[61] From a disability perspective, both parents have ideal bodies; Elimelech by virtue of his connection to God and king, and Naomi by her connection to beauty and a lovely disposition, in addition to the ability to have children. Yet the two sons with flawed bodies are insignificant to the story and the narrator kills them in the first five verses of the book. These sons and their father are without voice, value, or significant bodily presence, and remain a footnote as the text rushes to the unfolding story of the remaining female protagonists.

While the story is about women, a disability lens shows that the women are viewed as disabled by gender or ethnicity and without the

---

59. Queen-Sutherland, *Ruth & Esther*, 49.

60. Laffey and Leonard-Fleckman, *Ruth*, 7.

61. Laffey and Leonard-Fleckman, *Ruth*, 7.

ideal bodies. Hence, they continue to struggle throughout the text until a man appears. That man is Boaz, the 'îsh *gibbôr ḥayil* (a man of great worth), a man with the ideal body like that of a mighty warrior (2:1). He has status, wealth, and reputation, and owns the land. He provides for Ruth and Naomi and protects Ruth in the field because she is physically unable to protect herself. The women are vulnerable and less able to perform because patriarchal social structures contribute to their experience of disability. Yet Boaz is a powerful landowner and employer. So, the women hatch a scheme to obtain the favor of an ideal man who can end their misery. By marrying Boaz, Ruth secures the perfect man who can provide for her and her mother-in-law permanently. Boaz becomes the great-grandfather of David, a man with the ideal body, power, reputation, and accomplishments. A disability perspective demonstrates that bodies matter, and some bodies matter more than others. The book about women is filtered through the lens of the ideal male body which can provide for the struggling imperfect-bodied women.

Survival Perspective

The survival of women in a male-dominated context is at the heart of the story of Ruth and Naomi. Kugler and Magori argue that the performance of *ḥesed* or acts of kindness is how these protagonists survive in a deeply patriarchal society.[62] Therefore, Ruth receives mixed reactions in different African contexts. Some claim that Ruth "shows an androcentric slant that reinforces the belief that a woman cannot survive without being bound to a man in a marriage relationship."[63] Ruth is popular in Sub-Saharan Africa because it reinforces patriarchal norms where Ruth is regarded as a model woman who engages in "heterosexual marriage, as the only career available for her survival in a patriarchal society."[64]

Writing from a South African Indian woman's perspective, Sarojini Nadar finds Ruth helpful as "a positive role model for women in similar circumstances," because "Ruth emerges as a woman who takes control of her destiny and who changes it from hopelessness to happiness. She is a survivor, not a victim of circumstance, waiting for a man to change her

---

62. Kugler and Magori, "*Hesed* in Ruth," 9–10.
63. Masenya and Kondemo, "What of the Problematic Norm?," 125.
64. Masenya and Kondemo, "What of the Problematic Norm?" 126.

fate."⁶⁵ To Ruth's model of "success" in an oppressive patriarchal system, Tinyiko Maluleke responds that "the stubborn insistence that Ruths are successful and that they are succeeding, even though and even when they are not, may be as cruel as subjecting them to physical oppression."⁶⁶

Masenya and Kondemo find Naomi and Ruth's actions problematic for Congolese women. They argue that "so many young Mongo women are sent by their mothers to look for rich men to marry."⁶⁷ When they cannot afford basic things like school fees, "many Mongo women teach their daughters at a young age how to seduce a man, how to cook for him and how to attract and make a man comfortable in every way so that they would be good candidates for marriage."⁶⁸ However, the authors wish modern African women could extricate themselves from the clutches of heterosexual marriage, especially in the context of sexually transmitted diseases to which they are susceptible. Since women stay in wrong marriages for fear of losing economic support, they find Ruth "unhelpful to Mongo women in their fight against HIV and AIDS."⁶⁹

When Africans read the ending of the book of Ruth, they may appreciate the survival and restoration of the family unit as families are the most important social support system. According to Iliffe, "families were and are the main sources of support for the African poor."⁷⁰ The desire for many children is typical of African culture. Due to poverty, disease, death, and the need for field labor, large families were traditionally ideal, but in the modern world, it can lead to poverty.⁷¹ Despite how the book of Ruth is read, the story remains "the tale of two women who played according to the rules of the patriarchal game in order to survive" because they navigated the system "to change their lives and turn things to their advantage."⁷² This analysis has implications for reading and interpreting other biblical texts.

---

65. Nadar, "A South African Indian Womanist Reading," esp. 172.
66. Maluleke, "African 'Ruths,' Ruthless Africas,'" esp. 245.
67. Masenya and Kondemo, "What of the Problematic Norm?" 131.
68. Masenya and Kondemo, "What of the Problematic Norm?" 131.
69. Masenya and Kondemo, "What of the Problematic Norm?" 132.
70. Iliffe, *The African Poor*, 7.
71. Iliffe, *The African Poor*, 277.
72. Masenya and Kondemo, "What of the Problematic Norm?" 130.

Homiletic Overtures

This section transitions to a homily based on the above analysis. The setting is a Women's Day Sunday morning service at Progress Baptist Church, and I am the invited speaker. Both women and men typically attend church but today's focus is on women's issues. I seek to address women, but I am cognizant of the role men play. I suspect this is why the pastor asked me to preach, instead of inviting a woman as usual. So, I feel particularly concerned about honoring my assignment and preaching a relevant sermon. My goal is to address women's concerns, but I also want the men to learn something new. My sermon is entitled, "Against All Odds."

Homily

Thank you, Pastor Goredema, for the opportunity to preach on this Women's Day service. I know you could have chosen a woman preacher but you did not. Thank you for your trust and confidence in me. There is a word for the women and men assembled here today.

On this special occasion, I wish to preach on the subject, "Against All Odds." Life seldom conforms to our expectations. We make plans, but God makes God's own plans. So is the story of Naomi and Ruth. Many of you are familiar with this historical narrative. Uniquely, the book of Ruth is one of two books named after a woman in the Protestant canon. The other is the book of Esther. This makes Ruth special because it is an exception in the Bible. We should note that most of the biblical books were written by men to reflect their interests. So, when a woman is mentioned by name or has a book named after her, she is no ordinary woman. She is either a jewel or a Jezebel. Indeed, we know all the good girls of the Bible, but we also know all the bad ones.[73] You remember Shifrah and Puah (Exod 1:15) because they were deceptive midwives. Some of the women we know about are attached to a man even when they play key roles on their own. Do you remember the judge and prophetess Deborah, the *wife of Lappidoth* in Judges 4? There is also Samson's mother, the barren *wife of Manoah* (Judg 13:2). We remember the *daughters of Zelophehad* in Numbers 26 (v. 33) and

---

73. Higgs, *Bad Girls of the Bible*; Higgs, *Really Bad Girls of the Bible*; Higgs, *Slightly Bad Girls of the Bible*.

36 (v. 11) precisely because he had no sons. If Zelophehad had had sons, surely, we would never have known the names of his daughters!

On the notorious side are women like Jezebel, Delilah, and of course, the libidinous wife of Potiphar. The men who wrote about these women exhibit them as billboards of transgressive behavior. That is why Jezebel dies a particularly gruesome death. We don't really know the majority of biblical women. They exist on the margins of scriptures in both silence and anonymity. Schüssler Fiorenza's book *In Memory of Her* commemorates the mysterious woman who anointed Jesus before his death (Mark 14:9).[74]

This woman is nameless, but Ruth is named, and so also is her mother-in-law, Naomi. One Moabite and the other Israelite; foreigner and native; both attached to the men in their lives. After their men die, they struggle to survive in a man's world. These were the days of the judges, indeed a man's world. The judges ruled before kingship in Israel and people did whatever they pleased. These were chaotic times and women were treated as objects and could be raped by men with impunity. While men ruled in public spaces, women ran the household economy and were involved in the painstaking process of food processing and preparation. And when the men were missing, women did everything to survive.

The deaths of the husbands of Naomi and Ruth plunge them into a precarious situation, but it also sharpens their will to survive. Back in Bethlehem, Ruth takes charge of matters and goes to glean in Boaz's fields. If you grew up in the city, you might not know what this custom was. But country folk surely know. Legally, the poor could gather felled grain after harvesting crops. Even in their poverty, they had the dignity of work. A timely moment of divine intervention has brought Ruth to the right place, at the right time, to meet the right man.

As a foreigner in a strange land, Ruth stands out. This we know as people of African descent in America. Ruth's ethnicity, language, accent, and demeanor stand out. She works but she could be physically assaulted or raped by her male co-workers. Yet the problem is not with her, but with the men who are predisposed to such bad behavior! Think about it, brothers.

Ruth secures temporary security, but Naomi plans for permanent security for both of them. Against all odds, she hatches a daring plan. Full of potential dangers; Ruth implements it slyly. Naomi sends Ruth to

---

74. Schüssler Fiorenza, *In Memory of Her*.

meet a man at night and we wonder if she is pimping her daughter-in-law. Her dress suggests it, her perfume suggests it, the cover of darkness suggests it, lying next to a man's lap suggests it, and the drunken Boaz might be too impaired to resist a woman lying in his bosom. To survive, the women transgress social, cultural, and sexual boundaries. Yet their struggle is against a culture that says a woman needs a man to survive.

In the Congo, some mothers encourage their daughters to emulate Ruth and secure a man for marriage and security. They also struggle against all odds and put security in the control of a man. Like Ruth and Naomi, they feel incomplete without a man. We never question why. We take it for granted this is normal. We are conditioned to think a certain way. But what if we thought about it differently? What could women do if we empowered them? What if a woman did not need a man to survive? What if we changed the paradigm?

Ruth and Naomi struggle against all odds and their story is not complete until a man shows up. So, Ruth marries Boaz and they have a son who will maintain the family line. This child leads to the Davidic line and ultimately Jesus the Messiah. Yet Ruth is a foreigner and Boaz is an Israelite. A despised Moabite, and a beloved Israelite! In this transgressive moment, God is working a miracle, a messianic miracle. What can we learn from this story?

The first lesson is that liberation is a transgressive act. The book begins with a transgressive moment. Elimelech and his family liberate themselves and cross the border into Moab to survive a famine. They cross physical, social, emotional, and cultural boundaries. They forsake the "house of bread" for a place that now has the bread they need to survive for a decade. The sons also transgress racial, ethnic, and matrimonial boundaries by marrying Moabite women. Unfortunately, all the men transition from life to death in a foreign land. When fortunes change in Judah, Naomi retraces her steps back, but Ruth crosses her own geographical, social, cultural, and religious boundaries. Her assimilation into Israelite society is a transgressive act. Always a Moabite, but now an Israelite!

Back in Judah alone, the women continue to transgress social structures to survive. Ruth is surrounded by lurking dangers in the field. Naomi vitiates marriage norms by encouraging Ruth to meet a man at night when she is exposed to danger. She could be physically attacked, verbally abused, raped, or get a bad reputation if someone saw her going to and from the threshing floor at night. This was the place where prostitutes met their customers and Ruth could be mistaken for one. Ruth's final act of transgression and liberation is marrying Boaz, another foreigner to her as was Mahlon her first husband. Therefore, liberation is a truly transgressive act. The characters experience liberation only by moving away from the known to the unknown. Moab is a land of death for the men, and Ruth's desertion of her homeland is her liberation and messianic claim. Only in such transgressive moments can hope be experienced!

The second point is that liberated women can thrive and live independently. When Naomi and Ruth lose their husbands, they take matters into their own hands. While the culture dictated that a woman needed a man to survive, they survived without any men around them for a while. Sisters, you can make it on your own. Were it not for the culture, perhaps they could have been landowners rather than gleaners in some man's land. In ancient Israel, women took care of each other through their support circles and social networks. This is also true in Africa where daughters-in-law care for their mothers-in-law who are now their new mothers. In fact, they call them "mothers." In African culture, remembering family and your roots is important, and so is going back home to family. Orpah abandons her new mother, but Ruth embraces her completely. Such devotion to the mother-in-law is the hallmark of African culture.

The final point is that God works in transgressive ways beyond our expectations. The whole story of the book of Ruth is an act of transgression. Only in moving beyond the familiar can we experience the joy of liberation. All the characters transgress one boundary or another to experience transformation, whether from famine to fulfillment, from life to death, or from despised foreigner to revered great-grandmother of Davidic kings. Only God can do such a thing! Ruth may never have contributed to the genealogy of the Jewish messiah had she not acted in decisively transgressive ways. While we may be horrified and terrified by what Naomi and Ruth do to survive in a man's world, these are God's transgressive and transformative moments. Truly, God works in mysterious ways beyond our expectations. Surely, God often writes with crooked strokes and blesses the undeserving. Amazingly, the genealogy of the Messiah is undergirded by the transgressive and courageous act of a vulnerable foreign woman. And God's final transgressive act was the resurrection of this Israelite-Moabite descendant from death to life for our salvation. Truly, there is no situation against us that God cannot turn around. Amen!

Conclusion

The book of Ruth is a simple narrative that can be read from many different perspectives. This essay has used the hermeneutical frameworks of socio-economic analysis, decoloniality, masculinity, disability, and an African perspective to supplement traditional interpretations. The socio-cultural setting of the book has many resonances with African life and culture. Re-reading Ruth from these perspectives clarifies problems that women experienced in ancient Israel, such as dependence on men and their absence in the family. By interpreting Ruth from an African perspective, African women can relate to the experiences of marginality and problems of gender, inequality, sexuality, and patriarchy. The agrarian setting of both ancient Israel and traditional Africa makes the biblical text more accessible to African readers, especially women who are often victimized by societal norms and the expectations of a patriarchal culture, including heterosexual marriage. These reading methodologies have ramifications for biblical scholarship, and other biblical texts read in many African contexts.

The analysis of the book of Ruth led to the homiletical move on the power of transgressive moments. Ruth and Naomi survive in a male-dominated society, yet they also endure by negotiating the limitations of this cultural environment. Only by taking daring actions and crossing certain boundaries do they find their freedom and fulfillment. In the end, liberation is a transgressive act, and liberated women can thrive. Above all, God acts in unexpected and transgressive ways to effect human transformation.

PART THREE

Interpreting Matthew 15:21–28 and Homiletic Overtures

10

A Womanist Reading of the Canaanite Woman (Matt 15:21–28)

Dehumanization, and the Politics of Respectability and Inclusion

MITZI J. SMITH

Introduction

IN THE STORY OF the Canaanite woman's encounter with Jesus (Matt 15:21–28), this mother, sobbing loudly, pleads with Jesus and his disciples to heal her daughter who is being tormented by a demon. The frantic mother endures mistreatment and verbal abuse so that she might access the healing power that Jesus possesses for her daughter. The encounter itself is traumatic. Ultimately, Jesus declares that the woman demonstrated "great faith," and as a result, the daughter has been healed. This essay interprets this story through the lens of womanist biblical criticism that privileges the trauma of racism that poor Black women, children, and men face within the health care system. The dehumanization of racism, classism, xenophobia, sexism, and queerphobia insist that Black women and their children, and marginalized persons generally, conform to the politics of inclusion and respectability, two sides of the same racialized coin, in order to access the quality health care that they deserve.

A womanist interpretation of Matt 15:21–28 and the homily it inspires challenges a homiletical tradition that uncritically celebrates Jesus's declaration of the Canaanite woman's exercise of "great faith," which is manifested in her relentless advocacy for her chronically and fatally ill daughter.[1] When interpreting this narrative, preachers and scholars often apologetically engage in what I call *Jesussplaining*. Similar to *mansplaining*, *Jesussplaining* is when men and women explain in spiritually condescending, patronizing, and gaslighting ways Jesus's conduct (as depicted in the biblical text) in order to preserve or protect their uncritical and exalted view of Jesus as God. Jesus must always be viewed as flawless because he *is* God, although Jesus does not refer to himself as God and refuses to be worshipped (e.g., Matt 4:10; Luke 4:8; John 4:21; Acts 7:7; Rev 19:10; 22:9).[2] Jesus must be the reason for the hoop *and* the holler, for the celebration in the sermon, regardless. Jesus is very human, but thanks to Nicea, he is always read as God. This simplistic homiletical move is low-hanging unripe or rotten fruit that ignores the very problematic and horrible mistreatment of the woman and provides fodder for the weaponization of faith. A demonstration of "great faith" is required for the internal or external othered human beings; they must behave exceptionally to have even partial access to the resources and power necessary for survival and thriving. They must behave, dress, and speak respectably, as determined by the dominant. Respectability might gain them some degree of access or inclusion or none at all.

The weaponization of faith places the burden or responsibility on the person needing justice or health care and relieves the church, community, and society of the transformation of systems, structures, policies, and practices that create equality and equity for all. The weaponization of faith as the answer to all injustice and wholeness, excuses and permits the immortality of oppressive systems and structures. We preach that God is in control through problematic and violent depictions of Jesus (and God). Thus, the oppressed must develop a tougher spiritual skin or greater faith.

The rhetoric of governments, systems, and institutions may shift, and the faces of their upper management may change, but enduring racial religio-political ideologies remain embedded in the grammar,

---

1. In the case of the Canaanite woman, see Crowder, *When Momma Speaks*, xiv. Crowder coins the term "womanist maternal thought" hermeneutics, which focuses on advocacy and representation (22).

2. See Kim, *Truth, Testimony, and Transformation*.

syntax, and interpretation of the unchangeable founding documents (e.g., bylaws, constitutions, historical records) that ensure the perpetuity of existing oppressive and exclusionary structures, systems, policies, and practices. Liberation requires that we challenge problematic foundational sacred texts.

This essay proceeds as follows: First, I discuss the womanist lens of health care disparities that disproportionately impact Black women and their children through which I interpret the story of the Canaanite woman's encounter with Jesus and his disciples in Matt 15:21–28. Using a womanist lens privileges the voices, concerns, and experiences of poor Black women, and by extension the Black community and other blackened, dehumanized, and/or oppressed stigmatized peoples.[3] In conversation with Dayna Bowen Matthew's *Just Medicine* and Harriet Washington's *Medical Apartheid,* as well as my own personal experience with the health care system as the daughter of a chronically ill mother, Flora O. Carson Smith (1929–2009) and as a stroke victim myself, my womanist framework focuses on the dehumanizing treatment that Black women and their children and communities experience as a result of racism, sexism, and classism, which impact their (mis)treatment in the health care system.

Second, I offer a critical interpretation of the story of the Canaanite mother from my womanist perspective and in conversation with Black women's experiences, voices, and concerns. I attempt to humanize both the Canaanite woman and Jesus. I examine how Jesus and his disciples increase the woman's trauma. I humanize her by exposing the oppression to which she is subjected and naming the extra burden she bears of exercising her agency of contextual talk back while balancing the social mandates of respectability and inclusion politics imposed on women in a patriarchal society, on the ethnic othered, and those with health care needs without means of meeting them within biased systems.[4] This Canaanite mother knows that her silence will not save her daughter's life or her own; it will merely ensure that Jesus and his disciples, and the oppressive systems, structures, and policies they embody and represent, remain unchallenged.

Finally, I offer a homily or a homiletical transfer, a shift from interpretation to sermon or sermonic reflection. The audience I envision includes

3. Jackson, *Becoming Human,* 1–44.
4. Sechrest (*Race and Rhythm*) argues that the Canaanite woman's demonstration of agency is seen in "foregrounding urgent and necessary action," 82.

persons of faith and persons of no faith who are or have been troubled and harmed by oppressive biblical texts, interpretations, and interpreters; serious preachers, pastors, and students of the biblical text; and lay teachers and congregations, all of whom are committed to social justice and interested in working through difficult or complex texts.

Hermeneutical Horizon

Health care providers can be "nice" and biased simultaneously. My mother, Flora Smith used the term "nice nasty." The nasty dehumanization, oppression, and harmful biases committed against Black women, the poor, and other minoritized people are killing us. In Harriet Washington's book *Medical Apartheid*, she recounts the painful dehumanizing history of gynecological experimentation on enslaved Black women's bodies by J. Marion Sims, the father of modern gynecology, for the benefit of White women's survival and health.[5] An August 2024 National Bureau of Economic Research (NBER) report based on a study of almost one million births at sixty-eight New Jersey hospitals discovered that Black women are 25% more likely to undergo unnecessary C-sections compared to white women and apparently due to provider discretion.[6]

Overt racism in health care is illegal and generally not tolerated, but racial biases still pervade the system. As a master of arts student in the Black Studies program at The Ohio State University (OSU) in the mid-1980s, I researched cancer incidence and mortality rates for Black and white women and men in the Ohio Counties with the largest Black populations. At the time, statistics showed that incidence rates in almost every form of cancer were lower for Black people, but the mortality rate was higher, apparently due partly lack of access to the best cancer treatment facilities and care, adequate health insurance, and distrust of the system. Washington states that today Black women are 2.2 times more likely than white women to die of breast cancer.[7]

During my research, I also uncovered a news article about a white doctor who admitted that many of his peers did not believe Black people deserved the best care, even when they had good insurance. Before the

---

5. Washington, *Medical Apartheid*.

6. Corredor-Waldron, Currie and Schnell, "Drivers of Racial Differences in C-Sections."

7. Washington, *Medical Apartheid*, 4.

Trump-era presidency, it was socially unacceptable to be overtly racist, but now many US citizens want to march us back to a time when overt racism was acceptable and before the Affordable Care Act (Obama Care improved under the Biden/Harris Administration), women's rights, and civil rights. Donna Christian-Christensen, MD, former chair of the Congressional Black Caucus Health Braintrust states that "health disparities are the civil rights issue of the 21st century."[8]

While overt racism, sexism, and other civil rights violations are generally illegal and intolerable in most US public institutions,[9] covert racism or implicit racial biases exist in our health care system, and throughout our society. The impact of implicit biases is deadly. Implicit bias can be reversed if we admit it exists, if we expose, name, and work to heal it in our individual selves and our institutions, systems, and structures. According to Dayna Matthew, research shows that "implicit bias can be *intentionally* reversed. Therefore, the preponderance of malleability evidence warrants a complete reconceptualization of when and how providers could and should be held accountable to intervene and thwart the discriminatory impact of unintentional racial and ethnic discrimination."[10] But Matthew states "Implementing the transformation to an equitable health care model must be borne of the conviction that continued avoidance of the evidence that implicit bias causes disparities, and that disparities ruin lives, will be unethical at best, unjust in deed, and patently unforgivable."[11]

Within the matrix of (implicit or explicit) racism, the oppressed must submit to respectability politics as the price of access to resources (material and social), and access is contingent upon the system's representatives. Dominant systems and their representative gatekeepers can change the price, refuse access despite the performance of respectability, and permit access or inclusion that does not revise the founding documents that prioritize and protect the interests and privileges of the dominant. Respectability politics insists that the oppressed, marginalized, and othered "quietly lift themselves up, acquiescing and genuflecting to

---

8. Washington, *Medical Apartheid*, 3.

9. That is until we entered the MAGA Trump era, which began during the presidential election season of 2016 and continues to the present day; almost half of the US electorate unapologetically and blatantly supports and justifies overt racism, misogyny, xenophobia, and queerphobia society.

10. Matthew, *Just Medicine*, 170.

11. Matthew, *Just Medicine*, 172.

unjust laws and practices, which results in victim-blaming."[12] Respectability politics serves as a prerequisite for access to needed resources and inclusion at the table (as a guest), but it never guarantees survival, equality, parity, or justice.[13] Audre Lorde has warned that Black women's silence will not save us: "I remind myself all the time now that if I were to have been born mute, or had maintained an oath of silence my whole life long for safety, I would still have suffered, and I would still die."[14]

Womanist theologian Elaine Crawford demonstrates in her book *Hope in the Holler* that for Black enslaved women the holler is the horror of their enslavement. Crawford describes the "holler" this way:

> The hope that emerges in the echoes of the holler during slavery is the quest for freedom and humanity. We explored the narratives of slavery as the foundational genre out of which black women's hope can be gleaned. The narratives of slave women elucidate the dehumanizing horrors and the distinctive hopes of life during de jure slavery. Hope, the passion for the possible in their lives, was expressed by slave women as an undauntable seizing of life in spite of abuse. Slave women lived in the daily personal humiliation of the Holler. Their bodies and being were disregarded, disrespected, and despised.[15]

For contemporary Black women, the holler is the devastating impact of racism, classism, sexism, heterosexism, and other intersecting oppressions. And in the midst of the holler, Black women embody hope. The "context of abuse" changes and with it the "function of 'hope'" shifts in Black women's lives.[16] Similarly, despite being dismissed, disrespected, and despised, the Canaanite mother in Matt 15:21–28 expresses hope in and through her body. She musters hope under the duress of her daughter's illness but also amidst the dehumanization that the man (and his male companions) who ostensibly holds the power she needs subjects her. Hope manifests or functions as audacity, talk back, and resilience. Jesus may call it "great faith"; we might name it *hope despite the horror or the holler*. Crawford states that Black women "endured,

---

12. Smith, *Insights from African American Interpretation*, 78.
13. See Smith, "Paul, Timothy, and the Respectability Politics of Race."
14. Lorde, *Sister Outsider*, 43.
15. Crawford, *Hope in the Holler*, 110.
16. Crawford, *Hope in the Holler*, 75.

survived and at times transformed their lives and their communities into vessels of hope."[17]

Interpretation

In the first century CE, healing and healers were not rare. In his book *Zealot: The Life and Times of Jesus of Nazareth*, Reza Aslan argues that Jesus was known as one of those healers who healed people without monetary payment.[18] Certainly, we get this impression in the Gospels, and in Matthew particularly. Matthew 4:23–25 provides a synopsis of the miracles Jesus performed throughout the region of Galilee. He performed miracles that cured every disease and every malady among the people. As his reputation as a healer spread to everyone living in Syria, they too brought their sick to be healed, including those possessed by demons. Thus, the area formerly known as the land of Canaan is where Jesus gained notoriety as a miracle worker. We can assume that persons of Canaanite ancestry survived or remained in the region, including the Canaanite woman whose daughter is suffering from a demoniac attack on her body (15:21–28). There is more than one way to exact a price from the foreigner, outsider, the othered, or the marginalized, to tax them for access to power and other resources.

Jesus crossed the border into the district of Tyre and Sidon when the Canaanite woman confronts him with her need (15:21). Consider that Tyre and Sidon are located in the country of Syria, and people from that region had already crossed the border into Galilee with their ailing neighbors and loved ones seeking Jesus' healing power (4:24). The Canaanite mother had probably heard about or saw neighbors who returned home after Jesus healed them or their friends and family members. Perhaps, she was the only caregiver for her daughter and was unable to transport her to Galilee or had no one to assist her. But now Jesus has come to her hometown.[19] While Tyre and Sidon may be regarded as Gentile areas, it is not necessarily the case that no or few Jewish persons live in the region. Many Jewish persons lived in the diaspora in the first century CE (e.g., in the Acts of the Apostles; and Galatians). And people crisscrossed back

---

17. Crawford, *Hope in the Holler*, 75.
18. Aslan, *Zealot*.
19. Kgatle, "Crossing Borders," argues that the Canaanite woman crosses the borders of "gender and sexuality, landscape and spatiality, ethnicity, purity and social status," 606.

and forth in the same way that Matthew depicts people bringing their sick to Galilee for healing and returning home.

The Canaanite woman is identified broadly by her ethnicity or ancestry; she likely is not Jewish, not a proselyte. She differs from Jesus in terms of gender (woman), ethnicity (unknown; could be Sidonian, Tyrian, Syrophoenician[20] and so on), race (Canaanite), religion (not Jewish, broadly "pagan"), and culture. Mookgo Kgatle argues that "with the specific reference to the place as Tyre and Sidon (Gentile territories) and the designation of the woman as Canaanite (indigenous people of Canaan and ancient enemies of Israel), Matthew presents the woman as a political enemy of, and religious outsider for, the Jews."[21] According to the Hebrew Bible, the relationship between the Israelites and Canaanites was complex: Noah's genealogy charts them as biologically related; the two groups intermarried and co-existed as neighbors; and they fought against and enslaved each other (Gen 10:15–20; Esau married Canaanite women, Gen 36:2; Exod 23:28; 33:2; Judg 1:28, 32).

Two Canaanite women, Tamar and Rahab, are mentioned in Matthew's genealogy, but they are *included* because they birthed significant male children whose fathers were Israelites (1:3, 5). Genealogy as a foundational document of origins and ancestry is about the sons, the male children, and their fathers. Jesus is related to the sons of Israelite men *by* Canaanite women. The names of Canaanite and other foreign women are written into the genealogy, but they are valued more for their secondary wombs, as incubators of Jewish male sperm; they birthed baby boys conceived by Israelite men. Both Tamar and Rahab are identified in the Hebrew Bible as prostitutes or practicing prostitution (Gen 38; Josh 2:1–21; 6:22–25; 1 Chr 2:4). I agree with Daniel Gullotta that the *inclusion* of both Rahab and the Canaanite woman in Matthew is no coincidence; it is intentional.[22] Is it possible that Matthew expects his Jewish readers to associate the anonymous Canaanite mother with Tamar and Rahab and thus with prostitution?[23]

---

20. If we conflate Mark's story (7:24–31) with Matthew's (15:21–28), she could be Syrophoenician.

21. Mookgo, "Crossing Boundaries," 596. Sechrest (*Race and Rhyme*) regards this story is a thematic example of encountering enemies, more specifically of loving them, 75, 147; she likens the Caananites to contemporary white allies as identified in white anti-racist scholarship, 84.

22. Gullotta, "Among Dogs and Disciples," 331–32; he views the Canaanite Woman as "Matthew's model for Gentile conversion," 332.

23. Kgatle, "Crossing Boundaries," surmises that the woman is at the bottom of

How is the Canaanite woman like Rahab and Tamar? In Deut 23:18, money earned from prostitution is likened to the wages of a dog and is forbidden to be used in payment of a vow in Yahweh's house. This prohibition is echoed in Matt 7:6: "Do not give the holy thing to the dogs" (Μὴ δῶτε τὸ ἅγιον τοῖς κυσίν). Thus, for Jewish readers images of prostitution and dogs are connected similarly both in the Torah and in Matthew's Gospel. Further, the three characterizations of Canaanite women in Matthew have the impact of constructing and persuading a collective knowledge about Canaanite women as a group. Two of the three mentioned Canaanite women in Matthew are explicitly known by Jewish readers for their association with prostitution. The anonymity of the Canaanite woman increases the likelihood that she is associated with Tamar and Rahab and prostitution; Matthew's readers are presented with no other linguistic register for understanding her. Majority representations and stereotypes construct group identity and impact individual identity especially when imposed upon perceived outsiders. By calling the Canaanite woman one of the "dogs" (τοῖς κυναρίοις) in Matt 15:26, Jesus increases the likelihood that Matthew's audience familiar with the Torah, and Deut 23:18 in particular (also 1 Kgs 22:38), will assume a negative attitude toward her. We find very few if any, positive views of dogs in the Hebrew Bible; they are overwhelmingly negative and derogatory (e.g., 1 Sam 17:43, 24:14; 2 Sam 31:8; Ps 22:6; Isa 56:10). Matthew's Jesus definitely has insulted this woman.

This Canaanite mother approaches Jesus and his Jewish male disciples already with that socio-cultural religious baggage hoisted on her back. Her climb is an uphill one. Expressing her desperation and the urgency of the need, she cried intensely or audibly (ἔκραζεν, Matt 15:22); some translations read that she was "shouting" (OJB, NRSV, NRSVue), giving the impression that she is angry. The Canaanite woman's plea is concise, direct, and to the point. "Show me mercy. Master, King David's son, my daughter is tormented by a demon" (15:22). The Gadarene (aka as Gerasene) demoniacs cried out (ἔκραξαν, Matt 8:29a), needing to know if Jesus had come to torment them, prematurely. Demons torment human beings and can be tormented by Jesus. Jesus is a son; her child is a daughter. In patriarchal societies, sons are valued above daughters.

---

the social ladder: "What if the woman was a widow? Or she was a slave? From what we know about how families or households were constructed along gender and power imbued lines in the Greek-Roman world of 1st century Palestine, there could be many factors, which would make the woman and her daughter extremely marginal," 600.

Jesus meets the woman's desperate plea with silence: "And he did not answer her a single word!" (ὁ δὲ οὐκ ἀπεκρίθη αὐτῇ λόγον,15:23a). Amidst Jesus's silence, the woman is subjected to the harmful words of his disciples who ask that Jesus dismiss her because she is crying (κράζει) and following them (15:23b). The other time Jesus says nothing (οὐδὲν) is when the chief priests and elders accuse him of crimes as he stands before Pilate (27:12).

The disciples unanimously advise Jesus to send the Canaanite mother away. They appear heartless. Similarly, two blind men cry out for mercy from Jesus (ἔκραξαν, 20:30), and the crowd attempts to shut them up, but they, like the Canaanite woman, will not be intimidated or silenced (ἔκραξαν, 20:31). An immediate need is greater than the imminent threat of crowds and men. Like, Rachel and the slaughter of innocent children, the Canaanite mother cannot be consoled without justice, which means wholeness or freedom from evil forces in the case of her daughter (Matt 1:18).

Jesus's response to the Canaanite mother's continual pleading is an insulting metaphorical re-imagining, and a rhetorical performance that insists on Israel's priority over othered peoples: "It is not fair to take the children's (τῶν τέκνων) bread and cast it to the dogs (τοῖς κυναρίοις)" (15:26). As noted above, we need not think that Jesus had never encountered a Canaanite woman from her side of the border. He has, and he is referring to her and her people as dogs. Perhaps this encounter is different since Jesus is the visitor, and the encounter is more personal or intimate (cf. Matt 20:20–23 where the anonymous mother of the sons of Zebedee confronts Jesus). The Canaanite woman/mother does not approach Jesus in or with a crowd; Jesus is the one surrounded by a group of people, his Jewish disciples. Does Jesus succumb to group ethnonationalism peer pressure?

After the Exodus event, Moses, as Yahweh's spokesperson, instructed the children of Israel to eat no meat mauled by beasts; it should be thrown to the dogs (Exod 22:31). Any Canaanite, any human being, would be offended, to say the least, by Jesus's dehumanizing and exclusionary reference to them as dogs, as animals and scavengers. The Canaanites were the children of the land, planting and harvesting "bread" before the "children's" ancestor Abram arrived (Gen 12:5–6; Matt 3:9), in the same way that the Native Indigenous Peoples were present when Christopher Columbus arrived in the fertile land he claimed to have discovered. Father Abraham is mentioned often in Matthew beginning at 1:1 in the genealogy; Jesus Christ is the son of David and of Abraham (1:1, 2, 17; 3:9; 8:11; 22:32). The Israelites are children of Abraham (1:18; 3:9). The bread belongs to the children; those considered outsiders and scavengers will eat none of it. Chris Shannahan asserts that Jesus as "an insider dismisses an 'outsider' as theologically insignificant. It is not a surprise that this passage is regularly smoothed over, ignored, or spiritualized by preachers. However, the blunt truth, as we read it in scripture, is that Jesus too was hemmed in by xenophobia . . . he rejects this Canaanite woman as a cultural 'other.'"[24] She, as an outsider, is dismissed theologically and anthropologically.

As Dayna Matthew writes in *Just Medicine,* racism, whether intentional or unintentional is harmful. Further, patients as well as doctors show up in the hospital or doctor's office with their own experiences and expectations. The doctor's conduct will be filtered through those experiences and expectations.[25] The doctor possesses her own stored "unconsciously held stereotypes" through which she may perceive the patient's conduct.[26]

The Canaanite woman and mother will not be silenced. She responds, realistically and wisely, to Jesus, knowing the gendered, religious, nationalistic, and cultural power dynamics at play. Her daughter's life depends on her response. The politics of respectability and inclusion demand her deference to her social superiors and to those who insist upon their own ethnic, racial, religious, and cultural superiority.[27] Having already genuflected her body in a position that demonstrates a recognition of her status as a woman in a patriarchal society and as a Canaanite seeking the help of a Rabbi with the gift of healing, she talks back to Jesus (15:25). Her words are palatable to a human being with a propensity for compassion that transgresses biases and oppressive ideological boundaries: "Yes, master, for even the pets (τά κυνάρια) eat of the crumbs falling from their master's table" (15:27). With her ναί (yes) she acknowledges his view and his patriarchal power over her. And changing

---

24. Shannahan, "The Canaanite Woman and Urban Liberation Theology," 18. Conversely, Lee, "The Faith of the Canaanite Woman," 16. Lee contrasts the Canaanite woman's faith to Peter's wavering faith as he attempted to walk on water. Also, Jesus's initial response to the woman was meant "to strengthen her faith," 17.

25. Matthew, *Just Medicine*, 52.

26. Matthew, *Just Medicine*, 53.

27. Sechrest (*Race and Rhyme*) argues that the Canaanite woman's "submissiveness is even more pronounced than the Centurion's because trust issues come to the forefront," 85.

his imagery, she challenges his denial, offering an alternative reality, a different religio-cultural perspective that values all life and members of the household as worthy of bread. Her words omit the children in her scenario (but they are implicitly at the table); thus, the pets are distinct from the children in her imagination (of which her daughter is one) *and* the pets are *not* scavengers in the household.[28] Pets and children access what they need to live. Shingirai Masunda argues the Canaanite woman rejects the negative implications of the dog metaphor and "argues that dogs, just as children are insiders; they belong to the same household."[29] Further, Masunda states that Jesus yields to the Canaanite woman demonstrating that she has transformed his "mission from one of shortage and boundaries into one of inclusion and community" that matches her social world.[30] Ma M. Ibita asserts that the Canaanite woman creates a "teaching moment for Jesus and the disciples, by subverting the dog metaphor to her advantage" and challenges "discrimination concerning healing based on ethnicity, religion, and gender at that time."[31] According to Amy-Jill Levine, the Canaanite woman demonstrates a "superior" theology that "is in keeping with the claim in Matthew that the eschatological banquet belongs to God and the Son of Man (e.g., 22.1–14; 25.1–13)."[32] The Canaanite mother's use of the dog metaphor does not mean that she acquiesces to his insult and oppression.

Verse 28 reads: Jesus answered and said to the Canaanite woman: "O Woman, great is your faith (μεγάλη σου ἡ πίστις); let it be done to you as you wish." Matthew 15:28 is the only place we find the words "great faith." This is the only place we find it in the NT. It is uniquely applied to or required of the Canaanite mother (cf. Matt 9:27–31). In fact, Jesus heals man's son who is a demon-possessed because of his "little faith"

---

28. Smith, *Womanist Sass and Talk Back*, 37–38. See also Luz, *Matthew 18–20*, 340.

29. Masunda, "Running the Metaphor Blend with Jesus," 151.

30. Masunda, "Running the Metaphor Blend with Jesus," 152. Similarly, Kgatle argues that "[s]he used her courage, the urgency of her need, and her wisdom to transform barriers of race and gender into inclusiveness. As a Canaanite, unaccepted by the Jews, and as a woman in a male-oriented society, she extends Jesus' ministry to a wider population. The woman teaches about the universality of God's grace; that God's unconditional love is available to all, no exceptions," 606.

31. Ibita, "#Choosetochallenge," 193, 194. This challenge to Jesus is possible because Matthew has centered the Canaanite woman, a marginal character, "by means of active engagement," 192.

32. Levine with Blickenstaff, *Feminist Companion to Matthew*, 144.

(ὀλιγοπιστίαν, 17:20).[33] Interpreters and preachers rejoice in Jesus' acknowledgment or declaration of the woman's great faith and ignore or justify the disrespect and trauma to which the men in the story subject this desperate mother during the encounter.[34] For contemporary preachers, the acknowledgment of the mother's great faith and the subsequent healing of her daughter by Jesus is the "shout" or the good news in the text. No other character in Matthew exercises or is required to exercise great faith or endure the abuse that this woman does. Also, how do we understand great faith in light of Jesus's teaching that all one needs to perform an exorcism is the faith of a mustard seed (Matt 17:14–20)? Did Jesus rethink how he left things with the Canaanite woman or does his statement in chapter 17 further demonstrate Jesus's gender, ethnic, racial, and religious bias against the Canaanite woman and her people and the greater burden of respectability he imposed on her? It is difficult to know, but I encourage modern readers who read for freedom or liberation to expose and name the abuse to which the woman is subjected and consider such deconstructing work as good news.

Homiletic Overtures

This homily humanizes both the Canaanite mother and Jesus as it raises the consciousness of listeners about the fatal impact of implicit biases on individuals and communities who need quality health care. It demonstrates how the politics of respectability and inclusion function in the story and how they hinder our ability to bear witness to a God who shows no favoritism. God wants us to bear witness to and embody God's desire to meet human needs regardless of gender, ethnicity, race, religion and faith, sexuality, ability, or culture. Hope emerges despite the holler, amid

---

33. Gullotta ("Among Dogs and Disciples," 338) argues that "If the faith of the Canaanite woman reflects some sort of historical reality within the Matthean community, it would be that these sorts of Gentiles were unusual and their faith was so extraordinary, only because it was so rare."

34. Sechrest (*Race and Rhythm*) asserts that "the faith and humility of the Canaanite woman are exemplary of the greatest in the kingdom of heaven (15:28; cf. 18:1–4)," 81. Brown ("Gospel of Matthew," 106) states the "story is somewhat disturbing" due to Jesus's initial refusal to help, but he too emphasizes her humility and faith; like Sechrest, Brown likens her to the centurion as "outsider" that humble themselves. She is trying to secure the survival of her daughter and herself.

the horror. My sermon title is "When Her Humanity Is Not Enough: The Politics of Inclusion and Respectability."[35]

Homily

We live in a country rich in resources, but we have determined that much of our resources are best spent on war than on alleviating poverty or providing quality free education and universal health care. In the first century CE, healing or healers were not rare. Dr. Reza Aslan argues that Jesus was known as a healer who healed people without cost. Certainly, we get this impression in the Gospels. People in and beyond Galilee heard that Jesus was healing destitute folks. The Canaanite woman heard the stories of Jesus's miracles from her neighbors and believed them to be true. So, when he arrived in her region of the world, she seized the opportunity to ask him to heal her daughter.

The Canaanite woman is identified explicitly by her gender, ethnicity, and race. And Jesus's exclusion of her from the "lost sheep of the house of Israel," implies her religion is not Judaism. Two Canaanite women, Tamar and Rahab, are mentioned in Matthew's genealogy. Both Canaanite women mentioned are known to be associated with prostitution. The two women are included in the genealogy because they birthed male children whose fathers are Israelites. Their sons are related to David and Jesus. Ancient readers are likely to associate the Canaanite woman with Tamar and Rahab as prostitutes. In the Hebrew Bible, both prostitutes and Canaanites are negatively associated with dogs. The Israelites and Canaanites have a complex history as warring enemies who have also lived peaceably as neighbors and have inter-married. This complexity is reflected in Matthew, and particularly in this story of the desperate Canaanite mother.

This Canaanite mother's daughter is facing a life-threatening health emergency. She has come to the only urgent care, Emergency Room (ER), Intensive Care Unit (ICU), hospital to which she has access. Unfortunately, the first response to her plea for mercy is dead silence from Jesus, the attending physician: He did not answer her one word, the text says. We don't know how long the silence lasts, but silence in a life-and-death situation is at least an inhospitable and painful response. At most, the

---

35. This homily is a revision of the first sermon I preached at Druid Hills Presbyterian Church, Atlanta, Georgia, on January 14, 2024, almost eight months after I suffered a hemorrhagic stroke.

response can be fatal. A desperate need met with silence is emotional and psychological violence and can inflict further physical harm like high blood pressure. The response of the church to the many missing trafficked children in Atlanta and nationwide is largely silence. Former President Trump's initial silence about the COVID-19 virus caused many unnecessary disproportionate deaths among Black people. Silence is not a compassionate response in a death-dealing situation. I know that we often want to give Jesus a pass, but I wish we could let him be human. Let Jesus be as human as the folks to whom he is related in his genealogy—people like King David. This is not the behavior we want to imitate.

Some folks preach that Jesus was testing this woman. It is cruel to test a person during a life-threatening situation. The silence is broken by the cruel words that Jesus's disciples speak to him *in the woman's presence*: Send her away! The last woman I shared a hospital room with after my stroke in Emory's rehab hospital was a Kenyan American who had worked in hospice care but suffered a stroke while having brain surgery. She understandably did not want to move when the therapist would come early in the morning to get her out of bed. She had paralysis; I did not. But I too didn't want to get up the first couple days in the rehab hospital. A few of the nursing staff, and most of them were Black women, gathered outside my room, in hearing distance. I could hear them say that she is not ready to be here; she needs to be sent home. I was mortified that this conversation was happening in our hearing.

The Canaanite woman is anonymous, but for hermeneutical and homiletical purposes, permit me, at this moment, to name her *eimi-anthropé*, which in Greek means *I am a human being*. *Eimi-anthropé's* humanity and human needs are not sufficient for the disciples to advocate for her or to encourage Jesus to help her. Instead of advocating for the woman, they turn on her; it seems because of their biases. Dayna Matthew states that the "racial biases held by health care workers other than physicians have been ignored: nurses, physician extenders, technicians, and even medical staff workers such as receptions, administrators, and insurers are also likely unconscious contributors to health disparities."[36]

Finally, Jesus breaks his silence. But he does so to deny *Eimi-Anthropé*'s plea with words that are exclusive, dismissive, and lack compassion: "I was only sent to the lost sheep of the house of Israel." Initially, *Eimi-Anthropé* is denied healing for her daughter because of her race, ethnicity,

---

36. Matthew, *Just Medicine*, 37.

and religion. It is because of what she is *not* and not because of what *Eimi-Anthropé* is that she has yet to receive the response she needs and deserves. *Eimi-Anthropé* cannot and does not give up. She cannot give up, despite the silence, disrespect, biases, and discouragement that Jesus and his disciples subject her to. Perhaps, she came knowing the hurdles she would be required to jump to get access to healing for her daughter.

When I was ill, I resisted going to the ER until my pain was unbearable. At times I felt I was improving; perhaps it was a virus. Also, I'd been in the ER too many times with my mother when she was living. Often the silent waiting was long and the treatment by staff disappointing, to say the least. I thought, "I'm likely to die in an ER." But when the pain became intolerable, I called 911 and was taken to the ER where I waited for hours shivering in the cold air conditioning for tests and an almost empty ICU room at 3 a.m. on May 24, 2023. As I waited, brain cells were dying and the stroke was destroying my body. It wasn't until I attempted to sign the ER admittance papers that I discovered I could not write my name. Although I felt I would die in the ER, I endured to get the help I needed. *Eimi-Anthropé* had no choice but to endure the insults in the hope of getting the help she needed for her daughter. So, *Eimi-Anthropé* knelt on the ground and repeatedly begged "Master, help me!

She is not treated as an insider but as an outsider, despite the mention of Tamar and Rahab in the genealogy. Outsiders can be guests, but they are never viewed as permanent residents or insiders. They are recipients of hospitality, but hospitality is earned by good behavior that does not challenge the foundational documents of an institution or that guides individual behavior. Guests have less or no say in the menu served at the table or how the table is set. They may be given an illusion of having a say but only when their voices, votes, and concerns overlap, agree with, or are acceptable to insiders. The insiders are the dominant charted in the foundational tradition. The politics of inclusion guarantees neither parity nor fairness to outsiders, but racial, ethnic, gender, and religious inequality are disguised as niceness or hospitality. Dayna Matthew writes "when differences [in care] are related solely to race and ethnicity, they become 'disparities' and are unjustifiable."[37]

Eimi-Anthropé refuses to quit. She has heard from her neighbors that Jesus can heal her daughter. She cannot give up. Despite the way we have mistreated many immigrants, they keep showing up at our borders

---

37. Matthew, *Just Medicine*, 30.

because their situation is dire. Jesus's response to this desperate mother's continual pleading is an insulting metaphorical saying that re-emphasizes Israel's priority over *othered* peoples: "It is not fair to take the children's bread and cast it to the dogs (τοῖς κυναρίοις)." *Eimi-Anthropé* challenges Jesus's words, she talks back while demonstrating respectability. In her experience and imagination, the children, her people, are implicitly at the table and their pets eat the children's crumbs: "Indeed, Master, for even the pets (τά κυνάρια) eat the crumbs that fall from the table of their master." This mother uses the language of *pets* (τά κυνάρια) and not the language of *dogs* (τοῖς κυναρίοις) that Jesus used. And her short narrative excludes the children that are explicit in Jesus's saying. In her story, the children are implicitly present; it presumes that the children, and more particularly the Canaanite children, sit at the table eating as crumbs fall and the pets eat them. At the table of a compassionate master, the pets are permitted to eat *as* the children eat. *Eimi-Anthropé* envisions an empathetic master or patriarchal household where all living creatures in the home eat; they don't have to wait. Not a living creature goes without what they need to live.

Jesus's words do not imagine the dogs in the room at all, let alone at the table; food is cast to the dogs in the alley; they are scavengers. *Eimi-Anthropé* plays with Jesus's words and respectfully spits out a different rap that makes the small dogs the grammatical subjects of the sentence with agency; they "eat the crumbs that fall from their master's table." And at the table sit all the children; under the table sit hungry pets. Her scenario assumes the children recline at the table and the pets rest under the table. She does not see herself or her people as dogs.

Our need is sufficient to receive the compassion of God and should be enough for us to demonstrate compassion toward our fellow humans and other living creatures. The God who has and does work through Jesus also works in other humans who believe in a compassionate God—the God who has no name—who shows no favoritism.

Jesus does not say that he himself healed *eimi-Anthropé*'s daughter but he prays "let it be done as you desire." It is the omnipotent narrator who tells the reader that the Canaanite woman's daughter was healed that very hour. The *eimi-Anthropé woman* endured silence or indifference to her desperate plea for help, hurtful words that urged Jesus to dismiss her, and racial, gendered, religious, and ethnic bias. But *Eimi-Anthropé* never gave up on her daughter. And she never relinquished her own humanity!

The Politics of Respectability and the Politics of Inclusion are two sides of the same coin. To be included at the table, one must behave in ways that are acceptable to the dominant. Respectability is the price of inclusion, but inclusion does not promise equity or equality.

Jesus commends *Eimi Anthropé* for her great faith. But, why must she demonstrate great faith for her daughter to be healed? *Eimi-Anthropé's* daughter's human need should be sufficient for a loving God to heal her. *Eimi-Anthropé's* story is the only place we find the Greek words μεγάλη σου ἡ πίστις (her great faith) in Matthew's Gospel. In fact, this is the only place we find the phrase in the NT. What is great faith? How is it measured? Is it measured by the level of trauma and dehumanizing bias one must endure for health care? In Matt 17:14–20, Jesus tells his disciples if they had the faith the size of a mustard seed they, themselves, could have healed the boy possessed of a demon; they could move mountains. Why should *Eimi-Anthropé* demonstrate great faith before her daughter is healed? *Eimi-Anthropé's* daughter's human need should be sufficient for a loving, all-powerful God to heal her.

Eimi-Anthropé's story reminds me of the respectability politics that marginalized people are subjected to. Respectability politics protects access and control of resources by dominant groups. Outsiders are deemed unworthy of fair treatment and equal access unless they should behave impeccably, especially compared to others in their oppressed group. Respectability politics maintains that a Black person must be exceptional to be invited to the table; simultaneously, their exceptional status is threatening. They must behave exceptionally when encountering the police, and still, their survival is not guaranteed. A few criminals among an immigrant group seeking safety in America can be leveraged to blacken an entire ethnic group, banning them as criminals.

The good news, a reason to hoop in the holler, is that the biased oppressive behavior of Jesus and his disciples toward *Eimi Anthropé* and her daughter is unacceptable and should not be replicated among God's people. It is good news that God opposes the respectability tax imposed by the dominant. It is good news that *Eimi Anthropé* refuses to see herself and her people as dogs. It is good news that God is no respecter of religion, race, ethnicity, or gender! God shows no favoritism.

When I was in Emory's rehab hospital, I shared a room with one other stroke victim in the old wing of the hospital. Our room had no shower, just a sink and toilet. I re-learned how to wash myself from a small plastic tub. I didn't know that some hospital rooms in the newer section of the building had showers. One day, one of the part-time nurses named Georgia popped into my room at around 6 a.m., and asked, "Do you want a shower?" In shock, I replied, "How are you going to do that?" She said, "Don't worry about it; do you want one?" I said "Yes." Evidently, it was Georgia's habit and hers alone to treat three patients of various degrees of immobility to a hot shower whenever she was at Emory; she had a full-time job at another health facility. That was my lucky day. I felt renewed after the shower. Georgia was my Angel. God is like Georgia or Georgia is like God. God can and will meet human needs and alleviate human suffering through us. This is the God we must embody to transform the spaces we occupy homes. May we find a way to do our part, individually and collectively? Let God's people say "amen"! Let the people be the hope in the holler!

Conclusion

I have interpreted the story of the Canaanite woman's encounter with Jesus and his male disciples through the framework of womanist criticism that privileges the intersectional trauma that Black women and their communities face within the health care system. While Black women, and other marginalized and racialized people, may no longer generally be subjected to overt intersectional racism, covert or implicit biases based on race, gender, class, and sexuality impact the quality of care the Black women and other oppressed persons receive. And the politics of inclusion and respectability—hoisted upon the Canaanite woman's back and the shoulders of Black women—impose upon oppressed marginalized others the additional burden of behaving impeccably, with extraordinary faith, in order merely to sit at the table where they might access resources and care. In the homiletical transfer from interpretative analysis to sermon, I have attempted to humanize both the Canaanite woman and Jesus while praising the God who shows no favoritism.

11

The Colonial Christ, the Canaanite Woman, and the Crumbs of Insufficiency

Demetrius K. Williams

Introduction

The story of an unnamed, non-Israelite woman in Matt 15:21–28 (par. Mark 7:24–30) who encounters Jesus and his disciples is an interesting and, to some degree, quite concerning pericope that should heighten the attention of astute readers and perceptive interpreters to some important issues hidden (in plain sight?) within this narrative. This is the only passage in the New Testament where Jesus uses a pejorative racial-ethnic slur against someone who sincerely seeks his help. It has so disturbed some readers and interpreters that it has been termed a "hard saying of Jesus."[1] The passage opens with Jesus and his disciples entering the region of Tyre and Sidon which is gentile territory (the region of Phoenicia that is now part of the Roman province of Syria), after having debated with the Scribes and Pharisees over interpretive traditions of hand washing and internal vs. external purity (Matt 15:1–20). Upon their arrival in the gentile territory (among those who are ritually unclean and outside

---

1. See Kaiser, *Hard Sayings of the Bible*. The comments regarding Jesus's reference to the woman (and other gentiles) as "dogs" is found on pp. 424–25. The "hard saying" description is derived from John 6:60 when some of Jesus's disciples respond to his saying to "eat his flesh and drink his blood" that "This is a hard saying [KJV] or teaching" (15).

of the covenant promises of Israel), this non-Israelite woman comes to Jesus desperately begging and seeking an exorcism/healing for her demon-possessed daughter. Jesus, however, despite her sincere entreaties, surprisingly ignores her and the disciples seek to silence her and send her away empty. In addition to this, it is important to note that her racial-ethnic epithet in Matthew is essential to the interpretation of this passage because Mark describes her as "a gentile, of Syrophoenician origin" (Mark 7:26). Matthew, on the other hand, describes her as a "Canaanite" (Matt 15:22). Such indicators should give any reader interpretive pause—especially, a reader who seeks to proclaim this passage to a contemporary listening audience/congregation with suggestions for life-application. Such cues are important because one's hermeneutical perspective, methodology, and approach determine the possibilities, perspectives, and lenses for what might be seen, uncovered, and retrieved.[2] Such interpretive or hermeneutical insights related to land/geography, ethnicity, and gender, among several other things, were lost upon me when I attempted to preach this passage several decades ago in the early years of my ministry, which began in 1982 when I was licensed as a minister in a church affiliated with the National Baptist Convention, USA, Inc. (a historically founded African American Christian denomination).[3]

Hermeneutical Horizon

As a young, nineteen-year-old minister and preacher who by the end of my first semester in college in December of 1982 was licensed to preach, but had not taken any formal classes in preaching (homiletics), I had nevertheless inculcated intuitively a style of preaching in the Black church tradition that emphasized storytelling or what my elders in the church called "telling the story."[4] Having been raised and nurtured in the Black Baptist church, I recognized from hearing numerous sermons in the black preaching tradition that it is both important and imperative to have a theme or subject for the sermon that is equally interesting and compelling in order to garner the attention of the listening audience.

---

2. A text such as Kim's *How to Read the Gospels* can greatly assist interested readers to the numerous interpretive possibilities for this pericope and other Gospel passages, offering insights from feminist, womanist, minoritized, and postcolonial perspectives to name a few.

3. "The National Baptist Convention." https://www.nationalbaptist.com.

4. See Jones, "Telling the Story."

Therefore, when I preached this Matthean passage in the late 1980s, I titled the sermon, "Ain't Too Proud To Beg." This was a familiar title of a song popularized by The Temptations of 1960s Motown fame. I believed at that time that such a title to my sermon would resonate with the audience, many of whom had grown up listening to and loving the "Motown Sound." Thus, I attempted to "tell the story" or "re-tell" it "in terms and notions applicable to the present situation"[5] that emphasized the Canaanite woman's willingness to "beg and plead" earnestly through faith in Jesus for his sympathy until he acquiesced or relented and she received what she wanted—healing for her demon-possessed daughter.[6] In this early "hermeneutically naïve" attempt to preach this passage, my reading of scripture focused on the promotion and formation of personal Christian spirituality and piety. So, I wanted to use the story of the Canaanite woman's faith in the face of adversity as an example for the audience to emulate, demonstrating the same kind of willingness to beg and plead to Jesus, and to persist through faith until they, like the Canaanite woman, got what they needed—some spiritual blessing, a physical healing, financial security, a better job, salvation for a family member, a more fulfilling life, etc. Thus, with an evocative title and through creative storytelling ("telling the story") or the "retelling" of it as an "extended description or re-creation of a Bible story, usually one with which the congregation is already familiar, but which is now repeated with an additional or new insight,"[7] I attempted to preach this passage in this way, as John L. Thomas avers, "narration and explanation become interrelated."[8] To achieve this goal, Richard Ward advises that preachers read the biblical text carefully so that they might in their narrative preaching offer a retelling of the biblical story "critically from the standpoint of the listeners in order to find fresh perspectives from which to tell them [the story]."[9] Finally, Ka-

---

5. This is the focus of black narrative preaching as noted by Thomas, *Voices in the Wilderness*, 29.

6. I knew that the audience was familiar with a line in the lyrics of the song that stated: "If I have to beg and plead for your sympathy, I don't mind 'cause it means that much to me..." "Ain't Too Proud to Beg" was written by Norman Whitfield and Edward Holland Jr. in 1966 and appeared on the Temptations album "Getting Ready," https://www.google.com/search?client=safari&rls=en&q=temptations+ain%27t+too+proud+to+beg+lyrics&ie=UTF-8&oe=UTF-8.

7. This is how Lyndrey A. Niles describes "telling the story" in black preaching. See Lyndrey, "Rhetorical Characteristics of Traditional Black Preaching," 47.

8. Thomas, *Voices in the Wilderness*, 30.

9. Ward, *Speaking of the Holy*, 99.

tie Cannon reminds us that "telling the story" in black preaching has a familiar rhetorical structure: "Black preaching is a narrative that exhibits all of the formal structures of rhetorical pros, such as text, title, introduction, proposition, body, and conclusion."[10] Several of these elements were a part of my first attempt at preaching this passage.

I sought, therefore, in this sermon to employ familiar and important features of black preaching to emphasize that spiritual transformation does not come without some struggle and persistence, not unlike that of the patriarch Jacob (in Gen 32:22–32) who wrestled with the angel and would not let the angel go until he received a blessing.[11] This untaught but culturally inculcated theological and hermeneutical perspective *trained my eye* to see within this text issues from an angle of personal spiritual struggle, possibilities for individual transformation, and piety formation while ignoring other issues that were in "plain sight"—issues like gender, disproportionate power relations, racial-ethnic marginalization, religious triumphalism, land (geography), colonialism, empire, ethnicity, and power. My unreflective and untrained hermeneutical gaze and theological perspective offered no critical analyses like those mentioned above, so it is no wonder that it offered no social analysis either, and thus blinded me to the necessity of addressing pressing social and political issues of concern for my community.

Although I had not taken a class on preaching or hermeneutics but had imbibed and inherited an intuitive ecclesial and cultural hermeneutical perspective, it is undeniable that "Every preacher preaches out of an articulated perspective. The perspective might be methodological, theoretical, philosophical, cultural, sociological, or theological."[12] My unarticulated theological and cultural hermeneutical perspective had been nurtured in a stream of black preaching that was imaginatively powerful, rhetorically eloquent, and organically creative to be sure, but was also theologically and socially conservative. My preaching might fall within the category of "traditionalist preaching" as described by John Thomas who states: "Preaching in this stream looks to the Bible as

---

10. Cannon, "Womanist Interpretation and Preaching," 115.

11. Like my message on the Canaanite woman, I preached this Genesis passage several years ago from the title, "Wrestling for a Blessing" to underscore the faith, struggle, and tenacity required for spiritual transformation.

12. Gibson and Kim, *Homiletics and Hermeneutics*, xi. The authors are interested in the presuppositions behind one's theology of preaching, indictive of their conservative Evangelical perspective.

the sole source for hope and inspiration. The primacy of Scripture is a given."[13] He goes on to suggest that a defense of traditional values (looking to "the good ole' days"), respect for authority (of tradition and scriptures), and themes of repentance feature significantly in this homiletic stream. Narrative preaching in this theological and homiletical stream is designed primarily to help navigate the community through the dark and difficult experiences of life.[14] The difficult life experiences, however, are usually addressed in terms of garnering personal spiritual power to overcome such difficulties without necessarily addressing them, in addition, socially or politically.

What is also clear to me is that my preaching and hermeneutical perspective in the traditionalist theological and homiletical stream sought primarily to emphasize and celebrate the work and person of Jesus; his love for the poor and downtrodden; and his power to save, heal, and deliver. In this preaching tradition, if Jesus is not the central focus and "hero" of every message, it is not the gospel. While this preaching focus remains relevant for me, to suggest that Jesus could have been biased or bigoted toward the Canaanite woman in this passage was a moot point at that time. Calling the Canaanite woman a "dog" had to be explained in such a way that exonerated Jesus from any blame or criticism. In my experience and inculcation of black preaching, moreover, one could say that the Black church has more of a "Jesusology" than a "Christology." This Jesus-centric focus concentrated more on the life and "humanness" of Jesus who preached to the poor and needy, and demonstrated his power to heal in his earthly ministry, rather than on the high Christology of many mainstream churches wherein "the Christ" is seen more in his cosmic role as celestial ruler of the universe (see Eph 6:12). In any case, the focus on Jesus as a healer and deliverer of the poor and downtrodden did not always translate into messages inspiring social activism or the offering of critical social analyses in sermons, but was customarily relegated to the personal and spiritual spheres of the individual.[15] For this reason, although the Black Church's preaching tradition is not and has not ever been monolithic,[16] it is accurate to say that it has been largely "orthodox" in that the theology it espouses holds to many of the tenets

---

13. Thomas, *Voices in the Wilderness*, 104.
14. Thomas, *Voices in the Wilderness*, 104–7.
15. Blount, "A Tale of Too Many Options."
16. See Thomas, *Introduction to the Practice of African American Preaching*.

that Christians have generally believed,[17] even if "Jesusology" has been a central homiletical focus in several streams of its preaching traditions. In many ways, its theology/Jesusology has also been (and remains in many respects) conservative—theologically and socially—which determines what one sees or looks for when interpreting or preaching a Biblical passage like Matt 15:21–28 on the Canaanite woman. Perhaps, had I been aware of more critical hermeneutical approaches at that time, I might have been alerted to some interesting insights in this pericope some of which will be explored in the following section.

Interpretation

This pericope is placed between two significant narrative events. Matthew, following Mark's literary sequence, connects the encounter with the Canaanite woman to the feeding miracles, which have strong Eucharistic overtones but have been toned down in Mark (Mark 6:30–44; 8:1–9; Matt 14:13–21; 15:32–39). The feeding motif is, therefore, highlighted in the encounter with the Canaanite woman. Walter Wessell suggests another reason for its placement, "It seems to be a natural sequence to be proceeding an incident in which Jesus breaks with the Jewish oral law and particularly the law of ceremonial cleanness."[18] So, Matthew follows Mark and places the incident after a feeding miracle and disputes with religious leaders about ritual purity.[19] It seems that Matthew wants to contrast the teachers of the law, the scribes and Pharisees—who belong to the covenant people but take offense at the conduct of Jesus and his disciples regarding ritual purity, challenge his authority, and lack understanding of the scriptures and how they relate to Jesus— to a non-Israelite individual, a Canaanite woman. This woman is interestingly a descendent of Israel's ancient enemies with no claim to the blessings, inclusion into covenant membership, or hopeful expectations of Israel's Messiah.[20] A believing gentile, therefore, poses a sharp contrast to un-

---

17. McCaulley, *Reading While Black*, 5. Keisha Krumm, a grassroots organizer and social justice worker, recalls a pastor remarking during a meeting of the Industrial Areas Foundation (IAF) in 2016: "What we fail to understand is that Black folks are like White evangelicals when it comes to justice." See Krumm, *Our Birthright*, 2.

18. Wessell, "Mark," 681.

19. Hare, *Matthew*, 178.

20. Carson, "Matthew," 353.

believing Pharisees and scribes from Jerusalem.[21] For this reason, it has been suggested that these verses guide Matthew's Jewish church and its relation to gentiles.[22] "The *Sitz im Leben* of this story is not missionary preaching to the gentiles as such," according to Schüssler Fiorenza, "but the inner-Christian debate over the mission to pagans and table sharing between them and Jewish Christians."[23] The story, therefore, attempts to ground the gentile mission in the ministry of Jesus.[24] Accordingly, Douglas Hare suggests that Matthew, writing for a church that was becoming an increasingly gentile church, wanted to protect Jewish Christians from ridicule for adherence to the Jewish lifestyle.[25]

In any event, Jesus's encounter with gentiles did not begin with the Canaanite woman. Earlier in his ministry, he was approached by a Roman centurion who sought healing for his beloved servant (Matt 8:5–13). Musa Dube notes that, "The divergent receptions accorded to the centurion and the Canaanite woman reflect the imperial and patriarchal currents at work in Matthew."[26] Such currents can be clearly perceived when the two encounters are compared. In both stories, a gentile individual approaches Jesus for healing for another person: one (a male) for a servant and the other (a female) for a daughter. Jesus speaks directly to and positively with the male Roman centurion, even offering to come to his home to perform the requested healing (which was normally prohibited).[27] But the centurion asks Jesus to "only speak the word, and my servant will be healed" (Matt 8:8), and his request was summarily granted. The centurion recognized Jesus as a man of authority, equal to his, and this recognition by the centurion seemed to resonate with him. So, Jesus did not seem to have trouble recognizing male power dynamics when he healed the centurion's servant. Although the centurion was a gentile, it must be remembered that he was Roman—a respected member of a powerful gentile group! The Canaanite woman, on the

21. Hare, *Matthew*, 179.

22. Carson suggests that "the accent falls on the question of mission to Gentiles" ("Matthew," 323). So also, Williamson, *Mark*, 137, and Wessell, "Mark," 682.

23. Schüssler Fiorenza, *In Memory of Her*, 137. See Gal 2:11–14, where Paul confronts Cephas (Peter) over this very issue.

24. Williamson, *Mark*, 13.

25. Hare, *Matthew*, 173.

26. Dube, *Postcolonial Feminist Interpretation*, 132.

27. For example, in Acts 10:28 where Peter is at the home of a centurion named Cornelius, the text states: "You yourselves know that it is unlawful for a Jew to associate with or to visit a Gentile."

other hand, was from a despised group and therefore was compelled to "beg and plead." Moreover, Jesus initially ignores her, and when he does speak, he uses a pejorative slur against her. What might Matthew's narrative agenda indicate to the reader regarding Jesus's two encounters with these gentiles? It appears to be the case, according to Dube that "mission to the nations is foreshadowed not by featuring Greek characters, who were never mythologized as conquest targets of Israel. Instead, there is an option to feature a Canaanite, a character, whose very image alludes to those who must be conquered and dispossessed."[28]

Thus, when the woman whom Matthew identifies as "a Canaanite" comes out to the border of Tyre and Sidon,[29] she is someone whom Matthew intimates that Jews do not customarily associate with because of historical animus between the two peoples.[30] Perhaps even more, because Matthew's framing hermeneutic "presupposes the Hebrew foundation myth of promised land," which embodies imperialist values, the ancient land of Canaan, which the woman represents, is an ideologically loaded geographical marker. Again, according to Dube, "Land and people are closely interconnected. Different lands have come to largely symbolize different people, and the cultural narratives ascribed to them. Geography is therefore not just a physical body, but a page of intrinsically entwined, narrative of power and disempowerment."[31] The Canaanite woman's body becomes the indicator upon which "the identity desires of the colonizer, and the colonized too, are written and can be read."[32] Historically, imperial ideologies employ gender relations to express ideas of subordination and domination with women becoming markers of different lands and cultures. Because people of foreign lands can be portrayed as inferior in all respects, while the writer's race is bestowed all that represents decency and excellence, the Canaanite woman is not accorded the same "respect" as the centurion.[33]

Unlike the portrayal of the Roman centurion, then, who simply asks Jesus for help, the Canaanite woman must beg and kneel, and even employ

---

28. Dube, *Postcolonial Feminist Interpretation*, 148.

29. Jesus may not have entered the region, but the woman came out to him on the border (Carson, "Matthew," 354).

30. For example, Ezra 9:1–2 states that Israel should not associate with Canaanites, among several other nations.

31. Dube, *Postcolonial Feminist Interpretation*, 128, 145, 146.

32. Dube, *Postcolonial Feminist Interpretation*, 73.

33. Dube, *Postcolonial Feminist Interpretation*, 73, 145.

messianic titles to garner Jesus's attention: "Have mercy on me Lord, son of David; my daughter is tormented by a demon."[34] Instead of Jesus responding to her, she gets an initial response from his disciples who shout, "Send her away, for she keeps shouting after us" (v. 22). The term, "send her away" (Gk. *apoluson*) can alternatively mean to "loose her," which could be the disciples' request for Jesus to perform the miracle for her.[35] D. A. Carson asserts that "sending her away" with her request granted is the only "interpretation [that] makes sense because verse 24 gives a reason for Jesus not helping her rather than for not sending her away."[36] Jesus, moreover, informs the disciples that he was "only sent to the last sheep of the house of Israel." Jesus's instructions to the disciples when they were sent out in Matt 10:6 was that they should "Go nowhere among the Gentiles or enter a town of the Samaritans, but rather go to the lost sheep of the house of Israel." But a time is coming when the mission to the gentiles would be undertaken by the church (Matt 28:18–20). For now, the disciples must not actively engage in such an enterprise.

Perhaps because of her more demonstrative entreaties (kneeling and imploring), Jesus then, speaks directly to the woman and says: "It is not fair to take the children's food (bread) and throw it to the dogs," referring to her and other gentiles in an undeniably pejorative manner. Matthew does not include Mark's concession to "Let the children be fed first" (Mark 7:27), possibly to intensify the impact of Jesus's statement on this despised individual. The Canaanite woman responds, moreover, "Yes Lord, yet even the dogs eat the crumbs that fall from their master's table" (v. 27. Unlike Mark's rendering, "children's table"). Carson asserts that "She does not argue that her needs make her an exception or that she has a right to Israel's covenant mercies. She simply asked for help. The dog that she is."[37] While Carson's last phrase ("The dog that she is")—can be read as ironic; that is, that she does not deny the *Jewish perception* of her and her status. Yet it can still be troubling for marginal readers because such a slur is not problematized by many mainline interpreters but accepted without question. "[Y]et, at least," Carson continues, "she may be allowed to receive a crumb of the uncovenanted merits

---

34. Interestingly Mark has "unclean spirit" (*daimonion*, 7:25) but Matthew has intensified her condition as demonic possession (*kakos diamonizetai*, 15:22).

35. Gale, "Matthew," 29.

36. Carson, "Matthew," 354.

37. Carson, "Matthew," 355.

of God" because "The faith that simply seeks mercy is honored."[38] In a similar vein, Douglas Hare states: "Matthew probably sees her humility as a necessary ingredient to her faith; it was appropriate that she acknowledged the historical (and therefore theological) priority of God's election of Israel."[39] Interpretive remarks such as these are indicative of a conservative hermeneutic that precludes any attempt to read against the grain. This evangelical interpretive perspective does not value a more transgressive assessment of this encounter. Moving more toward a more unconventional and progressive perspective, it could be noted that "the woman acknowledges her marginal position but still insists on her rights."[40] Unlike the passive portrayal of the woman in conservative hermeneutics, a more transgressive reading sees her actions as assertive and challenging. Jesus's argument that the children's (Israel's) bread should not be taken from them and given to the dogs (gentiles) is wittily countered by the woman who insists that there is enough food and room at the abundant messianic table of inclusive community.[41]

The woman, therefore, in our estimation, is a heroine who believes and asserts that she deserves Jesus's healing for her daughter.[42] And it turns out that "the major theologian and spokesperson for table sharing with gentiles is a woman. As distinct from other controversial dialogues Jesus does not have the last word. Rather the woman's argument prevails over that of Jesus . . . the woman won the contest because Jesus convinced by her argument, liberates her daughter from the demon."[43] For this reason, the woman "shares the stage with Jesus"[44] in a way that the centurion does not. Her daughter, as her future, is in bondage to evil and for this reason, she is tenacious and will not give up until she gets what she asks for because her future depends on it. The story should remind us that those who suffer from the oppressive forces of society must be bold and assertive in their quest for the transformation

38. Carson, "Matthew," 355–56.
39. Hare, *Matthew*, 179.
40. Gale, "Matthew," 29.
41. Schüssler Fiorenza, *In Memory of Her*, 138.
42. This idea is different from Dube who says, "The woman is not a heroine, but a victim of patriarchal and imperial ideology." Dube, *Postcolonial Feminist Interpretation*, 170. While I agree that the woman is a victim of imperial patriarchy, her action can be read as heroic in that she confronts such and gets what she needs for her daughter.
43. Schüssler Fiorenza, *In Memory of Her*, 137.
44. Williamson, *Mark*, 137.

of their circumstance. This is why "The woman is not content to be ignored because she is convinced that her daughter deserves to be given a chance at living a normal productive life."[45]

Homiletic Overtures

In my earlier attempt to interpret this passage many years ago, my reading of scripture (hermeneutic) focused on the promotion and formation of Christian piety filtered through my unarticulated theological-cultural hermeneutic. This perspective trained my eye to see issues from this angle while ignoring others that were in plain view: issues like gender, power relations, racial-ethnic marginalization, religious triumphalism, etc. Gaining newer hermeneutical perspectives and interpretive methods, demonstrated in a limited manner in the exegesis, expanded my engagement with the biblical text and broadened my vision of interpretive possibilities. While not explicit in the exegesis, African American biblical interpretation (hermeneutics) helped me to see race and class oppressions in the struggle for freedom and equality, but not as much as the gender dynamics in the text. It was feminist and womanist hermeneutics that helped me to see more clearly how Matthew's redaction of the story encapsulates an encounter between Jesus and "a Canaanite woman" that is rich with implications for understanding power dynamics, gender inequities, marginalization, race and ethnicity, identity, and the potential for liberation. Through the lens of postcolonial/decolonial hermeneutics, this passage unveils for me the dynamics of land possession, colonialism, and empire, in addition to layers of meaning that highlight the resilience and agency of marginalized voices in the text. All these hermeneutical approaches challenge conventional interpretations of Matthew's account of Jesus's encounter with an unnamed Canaanite woman (Matt 15:21–28) and offer more transgressive readings from that of traditional approaches.

If I were to preach this Matthean passage today, my hermeneutical lens and approach to interpretation would be informed by womanist and postcolonial analyses because this pericope is reminiscent of European Christian colonial encounters with indigenous and native "others," especially with indigenous women, as colonizers entered "alien" territories and cultural spaces touting their possession of cultural resources, knowledge, and religious power. The "others" who occupied the lowest rung of the

---

45. Hare, *Matthew*, 179.

European racial hierarchy were African-descended peoples. Encouraging this colonizing enterprise was a "colonial Christ" constructed as the celestial epitome of European expansionists' newly conceived self-image as White, chosen, and destined to rule the "others" of the world. It is possible to see through the lens of this Matthean passage that European colonialism colluded with Christianity to produce a White colonial savior figure who was content to welcome "others" into the fold, but only if they accepted a subordinate status, partial inclusion, and a pejorative designation ("dogs"/savages/heathens): in short, an identity as an inferior and perpetual "other." The colonizer's Christ encourages a faith that educates "others" to be content with the crumbs that fall from the master's (the colonizer's) table, offering few avenues for wholeness; only bits and pieces that leave subordinated "others" in a state of perpetual insufficiency.

A womanist and postcolonial optic, therefore, reads Jesus's encounter with the Canaanite woman as an idealized colonial missionary paradigm reflective of a normalized colonial legacy that continues to this day as epitomized in White evangelical Christianity's response to the pleas for justice by people of color in the U.S., which are met with silence, ambivalence, and annoyance. The continued ideation of the White colonial Christ thereby perpetuates practices that "others" people of color and attempts to convince them to be content with "crumbs," which ultimately retains the power of White supremacy and White privilege. This colonial Christ is insufficient to address the need for justice for people of color because the Christ of colonial encounters was not conceived and created to address the needs and concerns of colonial subjects.[46] This Christ "remains silent" in the face of the woman's initial plea for help for her child, and the followers of the colonial Christ (European disciples of colonial ventures and empire) desire to send the woman way (and all other "others") or at best, keep her at bay. When the woman's persistent plea is addressed, the colonial Christ responds only when the woman is self-deprecating and willing to accept an insulting identification with "dogs" (subordinated, inferior others). Her alterity is demonstrated with the offer of crumbs from the "master's table" (the dominant group). Only then can she receive "partial acceptance" into the religion of the dominant group because of her willingness to accept faith in the colonial Christ, but she should not expect or anticipate that her material condition will

---

46. Western mission disregarded the reality of the colonized. Cho, "Matthew," 65.

be transformed.[47] Such transgressive views and outlooks inform my new hermeneutical perspective and would find welcome resonance in my sermon on the Canaanite woman if preached today.

Based on the hermeneutical horizons of postcolonial and womanist hermeneutics, it has become clearer how one might preach this passage differently from traditional interpretations. As noted above, in examining Matt 15:21–28 through a postcolonial and womanist lens, parallels with colonial dynamics, gender, race, and power become evident. The scene opens with Jesus withdrawing to the region of Tyre and Sidon, stepping outside the familiar confines of his Jewish homeland into the territory of the gentiles. Here, he encounters a Canaanite woman, a member of a marginalized and despised racial group in Jewish society. The encounter between Jesus and the Canaanite woman mirrors colonial interactions. The socio-political landscape of first-century Palestine provides a crucial context, characterized by power differentials, with marginalized communities such as women and non-Jews experiencing systemic oppression. The Canaanite woman, situated at the intersection of multiple marginalized identities, stands as a potent symbol of resistance against these structures of domination. Colonialism, with its imposition of cultural hegemony and hierarchical power structures, echoes throughout the biblical narrative. The encounter between Jesus and the Canaanite woman exemplifies a colonial dynamic, with Jesus initially embodying the role of the colonizer, asserting his superiority over the woman by referring to her as a "dog."

At first glance, Jesus's response to the woman seems harsh and dismissive, as he initially ignores her cries for help. When pressed by his disciples to send her away, Jesus responds (to the disciples it seems) with a dehumanizing comparison, referring to her as a "dog." This language reflects the prevailing attitudes of the time, where some Jews viewed gentiles as unclean and unworthy of God's grace. Yet, the woman's response is one of profound resistance and persistence. Despite being labeled an outsider, she refuses to accept her marginalized status and boldly confronts Jesus, pleading for mercy for her daughter. Her unwavering faithful defiance and undeterred determination seem to even challenge Jesus to expand his own understanding of the scope of God's love and grace. The woman's witty response to Jesus's quip about taking the children's bread and giving it to dogs disrupts the power dynamic, reclaiming her

---

47. "Western foreign mission became in effect, spiritual imperialism." Cho, "Matthew," 64, referencing Song, *Christian Mission in Reconstruction*, 10.

agency as she challenges Jesus's assumptions. She refuses to accept her marginalized status, asserting her humanity and dignity, demanding recognition and "justice" for herself, and healing for her daughter. A womanist reading of this passage might foreground the intersectionality of the woman's identity, acknowledging the unique oppressions she faces as both a woman and a member of a marginalized ethnic group. Her boldness in confronting Jesus, moreover, reflects the strength and resilience of black and brown women who resist oppression and reclaim their voices in spaces dominated by patriarchal, male/White supremacist, and colonial rhetorics and ideologies. Furthermore, the woman's insistence on justice (healing) for her daughter underscores the maternal instinct and fierce love that drive women of color to fight for the well-being and liberation of their children *and* communities, even in the face of systemic injustice. In claiming her human dignity and liberation, the Canaanite woman compels Jesus to recognize her worth (exemplified in the woman's demonstration of faith-laden resistance) and he grants her request, revealing a shift from a stance of exclusion to one of inclusion and solidarity. Her actions inform the reader of the value of confronting biases, power, and privilege, and the work of actively dismantling systems of oppression that dehumanize and marginalize others.

In reimagining Matt 15:21–28 through postcolonial and womanist hermeneutics and perspectives, we unearth a narrative of resistance, resilience, and liberation that speaks powerfully to contemporary struggles for justice and equality. Through our engagement with this text from broadened hermeneutical perspectives, we can be inspired to stand in solidarity with the marginalized, amplifying their voices and working towards a world where all are recognized and valued as equals in the eyes of the divine. Through this encounter, the Canaanite woman inspires Jesus to dismantle the barriers of ethnicity, gender, and social status, affirming the inherent worth and dignity of all people. This unnamed, non-Israelite woman was not just a passive recipient of mercy and grace. She offered a clever and critical challenge to Jesus and the disciples which ultimately changed the course of Jesus's ministry. Before his encounter with the Canaanite woman, Jesus proclaimed nationalist sentiments ("I was sent only to the lost sheep of the house of Israel"), but after his encounter with her, he widened the scope of his mission to include marginalized and despised "others." This hermeneutical framework lays the foundation for a more reflective and responsible sermon.

Based on the homiletic overtures above, I will preach "The Defiant Daughter of Canaan." The intended or imagined audience for this sermon is a racially and culturally diverse one, with female and male clergy, and lay delegates at a regional denominational meeting of American Baptist Churches in my home state of Wisconsin. ABC WI consists of 55 cooperating churches: 20 African American congregations, 4 Hispanic congregations, 7 Asian congregations (1 Chinese, 3 Chin, 2 Karen, and 1 Burmese-speaking multi-ethnic congregation), 1 historically Native American (Ho-Chunk) congregation, 22 Euro-American congregations, and 1 multicultural congregation, where English, Karen, Mandarin, Spanish, and Telagu are spoken in worship together. Of the 22 Euro-American churches, two are welcoming and affirming congregations. Such an audience and setting are reflective of my actual preaching and teaching experiences in the past.

Homily

I would like to share with you today from the Gospel of Matthew 15:21–28 on the Canaanite woman who acted with determination to intercede on behalf of her demon-possessed daughter. Considering her impressive and commendable insolence, I'd like to preach on the subject, "The Defiant Daughter of Canaan."

A cursory reading of this passage offers a characterization of the Canaanite woman as far from defiant, far from a rebellious, bold, insolent individual. She abruptly enters the narrative scene as Jesus and his disciples enter her geographical locale of Tyre and Sidon and she pleads, crying out, "Have mercy on me Lord, Son of David; my daughter is tormented by a demon" (v. 22). She appears desperate and distraught, not defiant. When Jesus ignores her, "did not answer her at all," the text says, the disciples implore him to "send her away!" She is persistent but far from insolent or defiant. Then, when Jesus does speak, whether to her or the disciples is not clear in the text, he nevertheless seems indifferent and insensitive: "I was sent only to the lost sheep of the house of Israel" (v. 24). She then kneels before Jesus and pleads, "Lord, help me." Perhaps we'll also need the Lord to help us see the defiance in her encounter. It will certainly require some reframing of our interpretive perspectives and a reconsideration of received interpretive outlooks and reading traditions.

This is what I've had to do to understand this passage differently and relevantly for our contemporary world because I view the encounter between Jesus and the Canaanite woman as analogous to colonial interactions with indigenous "others." Jesus and his disciples move outside familiar Jewish territory into the non-Jewish region of gentile inhabitants where they encounter a "Canaanite woman," a member of a marginalized and despised racial group in Jewish society. Matthew offers this characterization of the woman's identity that is quite different from Mark who describes her as "gentile/Greek of Syrophoenician origin." Matthew, with a slight intertextual flourish that recalls for astute readers the Exodus-Promised-Land narrative of the Israelite invasion of the land of Canaan, describes her as one who is a "Canaanite." Matthew's intertextual flourish marks the woman as a descendant of a people who were invaded, annihilated, and their land colonized by the Israelite/Jewish predecessors of Jesus and the disciples. Matthew's slight textual move also provides crucial context for unpacking power differentials in which marginalized persons and their communities experience systemic oppression. The Canaanite woman is therefore situated at the axis of multiple marginalized identities: a woman, a foreigner, and a member of a colonized and annihilated people. Viewed from this perspective, she stands as a compelling symbol of resistance against the multiple structures of domination.

This perspective, to me, exemplifies a colonial dynamic in which Jesus, at least initially, embodies the role of the colonizer, ignoring her entreaties and asserting his power and superiority over the woman by referring to her and her people as "dogs." It may be difficult to admit that Jesus's response to the woman seems harsh and dismissive, as he ignores her cries for help and refers to her as a "dog." It is extremely important, therefore, that we are open to the challenges of different reading and interpretive perspectives that will push many of us and our congregations to the limit, but such growing pains are necessary for progress and the realization of a just and equitable future for the church and society. To be sure, our views and understandings of Jesus might be challenged also because, in our sermons and homilies, Jesus is usually the hero, the central figure of liberating sayings, acts, and actions. But in this reading that I'm offering, perhaps the woman is the "heroine," the central figure whose words and actions are notable, as Jesus himself recognized: "Woman, you have great faith! Your request is granted" (v. 28). The Canaanite woman's actions and words exemplify profound faith, persistence, *and* defiance.

Her defiance is particularly demonstrated when Jesus says, "It is not fair to take the children's food and throw it to the dogs" (v. 24). But she responds, "Yes, Lord, yet even the dogs eat the crumbs that fall from their masters' table" (v. 27). Her response indicates to me that despite being labeled an outsider, she refuses to accept this marginalized status and boldly confronts Jesus's assessment of her outsider status. Her unwavering faithful defiance and undeterred determination challenge Jesus to expand his own understanding of the scope of God's love and grace. The woman's clever response to Jesus's statement disrupts the power dynamic, reclaiming her agency as she challenges Jesus's assumptions. She refuses to accept a marginalized status and asserts her humanity and dignity, demanding recognition and "justice" for herself and healing for her daughter. Furthermore, the woman's insistence on justice (healing) for her daughter underscores her fierce love that drives marginalized women to defiant acts as they fight for the well-being and liberation of their children and communities in the face of systemic injustice. In claiming her human dignity and liberation, the Canaanite woman compels Jesus to recognize her worth. He did not seem to have trouble recognizing male power dynamics when he healed the centurion's servant (Matt 8:5–13), although he too was a gentile (but he was Roman—a respected member of a powerful gentile group)! Jesus even offered to come to his home to do so. But the centurion asked him to "only speak the word, and my servant will be healed" (Matt 8:8) and his request was granted. The centurion did not have to "beg and plead" as did the Canaanite woman. But her begging and pleading led eventually to faith-filled defiance. She is not only defiant, but I would add that she is "sassy" in her response and behavior. The womanist scholar and preacher Mitzi Smith understands her response to Jesus as "sass," a manner of response embodying bold speech.[48] Sass is the language of resistance. This bold, impudent, and feisty speech is important for marginalized communities, Smith asserts because it offers a sense and means of maintaining their human agency and dignity. She cannot get what she needs if she does not "speak up" for herself and her daughter. Jesus seems to insult her and her people, so she "claps back"[49] at his apparent insult in referring to them and her as "dogs." Because of her faith-filled defiance, Jesus grants her request, revealing a shift from a stance of exclusion to one of inclusion and solidarity. Her actions on

---

48. Smith, *Womanist Sass and Talk Back*, 29.

49. According to dictionary.com, clap back is defined as "to quickly answer or criticize someone who has criticized, insulted, or annoyed you."

behalf of her child inform us of the value of confronting biases, power, and privilege, and that we should also work to actively dismantle systems of oppression that dehumanize and marginalize others.

Reflecting on this passage, we might be confronted with uncomfortable truths about our own biases and prejudices. How often do we, like the disciples, seek to silence the voices of those deemed "other" in our society? How often do we fail to recognize the humanity and worth of those who differ from us? In the example of the Canaanite woman and Jesus who was willing to respond positively to her defiant words, we find hope and inspiration to broaden the scope of our own understanding around notions of inclusion. This passage can inspire us to emulate the Canaanite woman's defiance, courage, and persistence, advocating for justice and inclusion for all God's children. Like Jesus, we must be willing to step outside our comfort zones, listen to and engage with those on the margins, and work tirelessly for a world where all are welcomed and embraced as beloved children of God. AMEN!

Conclusion

I have attempted to chart and indicate through my own personal homiletical journey that the move towards a more transgressive reading of the Bible and defiant homiletic based upon non-traditional hermeneutical perspectives is not an easy one. It requires reading broadly with an open mind and heart, both of which will most likely be challenged. Nevertheless, such growing pains are necessary for preachers to advance the church's commitment to "do justice and love mercy." This will require reading the Bible from various perspectives that challenge us to think more critically and to preach more "transgressively" for the sake of creating a more just and inclusive world.

12

The Matthean Jesus and the Canaanite Blues

HUGH R. PAGE JR.

Introduction

A Sense of Gratitude and Urgency

IN WRITING THIS ESSAY, I experience a deep sense of both gratitude and urgency. The former derives from the invitation to be part of a cutting-edge project with esteemed colleagues and the serendipity of being asked to offer reflections on Matt 15:21–28 as a scholar of the Hebrew Bible and the ancient Near East. The latter grows out of my realization that fall 2024 marks the fortieth anniversary of my commencing doctoral studies. I began that phase of my professional journey neither "fresh faced" nor *naïve*. Ordained several years earlier and weathered by Anglicanism's peculiar brand of racialized socialization in the Episcopal Church, I had no illusions about the hardships of service within that body or the so-called "joys" of graduate education.[1] This is, in many respects, a "full circle" moment. Health, longevity, and visibility within the ecclesial and academic arenas for BIPOC (Black,

---

1. For a contemporary take on the challenge of inclusion in The Episcopal Church for African-Americans, see Fisher-Stewart, *Black and Episcopalian*. On the phenomenon of weathering, see Geronimus, *Weathering*.

Indigenous, People of Color) scholars are not promised. I consider myself fortunate to have advanced thus far and survived this long, with my physical health and overall well-being relatively intact.

My ruminations on this passage take place while wrapping up old projects, archiving personal papers, "thinning out" my library, gathering materials for a *memoir*, and considering what my next steps—as scholar and cleric—might entail. I agreed to offer these "transgressive" musings because such is the kind of interpretive foray that "matters," that promises in some way to "make a difference." It is so far outside of what many of my colleagues would likely consider mainstream that I anticipate receiving little to no recognition for it. I have made peace with that reality because the value of hermeneutical interventions of this kind has never been clearer to me. Having engaged the Bible (as Scripture) *via* ruminations on lectionary passages for the purpose of preaching; and (as a multifaceted anthology) continuing my own work on Early Hebrew Poetry and other topics, I recognize that exegetical "business as usual" is not appropriate at a time when critical thinking about texts and traditions has become a target for weaponized assessment and when intellectual labor in service to freedom and democracy is so crucial.

Therefore, I offer the following "experimental encounter" with Matt 15:21–28 as a model for the kind of expansive, liberative, and "responsibly playful" approaches we might promote among specialist and lay audiences—ways of "reading" that eschew despair and generate resistance to structures that dehumanize and disempower. I do so while embracing not only my identity as priest and academic, but also as a child of the African Diaspora who willingly embraces the richly textured cosmologies and embodied epistemologies of the American Blues Tradition as essential elements in all endeavors. This essay embodies the cadences of two genres that are mainstays for my work in these arenas: the twenty-minute conference paper and the seven-minute homily. Consider it a succinct "first word"—an opening "verse"—for a much longer interpretive "song" I trust others will continue to craft and perform.

Hermeneutical Horizon

By today's cultural competency standards, the encounter between Jesus and a nameless Canaanite woman in Matt 15:21–28 is difficult to abide by. Its vision of Jesus's mission is narrowly conceived. Its conception of those living in the region of Tyre and Sidon is anything but salutary (15:26). Moreover, its effort to highlight this unnamed individual's tenacity and Jesus's magnanimity in granting her request raise discomfiting questions about the Matthean vision of Christian community and the place of those deemed outside of the social mainstream within it. One wonders how the subaltern faired among those responsible for creating and passing on this gospel. Were they fully welcomed or simply tolerated? Did they thrive? Perhaps more importantly, might they have resisted efforts to "other" or marginalize them by embracing the Canaanite woman of this tale, rather than Jesus, as an icon of an emancipatory poetics and praxis for themselves and others that were dispossessed.

Read through one *Africana* (i.e., African and African-Diasporan) lens—that of a performative Blues hermeneutic—Matt 15:21–28 may be said to describe how those rendered invisible by structures inimical to human wellbeing give voice to their needs, confront structures of power, and push back against forces that might otherwise harm them. Furthermore, it provides an opportunity for reading in a manner that allows imprudent questions to be raised; preaching that cuts against the grain of approaches glossing over troubling statements and behaviors attributed to Jesus in gospel accounts; and—in the words of musician James Blood Ulmer—utilization of, "the concept of the Blues to feel our way around" this passage and others that perplex us.[2] Therefore, this essay will consider the liberating capacity of a "Canaanite Blues" on the Matthean Jesus we meet in Matt 15:21–28 and his adherents; as well as the implications of such for radical truth-telling today.

Using the Blues concept to "feel" my "way around" the larger hermeneutical horizon for engaging this text involves acknowledging the ways that systems of power and the structures advancing their interests, including authoritative texts, can disempower and render marginalized persons both invisible and hyper-visible. The identity of the Canaanite woman in this passage is erased. She is reduced to being a person with a problem: someone whose crisis offers the Matthean Jesus an opportunity to display his power. Reading in this way involves asking inappropriate questions while not yielding to respectability norms that predominate in ecclesial circles. It means encountering a text with a sensitivity to how marginalized, minoritized, and forgotten characters are portrayed, as well as a mistrust of heavy-handed meta-narration.

---

2. One hears this refrain in Ulmer, "There Is Power in the Blues."

Such a strategy places a premium on identifying what might be strategically left unsaid or understated. As is the case with a skillful "Blues Woman" or "Blues Man," this must involve employing a compassionate yet critical gaze; a willingness to engage in unabashed truth-telling; and the capacity to craft a compelling interpretive performance that mitigates harm and promotes thriving.

This approach involves, as it were, a re-embrace of my pre-seminary training as a historian and foregrounding of my complementary identity as a Blues artist. It means asking questions that I set aside in the interest of successfully navigating the ordination process and surviving graduate school. It involves coming to terms with an academic landscape where interventions by BIPOC biblical scholars have become more pronounced and influential over the past three decades, but where additional progress is sorely needed.[3] It also requires brokering conversations among works within the commentary, edited bible, and study bible genres that represent multiple theological and interpretive perspectives. In this instance, several works have been impactful. One is the anonymously compiled *Select Parts of the Holy Bible: For the Use of Negro Slaves in the British West-India Island*s, which includes Matt 15:21–28 among its passages.[4] Another is Alejandro Duarte's entry on Matthew in the one-volume *Global Bible Commentary*, which affirms that Matthew "becomes a useful tool for every diaspora or marginalized community, because it shows us the destructive or oppressive role of verbal manipulation and teaches us how to make a clear distinction between liberating and oppressive discourses."[5] A third is Michael Joseph Brown's chapter on this gospel for *True to Our Native Land: An African American New Testament Commentary*, which describes this episode as "somewhat disturbing" and notes that its focus is on the theme of "survival."[6] A fourth consists of Dennis C. Duling's textual notes on Matthew for *The SBL Study Bible: New Revised Standard Version Updated Edition*, which call attention to the Canaanite woman's "doubly marginal" status as a gentile woman.[7] Together, these resources make me wonder what it was about the Canaanite woman's

---

3. See, for example, the recent collection of essays edited by Crowder and Foskett, *Remapping Biblical Studies: CUREMP at Thirty*.

4. Anonymous, ed., *Select Parts of the Holy Bible for the Use of the Negro Slaves in the British West-India Islands*.

5. Duarte, "Matthew," 351.

6. Brown, "The Gospel of Matthew," 106.

7. Duling, "Matthew (Notes)," 1766.

story that made it appropriate for colonial encounters with enslaved populations in the Caribbean; what strategies might be employed to leverage the liberative dimensions of this gospel for people living through diaspora currently; how a passage with such troubling dimensions can be made palatable for those that are voiceless, dispossessed, or experiencing crisis in our world today; and what the implications of a text like Matt 15:21–28 might be for those in our world currently experiencing multiple, overlapping, and intersecting forms of oppression.

This interpretive horizon, though intentionally selective, is suggestive of historical, contextual, and more traditional scholarly points of reference that are at once intriguing and compelling. Passages like this are often treated favorably by some mainstream interpreters, perhaps to avoid highlighting potentially embarrassing blemishes in canonical traditions. Such readings offer apologias for troubling encounters like the one between Jesus and the Canaanite woman in order to limit reputational damage for the Jesus Movement as represented in Matthew. By contrast, those who the late Howard Thurman described as having "their backs against the wall" might be more inclined to acknowledge the questions that the narrative leaves unresolved.[8] What happens to the woman after the encounter with Jesus and his disciples? Is she now an "insider" because of her faith? Will she be a perennial "outsider" because of her ethnicity? What of others like her? Can faith—whatever its magnitude—bridge the chasm separating social or cultural groups? Issues like these are generative of the hard-edged probing that is the stock-in-trade of the Blues aesthetic.

Interpretation

Setting the Mood

This reading utilizes a composite of methods learned, discovered, developed, or applied over a career as a scholar–cleric spanning more than forty years: e.g., the exegetical principles taught to a great many seminarians in the 1970s that focused on extraction of a text's implicit meaning;[9]

---

8. Thurman, *Jesus and the Disinherited*, 108.

9. My own sensibilities were shaped initially by my first Greek instructor, the late James A. Walther, as well as a set of unpublished mimeographed guidelines for preparing exegetical papers authored by the late George M. Landes. Walther's grammar—Walther, *New Testament Greek Workbook: An Inductive Study of the Complete*

Anthony Arlotto's succinct guidelines for preparing critical editions and the unusual vision of Hans Gumbrecht for such work;[10] a piece of advice from Northrup Frye about the relationship between teacher and student that can be applied to interpretation in general—i.e., that "Unless something is kept in reserve, suggesting the possibility of better and fuller questions, the student's mental advance is blocked";[11] and a personal penchant for writing articles and preparing homilies accompanied by music from genres including Spirituals, hymns, Classical, Blues, Jazz, Soul, Hip Hop, Country, and the like. I thank the late James Walther of Pittsburgh Theological Seminary for encouraging my fledgling efforts as a first-year seminarian to bring contemporary Black music into my exegetical and related efforts. I begin, therefore, by acknowledging the artists constituting part of the Blues playlist inspiring and informing the approaches taken in this article, one of which involves preparing a different kind of critical edition (see below) to serve as its basis.[12]

MATTHEW 15:21–28 • A CRITICAL BLUES EDITION

No name, protector, or hometown; just a daughter with a problem.[13] A courageous fast-talking "sister"[14] on a desperate search for help. Erased or hyper-visible, depending on where she stands. "Othered" within a maelstrom of violent, colonized, and gendered cultural matrices.[15] The "brothers" don't have a

---

Text of the Gospel of John—along with the first iteration of Landes' wordlist—Landes, *Building Your Biblical Hebrew Vocabulary: Learning Words by Frequency and Cognate*, then titled *A Students Vocabulary of Biblical Hebrew*—have been formative in my philological training.

10. See Arlotto, *Introduction to Historical Linguistics*, 20–22; and Gumbrecht, *The Powers of Philology*.

11. See Frye, *The Great Code*, xv.

12. They include James Blood Ulmer, Victoria Spivey, Cree Summer, Marian Anderson, Tina Turner, the group LaBelle, and Buddy Guy.

13. Based on the model for biblical personhood proposed some time ago by Malina, "Dealing with Biblical (Mediterranean) Characters: A Guide for U. S. Consumers," a model derived from a pan-Mediterranean paradigm, the woman in question is very much an outsider having to navigate her way through an environment beyond the domestic arena. The author of the story denies both her and her daughter the dignity of specific names, further diminishing their status. We know the possible names and identities of the remaining *dramatis personae* in this episode (see Matt 10:2–4 for the names of the apostles).

14. I use this term intentionally, although she is not so designated in the text. After all, she "stands in" for all "outsiders," especially women, that make their way to the Matthean Jesus's community.

15. Per the dominant model for Mediterranean personhood posited by Malina,

clue. Apparently, neither does the "New Moses."[16] Sometimes, you need noise and persistence to survive on the margin and in Diaspora. And, if all you have are words, you better know how to "shield," wield," and "come correct."[17]

> She does.
> Gets what she needs, for now.
> But, even as an exceptional exemplar,
> Are she and her ilk still outsiders?
> As they say,
> "Nobody knows the trouble..."[18]
> "Damn right," she's "got the Blues..."[19]

The text above intentionally blurs the boundary between critical edition and translation. It is very much unlike what one encounters in some of the more well-known versions—for example, the King James Version (KJV), the New International Version (NIV), the New Revised Standard Version (NRSV), or the New Revised Standard Version, Updated Edition (NRSVue). Neither are you likely to see anything like it in the multitude of study bibles or theme bibles available on the market today.

The concerns animating my reflections on this passage and others in the Bible resist the monolithic scholarly and theological norms that seminary and graduate training encourage one to adopt. Reading within, around, through, and even beyond the apparent plain sense of

---

"Dealing with Biblical (Mediterranean) Characters: A Guide for U. S. Consumers," she can be legitimately seen as a woman out of place, i.e., outside of her domicile; and behaving inappropriately by engaging in discourse with men that are not part of her immediate kin group.

16. The "insiders" include the Matthean Jesus, who is the new mediator of divine revelation, and his disciples. All seem blissfully unaware of the reason for the woman's persistence. Her marginalization within a space with intersecting forces of oppression leaves little choice than to engage in verbal challenge and riposte—signifying, as it were—with male brokers of *numinous* healing power. On signifying, see Major, *Juba to Jive*, 416.

17. Words and performative actions have power. The woman understands this and is both selective and strategic in their deployment to protect herself, obtain what she and her daughter require, and situate herself properly in relation to those able to assist her.

18. This line is adapted from the famous Spiritual, "Nobody Knows the Trouble I've Seen." Hear, for example the version on—Anderson, *Spirituals*.

19. This line is adapted from the song, "Damn Right, I Got the Blues," by Buddy Guy. Hear, for example, the version on—Guy, *Best of the Silvertone Years 1991-2005*.

a text—doing so accompanied by music and literature spanning multiple genres; and mindful of the lived experiences of people of African descent around the world—is a cornerstone of my approach. Such does not involve ignoring the riches to be gleaned from established pre- and post-Enlightenment scholarship. Instead, it involves seeking to understand the contexts within which such critical work has evolved, looking probingly at my own circumstances, and bringing heretofore-excluded methodologies into the hermeneutical process. Pushing back against established practices and making room for suppressed voices, including my own, to be heard is one of my highest priorities. Consciously embracing my identity as *Africana* philologist, such also entails transgressing some of the customs associated with the curation of texts and doing so in conformity with a philosophy that does not attempt to flatten, domesticate, or tame them.

As noted above, what follows should not be treated as the last word on this passage, or even as a canonical reading appropriate for a particular community of faith. It is a set of musings offered within what might be termed an "Afro-surrealist Blues Imaginary"—a worldview in which African-American Vernacular English (AAVE),[20] *Africana* commonsense, and straightforward acknowledgment of the "jagged edges" of day-to-day life—are essential facets.

One cannot help but think of other women in desperate circumstances referenced elsewhere in the Bible when reading Matt 15:21–28. These include the "concubine" of the Levite who was raped and whose body was dismembered to call up a tribal militia (Judg 19–20); the "conjure woman"[21] at Endor from whom Saul seeks counsel and receives a last meal (1 Sam 28:3–25); and the "widow" to whom Elijah provides a miraculous increase in oil (2 Kgs 4:1–7). None have names. In some ways, they are reduced to caricatures or stereotypes. All seem to play supporting roles in stories with larger thematic purposes not specifically focused on the identities, agency, or pain of women. Nonetheless, they operate at a deeper structural level opening portals for reflection on marginal individuals and groups.

Absent protection or a *specific* place of residence, the Canaanite woman in this text is cast simply as a troubled—indeed troublesome—figure. She is gifted, nonetheless, in the art of strategic speech. Despite

---

20. On which, see in particular the *lexicon* of terminology in Major, *Juba to Jive*.

21. This is my preferred translation for this liminal figure, based on what she does within the tale.

being virtually invisible in public space, she uses this skill to gain an audience with Jesus, whose miraculous power she implicitly recognizes. She navigates her way past Jesus's inner circle and proves herself a surprisingly deft advocate for her daughter and herself. She obtains what she needs and then moves on. Yet her presence in this narrative is troubling in many respects. Her aura persists, even after her departure. She is a noisy body "out of place." Hers is a voice more eloquent than those of Jesus or his immediate disciples. Her sagacity and eloquence deconstruct ideologies that treat gentiles—particularly those identified as Canaanite—as insignificant. She is, to cite a more modern image, the exemplary "outsider," someone sufficiently skilled in "code switching" to cross a cultural threshold and perhaps be folded into the main body of the Matthean community. However, the question with which we are left is whether her somewhat agonistic experience disincentivizes further engagement with the movement of this "New Moses." Sometimes the steps one must take to enter or to access resources from exclusive groups incline one against the pursuit of full membership or even further tangential encounters. For the marginalized, the cost-benefit *calculus* of "belonging" is at times too demanding. Needing and not possessing, periodically being forced to "mortgage" one's integrity to care for family and having to fend for oneself even in the presence of a new mediator of hope are more than enough to give one "the Canaanite Blues," and encourage deployment of them as an ongoing survival strategy.

This passage forces us to think about belonging in ancient and modern settings as well as the thresholds erected either to facilitate or inhibit entry. What does it mean to be a person lacking some form of bounded social aggregate with structures that afford protection and nurture; or to be labeled pejoratively by a community one hopes to enter? How are we to think about the crossing of membership thresholds in colonial settings where resource scarcity and power differentials breed strife and mistrust among rival groups? How do such organizations position themselves for stability while avoiding the suspicion of imperial authorities? How do they deal effectively with competition for authority and status? The Matthean community was situated within a Greco-Roman *milieu* with contending visions of Judaism and Christianity and a cacophony of both exponents and adherents. Matthew 15:21–28 seems focused on justifying strict criteria for entry into the Matthean fold. Its tone, particularly the use of the term "Canaanite" (15:22) and the manner in which the disciples appear to be aggressive "gatekeepers" that limit access to Jesus

(15:23), are suggestive of a group under siege, perhaps courting respectability among its peers, and seeking to reify its boundaries.

The version of this story in Mark (7:24–30) has a different feeling altogether. The term "Syrophoenician" (7:26) used to describe the woman seems less emotionally freighted and Jesus's disciples have no role. In fact, the meeting between Jesus and the woman appears to be a clandestine encounter between two marginal figures—one (Jesus) trying to keep a low profile (7:24) and another (the woman) in search of healing for a child. It unfolds within a veil of secrecy. Some of the questions raised by the Matthean version remain, but the maintenance of social boundaries seems less important than the unusual parameters governing a secret exchange between a patron and a client. In this instance, I am reminded of the ways that certain practitioners of indigenous *Africana* healing arts have historically situated themselves within the African American religious landscape. Their visibility is not typically as pronounced as that of clergy or congregations that are part of the Black Church milieu. However, people learn of their location, at times by word of mouth, and seek them when the need is acute. While the relationships formed between such practitioners and those seeking their services are largely transactional, they may also serve as the basis for enduring—perhaps fluid—relational ties. Moreover, they open the possibility for treating not just church buildings, but those locales where one can meet, receive the ministrations of, or learn about these indigenous healers as sacred spaces—whether storefronts, bars, or other venues where Blues music is performed.

Although the historical and cultural distance between the first-century CE setting of Matthew and that of twenty-first-century readers is substantial, there are analogous issues relating to religious conversion, group membership, disaffiliation, and the like that can be meaningfully explored by Scriptural exegetes and expositors. Much of this work is important for effective preaching, particularly in a global environment where such efforts can be particularly impactful in the promotion of civic virtues and social cohesion.

Homiletic Overtures

Preaching Matt 15:21–28 is challenging for anyone mindful of how gender, ethnicity, colonialism, etc. operated in the Greco-Roman world;

and looking to offer hope for those experiencing overlapping forms of exclusion in modern environments. This is certainly the case for me within my diocese of The Episcopal Church. Working as a "supply priest" I often find myself presiding in parishes where I may be the only BIPOC person present and the receptivity of congregants to critical Bible scholarship as well as "transgressive" theological interpretation is difficult at best to intuit.

My experience over many years here in the Midwest has been largely positive. I've sensed a hunger for more daring interpretive readings, particularly given the economic crises that have destabilized life in the so-called "Rust Belt." Moreover, in the wake of the COVID-19 pandemic, my preaching on passages calling attention to belonging and communal life has been well received. However, there are limits to what I feel empowered to say. I am always mindful of what people, however open and receptive, are capable of hearing in particular ecclesial settings.

In the Sunday Eucharistic Lectionary for our *Book of Common Prayer*, Matt 15:21–28 is listed as "Proper 15" and is designated for reading in Year A, on the Sunday closest to August 17.[22] It is paired with Isa 56:1 (2–5), 6–7; Psalm 67; and Rom 11:13–15, 29–32.[23] Moreover, the contemporary language "collect" (brief liturgical prayer for this day in the calendar) is as follows:

> Almighty God, you have given your only Son to be for us a sacrifice for sin, and also an example of godly life: Give us grace to receive thankfully the fruits of his redeeming work, and to follow daily in the blessed steps of his most holy life; through Jesus Christ your Son our Lord, who lives and reigns with you and the Holy Spirit, one God, now and for ever. *Amen.*[24]

This short prayer provides a contemplative focus for the day. I preached a homily based on these readings in August 2023. In preparing it, I thought about the passage in Matthew while pondering what it means to live a "godly life," how one can be a recipient of Christ's "redeeming work," and what might be involved in embodying Christ's "most holy life." I brought the story of the unnamed Canaanite woman into conversation with the universalizing and inclusive trajectories of the passages

---

22. The Episcopal Church, *The Book of Common Prayer*, 898.

23. The *Revised Common Lectionary* (RCL) includes these same pairings (with Matt 15:1–10 being an optional expansion for the Gospel reading). It also adds Gen 45:1–15 and Ps 133 as alternatives for the initial reading and Psalm for the day.

24. The Episcopal Church, *The Book of Common* Prayer, 232.

in Second Isaiah, Psalm 67, and Romans 11. Given the setting of the homily—a small somewhat homogeneous semi-rural Midwestern parish with an average attendance of seven to eleven persons; where I was the principal celebrant and preacher and, if memory serves, the only BIPOC person present—this was somewhat difficult. Inviting listeners to ponder the unstated costs of inclusion shouldered by those whose race, gender, sexual identity, citizenship status, etc., seeking to become members of a congregation where they might not be part of the dominant social group was a daunting task. Brokering a conversation about the dynamics of minoritization within an Anglican Communion coming to terms with its colonial legacy was equally challenging.[25] A "godly life" focused on "redeeming work" in this light might well involve decolonial self-care, social disengagement, and seeing in the Canaanite woman's ambiguous "after story" an invitation to undertake a critical assessment of one's own commitments. Given the choice between aligning with social groups where one's membership is contested and being alone, sometimes strategic (and limited) contact or solitude is a superior choice. Matthew 15:21–28 urges us to think about what it means to be part of communities where there are still "insiders" and "outsiders," even if the distinctions between them are not easily parsed. I realized that such issues would be incredibly tough for this congregation to engage, so I tried to broach them with subtlety. My hope was to leave those in attendance with an invitation for further reflection, in light of my sense that this was not a place where prophetic preaching was the norm.

Were I to offer an expanded and more "edgy" version of this homily in a fictive location—e.g., a diverse (in terms of race, ethnicity, gender, socioeconomic status, and sexual orientation) Midwestern parish, with less than a dozen members (and, as a result, in danger of closure), in an urban enclave experiencing economic decline—it would contain much the same form as the original composition, with an expansion of the section dealing with the Gospel reading (entitled "Some Uncomfortable Truths"). The setting for this homily would likely be the principal Sunday service (a celebration of the Eucharist), likely a "Low Mass" without music. As a result, the homily would be no longer than five to seven minutes. As part of my contemplative preparation as presider, while in the sacristy I would "thumb through" Allan Rohan Crite's visual illuminations of the prayer of

---

25. For a treatment of this ongoing process, see Kwok, *The Anglican Tradition from a Postcolonial Perspective*.

consecration in the *1928 Book of Common Prayer*,[26] which reveal a vision of *Africana* sacred reality conjured by a Black priest.[27] This is my recurring grounding discipline when I preside at the Eucharist. The homily, when offered after the readings for the day, would proceed as follows. The title of the sermon is "Grace, Inclusion, and the Godly Life."

Homily

Overview—Grace and the Godly Life

The Christian life of faith presents us with no small number of mysteries to ponder. One to which our collect and readings this morning allude has to do with the intersection of grace, inclusion, and the "godly life." Regarding the first, our *Book of Common Prayer* says the following: "Grace is God's favor towards us, unearned and undeserved; by grace God forgives our sins, enlightens our minds, stirs our hearts, and strengthens our wills."[28] We've heard much about the second over the years, whether as part of efforts nationally to promote it along with diversity and equity; or as one of the elements essential to building societies that are welcoming and non-exclusive. From a theological perspective, one might think of the term as denoting a process by, or reality in which, the distinction between "insiders" and "outsiders" is erased; and what has been termed the "Beloved Community" is created. As to the third—i.e., "godly life"—our collect notes that we see it reflected in the life of Christ, which we are encouraged "to follow daily."

Spirit-Filled and Inclusive Anglican Spiritualities

While the meaning and relevance of these three concepts are contested today, there is value nonetheless in seeing them as complementary facets of spirit-filled and meaningful Anglican spiritualities—ways of living and of being positive change agents in our world. Today's lessons and Psalm offer some interesting ideas for us to ponder in this regard. For example, the reading from Isaiah (56:1, 6–8) articulates a Divine vision for the

---

26. The Episcopal Church, *The Book of Common Prayer and Administration of the Sacraments*.

27. Crite, *All Glory*.

28. The Episcopal Church. *The Book of Common Prayer*, 858.

ultimate destiny of humanity that is expansive, rather than narrow. In the Letter to the Romans (11:1–2a, 29–32), Paul's notion of God's promises to Israel is comparably far reaching. As for the story of the Canaanite woman seeking relief for her daughter, which we find in Matthew (15:21–28), it drives home the fact that old cross-cultural animosities can be mitigated through encounters with Jesus. These are all hopeful messages of God's blessing, guidance, and justice toward peoples—a theme we hear echoed in this morning's Gradual (Ps 67:1, 2, and 4).

Some Uncomfortable Truths

However, there are some uncomfortable dimensions that at least one of these readings—Matt 15:21–28)—raises. It has to do with the "rough edges" of community life and belonging. The story of the unnamed Canaanite woman's encounter with Jesus contains troubling allusions to "gatekeeping," the process by which membership in exclusive organizations is managed. It is an uncomfortable subject to discuss, but one on which we would do well to reflect. The woman in question is someone considered outside of the Jewish mainstream. She has a daughter in need of healing. She tries to approach Jesus for help but is rebuffed by his disciples. She persists and through her own verbal skills, receives the help she sought. An extended lesson of the story—one drawn from the Gospel in which it is contained—is that Christian communities large and small need to be attentive to the ways that they treat those seeking help and desirous of becoming members. We must be careful not to erect obstacles that stand in the way of connection; and to consider how our interactions with newcomers may make them feel unaccepted. Such behavior on our part may lead them to feel like permanent outsiders. Such may lead them to avoid attending parish events or regular worship services.

We would do well, therefore, to look critically at this account, to imagine ourselves in the place of the Canaanite woman, and to ask how she felt in the aftermath of the encounter with Jesus and what her feelings might have been about following him and his disciples as teachers and guides. Rather than seeing this as an inappropriate way of reading this passage, one can reasonably approach this as an opportunity to consider some of the broader analogous issues that the Gospel—and the gospels—invite us to consider in the realm of belonging and deep connectedness as contemporary persons of faith.

Onward—Next Steps

So, what might these things suggest to us? At a time when our country is so acrimoniously divided over a range of social, religious, and political issues, perhaps we could develop strategies to overcome these differences through the kind of prophetic, theologically sophisticated, and evocative thinking we see in this morning's readings—approaches that see inclusion as one of the marvelous outcomes of God's grace; and the "godly life" as one that mirrors Jesus's embrace of the marginalized, as well as the Canaanite woman's courage and rhetorical flair in advocating for her daughter's healing. At a moment when civic life and even connections within faith communities seem once again to be fraying, we need new and creative strategies to build bridges, improve communication, and strengthen interpersonal and communal linkages.

May the remaining days of this Season After Pentecost find us embracing this important work and helping make the "Beloved Community" a reality one day at a time, one relationship at a time. Amen.

Conclusion

Almost four years after the so-called "January 6 Insurrection," less than fifty days until the 2024 Presidential Election, and a few months until the conclusion of the United Nations' "International Decade for People of African Descent," I am preoccupied with thoughts about inclusion, exclusion, hierarchy, the meaning of Biblical Studies in an era of massive political upheaval, the use of sacred texts to foster belonging and (regrettably) to justify violence, and the like. As noted earlier, the Canaanite woman in Matt 15 could clearly be numbered among those Howard Thurman described as having "their backs against the wall."[29] Behind her verbal exchange with Jesus, I feel the searing realization of someone unsure if she is fully embraced by those from whom she sought help. In the distance echo the voices of Black Women singing of the struggles they have managed and the attenuated dreams they harbor. In my "sanctified scholarly imagination," I discern in the heart of the Canaanite woman whose story has been this essay's focus a kinship with all women who do what must be done to make it in a world governed by men. In the words of artist Cree Summer's song "Deliciously Down" on the album *Street*

---

29. Thurman, *Jesus and the Disinherited*, 108.

Faerie, may theirs be "high prayers to breathe through" that assure them that they are "not supposed to be for nothing."[30]

---

30. Summer, Cree. "Street Faerie." Audio CD, Sony Music Entertainment, 1999.

13

Crumbs Are Never Enough

Decentering the White Supremacist Jesus

KATHERINE A. SHANER[1]

Introduction

ON THE EVENING OF August 11, 2017, a group of "alt-right" protestors marched unimpeded with tiki torches chanting White supremacist slogans to the statue of Thomas Jefferson on the campus of the University of Virginia. A group of students, staff, and faculty met the marchers at the statue in counter-protest. The White supremacist crowd subsequently assaulted the students, staff, and faculty. Police intervention ultimately dispersed the melee, but their delayed response has been highly criticized.[2] The next day, a similar march and a set of counter-protests took place at the site of a Stonewall Jackson monument in downtown Charlottesville. Once again, the march turned violent when skirmishes between marchers and counter-protestors culminated with a White supremacist driving an automobile into a crowd of anti-racist protestors, leaving one person dead and many wounded.[3] This violence stunned many average middle-class

---

1. In addition to the editor of this volume, I extend gratitude to both Mallory Challis, my graduate research assistant, for her research and copyediting work and to Anna C. Miller for her incisive editorial suggestions.

2. See Jenkins, "Ethics under Pressure," 163–76.

3. For one timeline of the events as well as an argument demonstrating the failure

White liberal mainline Christians who were not already activists—even after a summer of controversy over the meaning and legacy of Confederate memorials throughout cities in the southern United States.

Just one week after the violence in Charlottesville, churches that use the Revised Common Lectionary encountered Matthew's story of the Canaanite woman and her daughter (Matt 15:21–28; see also Mark 7:24–30)—a story where Jesus acts based on ethnic and racialized difference. White mainline protestant churches often represent this story as a triumph of inclusion, or at least of learning inclusion. This insistence is grounded in the fact that Jesus eventually heals the woman's daughter. It is also grounded in a homiletic hermeneutic that Jesus must always be the perfect, liberative, equity-producing hero of the gospel's story. Yet this hermeneutic allows preachers and those receiving proclamation to ignore the system of racializing discourses at work in Matthew's redaction of the story. On Sunday, August 20, 2017, in light of the racialized violence in Charlottesville (and many other less-publicized places), this use of systemic racialized discourses created a sense of tension for preachers searching to dismantle White supremacy in mainline Christian homiletic traditions. While Jesus does heal the woman's daughter, no systemic changes in the relationship between the Israelites and the Canaanites are suggested (nor between Romans and Jews—the hidden power context within the text). No fundamental changes in health access are made. No community reparation is offered. No sense of equity is forged.

Using feminist critical reading methods as well as a homiletic hermeneutic that decenters singularly powerful individuals, this essay interrogates the way Matthew's story, within the homiletic moment, can parallel and perpetuate White supremacist logics inherent to American political contexts. I wrestle with the idea that Matthew's Jesus never offers the woman different circumstances and systems of repair, even as he heals her daughter. Matthew's narrative draws on a well-known imperial male savior complex in which small acts of kindness burnish the images of great, beneficent men—men whose power comes from a divine source. Yet this great man-power dynamic undergirds the increased presence and dangerous persistence of White supremacist power in protestant theology across the United States.[4] Preaching at a White, liberal, middle-

---

of media to connect the protests with White supremacist ideologies and groups, see: Chuang and Tyler, "An Obscured View of 'Both Sides,'" 9.

4. Jennings, *After Whiteness*, 12, characterizes this dynamic well when he writes: "White self-sufficient masculinity is not first a person or a people; it is a way of

class, mainline church just ten days after the White supremacist rally in Charlottesville necessitated a homiletic hermeneutic that challenges both the central interpretive premise that Matthew's Jesus changed his mind about the woman and that it is enough for her to receive "crumbs" since her daughter was healed. I challenge White mainline protestant communities to decenter a perfect Jesus in this story as a praxis of biblical encounter with injustice. In this decentering, such communities find ways to identify and wrestle with problematic aspects of contemporary assertions of similar power. Such wrestling opens new ways to demand wholeness apart from a White supremacist system of logic.

Hermeneutical Horizon

This kind of wrestling comes from my own formation and context. My context as a preacher, the context of my listeners, and the context of the socio-political times require me to examine the effects of interpretation for the communities in which I am preaching. As such, I am aware of alternate interpretations of the Canaanite woman story. I support and often teach these interpretations for students whose contexts are not my own. For example, I frequently teach a reading my womanist scholar-preacher students and colleagues might advance to great success in a different context: This woman, denigratingly named as Canaanite in Matthew's version of the story, can determine her and her daughter's future by making a way out of no way.[5] That is, the woman finds healing for her daughter out of her own persistence, not out of her dependence on the conquering royal figure of Jesus.[6] Such an interpretation is, indeed, ethically necessary in both Black church contexts and scholarly discourses about the interpretation of this story. My womanist mentors and colleagues, however, have taught me how to see the logics of White supremacy as it manifests in the mainline church world in which I preach. In such a context, I cannot

---

organizing life with ideas and forming a persona that distorts identity and strangles the possibilities of dense life together. In this regard, my use of the term "whiteness" does not refer to people of European descent but to a way of being in the world and seeing the world that forms cognitive and affective structures able to seduce people into its habitation and its meaning making."

5. Williams, *Sisters in the Wilderness,* 193–94, develops this idea in response to the question, "how can oppressed people develop a positive and productive quality of life in a situation where the resources for doing so are not visible?"

6. For examples of this perspective, see M. J. Smith, "Commentary on Matthew 15:[10–20] 21–28"; and Sechrest, "Enemies, Romans, Pigs, and Dogs."

conscionably preach womanist readings. The ethical response for me requires intentionally deconstructing these White supremacist logics, even if that means deconstructing a particular image of Jesus.

My feminist impulse to decenter kyriarchally[7] driven voices within biblical texts shapes my preaching framework. The most basic question I ask of any text, whether interpreting it for scholarly conversation, homiletic proclamation, or pedagogical purposes is: Who or what perspective is missing from the center of this story? Quite often, women, especially low-status, disenfranchised, and racialized women are missing from stories about Jesus and his movement.

Yet, feminist scholarship has proven that women were central to the Jesus movement.[8] Homiletic hermeneutics often center stories about men and highlight malestream rules in biblical texts. Yet scholars have shown time and time again that both privileged and low-status women were active participants in ancient public life. This historical correction needs to filter into homiletic interpretation.[9] Women were important actors in the Jesus Movement, not as exceptions to rules, but as leaders in their communities.

For many preachers who highlight biblical women in leadership, however, Jesus poses a problem. Women's leadership can only lead so far. Jesus must ultimately be the one whose words, actions, and teachings are the central theological point of any story. Furthermore, the assumption that he acts perfectly recenters a singular male figure for listeners. The Canaanite woman's story is a significant example of this kind of kyriarchal re-centering. The woman is in her own territory and Jesus is the foreigner/stranger, yet Jesus is the one who has the power

---

7. Schüssler Fiorenza, *But She Said*, 7–11, coins this term as a way of quickly referencing the fact that gender is not the only concern of feminist interpretation, rather intersecting modes of domination need to be part of the analytic framework.

8. For some examples demonstrating women's participation in the ancient world, see Parks, Warren, and Sheinfeld, *Jewish and Christian Women*; King, *The Gospel of Mary of Magdala*; Kraemer, *Her Share of the Blessings*; Schaberg, *The Resurrection of Mary Magdalene*; and Schüssler Fiorenza, *In Memory of Her*. For a critique of scholarship that continues to insist on both the absence of women from ancient history and the absence of women scholars who write about ancient history, see Graybill, "Where Are All the Women?"

9. Levine, "Matthew's Advice to a Divided Readership," decenters Jesus in favor of the "children"; Schüssler Fiorenza, *But She Said*, 96–101, asserts the Syrophnecian woman "wins" the argument with Jesus. Dube, *Postcolonial Feminist Interpretation of the Bible*, 172–77, 180–82, critiques both of these moves as needing post-colonial critiques of imperial power. I draw on Dube's critiques.

to dismiss, heal, or recognize the woman. The woman asks clearly for Jesus's help, and he refuses to answer her. She asks for divine intervention, and Jesus suggests she is only worthy of the "crumbs" of his divine power. Centering the Canaanite woman in the story should shift the power dynamic between her and Jesus. But Matthew's redactions create a racialized context in which Jesus's actions inevitably carry all the power. A different kind of decentering is needed in the light of the homiletic context of a White mainline church struggling with the aftermath of White supremacist violence.

I propose a hermeneutic that decenters the power structures within the text. This decentering hermeneutic illuminates systems of power in biblical stories that give theological grounding to contemporary inequities. In this story, Jesus's assumed role as a powerful exemplar of perfection highlights Matthew's ethnocentric editorial decisions and their analog to contemporary White supremacy logics.[10] Regardless of which character is centered or decentered in the story, their actions mobilize racialized logics that allow Canaanite women to be analogous to dogs and Judeans/Israel to be favored for the Messiah's attention. Neither character suggests an alternative to these logics. What would happen if the hermeneutical center of the story were not a character, but rather the racialized logics themselves and the ways characters fail to see them? While it may seem dangerous to decenter Jesus and anti-feminist to decenter the woman, the shift from singular personalities to systemic dynamics is needed in homiletic contexts, in which White supremacist logics are embedded but rarely exposed, let alone homiletically examined.[11]

Ultimately, my feminist framework insists that no single biblical interpretation is the "right" interpretation for all times and all places. Scholars and preachers alike must recognize the validity of multiple perspectives and multiple interpretations. Within this plurality of biblical interpretation, interpreters must attend to the ethical use of the story-specific contexts. I am a third-generation ordained pastor and a vocationally recognized scholar in the Evangelical Lutheran Church in America (ELCA). I am the only woman in these generations of pastors. I am also culturally and racially White. This cultural identification draws from my deep roots in the ELCA. A 2015 Pew Research study showed the ELCA was demographically 96% White, earning the denomination

---

10. Sechrest, *Race and Rhyme*, 27–40, calls this dynamic an ethical rhyme.

11. For one explanation of this need in American mainline protestant Christianity, see Harvey, *Dear White Christians*.

the moniker of "whitest denomination in America."[12] Until my early 20s, my formative faith years fit well within this 96%. I did not know the ELCA included vibrant communities of color until I began exploring pastoral career options. One such community, Gracious Saviour Lutheran Church in Detroit, MI, generously hosted and trained me in pastoral ministry during a year-long residency (internship) in 2002–2003. This community and communities like it have often borne the burden of teaching the denomination, and its leadership, about its participation in systemic racism. My experience transformed my worldview irrevocably. I learned how to preach, teach, and pray within a context where African-American life was central to vibrant faith even as the larger church marginalized this community through its assumptions about depravity and need. This ministry experience and others like it transformed me into a learner and a listener. Through this learning and listening, I began to see the depths to which White supremacist logics and racialized discourses permeate mainline protestant churches. My womanist mentors in Detroit and other ministry training programs issued a clarion call for me to raise questions about and proclaim reparation for both racial and gender injustice as a pastor and a scholar in primarily White contexts. As a tenured professor at a prominent and racially diverse Divinity School embedded in a primarily White institution, I preach about twice each month in both small, rural, southern churches, and in larger mainline churches in urban centers across the country.

Audience

As a White mainline preacher, I am called to clearly teach and preach with an awareness of power systems, their underlying logics, and my place with them. This call is quite difficult because it often means critiquing, and even rebuking, myself and my community for our perpetuation of racist systems. Preachers like me often offer a kind of catharsis born of virtuous guilt divorced from a call to action. We recognize the systemic problem and our complicity in it, but reify power systems that depend on a perfect Jesus. The task, however, should be to dismantle the socio-political power

---

12. Lipka, "The Most and Least Racially Diverse U.S. Religious Groups." The Lutheran Church Missouri Synod and the then United Methodist Church were not far behind at 95% and 94% respectively.

of White supremacy.[13] So often, Jesus's engagement with the Canaanite woman is characterized as above or apart from racialized systems. But at the end of the story in Matthew, the woman is still a dog, and crumbs are her due at the hands of God's own son. Implying that transformation comes from benevolence toward others who are pitiable, or wretched, or not worthy of being called humans gives proclamatory sanction to the supremacy of one group over another. Pity and benevolence assume a stance of superiority. In the context of a White mainline protestant congregation, with a White embodied preacher, living in the political and geographic context of White supremacist power assertions, the rhetoric of superiority and supremacy needs to be rejected—even if that means rejecting a rhetoric of a perfect Jesus's supremacy. How do we center divine power when Jesus's actions connect with White supremacist logics? Especially when those logics are the cause of suffering and fear?

Homiletic Issues

Preachers approaching this story enter a difficult tension inherent in the story's interaction with contemporary US socio-political contexts. So often preachers create a single synthesis of the synoptic stories rather than reading Matthew and Mark on their own terms. Although Matthew edits Mark's version of the story to include multiple markers of ethnic particularity and imperial power, preachers often preach Mark's less ethnically specific story instead.[14] Yet an analysis of the differences between the two versions of this story shows that Matthew draws on at least two historical imperial symbolic worlds that Mark does not: the conquest of Canaan by Joshua and the Roman victory over the Judeans.[15] Musa Dube challenges interpreters to recognize and critique the racialized discourses that Matthew creates: "Readers tend to enter the story world of Matthew and its rhetorical language of divine claims such as salvation history, servant king, universal mission, and absolute

---

13. Case, "Claiming White Social Location," 67, describes this dilemma well: "The ambiguities of our social location, as *white* anti-racist people, often create complexities that impede ethical clarity and decisive, liberative action. We must speak about our experience of this complexity, and we must give and receive the help we need to become clear and to act."

14. Dube, *Feminist Postcolonial Biblical Interpretation*, 146–50.

15. S. D. Moore, *Gospel Jesuses and Other Nonhumans*, 61–63. See also Lopez, *Apostle to the Conquered*, 6–16, for an explanation of the gender dynamics at work in imperial conquest.

claims of power without any decolonization of its intentions."[16] White supremacy logics follow a similar pattern in assuming White culture, religion, and politics are universal across differences in race. When we consistently neglect the ethno-racialization at work in Matthew's version of the story, preachers can (inadvertently) reinscribe racialized discourses for contemporary faith communities.

Setting the Scene

In the immediate wake of the violence in Charlottesville, my call was to dismantle the racializing logics of a perfect Jesus, to decenter both the woman and Jesus, and to challenge the audience to re-frame how both mercy and justice become manifest in the world. Naming the characteristics of White supremacy clearly is the first hermeneutical step in following this call. The hermeneutical horizon lies in both this identification of White supremacist logics and their connections to ancient text and contemporary homiletics. As such, I propose the following as a broad set of characteristics of White supremacist logics.

First, White supremacist logics are colonialist logics. They claim space for the most powerful regardless of previous habitation. Musa Dube notes the failure of interpreters to interrogate the embedded mission-oriented imperial claims made in Matthew's version of the text.[17] She demonstrates that Matthew's foreshadowing of mission to the nations with this story is an imperial claim to power at home and in "distant and inhabited lands."[18] While Dube describes this dynamic from her social location as a woman of sub-Saharan African origin, I identify a similar logic around racialized space within my own American context. White culture claims all spaces—cultural, religious, political, and physical—as a neutral or rightful space for White presence.[19] White supremacy logics suggest that White folks should be welcome and even empowered in any space—even those in which they are the foreigner, the minority, and/or the stranger. Similarly, most homiletic occasions for preaching

---

16. Dube, *Postcolonial Feminist Interpretation*, 168.
17. Dube, *Postcolonial Feminist Interpretation of the Bible*, 127–35, 144–55.
18. Dube, *Postcolonial Feminist Interpretation of the Bible*, 129.
19. For a historical and theological genealogy of this idea, see Jennings, *The Christian Imagination*.

Matthew's version of the story ascribe power to Jesus regardless of the fact he was not on his own cultural ground.[20]

Second, White supremacist logics in mainline protestant churches minimize differences based on race, ethnicity, and/or the logics of peoplehood. This minimalization claims that the Jesus story transcends such differences. Yet, this universalist logic erases differences in favor of the status quo: White masculine political and cultural power.[21] This logic forges a false dichotomy between universalism and racial/ethnic particularity. According to this logic, Jesus stands on the side of universalism when he heals the woman's daughter. Yet, his rhetoric throughout the story reifies the particularity of Israel over Canaan, men over women, children over dogs. This rhetoric creates dichotomies that implicitly value the former (Israel, men, children) as more desirable than the latter (Canaan, women, dogs). When we obfuscate this rhetoric in a context where White supremacy already infuses societal systems, we do little to counter the contributions of mainline Christianity to its perpetuation.[22]

Third, White supremacist logics maintain a singularly powerful, self-contained,[23] male figure as the universal savior figure. Feminist scholars have long noted that singularly concentrated power is problematic because such power constructions mirror exploitative systems in contemporary life. Especially in the case of Jesus, readers "expect a figure who is self-contained, singular, and heroic."[24] This perception of singularity is just that, a perception. Jesus cannot be a singularly powerful savior without a community that recognizes him as such.[25] Similarly, White malestream cultural supremacy must also have a communal sanction. Yet, when the Jesus we construct from this story in Matthew

---

20. For one analysis of the way that Christian readings of Jesus assert power across time and space, see Dube, "Savior of the World." Elsewhere Dube, "Reading for Decolonization," 38 writes: "Imperialism is, therefore, about controlling foreign geographical spaces and their inhabitants. By its practice and its goals, imperialism is a relationship of subordination and domination between different nations and lands, which actively suppresses diversity and promotes a few universal standards for the benefit of those in power."

21. Emerson and Bracey, *The Religion of Whiteness*, 49–55.

22. Buell, *Why This New Race?*, 11 and especially 175n30.

23. The term "self-contained" comes from Johnson-Debaufre, "'That One' Takes a Village," 3. It resonates with Jennings, *After Whiteness,* 12, which critiques formation in Western theological education that strives to mold students in the image "of a white self-sufficient man, his self-sufficiency defined by possession, control, and mastery."

24. Johnson-DeBaufre, "'That One' Takes a Village," 3.

25. Johnson-DeBaufre, "'That One' Takes a Village," 3.

is singularly self-contained, universally inclusive, holds power apart from time and space, and does these things perfectly, we start to see the ways White supremacy logics are embedded in the mainline protestant communal image of Jesus. Matthew's specific redaction of Mark's story suggests not a self-contained, singularly powerful, perfect Jesus, but one constructed from communal editorial power.

Once we see the logics of White supremacy that resonate with Matthew's version of this story, we need to make a few historical inquiries to see Matthew's redaction choices in light of both ancient and contemporary readers. Thus, I center the racialized rhetoric at the heart of the text and invite listeners to consider what it would mean to let go of our perfect, all-powerful, self-contained Jesus in a moment when identifying with such power is problematic. Matthew's Jesus did not propose a way toward undermining the system that engenders pity for the oppressed, exploitation through inequity, and the expectation that one singular person (even a divine one) can "fix" the system and be perfect within it. In the immediate aftermath of Charlottesville, letting go of the perfect Jesus is a praxis against White supremacy. What if Jesus is the one who shows us our own need to wrestle with systemic racism and dare to imagine more just systems?

Interpretation

When we analyze Matthew's redaction of Mark's story (Mark 7:24–30) with an eye toward power systems, a picture of deeply embedded systemic racialization emerges.[26] Matthew conflates multiple complexes of historical power to demonstrate Jesus's authority regardless of his socio-political and cultural context. This reshaping intensifies both the possibilities for Jesus's power and the subjection of the racialized woman in the story. Putting these possibilities into historical context illuminates Matthew's focus on systemic rhetoric that was already available to him through conquest narratives in Jewish scripture and his own contemporary imperial world of the Roman empire. Matthew places Jesus and the woman into a power system that pits divinely sent royal conquerors against their ethnically othered, non-human captives. This system fluidly draws on historical tropes of ancient Israel conquering Canaan,

---

26. For purposes of this essay, I am adopting the idea that Matthew has access to Mark's version of the story and redacts it to suit his purposes. See one argument for Markan priority in Rhoads, "Jesus and the Syrophoenician Woman in Mark," 343–75.

gendered imperial rhetoric from the first-century CE Roman Empire, and the power positionality of Jesus as the royal heir of David all within the same story. With every connection to a conquering or imperial authority (Joshua, Rome, David), Jesus holds the power while the woman is associated with conquered or imperially dominated people.

In Matthew's version of this story, Jesus has traveled from Gennesaret (Matt 14:24) north and east to the region of Tyre and Sidon, where he encounters a woman who asks him to heal her demon-possessed daughter (Matt 15:21). Tyre and Sidon, for Matthew's first readers, were not just geographic names—these places metaphorically represented Israel's enemies.[27] Here, Matthew identifies the woman as a Canaanite instead of a Syrophonecian of Greek origin (Matt 15:22; cf. Mark 7:26). The term Canaanite generally connotes Israel's multiple enemies during and after the post-exodus conquest (Judg 1). This redaction invokes the Israelite origin story of God promising the land of Canaan "for a perpetual holding" (Gen 17:8), and God's direction for Israel's domination over Canaanite people ("You shall annihilate them;" Deut 20:17a). In addition, Matthew draws on a history of Canaanite enslavement to the Israelites (Judg 1:28) throughout his redaction by connecting Jesus with enslaver titles such as "lord" (*kyrios*; Matt 15:22, 27) and "master" (*despotes*; Matt 15:27).[28] Matthew leads the reader to associate the woman with racialized domination. She is an idolator. She is a conquered person. She belongs to a class of enslaveable people.

On the other hand, Matthew chooses to emphasize Jesus as both an Israelite and a royal messianic figure—the heir to David's throne. In Matthew, the woman names Jesus "son of David" (v. 22; cf. Mark 7:25–26), a name not used in Mark. Matthew's Jesus also claims an exclusive mission to "the lost sheep of the house of Israel" (v. 24), another claim absent from Mark. Jesus, as the Davidic messiah and the leader of Israel with divine sanction for domination of the Canaanites, provides an intertextual, geographical, mythic mash-up for Matthew's construction of unquestioned power. Musa Dube, in an analysis of another foreign territory story in John 4:1–42, writes that this kind of assertion of boundaryless power sets up "the installation of Christianity as a universal religion:

---

27. O'Day, "Surprised by Faith," 115–16, cites Isa 23; Ezek 26–28; and Joel 3:4. Jackson, *Have Mercy on Me*, 70–86, traces the literary and historical construction of Canaanite in both the Hebrew Bible narratives and Matthew. See also Moore, *Gospel Jesuses and Other Nonhumans*, 62–63.

28. S. D. Moore, *Gospel Jesuses and Other Nonhumans*, 62.

an installation that proceeds by disavowing all geographical boundaries in order to claim power over the 'world' and to relegate all other religions and cultures to inadequacy."²⁹ This encounter is not simply an intercultural encounter; Matthew's Jesus asserts the superiority of Israel over Canaan.³⁰ Matthew's redaction places ethnic domination, divine sanction, and enslavement on the character of Jesus. In constructing Jesus as a Davidic messiah with a universal mission and absolute power, Jesus's actions align quite easily with White supremacist assertions of power despite geopolitical or religious boundaries.

Moreover, the gendered aspects of Matthew's story sharpen this racialized rhetorical claim to power. Feminist scholarship on this passage focuses much attention on the gendered power differential between Jesus and the woman. In the first few verses of the story, Matthew changes Mark's verbs so that their actions are gendered. Matthew writes that the woman "cried out" (ἔκραζεν) to Jesus (v. 22). This verb, κράζω, is used as a way to describe women's cries while in birthing labor.³¹ She does not speak to Jesus, she "shrieks" or "screams" at him in the imperfect, suggesting repeated action.³² On the other side of the exchange, Jesus "did not answer her, not a word" (ὁ δὲ οὐκ ἀπεκρίθη αὐτῇ λόγον; v. 23). The addition of the term λόγος as the object of ἀποκρίνω intensifies Jesus's silence. The term also emphasizes Jesus's rationality, reason, and control—qualities of masculinity—as well as the woman's lack of such qualities. Jesus first speaks in the story when the disciples ask him to send her away (v. 23). Some commentators suggest this lack of response is evidence of Jewish misogyny. Jewish men would not respond to women who audaciously approach them in public, especially gentile women.³³ Yet, as Amy-Jill Levine has pointed out, Jesus interacts with gentile women throughout Matthew with no hint of such misogyny.³⁴ When the disciples recommend Jesus

29. Dube, "Reading for Decolonization," 53.
30. Dube, *Postcolonial Feminist Interpretation*, 140.
31. Long, *Matthew*, 174–75, points to Rev 2:12 as one example.
32. Gench, *Back to the Well*, 6.
33. See Gench, *Back to the Well*, 6. This interpretation has its own racializing logic that plays into contemporary anti-Jewish rhetoric. The White supremacist participants in the Charlottesville events chanted anti-Jewish slogans during their marches as part of their messaging around the need for white male power to remain the default in American socio-political life.
34. Levine, "Canaanite Woman," 413, discredits the idea that this woman is thwarting social mores by citing three other places where Jesus interacts with women without comment in Matthew (9:20–22; 26:6–13; 27:55–56).

send the woman away, Jesus responds to them with a clear statement of his limited purpose (v. 23–24)—a statement found only in Matthew. Matthew focuses on this purpose throughout the gospel. Jesus deploys this same rhetoric in 10:5–6 to send the disciples on a preaching mission focused solely on "the lost sheep of the house of Israel." For Matthew, the Canaanite woman's racialized identity, not her gender, disqualifies her from Jesus's attention in this story.

These gendered and racialized dynamics intensify with Matthew's redaction of the woman's actions. While Mark's version of the story includes only one exchange between the woman and Jesus (Mark 26–29), Matthew extends the dialogue.[35] In adding a second dialogue exchange with Jesus, Matthew changes the verb for the woman's posture from προσπίπτω or falling down (Mark 7:25) to προσκυνέω or prostration (Matt 15:25). Instead of simply begging out of desperation, Matthew intensifies Jesus's royal status and the woman's subservience. Matthew's Jesus is the royal heir of the woman's conquerors, and therefore this second plea comes in the form of pious subjection. The woman worships Jesus in the manner of a supplicant to a god or an enslaved person to their enslaver (v. 25).[36] Using this vocabulary of royal subjection, Matthew also calls to mind the posture of captive subjects. Roman propaganda frequently used images of prostrate women in contrast to heroic divine emperors as a way to celebrate victories.[37] While this elision of divine power with political power is a mark of nationalism, it is also a key component in modern-day White supremacist rhetorics.

The combination of gender and ethnic designation creates the power differential between Jesus and the woman. In Matthew's symbolic universe, Jesus is the singular, kingly leader over both sheepy Israel and its canine Canaanite conquests. Matthew's gendered redactions play into a well-known trope in ancient imperial rhetoric, even before the Roman empire. Imperial regimes frequently feminize enemies as a way

---

35. O'Day, "Surprised by Faith," argues that this extension is a parallel literary construction with lament pleas found in the Psalms and the parallels with Psalms. She sees a lament plea in the literary structure that Matthew imposes. Another connection to Israel that Matthew makes that is nearly absent from Mark.

36. S. D. Moore, *Gospel Jesuses and Other Nonhumans*, 66, writes: "Confronted with a paragon of hegemonic masculinity, the only appropriate response from a social or ethnic inferior was fawning obeisance." See also Senior, *Matthew*, 182; and Harrington, *The Gospel of Matthew*, 235.

37. See Lopez, *Apostle to the Conquered*, 26–55.

of showcasing their superiority.[38] One clear example is the first-century Roman coin in Figure 1. Emperor Vespasian's portrait appears on the obverse. On the reverse, a woman crouches in a posture of subjection under a palm tree. The inscription declares, "*Judaea Capta*," Judea is captive.

Figure 1, Bronze coin struck in 71 CE by emperor Vespasian commemorating the Roman conquest of Judea. Copyright: Classical Numismatic Group, Inc., CC BY-SA 3.0, via Wikimedia Commons"

Roman misogyny meets the racialization of Judeans in this coin. Its imagery undergirds the subjected status of the Judeans at Vespasian's hand during and after the siege of Jerusalem. Simultaneously, the coin illustrates the gendered symbolism of subjection as a Canaanite woman in Matthew's version of this story.[39] Matthew exploits feminized images of subjugation to show Jesus's superiority, even as Jesus himself belongs to a conquered people under Roman occupation.[40] Matthew's Jesus re-

---

38. Dube, "Reading for Decolonization," 52, writes: "Imperialist ideology of subjugation constructs extremely gendered discourse. The lands that must be subjugated are equated to a woman, and narratives about the penetration of distant lands feature a woman."

39. Dube, *Postcolonial Feminist Interpretation*, 148, reiterates the idea that portraying the foreigner or conquered person as womanlike communicates her subordination to Jesus.

40. Dube, *Postcolonial Feminist Interpretation*, 127, argues that the Roman empire is the main historical power frame for the story: "How the implied author [Matthew] narratively constructs reality in the text will be associated with the power struggles that pertain to the Roman imperial occupation. Postcolonial theories show that these struggles are usually not only between the colonizer and the colonized but also between various interest groups of the latter . . ."

jects this woman's full participation in his mission because she belongs to a conquered and enslaved people group. Thus, racialized rhetoric that draws on the historical colonial myth-making of Israel's domination of Canaan combines with gendered rhetoric of Roman conquest to create subordinates to the woman in Matthew.

As the story continues, Jesus remains aloof and disengaged with the woman. He responds to her prostrate plea with an aphorism that obliquely calls her a dog: "It is not good to take the children's bread and throw it to little dogs" (v. 26). Inherent in the metaphor is a hierarchical system of relationships that make both dogs and children dependent on Jesus for sustenance—with the dogs always having second priority to children. Yet Matthew intensifies even this distinction by dropping the first phrase from Mark. Mark's Jesus begins this sentence with, "Let the children be fed first" (Mark 7:27). Mark implies the dogs will be fed, just after the children. By deleting this jussive, Matthew implies dogs (and Canaanite women) should not eat the children's food at all.[41] This shift in metaphor heightens the power differential between Jesus and the woman, placing an unassailable barrier between them.[42] Instead of seeing her with compassion, or accepting her prostrate positionality, Jesus dehumanizes the woman calling her a dog who is unworthy of the children's food. Matthew's version of the story judges her as other, diminutive, and less than human in relationship to Jesus.[43] The woman assents to the metaphor and its referent system and acknowledges that even in that inequitable and degrading system, there is an ecosystem of survival. Figuring fellow humans as animals resonates deeply with contemporary racist rhetoric.

Matthew's Jesus replies one last time in the story, "'Woman, great is your faith (πίστις)! Let it be done for you as you wish (θέλεις)" (v. 28). Without knowing her name, Jesus commends her faith and grants her wish. Her daughter is instantly healed. These two words, "faith" and "wish" are key components of Jesus's response. In commending her faith (πίστις), Jesus commends her trust in Jesus. Such trust connotes that she depends on Jesus. Thus Jesus's decision whether or not to use his power. Matthew also adds that the woman "wishes" (θέλω) or desires her daughter's healing. The connotation here is that her daughter's healing is

---

41. Dube, *Postcolonial Feminist Biblical Interpretation*, 164.

42. Some scholars soften Jesus's harsh dismissal in v. 26, noting that κυνάριον refers to a family pet or even a puppy. For one example, see Lawrence, "Crumb Trails and Puppy-Dog Tales," 262–78.

43. Dube, *Postcolonial Feminist Interpretation*, 164.

unlikely or even impossible to achieve. Both these connotations, when combined with the woman's prostrate posture, racialized and conquered status, and categorization as a secondarily valued dog, place her in a relationship of dependence. This dependence stands in stark contrast to Jesus's kingly lineage, self-sufficiency, and divine connections—precisely the qualifications that allow him to grant her wish. Here, Matthew's Jesus accepts the woman's assent to the inequity of the racialized system. The power to change the woman's situation in Matthew's version belongs entirely to Jesus. The woman's only action is prostration and pleading. In this way, Matthew has redacted the story so the woman and her daughter illustrate the power possibilities for Jesus as an object lesson. At the end of the story, the woman must accept whatever Jesus gives her, and Jesus looks good just because he changed his mind. But the argument Matthew puts forward is still about crumbs. Magnanimity about crumbs is another deeply embedded dynamic of White supremacy.

Homiletic Overtures

My primary preaching audience is White mainline protestant church communities that often have liberal/progressive political leanings (although not always) and in some cases are aware of their complicity in systemic racial injustice. On August 20, 2017, I preached at such a church in Winston-Salem, NC. I had often preached there, so I knew some of its character as a community. This community was established in the 1960s as a response to the needs of Lutherans who had moved into the fast-growing suburban developments west of the city. Its founding coincided with a demographic movement of White middle-class families away from the mixed-race and primarily African-American neighborhoods around downtown and on the east side of the city. That morning the gathered community was mostly White, aging, middle to upper-middle-class, well-educated, liberal-leaning Lutherans.

I knew the events in Charlottesville just two weeks prior had shocked and horrified this community. I had an opportunity to acknowledge their emotions and challenge them—with their vestiges of a perfect White Jesus—to recognize how faith communities participate in the rise of such violence. They had heard me question the perspective of the biblical text from the pulpit on other Sundays. The following is an edited version of my sermon manuscript for the eleventh Sunday after Pentecost (August

20), 2017. The context, described above in fuller detail, was a liberal, White, mainline Lutheran church in North Carolina.

Homily

It has been a week of our lives with the usual things: sending children off to college, holding vigil at hospital beds, babies born, school getting ready to start, and celebrating late-summer weddings. I've walked the dog, made dinner, talked to my parents, ribbed my friends, and pulled a weed or two from my garden (while wringing my hands about needing to pull more). I've done some pretty mundane stuff.

But Charlottesville and the events last weekend (specifically, August 11, 2017), along with the wrangling over blame, the scramble to characterize it correctly, and the expectation that someone will do something about it all hangs heavy over the whole week. In the midst of our very ordinary lives, we have been confronted with the sinful systems and machinations of White supremacy in ways that some of our lifetimes have never seen. And we have not heard words of mercy or consolation from the places where we expect to hear things like, "Racism is in the past, we need to move forward with equality and tolerance." Or "Let's live peacefully and learn how to love everyone." Nor have we heard words that resonate with our sense of justice, "The systemic practice of White supremacy is morally bankrupt." Or "Intimidation, threats, and insults against people of color in the US perpetuate unjust relationships among Americans." We have heard neither words of mercy nor words of justice. And I suspect, at times, we have wanted to hear some of both. Mercy that soothes our rent-apart souls. Justice that gives us a compass for moving forward.

And then we hear this morning's Gospel text. At the center of this morning's Gospel reading is a question about what it means to be morally just and divinely merciful. Jesus encounters a Canaanite woman desperate for him to heal her daughter (Matt 15:22). When she asks for his help, they fundamentally disagree on whether or not Jesus's ministry includes helping her (Matt 15:25–27). You see, she was a Canaanite woman. In the story of the Israelite people—their escape from slavery in Egypt, their wanderings in the wilderness for 40 years, and their settling in the promised land—we often don't tell the part where this woman's ancestors, the Canaanites, were happily residing in the Promised Land before the Israelites ever came. Jesus's ancestors conquered and enslaved this woman's ancestors. And so, in Jesus' time, Canaanites were seen as weak, ungodly, pagan, and certainly not worthy of the attention and healing power of Jesus, the kingly Messiah. Surely, as most people living with these realities do, the woman in the story knows this is how Jesus's people perceive her. But she has heard about this Jesus guy, with his compassion for crowds and his power to heal. She asks him—no, she shouts at him—in the streets "Jesus, Son of David, can you heal my daughter?" (Matt 15:22). The disciples, having little tolerance for the noise of protestors asking for things, urge Jesus to silence her and send her away. And Jesus seems to agree with them, noting that he had come for Israel's sake (Matt 15:24).

When the woman continues, changing her plea from a shout to a posture of worshipful vulnerability (Matt 15:25), we celebrate her recognition of Jesus and her willingness to be dependent on his power. This woman is no ordinary woman. And because she is so devout, Jesus's answer surprises us. We usually think of Jesus as the benevolent wish-granter, the compassionate healer, or the guy who was just plain nice to everybody. So his words sting quite sharply when he looks her in the eye and says, "It is not fair to take the children's food and throw it to the dogs" (Matt 15:26). Jesus, who are you? Jesus, how is that response compassionate, merciful, or even just?!

Jesus's comment dehumanizes the Canaanite woman in a way that ignores her desperation and her daughter's need. And it's here that I have always felt unsettled and unmoored whenever I read this story. Matthew's gospel shines a mirror on the ugliest part of Jesus. We see the hideousness of human tendencies to dismiss out of hand and with demeaning language our fellow human beings over matters of race, religion, or a litany of other differences. This hideousness shows up in Jesus. It's not the disciples (although they're not innocent) who say this to the woman. It's not the crowds, or the Pharisees, or the Priests who say this to the woman. It is Jesus who says this to the woman. Had he stopped with his insistence that he was "sent only to the lost sheep of the house of Israel" (Matt 15:24), we might not have seen it as clearly. After all, we often identify with this statement. We often think our resources are barely enough for our own folks.

But it's the analogy between children and dogs that cuts so sharply this morning. We would never call our own children dogs. Would I ever call my nieces dogs? Would I allow someone else to make that analogy? Would you?

At this point, we have a full-blown theological crisis on our hands. Our Jesus, who is the blameless lamb of the world; our Jesus, whose innocence on the cross is what shows us our own faults; our Jesus, the perfect one, God made flesh; our Jesus cannot possibly be rejecting a woman of a different race and her daughter as unworthy of his full grace, mercy, and power. Our Jesus cannot possibly be the one who grants the woman's daughter healing but shows no sign of re-thinking his comparison of Canaanites to dogs. Our Jesus in this morning's gospel relents—he never repents. What is our Jesus doing?!

One resolution to this crisis is to conclude that Jesus, whose perfection never changed, is noting that there are second-class people in the world who are worthy only of scraps. But this perspective sounds to me, in our current context, too much like White supremacist logic. This logic shows up when Christians insist that Jesus is working only for us. This logic shows up when Christians insist that God's blessing falls only on those who are like us. This logic shows up when Christians suggest that Jesus's—indeed God's—moral superiority is based on *our knowledge* of an unchanging perfection in God's very center.

But thank God, the story does not end here, and our theology need not be built on identifying with either character in the story. The woman in this morning's Gospel is understandably not satisfied with a Jesus who is perfectly compassionate, merciful, and just only for his own people. She points out the flaw in his insistence on excluding her daughter from his mercy. The woman in this morning's Gospel draws on Jesus's own argument to say, "Even dogs cannot be ignored under the table" (Matt 15:27). She insists that Jesus must provide for her daughter's healing. She probably didn't know Isaiah's words as she spoke with Jesus—those words about justice and salvation for the foreigner in Isa 56:3 ("Do not let the foreigner joined to the Lord say, "The Lord will surely separate me from his people")—but nevertheless, she reminds Jesus that his own tradition has something more compassionate in it. The very tradition he invokes to exclude her from his healing power also includes a radical receptivity on God's part toward those who are different. Jesus's own tradition carries reminders of the expansive reach of God's mercy in the world. In fact, the woman's rebuttal *reminds* Jesus just how radically merciful his own tradition and his God, *our* God, really is.

Here is where we get to the crux of the Good News this morning, to the heart of the Gospel *and* the challenge that remains from it. The woman prompts us to remember God's radical mercy. But the failings of systemic justice in this story hold up a mirror to our own world—to see in the story not our perfect exemplar in Jesus. Rather the mirror helps us see our participation in systems that perpetuate our separation of our siblings in God's creation into food-worthy and crumb-worthy groups. Crumbs, this story shows us, are never enough for a living, breathing, creation-sustaining God. You see, Jesus in our gospel stories does not always, everywhere, with flawlessness say the correct words. Nor does he enact justice instantly. He does not perceive systems of injustice in their totality and dismantle them in a flash.

Even Jesus, in this story, does not know how far and wide and deep God's compassion, healing, and love can spread. Certainly, he does not expect God's hand to stretch beyond his own community to systemic reparation. The Canaanite woman questions her own exclusion but does not give us a mandate toward equity. Rather *our* engagement with the story and its flaws shows us our need to widen our work for systemic justice. The text shows us how strong and impassioned our advocacy must be. And we see this not from Jesus, but from a woman who felt the pinch of God's love too narrowly exercised, too stingily given, too exclusively understood, reluctantly rather than repentantly given.

How do we stand back from the story and see a world in which the woman should not have to receive crumbs only because of her willingness to beg? How do we stand back from the story and see a Jesus who mirrors our flaws in understanding God's possibilities for reordering the whole world? You see, at the very heart of God, at the center of our theological world is an insistence that God's heart will always envelop us in both mercy and justice. It is mercy that soothes our soul's tears and forgives our inability to instantly love beyond the expanse of our imagination. It is justice that must always be our compass, shifting our understanding and our action in its direction. May Jesus's mercy be your companion in these days and may God's creative justice be your guide.

Conclusion

Over the seven years since I preached this sermon, this story has been part of the lectionary reading two more times (in 2020 and 2023). Its parallel in Mark has appeared three times (2018, 2021, 2024). None of the same White supremacist socio-cultural upheaval was as near in subsequent appearances of this text—although the same White supremacist dynamics were still present in the social systems surrounding White mainline protestant churches. Nevertheless, a different approach to using this text as a reflection on racial injustice and systemic racism would be needed in each of these subsequent years. Given the biblical text's ability to accompany communities across situations, I would argue that preachers in White mainline liberal or progressive faith communities should understand biblical interpretation for the homiletic moment as radically contextual. In other words, homiletic calls for racial justice, for naming of injustice, and for dismantling of White supremacist systems cannot and will not be useful until preachers also dismantle the logics created in the intersections of biblical, social, and political contexts—the preachers', the audiences', the geography, and the particularities of the political moment. If White supremacist logics are created and reinforced from biblical texts through these intersections, dismantling them requires preachers to decolonize, differentiate, and at times diminish the role of a singular, perfect, authority in the figure of Jesus.

14

The Good News of a Struggle to Care (Matthew 15:21-28)

Challenge and Opportunity for Intercultural Caregivers

DANIEL S. SCHIPANI

Introduction

IN MY DECADES-LONG VOCATIONAL journey, the overarching epistemological and methodological framework has been supplied by Practical Theology; in other words, action research that is empirically grounded, interdisciplinary, hermeneutically structured, normatively infused, and pragmatically and strategically oriented.[1] Furthermore, those practical and theoretical endeavors have been carried out with a Christian perspective on care and justice that informs both a vision of reality and normative criteria regarding human life in community.[2] From this religious

---

1. For a systematic, thorough study of the fourfold epistemological and methodological structure of practical theology, see Osmer, *Practical Theology*. Other complementary contributions consistent with my research and overall work in practical theology are Anderson, *The Shape of Practical Theology*; Bass and Dykstra, *For Life Abundant*; Miller-McLemore, *Christian Theology in Practice*; Swinton and Mowat, *Practical Theology and Qualitative Research*; and Volf and Bass, *Practicing Theology*.

2. From a philosophy of science viewpoint, practical disciplines concerned with the orientation and reorientation of human behavior, such as education and psychotherapy,

and theological location, I seek to contribute to this book together with the company of biblical scholars.

This chapter approaches Matt 15:21–28 as a case study. It does so by working on the gospel story with attention to the four dimensions, tasks, and movements of the discipline: empirical-descriptive (observation), interpretive (analysis), normative (evaluation), and pragmatic-strategic (application).[3] In what follows, through interdisciplinary lenses, this chapter will illuminate Jesus's stunning encounter with a Canaanite woman in the borderlands. The narrative is thus reframed as a paradigmatic illustration of a total stranger (the woman as an Other) opening up an *epiphanic space*. In light of that claim, the argument presented is that the story shows, on the one hand, how intercultural encounters risk misunderstanding and harm; on the other hand, how those very situations offer possibilities for gaining insight and welcoming collaboration and healing.

Consistent with the overarching statement in the subtitle of this book—"Transgressive Readings for Transformational Preaching"—this chapter articulates a twofold contribution: It is written with an explicitly *interdisciplinary* approach to a sacred text while assuming its inexhaustible reservoir of meaning; and it highlights the *theological* significance of the gospel story, which is of course an essential component of "transformational preaching" as a particular form of Christian ministry. In light of all those considerations, the following sections explicate the hermeneutical horizon and then offer an interpretation of the text resulting from such an approach. There follow homiletic overtures with a homily that was actually delivered in a workshop for Cuban chaplains.

Hermeneutical Horizon

As already asserted, my interdisciplinary approach to the text is informed by an application of Practical Theology as an inherently hermeneutical discipline. The core dimensions of practical theological interpretation

---

cannot be ethically neutral. They always involve visions of reality and normative criteria concerning "good" society, "healthy" human life, and way(s) "forward" in human development, whether explicitly or implicitly. For example, Don S. Browning systematically unveiled the implicit metaphysical and ethical assumptions of major modern psychologies. Browning and Cooper, *Religious Thought & the Modern Psychologies*, 1–20.

3. For a demonstration of the structural analogy between the case study method and practical theology as a discipline, see Schipani, "Case Study Method," 89–101.

can be characterized as a fourfold dimension process involving distinct activities or "tasks."[4] Practical theological interpretation can thus be applied, for example, to a caregiving episode or situation; and it can also supply hermeneutic lenses in the study of an ancient or sacred text such as Matt 15:21–28; further, in the latter case, the reference can be to both the text itself as written and read today, and to the event and situation presented in the text. A comprehensive methodological-epistemological process can be described with simply worded questions connected to each of the four "tasks": (a) "What is going on?" Gathering information necessary to discern patterns, dynamics, etc. is the *descriptive-empirical* dimension and task of practical theological interpretation; (b) "Why is this going on?" Drawing from theories of the arts and sciences to better understand and explain why those patterns and dynamics are taking place is the *interpretive* dimension and task; (c) "What should be going on?" Constructing interdisciplinary ethical norms (e.g. from biblical studies, theology and social sciences) to guide the responses and learning from good or better practices are the *normative* task; (d) "How might we respond?" Determining strategies for caregiving action will affect situations in desirable (e.g. "faithful", effective) ways. It should be obvious that the normative and strategic dimensions of practical theological interpretation are essential and distinctive features of Practical Theology as a theological discipline. It should also be apparent that this practical theological activity represents a special manifestation of the "turn to hermeneutics" during the last century.

Hans-Georg Gadamer is rightly associated with the systematic recognition of the interpretive dimension of scholarship.[5] Practical theologians have embraced his views of *hermeneutical experience* and hermeneutical circulation process with five "movements": *pre-understanding* (interpretive judgments and understandings with which we begin interpretations); the *experience of being brought up short* (a challenge to such preunderstanding); *dialogical interplay* (back and forth interplay between the horizon of the interpreter and the horizon of the text or the persons being interpreted); *fusion of horizons* (interpretations thus yields new insights as an epistemic result of the dialogue); and *application* (new insights point to new ways of thinking and acting in the world).

---

4. The rest of this section closely follows Richard R. Osmer's contribution in Osmer, *Practical Theology*, 4–29.

5. Gadamer, *Truth and Method*.

Interpretation

Seeing[6] the Text in Context

Jesus's unexpected encounter with a Syrophoenician/Canaanite woman appears only in Mark and Matthew. In fact, Mark 7 and Matt 15 are remarkably paralleled because of narrative content and sequencing. Nevertheless, we note some significant differences between the two accounts of Jesus's encounter with a foreign woman seeking healing for her daughter. Those dissimilarities suggest that Matthew has an agenda in intensifying some features of the story.

We also realize that prior to encountering the foreign woman, Jesus had been involved in a serious controversy with Pharisees and scribes concerning the "tradition of the elders" on the question of eating with defiled hands. Jesus responded by accusing them of breaking God's commandment and making void God's word for the sake of their tradition, including a damning quote from the prophet Isaiah (Mark 7:1–13; Matt 15:1–9). Then we are told that Jesus spoke with authority about the spiritual implications of his position. In fact, he did so by using both direct and indirect language, that is, parabolic communication that requires further explanation (Mark 7:14–23; Matt 15:10–20).

It is significant that before being surprised by the foreign woman[7] Jesus had been engaged in a serious conflict situation. We might say that his adversaries put the controversy in terms of socio-religious and cultural adaptation—the conventional wisdom of needing to follow the tradition of the elders. In other words, the gospel accounts suggest that the nature of their argument betrayed a two-dimensional vision: they understood holiness as conformity to the precepts and practices handed down through religious teaching and socialization. Observance of the tradition, therefore, defined one's belonging to the chosen people of Israel. With the same framework

---

6. I employ the familiar movements of an inductive Bible study process in popularized Latin American terms, especially among so-called ordinary readers in Christian faith communities: "ver," "juzgar," "actuar" (seeing, judging, acting). The "judging" movement in those situations includes both interpretation and evaluation (which correlate with the third and fourth tasks of a practical theological approach.

7. Among the many scholars who studied this story we find interesting observations and hypotheses concerning the ethnic identity of the woman ("a Greek, born in Syrian Phoenicia," according to Mark 7:26a; "a Canaanite from that region [the district of Tyre and Sidon], according to Matt 15:21). Questions linger such as, was she a widow?; not necessarily poor?, etc.

we can claim that Jesus perceived the question four-dimensionally;[8] accordingly, for him the real problem lied in accommodating tradition while disobeying the will of God, as in the case of the commandment to honor father and mother. In that light, Jesus contended that the very worship of God had been compromised. So, for Jesus, the transformation of the tradition of the elders itself was a necessary outcome of radical trust in, and obedience to the living God of Israel.

It is also interesting to visualize Jesus speaking firmly, with certainty and authority, about the way of authentic spirituality right before he met the woman in the borderlands and faced a seemingly different kind of conflict situation. Indeed, it may be argued that Jesus still needed to process more deeply, both existentially and theologically, the very meaning and implications of "tradition" being confronted by divine grace. Could it be that a difficult scanning process[9] requiring the collaboration of such a special stranger would eventually lead Jesus to further light? That way, a transformative learning would translate into deeper caring and liberating power and a clearer sense of vocation? With such a question in mind, we now turn to that eventful encounter.

Highlights of a Stunning Confrontation

A plain reading of the story presents a unique instance in which Jesus yields. The most striking and problematic part of the story is, of course, Jesus's initial response to the request of the woman: First, a deafening silence, then an uncharacteristic affirmation of boundaries, followed by parabolic refusal. At that moment he appears to regard the woman's request as inappropriate, even as outrageously out of place! Only in this particular gospel story does Jesus ignore a supplicant, place the barrier

---

8. This is an allusion to James E. Loder's view of the "fourfold knowing event," which involves the lived world, the self, the void, and the Holy. See Loder, *The Transforming Moment*, chapter 3. Loder writes that "being human entails environment, selfhood, the possibility of nonbeing, and the possibility of new being. All four dimensions are essential, and none of them can be ignored without excessive loss to our understanding of what is essentially human" (69).

9. Scanning here denotes the conscious and unconscious process of seeking resolution to a given conflict situation, hopefully leading to new insight and a path forward. In Loder's practical theological perspective, scanning follows a baffled struggle (or conflict) in a context of rapport. Like in a creative process, scanning can eventually lead to a new insight and release of energy (i.e. *Eureka!* effect). The creative process culminates with interpretation and verification, hence resolution.

of ethnicity before a plea for help, and then use offensive language to reiterate the barrier. Without question, "dog" is a disdainful metaphor, though Jesus uses a diminutive form ("puppy," "little bitch"). The implication, of course, is that the gentiles/dogs have no place at the table. The woman, however, appears to play along with that harsh image and simply urges Jesus to take it one step further. She appeals to him as "Lord," asserts her claim, and demonstrates her faith by arguing that at the very least both children (Jews) and dogs (gentiles) are under the same caring, compassionate authority.

We need not infer that the woman agrees with the gentile/dog analogy. Nor do we need to conclude that she considers herself unworthy and less than human, or that she identifies herself as a dog.[10] On the contrary, we may assume that she is requesting that she and her daughter be included, that she hopes for a place at the table while challenging Israel's excluding ideology. When she says, "Yes, Lord . . . ," she agrees with Jesus that it would be wrong to throw the children's bread to the dogs. But she also reminds Jesus that if even dogs may eat what their masters waste, she and her daughter should receive bread, too. The Canaanite woman seems to understand the grave meaning and the implications of Jesus's initial response, but she proceeds relentlessly and daringly to reframe and recast it.

Jesus's original challenge to the woman merely restates the status quo of gender, ethnic, cultural, religious, and political divisions. Her counter-challenge calls him to look to the place for new possibilities across and beyond the established boundaries. Instead of accepting the dichotomy of children (insiders/receiving food) versus dogs (outsiders/no food), she imagines that both the children and the dogs can be graciously fed inside, within the same household and from the same table.[11] Stated in other terms, the foreign woman is facing the "Void"[12] as she tries to deal with the painful reality of her daughter's torment, and begs for mercy. Jesus, however, initially appears to cling to the conventional wisdom that he had earlier rejected. He seems to be pushed to face the possibility of his

---

10. Several authors address the issue of "dogs" in the story, such as Asikainen, "Women Out of Place," 183–88.

11. Elaine M. Wainwright argues this point in *Shall We Look for Another?*, 86–92.

12. In Loder's model, the Void ultimately denotes human existence "destined to annihilation . . . irrevocable drift toward utter emptiness and nothingness which accompanies human existence from the time of birth [and] has many faces—such as loneliness, depression, and death." Loder, *The Transforming Moment*, 230.

own faithlessness and abandonment of God at this point. Personally and vocationally he is challenged to come face to face with the holiness of God "beyond the boundaries" at the prompting of the foreign woman.

The dramatic import of this encounter in the borderlands is heightened as we recall its historical and textual background. "Show them no mercy," Moses had said to the people of Israel (Deut 7:2). "Have mercy on me, Lord, Son of David," the Canaanite woman implores the (Matthean) New Moses of Israel. This Canaanite woman thus shatters the lingering image of wicked Canaanites, who presumably offer their children in sacrifice to their gods; she pleads on behalf of her daughter, who cannot speak for herself. Well aware of his people's position and privilege as "chosen," Jesus initially reasserts the exclusiveness of his mission. But in the end, he welcomes the woman and she receives what she had sought with passion, courage, and dogged determination.

We also notice that this story parallels that of the Roman centurion in Matt 8:5–13. These are the only two healings in this Gospel explicitly involving gentiles and accomplished from a distance. In both cases Jesus deems the people worthy of the gift of healing. In fascinating reversals, both gentiles even become exemplary figures. Most commentators indicate that although Matthew's final word on mission to the gentiles does not come until the last chapter of the Gospel (28:16–20), in these and related episodes the theme emerges that ethnicity does not define the identity of the people of God. Intertextual comparative studies show that Matthew's overall positive portrait of Jesus's response to the gentiles constitutes a partial reversal of the Exodus tradition by focusing on the missional goal of bringing outsiders to the knowledge of the God of Israel.[13] God's purposes include gentiles, and Jesus the Jew is the agent of divine grace on their behalf.[14] Transformation—that is, *systemic change* of mind, relationships, and structures—can happen in the borderlands.

---

13. Willard M. Swartley makes this point in *Israel's Scripture Traditions and the Synoptic Gospels*, 70.

14. See for instance, Carter, *Matthew and the Margins*, 320ff. Other studies done with a "decolonizing" interest and perspective present a different picture as they attempt to unveil and deconstruct certain perceived biases in the biblical text. See, for example, Dube, "A Postcolonial Feminist Reading of Matthew 15:21–28," in *Postcolonial Feminist Interpretation of the Bible*. For this African scholar, "the divergent receptions accorded to the centurion and the Canaanite woman reflect the imperial and patriarchal currents at work in Matthew . . . No doubt [sic], the implied author, writing in the post-70 C.E. period, wishes to present the Matthean community as a nonsubversive community" (132–33). Dube's thesis and overall discussion are provocative; nevertheless, she neglects to acknowledge inherent tensions and dialectical import within biblical text, thus

Judging (I): Interpreting the Text

In the previous section we raised the question whether Jesus, viewed as a pastoral caregiver, needed to undergo a difficult "scanning" process requiring the collaboration of a foreign woman in the borderlands in order to further discern the nature and contours of divine grace. Earlier in the gospel text we saw him responding with clarity and certainty in the face of challenge by Pharisees and scribes. Now he is treading unfamiliar territory and the support of his circle of disciples does not seem to be particularly helpful.

The text before us calls for recognizing several kinds of stretching. Geographic, ethnic, gender, religious, theological, socio-cultural, moral, and political dimensions are involved. No wonder, then, that the encounter with the foreign woman stunned Jesus. Because this narrative has much spatial and contextual import, it is fitting that our interpretation underscores that this marginal Canaanite woman emerges as the center of the story. In fact, the story is primarily her story. We observe a surprising, transforming reversal: Jesus acknowledges that she has *great* faith, and *her* faith becomes the means for her daughter's healing. Matthew's Gospel uses that adjective to describe faith only once. The woman's faith encompasses her persistent demand for inclusion in the face of Jesus's resistance and insulting words; her challenge to the gender, ethnic, religious, political, and economic barriers; her recognition of Jesus's authority over demons; and her reliance on his power.[15]

Perhaps Jesus's praise includes a realization that, in the encounter in the borderlands, the Canaanite woman became a prophetic and wise teacher. Out of her desire to heal her daughter, she acted and spoke counter-culturally and counter-politically. We can claim that she reminded Jesus of the larger vision of the reign of God and that she did so in a way consistent with the converging prophetic and wisdom traditions with which Jesus/Wisdom (Sophia) is interpreted in the Gospel of Matthew.[16] The Syrophoenician/Canaanite woman had approached Jesus as a care seeker on behalf of her daughter; in the process of her encounter with Jesus, she also ministered to him by eventually focusing on *negating*

---

failing to appreciate a key aspect of its liberating and transformational potential. Dube's readings is *neo-modern* (not *postmodern*); her welcome, transgressive reading—a decolonizing approach—becomes reductionist when absolutized.

15. Carter, *Matthew and the Margins*, 324–25.
16. Wainwright, *Shall We Look for Another?*, 88.

(or *contradicting*) *the negation* inherent in the dog-gentile analogy traditionally used by Jews at the time. In terms of transformational logic, her "bisociating"[17] insight amounted to a constructive act of the imagination, which eventually resonated with Jesus's own imagination. The encounter itself—the unique relationality linking Jesus and the foreign woman— was transformed: confrontation became a kind of collaborative work. And while the disciples seemed to fade into the background, the foreign woman became emotionally and spiritually closer to Jesus.[18]

The most vexing question from a pastoral/practical theology perspective is why Jesus would act as he initially did in this encounter. An answer requires that we keep in mind the tension between two realities pertaining to his socio-cultural experience or lived world. On the one hand, we assume that Jesus had been socialized into the conventional wisdom of his time and dominant culture. According to such socialization, prudence involves keeping clear boundaries; adhering to certain criteria of what is proper, clean, normal, and appropriate; and holding to the right categories and patterns of perception, thought, and relationships. This socialization was undoubtedly part of Jesus's identity as a first-century Jew. From a human science perspective, we do not expect that Jesus would have been exempt from dealing with prejudice. Nor do we expect that he

17. "Bisociation" denotes the surprising convergence of two incompatible frames of reference to compose an original and meaningful unity; bisociation is the basic unit of an insight, which may include several bisociations to form a complex new meaning. And "constructive acts of imagination" are those insights, intuitions, or visions that appear—usually with convincing force—in the borderline area between consciousness and unconsciousness; they convey, in a form readily available to consciousness, the essence of a conflict resolution. Loder, *The Transforming Moment*, 222.

18. "Systemic change" is a simple definition of transformation. For a study on transformation in intercultural Bible reading, see Schipani, "Transformation in Intercultural Reading of the Bible." For a comprehensive study on transformation in connection with reading the Bible, see Kim, *A Transformative Reading of the Bible*. He discusses four models of transformation depending on their emphasis on different forms of human existence—autonomy (a mode of rule by self), relationality (a mode of rule by community), and heteronomy (a mode of rule by Other). He asserts that these modes reflect scholars' views of an ideal transformation in terms of individual life (autonomy), communal life (relationality) and religious experience (heteronomy). The four models discussed are as follows: the usual Western model (*individual-autonomous* transformation), the liberation model (*social-relational* transformation), the religious community model (*traditional-communal* transformation), and the religious individual model (*mystic, charismatic* transformation). Kim then proceeds to present his *holistic* model of transformation seeking to integrate the aim of human transformation in personal and public life; by connecting those three modes of human existence; three moments of human life ("I am no-one, I am some-one, I am for-others"); and the three subjects of human transformation (self, neighbor, and God).

would have spontaneously developed the kind of understanding enabling him to readily appreciate and communicate with the woman across vast ethnic, social, cultural, and religious differences.

On the other hand, we also recognize that Jesus of Nazareth was himself a marginal person.[19] He was rejected by the dominant groups and became a friend of marginalized people such as tax-collectors, outcasts, women, the poor and oppressed, "sinners," and gentiles. In other words, Jesus related abnormally well to those people and was accepted by them, because he was himself an outsider, a homeless person (Matt 8:20) living in two worlds without fully belonging to either.[20] In sum, from a theological perspective, the historical and existential reality of the incarnation involves the "body" (*sôma*) as well as "soul" (*psyche*) and "spirit" (*pneuma*). Stated in other words, a normative Christology necessitates a holistic anthropology.

An outsider, a marginal person, challenged Jesus to relate and minister across and beyond those boundaries. She gave him an opportunity to respond in tune with God's alternative wisdom expressed in an ethic and politic of compassion and radical inclusiveness. It is fitting to conclude that Jesus faced a major conflict and temptation, indeed a temptation from within, so to speak, and that eventually he chose wisely, even as he was creatively challenged by the foreign woman. From a Christian practical theological interpretation, this conclusion need not compromise the Christological conviction about the nature and work of Jesus as Christ. As Heb 4:15 puts it, "We do not have a high priest who is unable to sympathize with our weaknesses, but we have one who in every respect has been tested as we are, yet without sin." Acceptance of that interpretation implies rejection of other interpretations, such as: (a) Jesus was testing (that is, playing games with) the woman while knowing all along what he should and would do; (b) he wanted to teach the disciples a dramatic lesson about loving outsiders and enemies; (c) Jesus had to be literally converted; (d) Matthew's Jesus reflects accommodation to, and implicit support for the Roman empire.[21] The biblical text supports none of these

19. For a scholarly treatment of the marginality of Jesus, see Meier, *A Marginal Jew*.

20. Jung Young Lee insightfully discussed the question of Jesus and marginality in *Marginality*. Writing from an Asian (Korean) American perspective, Lee proposed "a new theology based on marginality," which serves not only as a hermeneutical paradigm but as a key to the substance of the Christian faith," 1.

21. Such "postcolonial" reading disregards Jesus's ethical and political teaching presented by Matthew, especially in the Sermon on the Mount (Matt 5–7). His teaching can be understood as a countercultural and counter-political manifesto, that is, an

interpretations. Theologically and spiritually put, the text implies the triumph of Jesus's (and the foreign woman's) spirit grounded and sustained by the Spirit of God. This gospel story illumines the question of how the spiritual life can become transcendent and at the same time preserve its immanent integrity in the context of human experience.

Jesus appropriated the woman's insight significantly, expanding the contours of compassion and care. Viewed in terms of a creative process, energy was released (that is, the Eureka! effect): he praised the woman in unusual terms, and her daughter was healed. Afterwards, more "signs" and miracles followed that encounter. The personal drama and the behavior of the Syrophoenician/Canaanite woman became a catalyst of the multifaceted transforming encounter in the borderlands: barriers were broken, temptation was overcome, understandings were deepened, faith was affirmed, and a child was healed.

The story, as it unfolds, makes clear that both the woman and Jesus became boundary walkers and boundary breakers. By eventually choosing to relate and to minister "out of place," Jesus and the woman pointed the way to God's utopia. "Utopia" means literally "no place," not in the sense of never-never land, illusion, or fantasy, but as the stuff of prophetic dreams. Utopias are places that are not yet, not because they are mere ideals beyond reach, but because evil and sinful structures and behaviors resist and contradict Divine will for multidimensional (that is, ethnic, social, cultural, and religious) justice and reconciliation.

As we judge this text, we realize its significance in light of the social and existential realities of the Matthean community. On the one hand, we recognize that Matthew was written from the perspective of the "chosen people of Israel," beginning with "Jesus the Messiah, the son of David, the son of Abraham" (Matt 1:1). The author writes from the center of the tradition, and from a typically "centralist" point of view.[22] Within this framework Jesus instructs the disciples, "Go nowhere among the Gentiles . . . , but go rather to the lost sheep of the house of Israel" (Matt 10:5–6). The latter expression is unique to Matthew and repeated in our text. The author leaves no doubt about Israel's priority in salvation history. On the other hand, the story of the Canaanite woman can help undermine and even dismantle—that is, dialectically speaking, negate the negation imposed by—chosenness as ideology, as justification for excluding and

---

alternative to the ethics and politics of Empire to be contextually enacted by a messianic community in the midst of Empire.

22. Lee, *Marginality*, 116.

discriminating against the other, the stranger, the foreigner, the "pagan." Therefore, a powerful paradox is at work here.

We surmise that the early readers of Matthew were Jewish Christians separated from the synagogue and relating both to a largely gentile Christian movement and to the Jewish community. The story might have aided them to understand their new place and role in the faith community. This story might have helped them be freed from the ideology of chosenness so they could be transformed into a more liberating, just and inclusive faith community. Perhaps they were already beginning to experience such a community, but were unsure about how to cope with, legitimate, and reflect on it.[23] This transition and transformation of the Matthean community would have been crucial for their sense of identity as well as for testimony and generous service; they would become, in Paul's words, a faith community "where there is no longer Jew or Greek, slave or free, male and female, for all are one in Christ (Gal 3:28)." Such inclusive community would thus be called to celebrate, embody, and be an agent of the coming reign of God.

Judging (II): Evaluating the Text

As indicated in the introductory paragraphs of this chapter, from a practical theology perspective the story can be studied as a case study. In the previous sections we addressed the questions, what is going on? and why is that going on? We will now consider the third question—what ought to be going on?—that is, the normative task of highlighting valuable "lessons" or guidelines for Christian ministry in today's multicultural and multifaith world.

We can realize the creative and liberating potential of this story in many ways on personal and communal levels. The following interrelated guidelines illustrate how this text can become foundational for ministering persons and caregivers in particular. The story illumines at least three interrelated principles—that is, dependable guides to practice—for caregiving and other ministry practices. Those principles can be stated as pertaining to marginality, vulnerability and *vision*; conflict, suffering and *virtue*; and mutuality, mission, and *vocation*.[24]

23. Leticia A. Guardiola-Sáenz discusses this question in "Borderless Women and Borderless Texts," 69–81.

24. I have proposed to understand spirituality and "human spirit" functionally and transculturally in terms of the interrelated categories of *vision*, *virtue*, and *vocation*.

Marginality, Vulnerability, and Vision

First, contrary to what dominant cultures hold, the borderlands can become privileged places for the blessings of creative and transformative caring and for personal and communal growth and healing. In light of our interpretation, this is what happened in the gospel story: the clearest illustration of Jesus learning from a foreign, gentile woman.[25]

Conventional and pragmatic wisdom favors the safe havens of familiar territory, the shrewd and sensible stance of "playing it safe." The story of the Canaanite woman who confronts Jesus helps us realize that we can see reality better at places of marginality and vulnerability and from the vantage point available to us at the borders. Our vision may thus be transformed. Hence, we are called to creative "willful contextual dislocations."[26] This story compels us to move deliberately beyond our comfort zones, either by going out or by welcoming into our midst the stranger, the alien, or the different Other. By moving from the center to the margins, we find our perspectives significantly changed: we become aware of the lenses through which we view the world, and our cultural and ideological captivities are unveiled. We are thus open to see better how to live and care for others in creative, healing, and empowering ways wherever we are.

Intercultural and interfaith situations present unique challenges and opportunities for caregivers and others to grow in *vision*, in the sense of perceiving care seekers and the very relationship of care with the eyes of God. That growth includes a number of dimensions and practices such as these: attentiveness, contemplation, and respectful and appreciative awareness of the uniqueness and value of the care receiver; critical thinking and

---

For the latest version of such construct see, Schipani, *Spiritual Care in Our Multifaith World*, 20–39.

25. On this point, see McGrath, *What Jesus Learned from Women*, 91–107. From a liberationist practical theological approach, the gospel story illustrates the teaching authority of the Other, whether a suffering stranger, marginalized, oppressed, or a mother whose child is gravely ill. McGrath helpfully includes input from a number of sources, such as Asikainen, "Women Out of Place;" Connor, *Fierce;* Driscoll, *Reading Between the Lines*; Hartman, *Letting the Other Speak* ; Kinukawa, "De-colonizing"; Love, *Jesus and Marginal Women*; Ringe, "Gentile Women Story;" O'Day, "Surprised by Faith"; Ruiz, *Readings from the Edges*; Schüssler Fiorenza, *In Memory of Her*; and Wahlberg, *Jesus According to a Woman*.

26. For the notion of willful (or voluntary) dislocation in connection with transformative learning, see Schipani, "Liberation Theology and Religious Education," 308–10; and "Educating for Social Transformation," 37–38.

creative imagination to deal with and transform barriers to communication and understanding and collaboration; spiritual discernment: (a) to recognize the care receivers' actual needs, hopes, and resourcefulness in their own terms; (b) to make available specific, pertinent care; and (c) to be intentionally open to receiving the spiritual gifts provided by those of other faiths. Growth in *vision*, thus understood, must be considered together with growth in *virtue* and *vocation*, as defined below.

Conflict, Suffering, and Virtue

A second guideline suggested by our study is that situations of conflict and suffering can become opportunities for transformation, for renewal and healing, and for witnessing God's amazing grace.[27] People who hunger and thirst for wholeness, justice, freedom, and peace are especially close to the heart of God because their desire reflects God's own longing for all people. For this reason they are blessed (Matt 5:3–11). For this reason, the Canaanite woman was blessed. That is the meaning of the claim of liberation theologies, that God has a preferential option for the poor and oppressed, for the victim and the weak. According to the four Gospels, Jesus not only taught about this preference, he also showed concretely what it involves. In our story, the demonstration happened in a context of conflict and against Jesus's own inclinations. A blessing in disguise, so to say, hence the title of this chapter, "Good News of a Struggle to Care." Christian pastoral and spiritual caregivers are sent to continue his ministry and to embrace the ailing and suffering neighbor who longs for healing and hope. As they respond, their hearts are nurtured and transformed.

Intercultural and interfaith situations thus present unique challenges and opportunities for pastoral caregivers to grow in *virtue*, in the sense of their hearts being formed in the light of Jesus. In other words, the notion of "virtue" (singular) in this context denotes the moral character of the caregiver. It can be described in terms of our innermost dispositions and attitudes, that is, the "habits of the heart" which help define the content of *character*. These are the deep affections and passions and, especially, the kinds of virtues (plural)[28] that, at their best, faith communities seek to fos-

---

27. That is the reason why James E. Loder's "logic of transformation" is a helpful hermeneutic resource. See Schipani, "Transforming Encounters in the Borderlands."

28. "Virtues" (in the plural) are those specific moral strengths, skills or capacities, and habits, which have particular moral significance. They are values that become

ter and form in their members as genuine expressions of divine love and a way of life in the power of the Spirit. For pastoral caregivers, therefore, intercultural and interfaith situations may become special places of grace as they are led and empowered to practice the values and the virtues essential for caring as representatives of Jesus, such as humility, hospitality, love, compassion, patience, hope, generosity, and courage.

Mutuality, Mission, and Vocation

Third, as Jesus himself may have experienced, ministry at its best is a two-way street, a mutual practice and process.[29] For those in the United States, a powerful center in the ongoing globalization process, market capitalism, Christian nationalism, and white supremacy, this ministry poses special challenges. In order to become truly "other-oriented," faith communities need to make efforts to reach the margins. Many of them need to shed an exclusivist ideology of chosenness and better attend to their own deepest yearnings, limitations, and needs, as well as to the potential and resourcefulness of others. They can bless and, in turn, be blessed, sometimes the hard way, despite their ideological blinders and moral and political shortcomings. Often they will unexpectedly find themselves being ministered to. History illustrates repeatedly that well-intentioned movements and groups cannot truly participate in other people's liberation and healing without allowing them to participate in their own liberation and healing.

Intercultural and interfaith spiritual caregiving presents unique challenges and opportunities for pastoral caregivers to grow in *vocation*, in the sense of partnership with God as essential to faithful and effective ministerial practice. In caregiving, our common human vocation can be

---

character shaped by practice and discipline. Virtues are thus personal qualities constitutive of the moral character of pastoral caregivers, hopefully reflective of the character of the very faith communities they represent.

29. The hypothesis of mutual enrichment is creatively presented by Melanie S. Baffes in "What to Do with *This* Jesus?" Baffes interprets the story of Jesus and the Canaanite woman by employing the lens of a psychoanalytic theory—Winnicot's concept of True Self and Stolorow-Atwood model of inter-subjectivity. She argues that, for modern readers, the Canaanite woman and Jesus offer new possibilities for being human. That fuller humanity results from both of them moving from False Self to True Self *and* from the mutuality that characterizes their interaction. And that such reader response interpretation can lead to new understandings of: (1) *loving self—seeing* ourselves as empowered, refusing compliance as a response to oppression; (2) *loving other*—overturning the self/other paradigm to regard all persons in terms of their humanity; and (3) *loving God*—learning to be in mutual and authentic relationship with the Divine.

reconfirmed and sustained. The twofold blessing of mutuality and partnership may include an additional realization: Caring and being cared for in the borderlands, across and against boundaries of culture and faith, become the epiphanic experience of encountering the Divine anew. In due time it is revealed, as in the eschatological parable of Matt 25:31–46. Jesus says: "Truly I tell you, just as you did it to one of the least of these who are members of my family, you did it to me" (v. 40).

Homiletic Overtures

This final section completes the study of Matt 15:21–28 from a Practical Theology perspective that considers the popularized Latin American pattern, *seeing, judging, acting*. The third phase—*acting-embodying the text*—can logically lead to intersecting hermeneutics and homiletics aimed, for example, at enhancing formation in pastoral care as illustrated in the Textbox at the end of the homily.[30] What follows is the homily that was actually offered in that setting. The title of the homily is "Good News: Jesus struggles to Care When Meeting a Multiply *Other*."

Homily

Peace be with you! All of us gathered here today have much in common. A salient feature of commonality is that we have participated, and will participate, in caregiving situations involving intercultural and/or interfaith difference. Sometimes those encounters have required negotiating multiple difference including gender, socio-economic status, spiritual-religious, and ethnic-cultural, educational, and generational aspects. In any case, we recognize that those situations always present difficult challenges and also unique opportunities for personal and vocational growth.

---

30. The Textbox describes a two-hour workshop that took place in Cuba. I have collaborated with the Cuban Council of Churches in the formation of prison and health care chaplains since 2013. The workshop took place on June 5, 2024, at the Seminario Evangélico de Teología, in Matanzas, Cuba. It included a homily (in Spanish) based on the story of Jesus and the Canaanite woman. The event was designed according to the five "movements" of Thomas Groome's *shared praxis* approach in *Sharing Faith*, 133–293. Groome names the five movements thus: "naming present praxis," "reflecting on present praxis," "making accessible Christian story and vision," "dialectical hermeneutic to appropriate story/vision to participants' stories and visions," and "decision/response for lived Christian faith."

I could tell you about numerous situations where that has happened to me; and I know that it will happen again and again.

While keeping those situations in mind, I invite you to take a fresh look at the story of a Canaanite woman who meets Jesus seeking healing for her ailing daughter. My New Testament colleague always asks a simple question: "How does the text minister to me so that I can minister with the text?" So, let's reconsider the story from our unique location and vantage point as spiritual caregivers. We do so with a declared bias and interest and seek to be informed, inspired, and guided as both followers (disciples) of Jesus as well as ministers (apostles, "sent") committed to care well with the same Spirit.

As we reflect together on the story, we can follow similar steps to those we employ in pastoral companioning. We hear people's stories in their terms; we help them to make sense of their situation; and we guide them to find a way forward.

We start by listening well, just as we listen to care seekers in the jail or in the hospital. We are struck by Jesus's initial response to the request of the woman: first, silence without evidence of empathy; then a dubious assessment of the appropriate turf for caregiving action followed by brusque rejection without referral. He has concluded that the woman's request as inappropriate, impertinent and out of place . . . So far, we have a case of a caregiver overwhelmed with resistance who cannot activate emotional and interpersonal intelligence, let alone contemplative curiosity and respect for the other's dignity. Only in this particular Gospel story does Jesus ignore a supplicant, place the barrier of ethnicity before a plea for help, and then use offensive language to reiterate the barrier. The care receiver in our story happens to be a woman who understands the grave implications of Jesus's response; yet, she doesn't yield. This care receiver persists with determination seeking healing for her suffering daughter. And eventually she's able to reframe or recast Jesus's insulting words—there's food even for the dogs under the table.

Have you experienced an encounter like this as you face unattractive strangers? What's going on in Jesus' case that might somehow also apply to us today? His dubious assessment merely restates the status quo of gender, ethnic, cultural, religious, and political divisions as absolute impediment for the caregiving relationship move forward. The woman's *counter-resistance* calls him to look to the place of new possibilities across and beyond the established boundaries. It is she, rather than the caregiver who *reframes*[31] the response thus opening the way to new insight! She rejects the dichotomy of children (insiders who receive food) versus dogs (outsiders who get no food); the woman imagines that both the children and the dogs can be graciously fed inside, within the same household and from the same table.

The text helps us to recognize the importance of dealing with multiple variables: geographic, ethnic, gender, religious, theological, sociocultural, moral, and political. No wonder, then, that the surprising, stunning encounter with this woman challenged Jesus personally and vocationally! It is significant that this marginal Canaanite woman emerges as the center of the story; in fact, it is primarily her story. Not unlike our case studies: when all is said and done, the care receiver's story can become a life giving document.

Here's good news of Jesus's struggle to care. By the end of the gospel story a surprising and transformative reversal takes: Jesus arrives at the right assessment. This woman with "great faith" is the means for her daughter's healing. In this encounter in the borderlands, the Canaanite woman has become a prophetic and wise teacher. Her unflinching desire for her daughter's wellbeing has counter-cultural and counter-political significance. She might have reminded Jesus of the larger vision of a divine commonwealth of care and justice.

How can we further interpret the story today in light of our circumstances and caregiving agenda? Good listening and attentive observation leads us to assume that Jesus would have been socialized into the conventional wisdom of his time and dominant culture. According to such socialization as a first-century Jew, prudence involved keeping clear boundaries; adhering to certain criteria of what is proper, clean, normal, and appropriate; and holding to right categories and patterns of perception, thought, and relationships. Then an outsider, a total stranger and marginal person, challenges Jesus to relate and to care across and beyond those boundaries. She makes possible for him to set aside conventional wisdom and to access an alternative. Subversive wisdom includes an ethic and politic of compassion and radical inclusiveness. Jesus has faced a

---

31. To the readers: The use of the terms *resistance* and *counter-resistance* in this section evokes concepts pertaining to counsel and psychotherapy stemming from psychodynamic psychology. The reference to *reframing* is here deliberately used in reference as a therapeutic approach in clinical practice that helps care receivers to become aware of material previously "hidden" or subconscious.

conflict and dilemma, a temptation from within, so to speak. He struggles to care for the woman. She persists. Eventually he chooses well.

How does the story "speak" to us today? Or, as a beloved former colleague would often say, "how does the text minister to us so that we can minister with the text?" For sure, the story of the Canaanite woman can challenge us to grow in intercultural competence. It can help us to overcome discrimination and exclusion of "unbelievers" (or "pagans") or for some reason "undeserving." It can inspire us to develop cultural humility, sensitivity and respect, compassion, emotional and interpersonal intelligence, and more; in other words, all those character strengths with which we can love our care seekers/neighbors effectively and faithfully. There's much more for us to draw from the story. For now, I propose three ways in which this episode of Jesus's struggle to care in the face of significant difference can challenge, inform and guide our caregiving ministry.

First, intercultural and interfaith situations are like inhabiting "borderlands." We must deal with disorientation, unfamiliarity and significant difference. Yet, jails and hospitals can thus become privileged spaces for transformative care. Places of vulnerability and marginality are potentially *epiphanic,* that is, illuminating or revelatory; they can also become *epistemic,* that is, sources of transforming insight and new meaning. Second, caregiving situations of conflict—especially those involving resistance and counter-resistance—call for wise discernment. They can open to us transformative opportunities for clinical and other forms of knowing and learning. So we can welcome those conflict situations with courage and hope. Finally, despite the inherently asymmetrical nature of caregiving relationships, and of interfaith care in particular, creative collaboration can result in growth, liberation, and healing for both care seekers and caregivers. May it be so!

A Workshop for Spiritual Care Chaplains

Encountering Difference in Spiritual Care

The following paragraphs describe the structure and the content of the workshop process according to the pattern of the *shared praxis approach.* It was an event in which the intersection of hermeneutics and homiletics was actually enacted.

Focusing Activity

"Encountering difference in spiritual care" was the generative theme for the workshop. The twenty-seven participants belong to six Christian denominations. Those Cuban chaplains often meet care receivers who are either atheists, "spiritual but not religious", or members of Afro-Caribbean/Cuban religious groups. So the overarching goal of the event was for those caregivers to become better equipped to care faithfully and competently in those intercultural and interfaith[32] caregiving situations.

The chosen focusing activity consisted in listening to the account in Matt 15:21–28. Reading the gospel story was done expressively twice by four people whose voices represented the woman, the disciples, and Jesus, in addition to the narrator. The participants were invited to listen with closed eyes and to engage their imagination.

"Jesus left that place and went away to the district of Tyre and Sidon. Just then a Canaanite woman from that region came out and started shouting, 'Have mercy on me, Lord, Son of David; my daughter is tormented by a demon.' But he did not answer her at all. And his disciples came and urged him, saying, 'Send her away, for she keeps shouting after us.' He answered, 'I was sent only to the lost sheep of the house of Israel.' But she came and knelt before him, saying, 'Lord, help me.' He answered, 'It is not fair to take the children's food and throw it to the dogs.' She said, 'Yes, Lord, yet even the dogs eat the crumbs that fall from their masters' table.' Then Jesus answered her, 'Woman, great is your faith! Let it be done for you as you wish.' And her daughter was healed from that moment."

The workshop process was thus set in motion as a dialogical and collaborative learning-teaching interaction. Reference to the five-movement process is included in the paragraphs that follow.

---

32. As expected, significant "intra-faith" differences were also discussed in the workshop, including implications for both collegial collaboration and therapeutic communication.

Naming/Expressing Present Praxis

Participants were encouraged to respond to the reading with a simple question: what word or phrase stands out for you . . . ? A variety of highlights followed, such as: "answer," "shouting," "tormented," "help me," "not fair," "crumbs," "great faith," "healed," and others. In that way a connection began to be established involving personal experience, gospel story, and the challenges and opportunities of intercultural and interfaith caregiving. That connection defines the so-called first movement of an unfolding *shared praxis* process.

Reflecting on Present Praxis

Following that first step, workshop participants formed nine triads in order to discuss a couple of questions: "Do you have memories of personal experience somehow connected with, or similar to this gospel account;?" "does the story of Jesus being approached by a woman/stranger elicit some expectation or hope in you?" After half an hour conversation in subgroups, a plenary session followed. Summary reporting on the content of those dialogues brought forth a wealth of observations and insights together with new questions about the gospel story as such and its possible connection with personal and ministerial experience. Before a fifteen-minute break, workshop participants were told that I would make a short presentation in *homily*[33] form in the next plenary session to be followed by an invitation to respond and to look ahead.

---

33. Workshop participants were reminded that the etymological root of "homily" (*homilein*) suggests "having a conversation" rather than, merely, monological speech. The observation was pertinent also given the fact that those chaplains often offer homilies or "meditations," especially within the jail settings where they serve. Healthcare chaplains are beginning to be afforded an official status in Cuban hospitals, so the opportunity to offer homilies is for now limited to certain situations such as the death of a patient.

Making Accessible Christian Story and Vision

This third step, or movement, in the process consists in the presentation of substantive content appropriate to the generative theme—"encountering difference in spiritual care"—stemming primarily, though not exclusively, from the faith tradition. Further, such presentation must address the realities contextually and personally highlighted in the previous two movements. The text of the homily (originally offered in Spanish) was included in this chapter under the heading "Homily."[34]

Dialectical Hermeneutic Engaging the Previous Movements

The homily supplied substantive content delivered as "authorized" input by the workshop leader in the manner of an "authoritative" voice from the tradition and the spiritual care professions. Nevertheless, that input wasn't meant as the final word addressing the generative theme, "encountering difference in spiritual care." On the contrary, the homily was given as a meditation aimed at encouraging further critical dialogue and creative collaboration. Therefore, workshop participants were free to ask questions for clarification, highlight new learnings, express criticisms and points of agreement or disagreement, and visualize implications and ramifications for further reflection and ministry action. After about half an hour of interaction in a plenary session, the chaplains returned to the triads for the final activity.

Decision/Response for Lived Christian Faith and Ministry

The fifth and final movement in this process gave workshop participants an opportunity for making decisions about how to better live out their vocational commitment to care well in the face of significant difference. Within the triads they engaged

---

34. At the end of the homily workshop participants received an electronic copy of the text.

in a self-reflective exercise that includes assessment of one's profile of competence (or "pastoral wisdom") with a threefold focus and sets of distinct yet interrelated competencies: interdisciplinary-academic ("knowing"), professional-ministerial ("doing"), and personal-spiritual ("being").[35] In light of the twofold purpose of this exercise—to foster commitment to growth with accountability—the results of the self-assessment were discussed within the triads. Finally, the whole group of chaplains participated in a ritual of blessing.

Conclusion

The content of this chapter is a systematic response to the overarching statement in the subtitle of this book—"Transgressive Readings for Transformational Preaching"—intended as a twofold contribution. The essay is written with a practical theological approach to the text of Matt 15:21–28 and, therefore, with an explicitly *interdisciplinary* method while assuming its inexhaustible reservoir of meaning; further, the chapter highlights the *theological* significance of the gospel story as a sacred text, which is an essential component of *transformational preaching* as a particular form of Christian ministry.

Practical theology necessarily recognizes the special nature of a *sacred* text and employs a theological lens already in the study of the actual story, as indicated in connection with the notion of "fourfold knowing event." In addition, practical theology examines the homily as public communication and as a ministry art form; its interdisciplinary approach includes a theological lens that views the preaching event in a setting and a context characterized as a safe place of trust, respect, and collaborative and worshipful participation. In the experience with the Cuban chaplains, a space was created in which they expected the homily

---

35. I distributed a simple one-page instrument with a list of competencies within the three categories of) "knowing", "doing," and "being." Respondents can indicate self-assessment for each competence from 1 ("poorly") to 4 ("very well"); they can also add competencies not included on the list. On the other side of the sheet there are instructions about ways to increase competence and a possible timetable. For a thorough presentation of competence in spiritual care, see Schipani, *Spiritual Care in Our Multifaith World*, 108–22.

as a source of inspiration and orientation and a gift of the Holy Spirit. In that sense, the workshop experience serves as an illustration of a biblical text becoming contextually and situationally (*Holy*) *Scripture* anew; in Wilfred Cantwell Smith's words: "being scripture is . . . an interaction, a relationship between that text and a community of persons . . . 'scripture' is a bilateral term . . . it inherently implies, in fact, names, a relationship . . . People—a given community—make a text into scripture, or keep it scripture by treating it a certain way."[36]

Interdisciplinary hermeneutics are a fertile field of inquiry in many areas. In the case of pastoral and spiritual care, recent examples include the study of moral injury and trauma among many others.[37] The fruits of those studies demonstrate that biblical and practical-theological approaches can significantly illumine a given human situation with complementary insights; further, they show how each discipline can help enhance the other.

Finally, the response to the (implicit) question of what makes our reading transgressive is twofold: we intend to encourage moving beyond compartmentalized academic disciplines and research in theological education and ministerial formation; and to more creatively employ theological views and analysis in the study of both sacred texts and human life in community. This book offers manifold testimony that such movement is actually happening. May that continue be the case in the days ahead.

---

36. W. C. Smith, *What Is Scripture?* ix, 17, 18.

37. See, for example, Kelle, *The Bible and Moral Injury*; McDonald, ed., *Exploring Moral Injury in Sacred Texts*; De Wit and Schipani, *Intercultural Hermeneutics, Trauma y Acompñamiento Pastoral*.

Bibliography

Achebe, Chinua. *The African Trilogy: Things Fall Apart; No Longer at East; Arrow of God.* Everyman's Library 327. New York: Knopf, 2010.

———. *Things Fall Apart.* Everyman's Library 327. New York: Knopf, 2010.

Adamo, David T. *Africa and Africans in the Old Testament.* 1998. Reprint, Eugene, OR: Wipf & Stock, 2001.

———, ed. *Biblical Interpretation in African Perspective.* Lanham, MD: University Press of America, 2006.

Ahmed, Sara. *The Promise of Happiness.* Durham: Duke University Press, 2010.

Allen, Donna. *Toward a Womanist Homiletic: Katie Cannon, Alice Walker, and Emancipatory Proclamation.* New York: Lang, 2013.

Alpert, Rebecca. "Finding Our Past: A Lesbian Interpretation of the Book of Ruth." In *Reading Ruth: Contemporary Women Reclaim a Sacred Story,* edited by Judith A. Kates and Gail Twersky Reimer, 91–96. New York: Ballantine, 1994.

Anderson, Marian. *Spirituals.* Sony Classical, 1999.

Anderson, Ray. *The Shape of Practical Theology: Empowering Ministry and Theological Praxis.* Downers Grove, IL: InterVarsity, 2001.

Anonymous, editor. *Select Parts of the Holy Bible for the Use of the Negro Slaves in the British West-India Islands.* London: Law & Gilbert, 1807.

Arlotto, Anthony. *Introduction to Historical Linguistics.* New York: Houghton Mifflin, 1971.

Asante, Molefi Kete. *The Afrocentric Idea Revised.* Philadelphia: Temple University Press, 2001.

Aschkenasy, Nehama. "Reading Ruth through a Bakhtinian Lens: The Carnivalesque in a Biblical Tale." *Journal of Biblical Literature* 126 (2007) 437–53.

Asikainen, Susanna. "Women Out of Place: The Women Who Challenged Jesus." *Neotestamentica* 52 (2018) 179–93.

Aslan, Reza. *Zealot: The Life and Times of Jesus of Nazareth.* New York: Random House, 2014.

"Attention Span by Age." https://www.wellbrookrecovery.com/post/average-attention-span#:~:text=A%20study%20by%20the%20University,individual%20differences%20in%20cognitive%20abilities.

Avnery, Orit "On the Threshold: Liminality in the Stories of the Concubine of Gibeah and Ruth." *Journal for the Study of the Old Testament* 46 (2021) 232–45.

Baffes, Melanie S. "What to Do with This Jesus?" *Pastoral Theology* 63 (2014) 249–63.

Baird, Josephine. "Trans/National Queer Parenting." *Lambda Nordica* 24 (2019) 191–206.

Banks. Adam. *Digital Griots: African American Rhetoric in a Multimedia Age*. Carbondale: Southern Illinois University Press, 2011.

Bass, Dorothy C., and Craig Dykstra, eds. *For Life Abundant: Practical Theology, Theological Education, and Christian Ministry*. Grand Rapids: Eerdmans, 2008.

Bellis, Alice Ogden. "Ruth: Sweet or Salty." *Journal of Religious Thought* 52/53.2 (1996) 65–68.

Bennett, Harold V. *Injustice Made Legal: Deuteronomic Law and the Plight of Widows, Strangers, and Orphans in Ancient Israel*. Grand Rapids: Eerdmans, 2002.

Bennett, Milton J. *Basic Concepts of Intercultural Communication: Paradigms, Principles, & Practices*. Boston: Intercultural, 2013.

———. "Intercultural Communication." IDR Institute. https://www.idrinstitute.org/resources/intercultural-communication.

Bennington, Geoffrey and Jacques Derrida. *Jacques Derrida*. Translated by Geoffrey Bennington. Religion and Postmodernism. Chicago: University of Chicago Press, 1993.

Berlant, Lauren and Michael Warner. "Sex in Public." *Critical Inquiry* 24 (1998) 547–66.

Bernasconi, Robert. *Critical Philosophy of Race: Essays*. New York: Oxford University Press, 2023.

Berzon, Todd. "Ethnicity and Early Christianity: New Approaches to Religious Kinship and Community." *Currents in Biblical Research* 16 (2018) 191–227.

"Biblical Literacy in the Postliterate Age." Logos. https://www.logos.com/grow/biblical-literacy/.

"B Famine?" International Rescue Committee (IRC). https://www.rescue.org/article/

"Big Data." https://whatsthebigdata.com/data-generated-every-day/; https://edgedelta.com/company/blog/how-much-data-is-created-per-day.

Blount, Brian. *Cultural Interpretation: Reorienting New Testament Criticism*. 1995. Reprint, Eugene, OR: Wipf & Stock, 2004.

Blount, Farris. "A Tale of Too Many Options: Following Jesus in the Black Church Tradition." Respectful Conversations Blog. https://respectfulconversation.net/category/may-blount/.

Boer, Roland. "On the Feasibility of Subsistence Economics." In *Reading the Bible in an Age of Crisis: Political Exegesis for a New Day*, edited by Bruce Worthington, 109–29. Minneapolis: Fortress, 2015.

———. *The Sacred Economy of Ancient Israel*. Library of Ancient Israel. Louisville: Westminster John Knox, 2015.

Boesak, Allen Aubrey. *Children of the Waters of Meribah: Black Liberation Theology, the Mariamic Tradition, and the Challenges of the Twenty-First-Century Empire*. Eugene, OR: Cascade Books, 2019.

Booth, Wayne C. *A Rhetoric of Irony*. Chicago: University of Chicago Press, 1974.

"Born in Slavery: Slave Narratives from the Federal Writers' Project, 1936 to 1938." Library of Congress. https://dlg.usg.edu/record/loc_mesn041.

Brady, Christian M. M. "The Conversion of Ruth in Targum Ruth." *Review of Rabbinic Judaism* 16 (2013) 133–46.

Brenner, Athalya. "From Ruth to the 'Global Woman': Social and Legal Aspects." *Interpretation* 64 (2010) 162–68.

———. "Introduction." In *A Feminist Companion to Ruth*, edited by Athalya Brenner, 9–19. Feminist Companion to the Bible 3. Sheffield: Sheffield Academic, 1993, 2001.

———. "Naomi and Ruth." In *A Feminist Companion to Ruth*, edited by Athalya Brenner, 70–84. Feminist Companion to the Bible 3. Sheffield: Sheffield Academic, 1993, 2001.

———, ed. *Ruth and Esther*. Feminist Companion to the Bible 2nd Series. Sheffield: Sheffield Academic, 1999.

Bright, Laurie Lyter. "Woman in a Man's Pulpit: Incarnating Feminism in a Black and White Collar." *Feminist Theology* 27.1 (2018) 103–10.

Brintnall, Kent L. "Queer Studies and Religion." *Critical Research on Religion* 1 (2013) 51–61.

Brown, Michael. "The Gospel of Matthew." In *True to Our Native Land: An African American Commentary of the New Testament*, edited by Brian K. Blount, 85–120. Minneapolis: Fortress, 2007.

———, ed. *The Blackening of the Bible: The Aims of African American Biblical Scholarship*. African American Religious Thought and Life. Harrisburg: Trinity International, 2004.

Brown, Teresa Fry. "The Action Potential of Preaching." In *The Purposes of Preaching*, edited by Jana Childers, 49–65. St. Louis: Chalice, 2004.

———. *Delivering the Sermon: Voice, Body, and Animation in Proclamation*. Minneapolis: Fortress, 2008.

Browning, Don S., and Terry D. Cooper. *Religious Thought and the Modern Psychologies*. Minneapolis: Fortress, 2004.

Brueggemann, Walter. *Deep Memory, Exuberant Hope: Contested Truth in a Post-Christian World*. Minneapolis: Fortress, 2000.

———. *Money and Possessions*. Interpretation. Louisville: Westminster John Knox, 2016.

———. "The Social Nature of the Biblical Text for Preaching." In *Preaching as a Social Act: Theology & Practice*, edited by Arthur Van Seters, Chapter 4. Nashville: Abingdon, 1988. Reprinted in Brueggemann, *The Word Militant: Preaching a Decentering Word*, 84–102. Minneapolis: Fortress, 2007.

Budd, John. "The Eye Sees What the Mind Knows: The Conceptual Foundations of Invisible Work." In *Invisible Labor: Hidden Work in the Contemporary World*, edited by Marion Crain et al., 3–27. Oakland: University of California Press, 2016.

Buell, Denise Kimber. *Why This New Race: Ethnic Reasoning in Early Christianity*. New York: Columbia University Press, 2005.

Butler, Judith. *Gender Trouble: Feminism and the Subversion of Identity*. Routledge Classics. New York: Routledge, 2006.

Butler, Lee H., Jr. *Liberating Our Dignity, Saving Our Souls*. St. Louis: Chalice, 2016.

Byron, Gay. *Symbolic Blackness and Ethnic Difference in Early Christian Literature*. New York: Routledge, 2003.

Cannon, Katie. *Black Womanist Ethics*. American Academy of Religion Academy Series 60. Atlanta: Scholars, 1988.

———. *Katie's Canon: Womanism and the Soul of the Black Community*. Expanded 25th Anniversary ed. Minneapolis: Fortress, 2021.

———. *Womanism in the African American Sacred Rhetoric the Soul of the Black Community*. New York: Continuum, 1995.

———. "Womanist Interpretation and Preaching in the Black Church." In *Katie's Canon: Womanism and the Soul of the Black Community*, 75–84. Expanded 25th Anniversary ed. Minneapolis: Fortress, 2021.

Caputo, John D. *Hermeneutics: Facts and Interpretation in the Age of Information*. London: Pelican, 2018.

———. *John D. Caputo: The Collected Philosophical and Theological Papers*. Vol. 3: *1997–2000: The Return of Religion*. NP: John D. Caputo Archives. Kindle Edition.

———. "The Prayers and Tears of Devilish Hermeneutics: Derrida and Meister Eckhart." In *More Radical Hermeneutics: On not Knowing Who We Are*, 249–64. Studies in Continental Thought. Bloomington: Indiana University Press, 2000.

Carson, D. A. "Matthew." In *Matthew, Mark, & Luke*, edited by Frank Graebelien, 3–599. Expositor's Bible Commentary 8. Grand Rapids: Zondervan, 1984.

Carter, Warren. *Matthew and the Margins: A Sociopolitical and Religious Reading*. Bible & Liberation. Maryknoll, NY: Orbis, 2000.

Case, Karin A. "Claiming White Social Location as a Site of Resistance." In *Disrupting White Supremacy from Within: White People on What WE Need to Do*, edited by Jennifer Harvey et al., 63–90. Cleveland, OH: Pilgrim, 2004.

Catalano, Joseph S. *A Commentary on Jean-Paul Sartre's Being and Nothingness*. New York: Harper & Row, 1974.

Chapman, Cynthia. "'Oh that you were like a brother to me, one who had nursed at my mother's breasts': Breast Milk as a Kinship-Forming Substance." *Journal of Hebrew Scriptures* 12 (2012) 1–41.

Charney, Marvin. "The Political Economy of Peasant Poverty: What the Eighth-Century Prophets Presumed but Did Not State." *Journal of Religion and Society* 10 (2014) 34–60.

Cho, Jae Hyung. "The Gospel of Matthew." In *An Asian Introduction to the New Testament*, edited by Johnson Thomaskutty, 47–73. Minneapolis: Fortress, 2022.

Chuang, Angie and Autumn Tyler. "An Obscured View of 'Both Sides': Default Whiteness and the Protest Paradigm in Television News Coverage of the Charlottesville Unite the Right Rally." *Journalism & Mass Communication Quarterly* 100 (2023) 668–91.

"ClassicsWrites: A Guide to Research and Writing in the Field of Classics." Harvard University. https://projects.iq.harvard.edu/classicswrites.

Cobb, Christy. "Learning Design: Discussing Political Issues with Ruth." *Wabash Center Journal on Teaching* 1.3 (2020) 117–122.

Collins, John J. *Introduction to the Hebrew Bible: And Deutero-Canonical Books*. 3rd ed. Minneapolis: Fortress, 2018.

Collins, Patricia Hill. *Fighting Words: Black Women and the Search for Justice*. Minneapolis: University of Minnesota Press, 1998.

Cone, James H. *Black Theology and Black Power*. 1969. Reprint, Maryknoll, NY: Orbis, 1997.

———. *A Black Theology of Liberation*. Philadelphia: Lippincott, 1970.

———. *God of the Oppressed*. San Francisco: Harper & Row, 1975.

Connor, Alice. *Fierce: Women of Bible and Their Stories of Violence, Mercy, Bravery, Wisdom, Sex, and Salvation*. Minneapolis: Fortress, 2017.

Cook, Scott B. *Colonial Encounters in the Age of High Imperialism*. Upper Saddle, NJ: Pearson, 1997.

Coomber, Matthew J. M., ed. *Economics and Empire in the Ancient Near East*. Guide to the Bible and Economics 1. Center and Library for the Bible and Social Justice Series. Eugene, OR: Cascade Books, 2023.

Corredor-Waldron, Adriana et al. "Drivers of Racial Differences in C-Sections." National Bureau of Economic Research. August 2024. https://www.nber.org/papers/w32891.

Crawford, A. Elaine Brown. *Hope in the Holler: A Womanist Theology*. Louisville: Westminster John Knox, 2022.

Creangă, Ovidiu, and Peter-Ben Smit. *Biblical Masculinities Foregrounded*. Hebrew Bible Monographs 62. Sheffield: Sheffield Phoenix, 2014.

Crite, Allan Rohan. *All Glory: Brush Drawing Meditations on the Prayer of Consecration*. Cambridge, MA: Society of Saint John the Evangelist, 1947.

Crowder, Stephanie Buckhanon. *When Momma Speaks: The Bible and Motherhood from a Womanist Perspective*. Louisville: Westminster John Knox, 2016.

Crowder, Stephanie Buckhannon and Mary F. Foskett, editors. *Remapping Biblical Studies: CUREMP at Thirty*. Biblical Scholarship in North America 31. Atlanta: SBL Press, 2023.

Dagley, Kelly. "Women's Experience of Migration and the Book of Ruth." PhD diss., Fuller Theological Seminary, 2019.

Daniels, Arlene Kaplan. "Invisible Work." *Social Problems* 34 (1987) 403–15.

Davis, Andrew R. "The Literary Effect of Gender Discord in the Book of Ruth." *Journal of Biblical Literature* 132 (2013) 495–513.

De Wit, Hans, and Daniel S Schipani. *Intercultural Hermeneutics, Trauma y Acompañamiento Pastoral*. Matanzas: Seminario Evangélico de Teología, 2024.

Derrida, Jacques. "Hospitality, Justice and Responsibility: A Dialogue with Jacques Derrida." In *Questioning Ethics: Contemporary Debates in Philosophy*, edited by Richard Kearney and Mark Dooley, 65–83. New York: Routledge, 1999.

———. "Living On: Border Lines." In *A Derrida Reader: Between the Blinds*, edited by Peggy Kamuf, translated by James Hulbert, 256–57. New York: Columbia University Press, 1991.

———. *Of Grammatology*. Corrected ed. Translated by Gayatri Spivak. Baltimore: Johns Hopkins University Press, 1997.

———. "Psyche: Inventions of the Other." In *Psyche: Inventions of the Other*, Vol. 1, edited by Peggy Kamuf and Elizabeth Rottenberg, translated by Catherine Porter, 1–47. Stanford: Stanford University Press, 2007.

———. "The Rogue That I Am." In *Rogues: Two Essays on Reason*, 63–70. Translated by Pascale-Anne Brault and Michael Naas. Stanford: Stanford University Press, 2005.

———. "*Sauf le nom* (Post-Scriptum)." Translated by John Leavey Jr. In *On the Name*, edited by Thomas Dutoit, 33–85. Stanford: Stanford University Press, 1995.

———. "Violence and Metaphysics: An Essay on the Thought of Emmanuel Lévinas." In *Writing and Difference*, translated by Alan Bass, 79–153. Chicago: University of Chicago Press, 1971.

Desmond, William. *Being and the Between*. SUNY Series in Philosophy. Albany: State University of New York Press, 1995.

———. *Ethics and the Between*. SUNY Series in Philosophy. Albany: State University of New York Press, 2001.

"Dogmatism." In *The Oxford English Dictionary*. https://www.oed.com/dictionary/dogmatism_n?tab=factsheet#6378371.

Donaldson, Laura E. "The Sign of Orpah: Reading Ruth Through Native Eyes." In *The Postcolonial Biblical Reader*, edited by R. S. Sugirtharajah, 159–70. Oxford: Blackwell, 2006.

Douglas, Kelly Brown. *Stand Your Ground: Black Bodies and the Justice of God*. Maryknoll, NY: Orbis, 2015.

Duarte, Alejandro. "Matthew." *Global Bible Commentary*, edited by Daniel Patte, 350–60. Nashville: Abingdon, 2004.

Dube, Musa W., Andrew M. Mbuvi, and Dora R. Mbuwayesango, eds. *Postcolonial Perspectives in African Biblical Interpretations*. Global Perspectives on Biblical Scholarship 13. Atlanta: Society of Biblical Literature, 2012.

Dube, Musa. "Divining Ruth for International Relations." In *Other Ways of Reading: African Women and the Bible*, edited by Musa Dube, 179–195. Global Perspectives on Biblical Scholarship 2. Atlanta: Society of Biblical Literature, 2001.

———. *Postcolonial Feminist Interpretation of the Bible*. St. Louis: Chalice, 2000.

———. "Reading for Decolonization (John 4:1–42)." *Semeia* 74 (1996) 37–59.

———. "Savior of the World but not of This World." In *The Postcolonial Bible*, edited by R. S. Sugirtharajah, 118–35. Bible and Postcolonialism 1. Sheffield: Sheffield Academic, 1998.

———, ed. *Other Ways of Reading: African Women and the Bible*. Global Perspectives on Biblical Scholarship 2. Atlanta: Society of Biblical Literature, 2001.

Duling, Dennis C. "Matthew (Notes)." *The SBL Study Bible: New Revised Standard Version Updated Edition*, edited by Society of Biblical Literature, 1743–90. New York: HarperCollins, 2023.

Duncan, Celena M. "The Book of Ruth: On Boundaries, Love, and Truth." In *Take Back the Word: A Queer Reading of the Bible*, edited by Mona West and Robert Goss, 92–102. Cleveland, OH: Pilgrim, 2000.

Eccleston, Sasha-Mae and Dan-El Padilla Peralta. "Racing the Classics: Ethos and Praxis." *American Journal of Philology* 143 (2022) 199–218.

Edelman, Lee. *No Future: Queer Theory and the Death Drive*. e-Duke Books Scholarly Collection. Series Q. Durham: Duke University Press, 2004.

Elliott, John H. *What Is Social-Scientific Criticism?* Guides to Biblical Scholarship. Minneapolis: Fortress, 1993.

Eng, David L. "Transnational Adoption and Queer Diasporas." *Social Text* 21.3 (2003) 1–37.

The Episcopal Church. *The Book of Common Prayer*. Church Hymnal Corporation, 1979.

———. *The Book of Common Prayer and Administration of the Sacraments and Other Rites and Ceremonies of the Church According to the Use of the Protestant Episcopal Church in the United States of America*. The Church Pension Fund, 1928.

Eskenazi, Tamara Cohn, and Tikva Frymer-Kensky. *Ruth*. JPS Torah Commentary. Philadelphia: Jewish Publication Society, 2011.

Fanon, Frantz. *Black Skin, White Masks*. Translated by Charles Lam Markmann. New York: Grove, 1967.

Farris, Stephen, "Hermeneutics" In *The New Interpreter's Handbook of Preaching*, edited by Paul Scott Wilson et al., 31–37. Nashville: Abingdon, 2008.

Fee, Gordon D. and Stuart, Douglass. *How to Read the Bible for All Its Worth*. 3rd ed. Grand Rapids, Zondervan, 2014.

Felder, Cain Hope ed. *Stony the Road We Trod: African American Biblical Interpretation*. Minneapolis: Fortress, 1990.

———. *Troubling Biblical Waters: Race, Class, and Family*. Maryknoll, NY: Orbis, 1989.

Fentress-Williams, Judy. *Ruth*. Abingdon Old Testament Commentaries. Nashville: Abingdon, 2012.

Fewell, Dana Nolan, and David M. Gunn. *Compromising Redemption: Relating Characters in the Book of Ruth*. Literary Currents in Biblical Interpretation. Louisville: Westminster John Knox, 1990.

———. "A Son is Born to Naomi!": Literary Allusions and Interpretation in the Book of Ruth." In *Women in the Hebrew Bible*, edited by Alice Bach, 233–40. New York: Routledge, 1999.

Fischer, Irmtraud. "The Book of Ruth: A 'Feminist' Commentary to the Torah?" In *Ruth and Esther*, edited by Athalya Brenner, 24–49. Feminist Companion to the Bible, 2nd Series. Sheffield: Sheffield, 1999.

———. *Rut*. HThKAT. Freiburg: Herder, 2001.

Fisher-Stewart, Gayle. *Black and Episcopalian: The Struggle for Inclusion*. Church Publishing Inc., 2022.

Flagg, Fannie. *Fried Green Tomatoes at the Whistle Stop Cafe*. New York: Random House, 2016.

Floyd, Kevin and José Esteban Muñoz. "Queer Principles of Hope." *Meditations* 25 (2010) 107–13.

Floyd-Thomas, Stacey, ed. *Deeper Shades of Purple: Womanism in Religion and Society*. Religion, Race, and Ethnicity. New York: New York University Press, 2006.

Foskett, Mary. *Interpreting the Bible: Approaching the Text in Preparation for Preaching*. Elements of Preaching. Minneapolis: Fortress, 2007.

Foss, Sonja Kay, and Cindy L Griffin. "Beyond Persuasion, a Proposal for an Invitational Rhetoric." In *Contemporary Rhetorical Theory*, edited by Mark J. Porrovecchio and Celeste Michelle Condit, 77–89. 2nd ed. New York: Guilford, 2016.

Foucault, Michel. "Of Other Spaces: Utopias and Heterotopias." Translated by Jay Miskowiec. *Architecture/Mouvement/Continuité* (October 1984) 1–9. Reprinted in *Rethinking Architecture: A Reader in Cultural Theory*, edited by Neil Leach, 330–36. New York: Routledge, 1997.

———. "A Preface to Transgression." In *Language, Counter-Memory, Practice: Selected Essays and Interviews*, edited and translated by Donald F. Bouchard, 29–52. Ithaca: Cornell University Press, 1980.

Frye, Northrop. *The Great Code: The Bible and Literature*. New York: Harcourt Brace Jovanovich, 1982.

Gadamer, Hans-Georg. *Truth and Method*. Translated by William Glen-Doepel. Edited by John Cumming and Garrett Barden. New York: Continuun, 1975.

Gafney, Wil. "Mother Knows Best: Messianic Surrogacy and Sexploitation in Ruth." In *Mother Goose, Mother Jones, Mommy Dearest: Biblical Mothers & Their Children*, edited by Cheryl Kirk-Duggan and Tina Pippin, 23–36. Semeia Studies 61. Atlanta: Society of Biblical Literature, 2009.

———. "Ruth." In *The Africana Bible: Reading Israel's Scriptures from Africa and the African Diaspora*, edited by Hugh R. Page Jr. et al., 249–54. Minneapolis: Fortress, 2010.

Gaiman, Neil. *Coraline*. Tenth Anniversary ed. New York: HarperCollins, 2012.

Gale, Aaron M. "Matthew." In *The Jewish Annotated New Testament*, edited by Amy-Jill Levine and Marc Zvi Brettler, 9–66. Oxford: Oxford University Press, 2011.

Geronimus, Arline T. *Weathering: The Extraordinary Stress of Ordinary Life in an Unjust Society*. New York: Little, Brown Spark, 2023.

Gibson, E. Leigh, and Shelly Matthews, eds. *Violence in the New Testament*. New York: T. & T. Clark, 2005.

Gibson, Scott M. and Kim, Matthew D., eds. *Homiletics and Hermeneutics: Four Views on Preaching Today*. Grand Rapids: Baker Academic, 2018.

Glueck, Nelson. *Hesed in the Bible*. Translated by A. Gottschalk. Cincinnati: Hebrew Union College Press, 1967.

Goh, Samuel T.S. "Ruth as a Superior Woman of חיל? A Comparison between Ruth and the 'Capable' Woman in Proverbs 31.10–31." *Journal for the Study of the Old Testament* 38 (2014) 487–500.

Gordon, H. R., K. Willink, and K. Hunter. "Invisible Labor and the Associate Professor: Identity and Workload Inequity." *Journal of Diversity in Higher Education* 17 (2024) 285–96.

Gornick, Vivian. *The Situation and the Story: The Art of Personal Narrative*. New York: Farrar, Straus & Giroux, 2001.

Goss, Robert E. and Mona West, eds. *Take Back the Word: A Queer Reading of the Bible*. Cleveland, OH: Pilgrim, 2000.

Gottwald, Norman K. "Abusing the Bible: The Case of Deuteronomy 15." *Review & Expositor* 111 (2014) 196–198.

——— . *The Tribes of Yahweh: A Sociology of the Religion of Liberated Israel, 1250–1050 BCE*. 3rd printing. Maryknoll, NY: Orbis, 1985.

Graeber, David. *Debt: The First 5000 Years*. Brooklyn: Melville House, 2011.

Graybill, Rhiannon. "After the Idyll Ends: Ruth and the Uses of Disappointment." In *Ruth*, edited by Rhiannon Graybill and Philippe Guillaume. Themes and Issues in Biblical Studies. Equinox, 2023 (online advance publication).

——— . "Even unto This Bitter Loving": Unhappiness and Backward Feelings in Ruth." *Biblical Interpretation* 29 (2020) 308–31.

——— . "Sex in Public in the Song of Songs." In *Reading the Song of Songs in a #MeToo Era: Women, Sex, and Public Discourse*, edited by Elaine T. James and Simeon Chavel, 38–61. Biblical Interpretation Series 212. Leiden: Brill, 2023.

——— . "Where Are All the Women?" *Journal of Biblical Literature* 140 (2021) 826–30.

Greenstein, Edward L. "Reading Strategies and the Story of Ruth." In *Women in the Hebrew Bible*, edited by Alice Bach, 211–32. New York: Routledge, 1999.

Guardiola-Sáenz, Leticia A. "Borderless Women and Borderless Texts: A Cultural Reading of Matthew 15:21–28." *Semeia* 78 (1997) 69–81.

Guillaume, Philippe. "One Plus One Equals Three: The Economics of Land Shares According to Boaz." In *Ruth*, edited by Rhiannon Graybill and Philippe Guillaume, Themes and Issues in Biblical Studies. Equinox, 2023 (online advance publication).

Gullotta, Daniel N. "Among Dogs and Disciples: an Examination of the Story of the Canaanite Woman (Matthew 15:21–28) and the Question of the Gentile Mission Within the Matthean Community." *Neotestamentica* 48 (2014) 325–40.

Gumbrecht, Hans Ulrich. *The Powers of Philology: Dynamics of Textual Scholarship*. Urbana: University of Illinois Press, 2003.

Guy, Buddy. *Best of the Silvertone Years 1991–2005*. Sony Japan, 2005.

Halberstam, Jack. *The Queer Art of Failure*. Durham: Duke University Press, 2011.

Halperin, David M. *Saint Foucault: Towards a Gay Hagiography*. New York: Oxford University Press, 1995.
Halpern, Baruch. *David's Secret Demons: Messiah, Murderer, Traitor, King*. The Bible in Its World. Grand Rapids: Eerdmans, 2001.
Halton, Charles. "An Indecent Proposal: The Theological Core of the Book of Ruth." *SJOT* 26 (2012) 30–43.
Hamad, Rita. "Immigrants to the United States Contribute to Society: Here Are 3 Ways to Support Their Transition." *Health Affairs Scholar* 2 (2024) 1–3.
Hammer, K. Allison. "Epic Stone Butch: Transmasculinity in the Work of Willa Cather." *Transgender Studies Quarterly* 7 (2020) 77–98.
Häner, Tobias, Virginia Miller, and Carolyn J. Sharp, eds. *Irony in the Bible: Between Subversion and Innovation*. Biblical Interpretation Series 209. Leiden: Brill, 2023.
Hare, Douglass R. A., *Matthew*. Interpretation. Louisville: Westminster John Knox, 1993.
Harrington, Daniel J. *The Gospel of Matthew*. Sacra Pagina 1. Collegeville, MN: Liturgical, 1991.
Harris, James H. *Beyond the Tyranny of the Text: Preaching in Front of the Bible to Create a New World*. Nashville: Abingdon, 2019.
———. *The Word Made Plain: The Power and Promise of Preaching*. Minneapolis: Fortress, 2004.
Hartman, Tracy. *Letting the Other Speak: Proclaiming the Stories of Biblical Women*. Lanham, MD: Lexington, 2012.
Harvey, Jennifer. *Dear White Christians: For Those Still Longing for Racial Reconciliation*. Grand Rapids: Eerdmans, 2014.
Havea, Jione. *Losing Ground: Reading Ruth in the Pacific*. London: SCM, 2021.
Havice, Harriet K. "The Concern for the Widow and Fatherless in the Ancient Near East: A Case Study in Old Testament Ethics." PhD diss., Yale University, 1978.
Heidegger, Martin. *Ontology—The Hermeneutics of Facticity*. Translated by John Edward van Buren. Studies in Continental Thought. Bloomington: Indiana University Press, 1999.
Hesselgrave, David J. *Communicating Christ Cross-Culturally: An Introduction to Missionary Communication*. Grand Rapids: Zondervan Academic, 1991.
Hiebert, Paula S. "'Whence Shall Help Come to Me?' The Biblical Widow." In *Gender and Difference in Ancient Israel*. Edited by Peggy L. Day, 125–41. Minneapolis: Fortress, 1989.
Higgs, Liz C. *Bad Girls of the Bible: And What We Can Learn from Them*. Colorado Springs, CO: Waterbrook, 1999.
———. *Really Bad Girls of the Bible: More Lessons from Less-Than-Perfect Women*. Colorado Springs, CO: Waterbrook, 2000.
———. *Slightly Bad Girls of the Bible: Flawed Women Loved by a Flawless God*. Colorado Springs, CO: Waterbrook, 2007.
Hill Collins, Patricia and Sirma Bilge. *Intersectionality*. Key Concepts. Cambridge, UK: Polity, 2016.
Hirschman, Charles. "The Contribution of Immigrants to American Culture." *Daedalus* 142 (2013) 26–47.
Hochschild, Arlie. *The Second Shift: Working Families and the Revolution at Home*. New York: Penguin, 2012.
hooks, bell. *Teaching Community A Pedagogy of Hope*, Milton Park: Taylor & Francis, 2004.

"How to Sharpen Your Attention." https://www.universityofcalifornia.edu/news/how-sharpen-your-attention-and-meet-your-goals-2024.
Hubbard, Robert L., Jr. *The Book of Ruth*, Grand Rapids: Eerdmans, 1988.
Hudson, Michael. *The Lost Tradition of Biblical Debt Cancellations*. New York: Henry George School of Social Science, 1993.
———. "Reconstructing the Origins of Interest-Bearing Debt and the Logic of Clean Slates." In *Debt and Economic Renewal in the Ancient Near East*. International Scholars Conference on Near Eastern Societies. Vol. 3. Edited by Michael Hudson and Marc Van De Mieroop, 7–58. Bethesda, MD: CDL, 2002.
Hudson, Michael, and Marc Van De Mieroop, eds. *Debt and Economic Renewal in the Ancient Near East*. International Scholars Conference on Near Eastern Societies. Vol. 3. Bethesda, MD: CDL, 2002.
Human, D. J. "Re-interpretation as Transformation; Perspectives and Challenges for Old Testament interpretation." *Acta Theologica*, Supp 32 (2021) 195–219.
Ibita, Ma. M. "#Choosetochallenge: Covid-19, Community Research, and the Canaanite Woman." *Acta Theologica*, Supp 39 (2023) 180–99.
Iliffe, John. *The African Poor: A History*. African Studies Series 58. New York: Oxford University Press, 1987.
Isaac, Benjamin. *The Invention of Racism in Classical Antiquity*. Princeton: Princeton University Press, 2013.
Jackson, Glenna S. *'Have Mercy on Me': The Story of the Canaanite Woman in Matthew 15.21–28*. Copenhagen International Seminar 10. London: Sheffield Academic, 2002.
Jackson, Zakiyya Iman. *Becoming Human: Matter and Meaning in an Antiblack World*. New York: New York University Press, 2020.
Jenkins, Willis. "Ethics under Pressure: An Autoethnography of Moral Trauma." In *Charlottesville 2017: The Legacy of Race and Inequity*, edited by Claudrena N. Harold and Louis P. Nelson, 163–176. Charlottesville: University of Virginia Press, 2018.
Jennings, Willie James. *After Whiteness: An Education in Belonging*. Grand Rapids: Eerdmans, 2020.
———. *The Christian Imagination: Theology and the Origins of Race*. New Haven: Yale University Press, 2010.
Jones, Clifford R. "Telling the Story: A Brief Survey of African American Preaching." *Asia Aadventist Seminary Studies* 8 (2005) 44–62.
Johnson-DeBaufre, Melanie. "'That One' Takes a Village: The Uniqueness of Jesus and the Beelzebul Controversy (Q 11:14–26)." *The Fourth R* 22.5 (2009) 3–22.
Kaiser, Walter C., Jr. et al. *Hard Sayings of the Bible*. Downers Grove, IL: InterVarsity, 1996.
Kelle, Brad E. *The Bible and Moral Injury: Reading Scripture Alongside War's Unseen Wounds*. Nashville: Abingdon, 2020.
Kelley, Shawn. *Racializing Jesus: Race, Ideology, and the Formation of Modern Biblical Scholarship*. Biblical Limits. London: Routledge, 2002.
Kierkegaard, Soren. *Works of Love*. Edited by Robert Perkins. The International Kierkegaard Commentary 16. New Jersey: Mercer University Press, 2021.
Kim, Hyun Chul Paul. "Ruth vis-a-vie Esther: Reading Intertextually Ruth 'the Widow' and Esther 'the Orphan' as Diasporic Immigrants." *Korean Journal of Old Testament Studies* 74 (2019) 20–34.

Kim, Yung Suk. *Biblical Interpretation: Theory, Process, Criteria*. Eugene, OR: Pickwick Publications, 2013.

———. *How to Read the Gospels: An Introduction*. New York: Rowman & Littlefield, 2024.

———. *A Transformative Reading of the Bible: Explorations of Holistic Human Transformation*. Eugene, OR: Cascade Books, 2013.

———. *Truth, Testimony, and Transformation: A New Reading of the "I Am" Sayings of Jesus in the Fourth Gospel*. Eugene, OR: Cascade Books, 2014.

Kim-Cragg, HyeRan. "Unfinished and Unfolding Tasks of Preaching: Interdisciplinary, Intercultural, and Interreligious Approaches in the Postcolonial Context of Migration." *Homiletic* 44.2 (2019) 4–17.

King, Karen L. *The Gospel of Mary of Magdala: Jesus and the First Woman Apostle*. Santa Rosa, CA: Polebridge, 2003.

King, Martin Luther, Jr. *Strength to Love*. 1977. Reprint, Philadelphia: Fortress, 1981.

Kinukawa, Hisako. "Decolonizing Ourselves as Readers: The Story of the Syrophoenician Woman as a Text." In *Distant Voices Drawing Near: Essays in Honor of Antoinette Clark Wire*, edited by Holly E. Hearon, 131–44. Collegeville, MN: Glazier, 2004.

Kirk, Russell. "The Moral Imagination." *Literature and Belief* 1 (1981) 37–49.

Koosed. Jennifer L. *Gleaning Ruth: A Biblical Heroine and Her Alternatives*. Columbia: University of South Carolina Press, 2011.

Kowalski, Beate. "The Rewriting of the Old Testament in the Book of Ruth and the Rewriting of Ruth in Jewish and Christian Literature." *Proceedings of the Irish Biblical Association* 33–34 (2010) 1–35.

Kraemer, Ross Shepherd. *Her Share of the Blessings: Women's Religions among Pagans, Jews, and Christians in the Greco-Roman World*. New York: Oxford University Press, 1992.

Kruizinga, Renske et al., eds. *Learning from Case Studies in Chaplaincy: Towards Practice Based Evidence and Professionalism*. Utrecht: Eburon, 2020.

Krumm, Keisha. *Our Birthright: The Politics of Jesus for Black People Today*. Niles, IL: ACTA, 2024.

Krutzsch, Brett. "Un-Straightening Boaz in Ruth Scholarship." *Biblical Interpretation* 23 (2015) 541–52.

Kugler, Gili, and Ohad Magori. "*Hesed* in Ruth: A Frail Moral Tool in an Inflexible Social Structure." *Religions* 14.604 (2023) 1–13.

Kwok, Pui-Lan. *The Anglican Tradition from a Postcolonial Perspective*. New York: Seabury, 2023.

———. "Worshipping with Asian Women: A Homily on Jesus Healing the Daughter of a Canaanite Woman." In *Feminist Theology from the Third World: A Reader*, edited by Ursula King, 236–42. 1994. Reprint, Eugene, OR: Wipf & Stock, 2015.

LaCocque, André. *Ruth*. Translated by K. C. Hanson. Continental Commentaries. Minneapolis: Fortress, 2004.

Laffey, Alice, and Mahri Leonard-Fleckman. *Ruth*. Wisdom Commentary 8. Collegeville, MN, Liturgical, 2017.

Landes, George M. *Building Your Biblical Hebrew Vocabulary: Learning Words by Frequency and Cognate*. 2nd ed. Resources for Biblical Study. Atlanta: Society of Biblical Literature Press, 2001.

———. *Students Vocabulary of Biblical Hebrew*. New York: Scribner, 1961.

LaRue, Cleophus J. "Preaching Out of the Overflow." In *The New Interpreter's Handbook of Preaching*, edited by Paul Scott Wilson et al., 243–46. Nashville: Abingdon, 2008.

Lau, Peter H. W. "Another Postcolonial Reading of the Book of Ruth." In *Reading Ruth in Asia*, edited by Jione Havea and Peter H. W. Lau, 15–34. International Voices in Biblical Studies 7. Atlanta: SBL Press, 2015.

———. *The Book of Ruth*. International Critical Commentary on the Old Testament. Grand Rapids: Eerdmans, 2023.

Lawlor, Leonard. *Thinking Through French Philosophy: The Being of the Question*. Bloomington: Indiana University Press, 2003.

Lawrence, Louise Joy. "'Crumb Trails and Puppy-Dog Tales': Reading Afterlives of a Canaanite Woman." In *From the Margins 2: Women of the New Testament and Their Afterlives*, edited by Christine E. Joynes, 262–78. Bible in the Modern World 27. Sheffield: Sheffield Phoenix, 2009.

Lee, Dorothy. "The Faith of the Canaanite Woman (Mt. 15.21–28): Narrative, Theology, Ministry." *Journal of Anglican Studies* 13 (2014) 12–29.

Lee, Eunny P. "Ruth." In *The Women's Bible Commentary*, edited by Carol Newsom et al., 142–49. 3rd ed, twentieth anniversary ed. Louisville: Westminster John Knox, 2012.

Lee, Jung Young. *Marginality: The Key to a Multicultural Theology*. Minneapolis: Fortress, 1995.

Levine, Amy-Jill. "Matt. 15:21–28, Canaanite Woman." In *Women in Scripture: A Dictionary of Named and Unnamed Women in the Hebrew Bible, the Apocryphal/Deuterocanonical Books, and the New Testament*, edited by Carol Meyers, 413. Boston: Houghton Mifflin, 2000.

———. "Matthew's Advice to a Divided Readership." In *The Gospel of Matthew in Current Study: Studies in Memory of William G. Thompson, S.J.*, edited by David E. Aune, 22–41. Grand Rapids: Eerdmans 2001.

Levine, Amy-Jill, with Marianne Blickenstaff. *A Feminist Companion to Matthew*. Feminist Companion to the New Testament and Early Christian Literature 1. Sheffield: Sheffield Academic, 2001.

Lévinas, Emmanuel. *Ethics and Infinity: Conversations with Philippe Nemo*. Translated by Richard A. Cohen. Pittsburgh: Duquesne University Press, 1985.

———. *Otherwise than Being: Or, Beyond Essence*. Translated by Alphonso Lingis. The Hague: Nijhof, 1981.

———. "The Paradox of Morality: An Interview with Emmanuel Lévinas." Translated by Andrew Benjamin and Tamra Wright. In *The Provocation of Lévinas: Rethinking the Other*, edited by Robert Bernasconi and David Wood, 168–80. Warwick Studies in Philosophy and Literature. London: Routledge, 1988.

Linafelt, Tod. "Narrative and Poetic Art in the Book of Ruth." *Interpretation* 64 (2010) 117–29.

———. *Ruth*. Berit Olam. Collegeville, MN: Liturgical, 1999.

Lindsay, Lisa A., and Stephan F. Miescher, eds. *Men and Masculinities in Modern Africa*. Portsmouth: Heinemann, 2003.

Lipka, Michaele. "The Most and Least Racially Diverse U.S. Religious Groups." Pew Research Center. 27 July 2015. https://www.pewresearch.org/short-reads/2015/07/27/the-most-and-least-racially-diverse-u-s-religious-groups/.

Loder, James E. *The Transforming Moment*. 2nd ed. Colorado Springs: Helmers & Howard, 1989.

Long, Thomas G. *Matthew*. Westminster Bible Companion. Louisville: Westminster John Knox, 1997.

Lopez, Davina. *Apostle to the Conquered: Reimagining Paul's Mission*. Paul in Critical Contexts. Minneapolis: Fortress, 2008.

Lorde, Audre. *Sister Outsider: Essays and Speeches*. Berkeley: Crossing, 1984.

Love, Heather. *Feeling Backward: Loss and the Politics of Queer History*. Cambridge: Harvard University Press, 2007.

Love, Stuart L. *Jesus and Marginal Women: The Gospel of Matthew in Social-Scientific Perspective*. Matrix 5. Eugene, OR: Cascade Books, 2009.

Luibhéid, Eithne. "Queer/Migration: An Unruly Body of Scholarship." *GLQ* 14 (2008) 169–90.

Luther, Martin. *Commentary on the Epistle to the Romans*. Translated by J. T. Mueller. Grand Rapids: Zondervan, 1962.

Major, Clarence. *Juba to Jive: A Dictionary of African-American Slang*. New York: Viking, 1994.

Malina, Bruce J. "Dealing with Biblical (Mediterranean) Characters: A Guide for U. S. Consumers." *Biblical Theology Bulletin* 19 (1989) 127–41.

Manalansan, Martin F. "Queer Intersections: Sexuality and Gender in Migration Studies." *International Migration Review* 40 (2006) 224–49.

Maluleke, Tinyiko. "African 'Ruths,' Ruthless Africas: Reflections of an African Mordecai." In *Other Ways of Reading: African Women and the Bible*, edited by Musa Dube, 237–51. Global Perspectives on Biblical Scholarship 2. Atlanta: Society of Biblical Literature, 2001.

Masenya, Madipoane, and Kenneth Ngwa, eds. *Navigating African Biblical Hermeneutics: Trends and Themes from Our Pots and Our Calabashes*. Newcastle: Cambridge Scholars, 2018.

Masenya, Madipoane, and Marthe M. Kondemo. "What of the Problematic Norm? Rereading the Book of Ruth within the Mongo Women's Context." In *Navigating African Biblical Hermeneutics: Trends and Themes from Our Pots and Our Calabashes*, edited by Madipoane Masenya and Kenneth Ngwa, 122–136. Newcastle: Cambridge Scholars, 2018.

Masenya, Madipoane. "*Ngwetši* (Bride): The Naomi–Ruth Story from an African-South African Woman's Perspective." *Journal of Feminist Studies in Religion* 14 (1998) 80–90.

———. "Ruth." In *Global Bible Commentary*, edited by Daniel Patte, 86–91. Nashville: Abingdon, 2004.

Masunda, Shingirai Eunice. "Running the Metaphor Blend with Jesus: How the Canaanite Woman Transformed Jesus' Metaphor." *Journal of the European Society of Women in Theological Research* 30 (2022) 147–52.

Matheny, Jennifer M. "Ruth in Recent Research." *Currents in Biblical Research* 19 (2020) 8–35.

Matthew, Dayna Bowen. *Just Medicine. A Cure for Racial Inequality in American Health Care*. New York: New York University Press, 2015.

Matthews, Victor H. *Judges and Ruth*. New Cambridge Bible Commentary. Cambridge: Cambridge University Press, 2004.

Mbiti, John S. *African Religions and Philosophy*. 2nd ed. London: Heinemann, 1990.

Mbuvi, Andrew M. *African Biblical Studies: Unmasking Embedded Racism and Colonialism in Biblical Studies*. London: T. & T. Clark Bloomsbury, 2023.

McCaulley, Esau. *Reading While Black: African American Biblical Interpretation as an Exercise in Hope.* Downers Grove, IL: IVP Academic, 2020.

McClure, John. *Otherwise Preaching: A Postmodern Ethic for Homiletics.* St. Louis: Chalice, 2001.

McCray, Donyelle C. "Black Feminist Triptych." *Homiletic* 45.2 (2020) 5–13.

McDonald, Joseph, ed. *Exploring Moral Injury in Sacred Texts.* Studies in Religion and Theology Series. London: Kingsley, 2017.

McGrath, James F. *What Jesus Learned from Women.* Eugene, OR: Cascade Books, 2021.

McKenna, Megan. "Navigating Mystery: The Preacher as Prophet and Mystic." In *Preaching as Spiritual Leadership: Guiding the Faithful as Mystic and Mystagogue,* edited by Michael E. Connors, 19–33. Chicago: Liturgy Training Publications, 2021.

Meier, John. *A Marginal Jew: Rethinking the Historical Jesus.* New York: Doubleday, 1991.

Melgar, César. "Ruth and the Unaccompanied Minors from Central America: Ethical Perspectives on a Socio- Economic Problem." *Review and Expositor* 112 (2015) 269-279.

Meyers, Carol. "Hierarchy or Heterarchy? Archaeology and the Theorizing of Israelite Society." In *Confronting the Past: Archaeological and Historical Essays on Ancient Israel in Honor of William G. Dever,* edited by Seymour Gitin et al., 245–54. Winona Lake, IN: Eisenbrauns, 2006.

———. *Discovering Eve: Ancient Israelite Women in Context.* New York: Oxford University Press, 1988.

———. "'Women of the Neighborhood' (Ruth 4:17): Informal Female Networks in Ancient Israel." In *Ruth and Esther,* edited by Athalya Brenner, 110–27. Feminist Companion to the Bible Second Series. Sheffield: Sheffield Academic, 1999.

Miller, Claire Cain, Sarah Kliff, and Larry Buchanan. "Childbirth Is Deadlier for Black Families Even When They're Rich, Expansive Study Finds." *New York Times* (February 2023) n.p., https://www.nytimes.com/2023/06/27/well/mind/postpartum-depression-mental-health.html.

Miller-McLemore, Bonnie. *Christian Theology in Practice: Discovering a Discipline.* Grand Rapids: Eerdmans, 2012.

Mills, Charles. *The Racial Contract.* Ithaca: Cornell University Press, 2014.

Milton J. Bennett. "Intercultural Communication, Intercultural Development Institute, Extended Encyclopedia Entries." In C. Cortés, ed., *Multicultural America: A Multimedia Encyclopedia.*

Moogkok, Kgatle S. "Crossing Boundaries: Social-scientific Reading of the Faith of a Canaanite Woman (Matt 15:21–28)." *Stellenbosch Theological Journal* 4 (2018) 595–613.

Moore, Michael. "Ruth the Moabite and the Blessing of Foreigners." *CBQ* 60 (1998) 203–17.

Moore, Stephen D. *Gospel Jesuses and Other Nonhumans: Biblical Criticism Post-Poststructuralism.* Semeia Studies 89. Atlanta: SBL Press, 2017.

Moore, Steven D., and Fernando F. Segovia, eds. *Postcolonial Biblical Criticism: Interdisciplinary Intersections.* London: T. & T. Clark, 2005.

Morrison, Toni. *The Origin of Others.* Cambridge: Harvard University Press, 2017.

Moyo, Fulata Lusungu. "'Traffic Violations': Hospitality, Foreignness, and Exploitation: A Contextual Biblical Study of Ruth." *Journal of Feminist Studies in Religion* 32 (2016) 83–94.

Mtshiselwa, V. Ndikhokele N. "Reading Ruth 4 and Leviticus 25:8–55 in the Light of Landless and Poor Women in South Africa: A Conversation with Fernando F. Segovia and Ernesto 'Che' Guevara." *HTS Teologiese Studies/Theological Studies* 72.1 (2016) 1–5.

Muñoz, José Esteban. *Cruising Utopia: The Then and There of Queer Futurity*. Sexual Cultures. New York: New York University Press, 2009.

Myers, Jacob D. *Making Love with Scripture: Why the Bible Doesn't Mean How You Think It Means*. Minneapolis: Fortress, 2015.

———. *Preaching Must Die! Troubling Homiletical Theology*. Minneapolis: Fortress, 2018.

Myers, Jacob D., and Sunggu Yang. *Preaching Philosophy: French Thought for Gospel Proclamation*. Waco: Baylor University Press, 2024.

Nadadur, Ramanujan. "Illegal Immigration: A Positive Economic Contribution to the United States." *Journal of Ethnic and Migration Studies* 35 (2009) 1037–52.

Nadar, Sarojini. "A South African Indian Womanist Reading of the Character of Ruth." In *Other Ways of Reading: African Women and the Bible*, edited by Musa Dube, 159–75. Global Perspectives on Biblical Scholarship. Atlanta: Society of Biblical Literature, 2001.

Nadella, Raj. *Dialogue not Dogma: Many Voices in the Gospel of Luke*. Library of New Testament Studies 431. London: T. & T. Clark, 2011.

Nelavala, Surekha. "Patriarchy, a Threat to Human Bonding: Reading the Story of Ruth in Light of Marriage and Family Structures in India." In *Reading Ruth in Asia*, edited by Jione Havea and Peter H. W. Lau, 89–97. International Voices in Biblical Studies 7. Atlanta: SBL, 2015.

Ngũgĩ, wa Thiong'o. *Decolonising the Mind. The Politics of Language in African Literature*. Nairobi: EAEP, 1986.

Nielsen, Kristen. *Ruth*. Interpretation. Louisville: Westminster John Knox, 2015.

Niggemann, Andrew J. "Matriarch of Israel or Misnomer? Israelite Self-Identification in Ancient Israelite Law Code and the Implications for Ruth." *Journal for the Study of the Old Testament* 41 (2017) 355–77.

Niles, Lyndrey A. "Rhetorical Characteristics of Traditional Black Preaching." *Journal of Black Studies* 15.1 (1984) 41–52. https://www.jstor.org/stable/2784116.

Ochs, Peter. *Peirce, Pragmatism and the Logic of Scripture*. Cambridge: Cambridge University Press, 2005.

O'Day, Gail. "Shaped by Hearing: Living Our Stories Together." In *Questions Preachers Ask: Essays in Honor of Thomas G. Long*, edited by Scott Black Johnson et al., 3–11. Louisville: Westminster John Knox, 2016.

———. "Surprised by Faith: Jesus and the Canaanite Woman." In *A Feminist Companion to Matthew*, edited by Amy-Jill Levine with Marianne Blickenstaff, 114–25. Feminist Companion to the New Testament and Early Christian Writings 1. Cleveland, OH: Pilgrim, 2004.

Organ, Deborah S. "Cultural Hermeneutics." In *The New Interpreter's Handbook of Preaching*, edited by Paul Scott Wilson et al., 143–46. Nashville: Abingdon, 2008.

Osmer, Richard R. *Practical Theology: An Introduction*. Grand Rapids: Eerdmans, 2008.

Page, Hugh R., Jr., ed. *The Africana Bible: Reading Israel's Scriptures from Africa and the African Diaspora*. Minneapolis: Fortress, 2010.

Palmer, Carmen. "Naomi the Nurse: Obed's Ambiguous Identity Transmission." *Journal for the Study of the Old Testament* 47 (2023) 277–88.

Pardes, Ilana. *Ruth: A Migrant's Tale*. New Haven: Yale University Press, 2022.
Park, Song-Mi Suzie. *Love in the Hebrew Bible*. Louisville: Westminster John Knox, 2023.
Parker, Angela N. "Rethinking "God-breathed" in the Age of #BLM : A Womanist Reading of 2 Tim 3:10–17." In *Bitter the Chastening Rod: Africana Biblical Interpretation after Stony the Road We Trod in the Age of BLM, SayHerName, and MeToo*, edited by Mitzi J. Smith et al., 211–28. Lanham, MD: Lexington, 2022.
Parks, Sara et al. *Jewish and Christian Women in the Ancient Mediterranean*. Abingdon, UK: Routledge, 2021.
Patte, Daniel, ed. *Global Bible Commentary*. Nashville: Abingdon, 2004.
Pearson, Catherine. "Life in the Throes of Postpartum Depression." *New York Times* (June 2023) n.p., https://www.nytimes.com/2023/06/27/well/mind/postpartum-depression-mental-health.html.
"The President and Fellows of Harvard College, Classics Write a Guide to Research and Writing in the Field of Classics." https://projects.iq.harvard.edu/classicswrites.
Peters, Torrey. *Detransition, Baby*. New York: Random House, 2021.
"Polyphony" is "a multiplicity of sounds or voices," per the OED online. https://www.oed.com/dictionary/polyphony_n?tab=factsheet#29580040.
Pindi, Gloria Nziba, and Antonio Tomas De La Garza. "The Colonial Jesus: Deconstructing White Christianity." In *Interrogating the Communicative Power of Whiteness*, edited by Dawn Marie D. McIntosh et al., 218–38. New York: Routledge, 2018.
Powell, Stephanie Day. *Narrative Desire and the Book of Ruth*. Library of Hebrew Bible / Old Testament Studies 662. New York: T. & T. Clark, 2018.
Preser, Ruth. "Things I Learned from the Book of Ruth." *De/Constituting Wholes: Towards Partiality Without Parts* 11 (2017).
Pritchard, James B. *Ancient Near Eastern Texts Relating to the Old Testament*. 3rd ed. Princeton: Princeton University Press, 1969.
Puar, Jasbir Puar, and Maya Mikdashi. "Pinkwatching and Pinkwashing: Interpenetration and Its Discontents." *Jadaliyya* (blog). August 9, 2012. http://www.jadaliyya.com/pages/index/6774/pinkwatching-and-pinkwashing_interpenetration-and-.
Punt, Jeremy. "Postcolonial Approaches: Negotiating Empires, Then and Now." In *Studying Paul's Letters: Contemporary Perspectives and Methods*, edited by Joseph A. Marchal, 191–205. Minneapolis: Fortress, 2012.
Queen-Sutherland, Kandy. *Ruth & Esther*. Smyth & Helwys Bible Commentary. Macon, GA: Smyth & Helwys, 2016.
Quick, Laura. "The Book of Ruth and the Limits of Proverbial Wisdom." *Journal of Biblical Literature* 139 (2020) 47–66.
Rabin, Roni Caryn. "One in Five Women Feels Mistreated During Maternity Care, C.D.C Reports." *New York Times* (August 2023) n.p., https://www.nytimes.com/2023/08/22/health/pregnancy-mistreatment-health-care.html.
Raboteau, Albert. *Slave Religion: The Invisible Institution in the Antebellum South*. New York: Oxford University Press, 2004.
Rashkow, Ilona. *Taboo or Not Taboo: Sexuality and Family in the Hebrew Bible*. Minneapolis: Fortress, 2000.
"Reading is Fundamental." https://www.idealist.org/en/nonprofit/3338ee0688894df1bccf20a4bcc8b8a1-reading-is fundamental-washington.

Rees, Anthony. "The Boaz Solution: Reading Ruth in Light of Australian Asylum Seeker Discourse." In *Reading Ruth in Asia*, edited by Jione Havea and Peter H. W. Lau, 99–110. International Voices in Biblical Studies 7. Atlanta: SBL Press, 2015.

Rhoads, David. "Jesus and the Syrophoenician Woman in Mark: A Narrative-Critical Study." *Journal of the American Academy of Religion* 62 (1994) 343–37.

Rich, Adrienne. "Compulsory Heterosexuality and Lesbian Existence." *Signs* 5 (1980) 631–60.

Ricoeur, Paul. *Oneself as Another*. Chicago, IL: University of Chicago Press, 1990.

———. "The Hermeneutical Function of Distanciation." *Philosophy Today* 15.2 (1973) 120–41.

———. *Interpretation Theory: Discourse and the Surplus of Meaning*. Fort Worth: Texas Christian University Press, 1976.

———. "Metaphor and the Main Problem of Hermeneutics." *New Literary History* 6.1 (1974) 95–110.

———. *Time and Narrative*. Vol. 1. Translated by Kathleen McLaughlin and David Pellauer. Chicago: University of Chicago Press, 1984.

Ringe, Sharon H. "A Gentile Woman Story." In *Feminist Interpretation of the Bible*, edited by Letty Russell, 65–72. Louisville: Westminster John Knox, 1985.

Rosenberg, Gil. "New Authorities, New Readings." *Biblical Interpretation* 23 (2015) 574–600.

Rouhani, Farhang. "Queer Diasporas," in *Global Encyclopedia of Gay, Lesbian, Bisexual, Transgender, and Queer History*. Farmington Hills, MI: Cengage Learning, 2018.

Ruiz, Jean-Pierre. *Readings from the Edges: The Bible and People on the Move*. Studies in Latino/a Catholicism. Maryknoll, NY: Orbis, 2011.

Sakenfeld, Katharine Doob. *The Meaning of* Hesed *in the Hebrew Bible: A New Inquiry*. Harvard Semitic Monographs 17. Missoula, MT: Scholars, 1978.

———. *Ruth*. Interpretation. Louisville: John Knox, 1999.

Sartre, Jean-Paul. *Being and Nothingness: An Essay on Phenomenological Ontology*. Translated by Hazel E. Barnes. New York: Philosophical Library, 1956.

Sasson, Jack M. *Ruth: A New Translation with a Philological Commentary and a Formalist-Folklorist Interpretation*. 2nd ed. Biblical Seminar 10. Sheffield: JSOT, 1989.

Saxegaard, Kristin Moen. *Character Complexity in the Book of Ruth*. Forschungen zum Alten Testament 2. Tübingen: Mohr Siebeck, 2010.

Schaberg, Jane. *The Resurrection of Mary Magdalene: Legends, Apocrypha, and the Christian Testament*. New York: Continuum, 2002.

Schipani, Daniel S. "Biblical Foundations: Challenges and Possibilities of Interfaith Caregiving." In *Interfaith Spiritual Care: Understandings and Practices*, edited by Daniel S. Schipani and Leah D. Bueckert, 51–77. Kitchener, ON: Pandora, 2009.

———. "Case Study Method." In *The Wiley-Blackwell Companion to Practical Theology*, edited by Bonnie J. Miller-McLemore, 91–101. Wiley-Blackwell Companions to Religion. Malden: Blackwell, 2013.

———. "Educating for Social Transformation." In *Mapping Christian Education: Approaches to Congregational Learning*, ed. Jack L. Seymour, 23–40. Nashville: Abingdon, 1997.

———. "Liberation Theology and Religious Education." In *Theologies of Religious Education*, edited by Randolph Crump Miller, 286–313. Birmingham: Religious Education Press 1995.

———. "Transformation in Intercultural Bible Reading: A View from Practical Theology." In *Bible and Transformation: The Promise of Intercultural Bible Reading*, edited by Hans De Wit and Janet Dyk, 99–116. Semeia Studies 81. Atlanta: SBL, 2015.

———. *Spiritual Care in Our Multifaith World: A Primer on Practice and Theory*. Eugene, OR: Wipf & Stock, 2024.

Schipper, Jeremy. *Ruth: A New Translation with Introduction and Commentary*. Anchor Yale Bible 7D. New Haven: Yale University Press, 2016.

Schottroff, Willy, and Wolfgang Stegemann, eds. *God of the Lowly: Socio-Historical Interpretations of the Bible*. Translated by Matthew J. O'Connell. Maryknoll, NY: Orbis, 1984.

Schüssler Fiorenza, Elisabeth. *But She Said: Feminist Practices of Biblical Interpretation*. Boston: Beacon, 1992.

———. *In Memory of Her: A Feminist Theological Reconstruction of Christian Origins*. New York: Crossroad, 1986.

———. *Jesus and the Politics of Interpretation*. New York: Continuum, 2000.

"Scriptures, Creeds, and Confessions." ELCA.org. https://www.elca.org/Faith/ELCA-Teaching/Scripture-Creeds-Confessions.

Sechrest, Love. "Enemies, Romans, Pigs, and Dogs: Loving the Other in the Gospel of Matthew." *Ex Auditu* 31 (2015) 71–105.

———. *Race and Rhyme: Rereading the New Testament*. Grand Rapids: Eerdmans, 2022.

Segovia, Fernando F. *Decolonizing Biblical Studies: A View from the Margins*. Maryknoll, NY: Orbis, 2000.

Segovia, Fernando F., and Mary A. Tolbert, eds. *Reading from this Place*. Vol. 1: *Social Location and Biblical Interpretation in the United States*. Minneapolis: Fortress, 1995.

———, eds. *Reading from this Place*. Vol. 2: *Social Location and Biblical Interpretation in Global Perspective*. Minneapolis: Fortress, 1995.

Segovia, Sofía. *The Murmur of Bees*. Translated by Simon Bruni. Seattle: Amazon Crossing, 2019.

Senior, Donald. *Matthew*. Abingdon New Testament Commentaries. Nashville: Abingdon, 2011.

Shafer-Elliott, Cynthia. "Women and Economics in Ancient Israel and Judah." In *Economics and Empire in the Ancient Near East: Guide to the Bible and Economics*. Vol. 1. Edited by Matthew J. M. Coomber, 108–27. Eugene, OR: Cascade Books, 2023.

Shaner, Katherine A. "The Danger of Singular Saviors: Vulnerability, Political Power, and Jesus's Disturbance in the Temple (Mark 11:15–19)." *Journal of Biblical Literature* 140 (2021) 139–161.

———. "Slaves of the Gods or Enslaved to the Gods? Enslaved Labour and the βασιλεία τοῦ θεοῦ." *Religion in the Roman Empire* 10 (2024) 107–126.

Shannahan, Chris. "The Canaanite Woman and Urban Liberation Theology." *Expository Times* 125.1 (2013) 13–21.

Sharp, Carolyn J. "Embodying Moab: The Figuring of Moab in Jeremiah 48 as Reinscription of the Judean Body." In *Concerning the Nations: Essays on the Oracles against the Nations in Isaiah, Jeremiah and Ezekiel*, edited by Else K. Holt et al., 95–108. Library of Hebrew Bible / Old Testament Studies 612. New York: Bloomsbury T. & T. Clark, 2015.

———. "Feminist Queries for Ruth and Joshua: Complex Characterization, Gapping, and the Possibility of Dissent." *Scandinavian Journal of the Old Testament* 28 (2014) 229–52.

———. *Irony and Meaning in the Hebrew Bible*. Indiana Studies in Biblical Literature. Bloomington: Indiana University Press, 2009.

———. "Is This Naomi? A Feminist Reading of the Ambiguity of Naomi in the Book of Ruth." In *Feminist Frameworks and the Bible: Power, Ambiguity and Intersectionality*, edited by L. Juliana Claassens and Carolyn J. Sharp, 149–61. Library of Hebrew Bible / Old Testament Studies 630. New York: Bloomsbury T&T Clark, 2017.

———. *Jeremiah 26–52*. International Exegetical Commentary on the Old Testament. Stuttgart: Kohlhammer, 2022.

Shepherd, David. "Ruth in the Days of Judges: Women, Foreigners and Violence." *Biblical Interpretation* 26 (2018) 528–43.

Shercliff, Liz. "Towards a New Homiletic." *Feminist Theology* 29/1 (2020) 48–60.

Sinnott, Alice M. *Ruth: An Earth Bible Commentary*. London: T. & T. Clark, 2022. doi: 10.5040/9780567676245.

Siquans, Agnethe. "Foreignness and Poverty in the Book of Ruth: A Legal Way for a Poor Foreign Woman to Be Integrated into Israel." *Journal of Biblical Literature* 128 (2009) 443–52.

Smith, Mitzi J. "Commentary on Matthew 15:[10–20] 21–28." *Working Preacher*. https://www.workingpreacher.org/commentaries/revised-common-lectionary/ordinary-20/commentary-on-matthew-1510-20-21-28-4.

———, ed. *I Found God in Me: A Womanist Biblical Hermeneutics Reader*. Eugene, OR: Cascade Books, 2015.

———. *Insights from African American Interpretation*. Minneapolis: Fortress, 2017.

———. "Paul, Timothy, and the Respectability Politics of Race: A Womanist Inter(con)textual Reading of Acts 16:1–5." *Religions* 10.3 (2009) 190. https://doi.org/10.3390/rel10030190

———. *Womanist Sass and Talk Back: Social (In) Justice, Intersectionality, and Biblical Interpretation*. Eugene, OR: Cascade Books, 2018.

Smith, Mitzi J. and Yung Suk Kim. *Toward Decentering the New Testament: A Reintroduction*. Eugene, OR: Cascade Books, 2018.

Smith, Wilfred Cantwell. *What Is Scripture? A Comparative Approach* Minneapolis: Fortress, 1993.

Song, Choan-Seng. *Christian Mission in Reconstruction: An Asian Analysis*. Maryknoll, NY: Orbis, 1977.

St. Clair, Raquel. "Womanist Biblical Interpretation." In *True to Our Native Land: An African American New Testament Commentary*, edited by Brian Blount, 54–62. Minneapolis: Fortress, 2008.

Stampp, Kenneth M. *Peculiar Institution: Slavery in the Antebellum South*. 1956, Reprint, New York: Vintage, 1989.

Stone, Ken. *Queer Commentary and the Hebrew Bible*. Journal for the Study of the Old Testament Supplements 334. Cleveland, OH: Pilgrim, 2001.

Streete, Gail Corrington. *The Strange Woman: Power and Sex in the Bible*. Louisville: Westminster John Knox, 1997.

Strong, Justin David. "The Rape of Men in the Hebrew Bible, the Syrian Civil War, and the MeToo Movement." In *Doing Biblical Masculinity Studies as Feminist Biblical Studies: Critical Studies*, edited by Susanne Scholz, 66–84. Hebrew Bible Monographs 107. Sheffield: Sheffield Phoenix, 2023.

Stuckey, Sterling. *Slave Culture: Nationalist Theory and the Foundations of Black America*. New York: Oxford University Press, 2014.

Sugirtharajah, R. S. *The Bible and the Third World: Precolonial, Colonial and Postcolonial Encounters*. Cambridge: Cambridge University Press, 2001.

———. *Postcolonial Reconfigurations: An Alternative Way of Reading the Bible and Doing Theology*. St. Louis: Chalice, 2003.

Summer, Cree. "Street Faerie." Audio CD, Sony Music Entertainment, 1999.

Sun, Chloe. "Recent Research on Asian and Asian American Hermeneutics." *Currents in Biblical Research* 17 (2019) 238–65.

Swartley, Willard M. *Israel's Scripture Traditions and the Synoptic Gospels: Story Shaping Story*. Peabody, MA: Hendrickson, 1994.

Swinton, John and Harriet Mowat. *Practical Theology and Qualitative Research*. 2nd ed. London: SCM, 2016.

Tan, Nancy Nam Hoon. *The "Foreignness" of the Foreign Woman in Proverbs 1–9: A Study of the Origin and Development of a Biblical Motif*. Beihefte zur Zeitschrift für die alttestamentliche Wissenschaft 381. Berlin: de Gruyter, 2008.

Taylor, Charles. *Modern Social Imaginaries*. Durham: Duke University Press, 2004.

Taylor Gench, Frances. *Back to the Well: Women's Encounters with Jesus in the Gospels*. Louisville: Westminster John Knox, 2004.

Thomas, Frank. *How to Preach a Dangerous Sermon*. Nashville: Abingdon, 2018.

———. *Introduction to the Practice of African American Preaching*. Nashville: Abingdon, 2016.

Thomas, John L., Jr. *Voices in the Wilderness: Why Black Preaching Still Matters*. Eugene, OR: Cascade Books, 2018.

Thurman, Howard. *Jesus and the Disinherited*. 1949. Reprint, Boston: Beacon, 1996.

Tillich, Paul. *Systematic Theology*. Vol. 1: *Reason and Revelation, Being and God*. Chicago: University of Chicago Press, 1951, 1973.

———. *Systematic Theology*. Vol. 2: *Existence and the Christ*. Chicago: University of Chicago Press, 1957, 1975.

Tolstoy, Leo. *Anna Karenina*. New York: Random House, 2000.

Travis, Sarah. *Decolonizing Preaching: The Pulpit as Postcolonial Space*. Lloyd John Ogilvie Institute of Preaching Series 6. Eugene, OR: Cascade Books, 2014.

Trible, Phyllis. *God and the Rhetoric of Sexuality*. Overtures to Biblical Theology. Philadelphia: Fortress, 1978.

Troeger, Thomas. *Imagining a Sermon*. Nashville: Abingdon, 1990.

Ulmer, James Blood. "There Is Power in the Blues." *Greatest Blues Hits*, Hyena, 2011.

Valle-Ruiz, Lis, and Andrew Wymer, eds. *Unmasking White Preaching: Racial Hegemony, Resistance, and Possibilities in Homiletics*. Postcolonial and Decolonial Studies in Religion and Theology. Lanham, MD: Lexington, 2022.

Van De Meiroop, Marc. "A History of Ancient Near Eastern Debt." In *Debt and Economic Renewal in the Ancient Near East*, edited by Michael Hudson and Marc Van De Mieroop, 59–94. International Scholars Conference on Near Eastern Societies 3. Bethesda, MD: CDL, 2002.

Volf, Miroslav, and Dorothy C. Bass, eds. *Practicing Theology: Beliefs and Practices in Christian Life*. Grand Rapids: Eerdmans, 2002.

Wafawanaka, Robert. *Am I Still My Brother's Keeper? Biblical Perspectives on Poverty*. Lanham, MD: University Press of America, 2012.

———. "The Global Crisis of Debt in Context: Biblical and Postcolonial Reflections on the Ideology of Empire." In *Reading the Bible in an Age of Crisis: Political Exegesis for a New Day*, edited by Bruce Worthington, 163–90. Minneapolis: Fortress, 2015.

———. "In Quest of Survival: The Implications of the Reconstruction Theology of Ezra-Nehemiah." In *Postcolonial Perspectives in African Biblical Interpretations*, edited by Musa W. Dube et al., 349–58. Global Perspectives on Biblical Scholarship 13. Atlanta: Society of Biblical Literature, 2012.

———. "'The Land Is Mine!' Biblical and Postcolonial Reflections on Land with Particular Reference to the Land Issue in Zimbabwe." In *Postcolonial Perspectives in African Biblical Interpretations*, edited by Musa W. Dube et al., 221–34. Atlanta: Society of Biblical Literature, 2012.

———. "Righteous Rage and the Politics of Subsistence Economies: A Socio-economic Reading of the Books of Amos and Micah from an African Perspective." In *Contemporary African Perspectives on the Bible*, edited by Tobias Marevesa et al., 163–84. London: Palgrave Macmillan, 2024.

———. "Toxic Masculinity in Africa and the Bible: The Strong-Man Model and the Co-optation of Feminist Biblical Interpretation." *Old Testament Essays* 34 (2021) 806–34.

Wahlberg, Rachel Conrad. *Jesus According to a Woman*. New York: Paulist, 1986.

Wainwright, Elaine M. *Shall We Look for Another? A Feminist Rereading of the Matthean Jesus*. Bible & Liberation. Maryknoll, NY: Orbis, 1998.

Walker, Alice. *In Search of Our Mother's Gardens: Womanist Prose*. San Diego: Harcourt Brace Jovanovich, 1983.

Walther, James A. *New Testament Greek Workbook: An Inductive Study of the Complete Text of the Gospel of John*. 2nd ed. Chicago: University of Chicago Press, 1981.

Ward, Richard F. *Speaking of the Holy: The Art of Communication in Preaching*. St. Louis: Chalice, 2001.

Warnock, Raphael. *The Divided Mind of the Black Church: Theology, Piety, and Public Witness*. Religion, Race, and Ethnicity 9. New York: New York University Press, 2014.

Warrior, Robert Allen. "Canaanites, Cowboys, and Indians: Deliverance, Conquest, and Liberation Theology Today." *Christianity and Crisis* 49.12 (1989) 261–65.

Washington, Harriett A. *Medical Apartheid: The Dark History of Medical Experimentation on Black Americans from Colonial Times to the Present*. New York: Harlem Moon, 2006.

Wessell, Walter W. "Mark." In *The Expositors Bible Commentary*, vol. 8, edited by Frank Graebelien, 603–93. Grand Rapids: Zondervan, 1984.

West, Gerald O. "1 and 2 Samuel." In *Global Bible Commentary*, edited by Daniel Patte, 92–104. Nashville: Abingdon, 2004.

———. *The Stolen Bible: From Tool of Imperialism to African Icon*. Biblical Interpretation Series 144. Leiden: Brill, 2016.

———. "Tracking an Ancient Near Eastern Economic System: The Tributary Mode of Production and the Temple-State." *Old Testament Essays* 24.2 (2011) 511–32.

West, Gerald O., and Musa W. Dube, eds. *The Bible in Africa: Transactions, Trajectories, and Trends.* Leiden: Brill, 2000.

———. "Reading with African Overtures": An Exploration of the Interface between Critical and Ordinary Readings of the Bible." *Semeia* 73 (1996) 1–284.

West, Mona. "The Book of Ruth: An Example of Procreative Strategies for Queers." In *Our Families, Our Values: Snapshots of Queer Kinship,* edited by Robert Goss and Amy Adams Squire Strongheart, 51–60. Haworth Gay & Lesbian Studies. New York: Routledge, 2019.

West, Mona, and Robert E. Shore-Goss, eds. *The Queer Bible Commentary.* 2nd ed. London: SCM, 2022.

Westphal, Merold. *Whose Community, Which Interpretation? Philosophical Hermeneutics for the Church.* Church and Postmodern Culture. Grand Rapids: Baker Academic, 2009.

Walter, Jess. *The Cold Millions.* New York: HarperPerennial, 2021.

"What Is Reception History?" *Bible Odyssey.* https://blog.bibleodyssey.org/articles/what-is-reception-history/.

Willamon, William, and Richard Lischer, eds. *Concise Encyclopedia of Preaching.* Louisville: Westminster John Knox, 1995.

Williams, Delores S. *Sisters in the Wilderness: The Challenge of Womanist God-Talk.* Maryknoll, NY: Orbis, 1995.

Williamson, Lamar, Jr. *Mark.* Interpretation: A Bible Commentary for Preachers and Teachers. Louisville: Westminster John Knox, 2009.

Wilson, Robert R. *Prophecy and Society in Ancient Israel.* Philadelphia: Fortress, 1980.

———. *Sociological Approaches to the Old Testament.* Guides to Biblical Studies. Philadelphia: Fortress, 1984.

Winterson, Jeanette. *Oranges Are not the Only Fruit.* New York: Grove, 1985.

Yarber, Angela M. *The Gendered Pulpit: Sex, Body, and Desire in Preaching and Worship.* Cleveland: Parson's Porch, 2013.

Yee, Gale. "'She Stood in Tears Amid the Alien Corn': Ruth, the Perpetual Foreigner and Model Minority." In *They Were All Together in One Place? Toward Minority Biblical Criticism,* edited by Randall C. Bailey et al., 237–58. Semeia Studies 57. Atlanta: Society of Biblical Literature, 2009.

———. "'Take This Child and Suckle It for Me': Wet Nurses and Resistance in Ancient Israel." *Biblical Theology Bulletin* 39 (2009) 1–10.

www.ingramcontent.com/pod-product-compliance
Lightning Source LLC
Chambersburg PA
CBHW071158300426
44113CB00009B/1248